TWO ROOMS

TWO
ROOMS

The Life of Charles Erskine Scott Wood

Robert Hamburger

UNIVERSITY OF NEBRASKA PRESS Lincoln & London

© 1998 by

The University of Nebraska Press

All rights reserved

Manufactured in the United States of America

☉ The paper in this book meets the minimum
requirements of American National Standard for
Information Sciences—Permanence of Paper
for Printed Library Materials, ANSI Z39.48-1984.

Library of Congress Cataloging-in-Publication Data

Hamburger, Robert, 1943–

Two rooms : the life of Charles Erskine Scott Wood /
Robert Hamburger.

p.   cm.

Includes bibliographical references and index.

ISBN 0-8032-2389-7 (cl : alk. paper).

ISBN 0-8032-7315-0 (pbk. : alk. paper).

1. Wood, Charles Erskine Scott, 1852–1944—Biography.

2. Authors, American—19th century—Biography.

3. Authors, American—20th century—Biography.   I. Title.

PS3545.0465Z69 1998   811′.52—dc21   [B]   97-50390   CIP

FOR
MY MOTHER
AND
FATHER

To me, the doublenesses in Grandfather Camoens reveal his beauty; his willingness to permit the coexistence within himself of conflicting impulses is the source of his full, gentle humaneness. If you pointed out the contradictions between, for example, his egalitarian ideas and the olympian reality of his social position, he would answer with no more than an owning-up smile and a disarming shrug. 'Everyone should live well, isn't it,' he was fond of saying.—Salman Rushdie: *The Moor's Last Sigh*

Contents

Love and Anarchy
1910–1918

Precious Hours
1918–1944

Illustrations

Preface

I first came upon Charles Erskine Scott Wood some fifteen years ago during a summer I spent on the cusp of Oregon's high desert country, territory that preoccupied Wood for many years and for many reasons. I was visiting a close friend from my graduate school days who lived in a hand-built cabin set on an idyllic meadow laced with spring-fed streams surrounded by stately ponderosa pines. The snow-covered summits of Mount Jefferson, Three-Fingered Jack, and Three Sisters hovered above the trees—part of the glorious Cascade Range that Wood first saw some one hundred years before. I was browsing through my friend's books one day when I came upon a thin, privately printed volume:

Life of
CHARLES ERSKINE SCOTT WOOD
By His Son
ERSKINE WOOD
A RENAISSANCE MAN

West Point graduate, soldier, explorer, Indian fighter—and friend, General's aide, lawyer, orator, politician, bibliophile, as much at home in the salons and studios of New York, as on the plains of the Far West, patron of the arts and artists, himself a painter and bon vivant, lover, poet and satirist, champion of the oppressed, righter of wrongs, author of "Heavenly Discourse" and "Poet in the Desert," and kind and indulgent father—such was the man of whom I write.

Wood was my friend Bruce's great-grandfather, that I knew, but Bruce had only mentioned him in passing. I took Wood to be a colorful figure in the family's past—the man who had made several lovely paintings that hung in Grandma Ruth's home across the meadow. But a "Renaissance Man"—an Indian fighter, bon vivant, and champion of the oppressed—all this was news to me. I read Erskine's affectionate narrative in a single sitting.

What struck me then, and what even now seems noteworthy, was the sheer size of Wood's life. As a boy, Wood cheered president-elect Lincoln on his train journey to Washington; as a young army officer he pursued the Nez Perce Indians across the mountains and high plains of Idaho and Montana. Later, as a prominent lawyer and philosophical anarchist, he supported woman's suffrage, the IWW, and unpopular First Amendment cases. Along with this, he was, indeed, a bon vivant: a dandy, a connoisseur of just about everything, a dedicated (but mediocre) poet, a friend and supporter of some of the finest artists of his day. The arc of Wood's ninety-one years spans from antebellum America to the brink of the nuclear age. His long life placed him in contact with many notable people, and, it seemed, he always won their affection and respect. Chief Joseph, Mark Twain, Albert Pinkham Ryder, Clarence Darrow, Emma Goldman, Margaret Sanger, Lincoln Steffens, James J. Hill, Woodrow Wilson, John Cowper Powys, Langston Hughes, Ezra Pound, and Ansel Adams—these are just some of the figures Wood encountered.

If I was drawn to Wood by the incredible compass of his life, I was also intrigued by an unresolved tension that marked every phase of his story. Rebellious from his earliest childhood, Wood was combatively critical of the social and economic inequalities spawned by the so-called "Gilded Age" that followed the Civil War. He despised what he called "feudalism" in all its forms: organized religion, monopolistic enterprise, plutocratic government, militarism, imperialism, and the authoritarian silencing of dissident voices. He cared about these issues passionately, and throughout his life he fought to make America worthy of the democratic principles on which it was founded. But Wood also had a passion for good living. He dressed impeccably, creatively, expensively. The wines and cheeses he served in his Portland home came from the finest purveyors in San Francisco. He enjoyed opera, theater, and classical music. He took pleasure in his exquisitely bound collection of rare books. His home was a palace of art. He had an eye for fine carpets, for Greek and Roman artifacts, for contemporary painting and sculpture. All this cost money—far more than Wood earned. As a result, this eloquent critic of the status quo spent most of his adult life struggling to pay off sizable debts to the very banks and investment houses that he criticized. Though he openly supported the forces of radical and progressive change, he earned his living in the service of some of the most powerful financial interests in America. Wood's situation intrigued me. I wondered how he sustained these contradictory commitments and to what degree they either inhibited or sharpened his wish for fundamental change.

These were some of the concerns that drew me to Wood. I think, too, that I was drawn to the fact that he is virtually unknown. In one way or another, my books on the Civil Rights movement, on black women working as maids, and on people living in single-room occupancy hotels have all been driven by a conviction that there is something intrinsically valuable in bringing the words and lives of "insignificant" people into the overlapping discourse that we call social history. In his time, Charles Erskine Scott Wood existed at the opposite end of the social spectrum from the subjects of my other books. And he was hardly unknown. Today, however, he is an obscure figure: he remains a local hero in Oregon, but he's either a forgotten name or a "footnote to history" just about everywhere else. What we choose to call history depends largely on the existence (or nonexistence) of documentary evidence, as well as on the preoccupations of those who research and write and teach about the past for a living. Out of necessity, historians practice a kind of triage and, inevitably, "lesser lives" are often ignored. You can find Wood mentioned here and there: a paragraph in a literary history; brief mention in biographies of some of the remarkable people he knew—but until Geoffrey Cowan's recent book, *The People v. Clarence Darrow*, Wood had little place in the published texts that constitute an essential part of what we call history.

In one sense, Wood has been treated justly. He did not change history or produce some ignored masterpiece worthy of reexamination. For all that he did, it would not be unfair to call him a "bit player" in the great events of his time. Nonetheless, Wood's life has a resonance far richer than any of his written works and more significant than any of his individual accomplishments. In the sweep of years his life covers, in his heartfelt ideals, and in the uncanny way his words and deeds expressed the spirit of the times in which he lived, Charles Erskine Scott Wood's story brings together an absorbing personal saga with vital forces in American history. A current of restless energy streams through his life. He never relinquished his bright-eyed dreams even when they brought pain to himself and those he loved. His actions stemmed from a need to experiment with possible selves, from a rebellious impulse to leap at opportunities for a richer, more spontaneous existence whenever possible. It is hard not to admire a person who lived with such verve, yet it is impossible not to feel frustrated by the compromises and rationalizations he made in his protracted struggle to live on his own terms. Torn between irreconcilable pursuits, Wood maintained two offices. In one he conducted his legal practice, representing some of the most powerful business interests in the country. In the other, his private office, he met with radical labor leaders, anarchists, suffrage activists, and others who challenged fundamental aspects of the American system. Those two rooms are a vivid metaphor for his divided life—and, in a sense, for essential divisions in the life of the nation in which he lived.

The radical activist and writer Michael Gold must have understood the scope and resonant strains of Wood's life when he urged him to tell his own story. "I still ask," Gold wrote, "when is Erskine going to write the Great American Autobiography? From the Indians right smack into the trusts and skyscrapers—it could be the story of America, better and more representative than that of the bookish Henry Adams—if only Gods ever stooped to autobiography." When he was old and nearly blind; when the idyllic settings of his youth had vanished; when General Howard, Chief Joseph, Mark Twain, Albert Pinkham Ryder, Lincoln Steffens—so many of his beloved friends—were all dead; with Darrow senile and Emma Goldman living in exile; with America itself changed utterly—Wood set out to fulfill Gold's request. After years of writing poetry, political commentary, satire, and didactic tales, he seemed to understand that the finest story he had to tell was his own. Though he never said it in so many words, he lived with the conviction that his experiences were more than a mere succession of events: he saw his life as a kind of novel, a narrative with structure and meaning, in which he was both protagonist and storyteller. To this end, he had saved his correspondence and journals, drafts of speeches and poems, articles he wrote, photos, and memorabilia.

Wood was close to ninety when he began. He knew he had very little time, but he still hoped to tell his story. In crabbed, barely legible script he set down whatever fragments his shattered memory retrieved: a seafaring father who filled his home with alluring treasures from distant lands. A beloved mother who languished at home. A dress ball at West Point. A kiss from a dazzling Washington socialite. The magnificent high desert of eastern Oregon—and above the desert vastness, brilliant starlit heavens. It was barely a beginning. . . .

Had Wood been magically restored to his youthful vigor, or had he found the time to continue his first effort to write his autobiography when he was in his sixties, he might have produced a unique personal narrative evoking the great span of American history in which he played a part. But we will never have that story—not as Wood himself would have told it. The story I have told is no doubt different than what Wood might have written. To the questions what did the man do? what did he achieve? what did he make?—I would reply that he lived with a keen curiosity about the world in which he moved; that he was drawn to men and women who displayed vision, creativity, and moral courage; and that he was driven by a wish for social justice that brought him close to the pressing issues of his time. He did not make history, but few people do. Still, Wood's story has its own kind of magnitude and importance. Certain people gather about them the contradictory forces and interlocking narratives that make their personal histories, for all their unique details, strikingly "representative." Wanting so much, living so fully, Wood was, to borrow a phrase from Henry James, a "reverberator," a living mirror who vividly reflected the spirit of the age. Unlike those works that redefine the achievement of some canonized figure—a Walt Whitman, Edith Wharton, or Theodore Roosevelt—my narrative does not make a case for the unacknowledged merit of neglected books and barely remembered deeds. My purpose is to present Wood's life as an engrossing story, the telling of which gives a human dimension to issues that divided and defined our changing nation over nine decades.

The Perfect Product of a Perfect System

1852–1883

1. An Enchanted Land

In the autumn of 1874, Second Lieutenant Charles Erskine Scott Wood bid farewell to his mother and father at their farm outside of Baltimore and traveled West to report for military duty. For four years he had habitually defied the exacting regulations of the United States Military Academy at West Point, accumulating a perilous record of demerits; but all that was behind him now. Lieutenant Wood was on his way West. With resolute chiseled features, curly black hair, and keen, penetrating eyes he cut a dashing figure. He was cultured, self-assured, immensely charming—in love with the most sought-after belle in Washington DC. Life could hardly have been better. For a young man with high connections and impeccable lineage it was a time of golden opportunity. True, it would have been helpful if Wood could have counted great wealth among his many blessings. But for a person of such promise, good fortune would surely come in time.

Years later, Wood wrote a short story in which the protagonist resembled himself in many ways:

> Lieutenant Bastian [was] . . . a graduate of West Point, and with a conceit quite characteristic of that insular institution, and of young people in general, believed himself the perfect product of a perfect system. . . . Lieutenant Bastian had good ground for his conceit. He was tall, straight and handsome. He found that he had more positive and exact information than most people he met. He felt himself part of the bulwark of the country; and, believing himself irresistible, he was so.[1]

In time, Wood grew to question that "perfect system" that had given him his running start in life. The privileges of race, sex, and social standing; the use of American military might; the power of concentrated wealth: in years to come, he would join the men and women who opposed all that. For now, though, Wood was free of the irony—aimed at himself and his nation—evident in his description of Lieutenant Bastian. As the train spirited him across the open country of the American West, his days were filled with anticipation and discovery, with boundless hope. Truly, Lieutenant Charles Erskine Scott Wood was one of fortune's favorites: a young man of the East, heading West.

To make that journey at that time, when the Union Pacific Railroad was only five years old, was to know the tangible reality of the American dream: immense physical space and restless, deliberate progress through it. America's first transcontinental railroad itself was a remarkable expression of the national will: the bold effort of capital and labor to subdue nature and make it profitable.

Lieutenant Wood traveled from Baltimore to Chicago, west to the Mississippi, and on to Omaha at the junction of the Missouri and Platte Rivers. From there the railroad followed the old route of the first trappers and explorers, the trail of the Mormon migration and the gold-seeking California forty-niners, into a vastness that filled Wood with "excitement and wonder."[2] There was Nebraska and the Great Plains where, only a few years before, the Sioux, Pawnee, and Cheyenne had struggled to defend their territories. Then came Wyoming and the Rocky Mountains. The railroad picked its way through mountain passes and cut through Echo Tunnel into Utah, where it passed the Great Salt Lake. Nearby, on May 10, 1869, in the town of Promontory, T. C. Durant and Leland Stanford pounded gold spikes to join the Union Pacific and Central Pacific railroad lines, completing an extraordinary five-and-a-half-year venture that fulfilled America's vision of itself: a great nation stretching "from sea to shining sea."

Wood's train skirted the alkali flats along the northern fringe of the Great Salt Lake Desert. It cut through the Pequop Mountains and the Ruby Range; then it picked up the Humboldt River northeast of Elko to follow the old California Trail across Nevada and into

California just north of Lake Tahoe. After a series of tunnels through the Sierra Nevada Range, the line joined the American River, cleaving to its shore, descending through fertile fields into Sacramento. From there, it was on to Oakland Terminal.

Upon his arrival, Wood received orders to join the Twenty-first Infantry at Camp Bidwell in the northeast corner of California. Within a few days he was off to Reno where he hoped to catch a stage north to his post.

In Reno the stage company informed Lieutenant Wood that early winter storms had blocked the mountain trails. They could take him as far as Susanville, but it might be months before he would be able to complete his trip. Wood was too caught up in his adventure to think of turning back. He took the stage as far as Susanville; then, with only a rough idea of what course to follow, he set out by saddle horse on his own. A few days earlier, he had been peering out at majestic mountain scenery from the comfort of his railroad car. Now he was a figure in that landscape, and he wished himself "well out of it."[3] Lieutenant Wood had reason to recall how, eight years before, at almost the same time of year, a group of settlers, California-bound, had attempted to cross the Sierras just north of Lake Tahoe. Trapped by heavy snows, they were driven to desperate measures. When rescuers reached the Donner party's camp in early spring, they found grisly evidence of cannibalism.

As Wood made his way across a frozen lake, a band of coyotes loped along in pursuit, howling dismally. He worried that his horse might give in to fatigue, allowing the coyotes to "begin their savage feast."[4] Wood drew his revolver and shot the leader of the pack. In moments, the other coyotes tore the creature to pieces, shaking its intestines over the snow. Their hunger satisfied, the animals abandoned their pursuit, and Wood continued on into the mountains.

Before nightfall Lieutenant Wood came upon a cattle tender's cabin dug into the side of a small hill. He built a fire and forced himself to eat some bacon and beans that he found buried in a skillet full of congealed grease. In that dingy shelter, with its dirt floor and sleeping bunk covered with rotting straw, Wood was not much elated by his first western adventure. He crawled into his dismal bed and promptly fell asleep.[5]

Wood was back on the trail before sunup. In three hours he reached the next stage station, where he announced that he was an army officer on orders to report for duty at Camp Bidwell. He was told that with snow on the ground and winter ahead, Camp Bidwell was out of the question until the spring thaw.

As Wood finished his breakfast, he noticed that a mail coach was preparing to head north. When he asked what was going on, the driver explained that the station had a lot of mail piling up, so he thought he would attempt a run to Camp Bidwell. Wood insisted on accompanying him, but the driver flatly refused and went off to fortify himself with whiskey at the tavern. He emerged loading a pint bottle of whiskey into the side pocket of his sheepskin coat.

"Where do I go?" Wood asked.

"Why you and your government can go to hell!"

Lieutenant Wood put his foot on the hub of the coach wheel and vaulted into the driver's seat. He drew his revolver from his shirt and pressed its muzzle against the driver. The driver spit out a quid of tobacco; he picked up the reins, cracked his long whip lash, and Lieutenant Wood was on his way.[6]

For all his brazen behavior, Wood was scared. He was twenty-two and untested in life. What he knew of weapons he had learned at West Point with its accompanying code of gentlemanly behavior. But he had a reckless streak: "I was just out of the Academy and anxious to do startling things—that is to say, foolish things."[7]

It was hard going. Straining toward the summit of the mountain pass, the horses bogged down in heavy snowdrifts. Again and again, Wood and the driver had to unload the coach, then dig with fenceposts to free the wheels. By day's end they had cleared the summit and made it down to the stage station in Surprise Valley. The following day, Lieutenant Wood reported for duty at Camp Bidwell.

Wood was welcomed "as Columbus might have been received on his return from his celebrated voyage."[8] To Captain Robert Pollock, the commanding officer, Wood's arrival came as a blessing. Pollock was a Civil War veteran, a fearless foot soldier who had worked his way up the ranks but never gained more than a rudimentary knowledge of reading and writing. He promptly assigned Wood to take over the company's record keeping and report writing, a task that involved little effort and many pleasures. One of the tasks at Camp Bidwell was to survey the area and construct military roads where they were needed, and Captain Pollock was not adverse to using his surveys for occasional holidays. Pollock would say, "Charley, don't you think we ought to have a military road survey over on the other side of the divide over the mountain? There's splendid trout fishing over there and swans in the lake and good deer shooting, and I think if we just took a little party and surveyed that neck of the woods it would be a very valuable thing for the government to have."[9]

Over the next months, Wood and Pollack made several such excursions, charting and mapping lands that extended into Oregon and Nevada—territory few white men had traveled.[10] Wood became friendly with a Piute Indian named Debes, with whom he often went hunting. On several occasions he spent the night in Debes's tepee, nestled under a bearskin blanket alongside Debes's wife and young baby. For weeks at a time, he lived the life of a latter-day Natty Bumppo.

That spring Wood's company was ordered to Fort Vancouver in the Washington Territory, just across the Columbia River from Portland, Oregon. Portland was then the busiest port in the Pacific Northwest, a boom town of almost twenty thousand people, and growing by leaps and bounds. "What could be better than that?" Wood reflected. "I was going into the very midst of civilization."[11]

But whatever momentary attractions "civilization" held, it was the untouched land between Camp Bidwell and Portland that captured the young man's heart. The company marched north into the Warner Valley, along a string of lakes, and on into the Harney Desert. The Harney Desert is the northernmost section of the Great Basin, a unique ecological system spread over thousands upon thousands of acres between the Rockies and the Cascade Range, where melting snow streams down from mountain heights and drains into sprawling salt marshes. There Wood's company camped beside hot springs and feasted on sage hens and snipe. Close by, Wood looked upon the gigantic morass known as Harney Marsh, thirty miles across, a wilderness of giant tulle grass sprinkled with small lakes. It was, and remains, one of the largest nesting areas for waterfowl and migratory birds in the Western Hemisphere. Wood marveled at this desert paradise with its ducks, geese, egrets, blue heron, owls, songbirds, blackbirds, and waders. "Away out there in the middle of the world amidst utter loneliness . . . it was all tremendously beautiful, breath-taking. That desert was as if it were the whole world. The sky above was a million worlds. It was enough to impress the most calloused heart."[12]

The next morning the company headed north toward Fort Harney, across high desert bounded to the east by the Steens Mountains. Wood quickly came to love that land: the delicate colors of sagebrush, rabbit brush, and juniper; its sage hens, scurrying rabbits, and horned toads; buzzards, hawks, and eagles circling in the sky. They made camp by the Silvies River, the site of what is now the town of Burns. Then they headed on to Fort Harney, just south of the Blue Mountains.

The Twenty-first Infantry continued north to Canyon City and on to Dalles, a small town on the Columbia River, where a steamboat awaited them. With horses, baggage, and freight piled aboard, the vessel swung out into the great river: the same western passage that Lewis and Clark had traveled seventy years before. The men had nothing to do but relax and enjoy the dramatic scenery. For lunch they dined on caviar and smoked salmon, provided by Russian fish-ermen who worked at the mouth of the river. To the south rose the snowy summit of Mount Hood, over eleven thousand feet high; to the north the snow-capped peaks of Mount Saint Helens, Mount Adams, and Mount Rainier. "It was all wonderful," Wood remembered, "an enchanted land. We were being taken slowly and majestically on from one wonder to another and all beyond our comprehension."[13]

It is hard not to envy Lieutenant Wood as he savored the glories of the unspoiled Northwest Territory. His sense of his own rightful place amidst this natural splendor was not burdened by disturbing questions. He thrilled to his railway journey West without much knowledge of the manipulation and chicanery that went into the railroad's financing—or the terrible conditions suffered by laborers, especially the Chinese, in the railroad's construction. He hunted and lived with his Indian friend Debes, untroubled by reflections on how the western progress of his people had disrupted the Piutes' ancient way of life. Traveling with the Twenty-first Infantry, he hunted and fished and camped and made his way through the sacred land of various Indian nations with utter certainty that this territory belonged in the American domain. In short, he was innocent.

American innocence—how easily the two words fit together! We know this from the canonized masterpieces of our literature: from *The Deerslayer;* from Thoreau and Whitman; from Tom Sawyer, Daisy Miller, Jay Gatsby. And we know, too, that sustained innocence can be self-destructive, tragic, dangerous to others. If young Lieutenant Wood is to become worthy of our attention, he will have to shed his innocence, to absorb unsettling facts that explain his privileged place in the world; he will have to find ways to act upon his burdensome knowledge; and he will have to face the consequences of these actions—alienation from his community, the suffering of those he loves, spiritual solitude, and personal despair.

There will be time for all this, but there is no need to be impatient. For the lucky few, youth itself is an enchanted land. And though we understand that even the most potent spells must end, that is no reason to spurn this young man's enraptured impressions of a new world. For generation after generation, the West has been a theater of enchantment where the adventurous have pursued dreams of wealth and boundless freedom. In a sense, the story of the West is one of enchantment: of Native Americans' covenant with the land itself; of Lewis and Clark's enticing account of their travels; of General John C. Frémont's Byronic adventures in Mexican California; of the heavenly ordained migration of Brigham Young and his Mormon battalion; and, soon to come, of General George Armstrong Custer's fatal pursuit of glory. Later, the West will attract cattle barons, land grant speculators, and empire builders possessed by dreams of subduing the land and using its vast resources for their own ends.

The Columbia River widens. Up ahead lies Fort Vancouver. For now, let us leave Lieutenant Wood on the steamboat deck savoring a magnificent mountain panorama along with the aftertaste of his smoked river salmon. Perhaps he is mentally composing a letter to his sweetheart in the nation's capital, a continent away. What could be finer than this, or more promising: a keen young man, the perfect product of a perfect system, whose pride and derring-do have carried him into the enchanted land of the American dream?

2. Noah's Ark

When he was old and barely able to read the words he scrawled with painstaking effort, Charles Erskine Scott Wood gave his waning energy to recollecting his childhood. "My education resembled the building of Noah's Ark," he began. "It was fearfully and wonderfully made. My father saw little of his family but was absent three years at a time as fleet surgeon in foreign seas. My dear sweet grey eyed mother laid herself on the altar of the home."[1] When he looked back on those times, his most vivid memories were of the canal that flowed past his family's small brick house; of Lake Erie only a mile or so away; and of his seafaring father, the source of both wonder and fear, whose career as naval surgeon took him far from his family.

Charles Erskine Scott Wood was born on February 20, 1852, in Erie, Pennsylvania, where he grew up beside the Erie-to-Pittsburgh Canal. During Erskine's childhood (he never used the name "Charles"), Erie was a busy shipping center that linked the Great Lakes to a network of inland waterways, railroad trunk lines, and toll roads reaching into the Pennsylvania interior. Three quarters of the American continent lay west of Erie, but the vital centers of American life lay to the east. The narrow band of water outside his door joined his home to that larger world: to Pittsburgh, Philadelphia, New York, and, beyond that, the Atlantic Ocean, Europe, South America, and exotic distant lands.

Erskine had an exceptional interest in foreign shores, for his father, William Maxwell Wood, was a man of the sea. By the time Erskine was born, his father, who was then forty-two, had spent close to half his life on naval vessels. As a surgeon in the United States Navy, he visited Mexico, Rio, Lima, Valparaiso, the Marquesas, Hawaii, the Sandwich Islands, Japan, China, and Siam. He had eaten strange foods, explored natural wonders, visited half-naked natives, engaged in exciting secret missions, and proven equal to every danger he had faced. His rooms were filled with artifacts from his travels, and each treasured article summoned a beguiling narrative of its origins. Erskine was spellbound. He remembered his father as "ruddy, robust in every way, looking strong wholesome and rigorous . . . [with] piercing alert intellectual blue eyes . . . [that] could twinkle with merriment."[2] But Erskine added that those eyes "could become very steely and look through and through you cruelly."[3]

William Maxwell Wood grew up in Baltimore, the eldest son of John Wood, a prosperous commodities dealer in the early decades of the American republic. Emboldened by his success, John Wood tried to corner the wheat and flour market, and lost his entire fortune in the attempt. He was a hard drinker and died in 1827, in his early forties. At eighteen, William was forced to look after his widowed mother, two brothers, and three sisters. He provided for them by working in an apothecary shop while still managing to complete his studies in medicine at the University of Maryland. During those years he struggled grimly to make ends meet. He lived in a barren room and prepared his meager meals in a blacking-box cover over an alcohol lamp.[4] He graduated before he was twenty-one. Immediately, he entered the navy as surgeon's mate, beginning a lifetime of service.[5]

The duties of a naval surgeon are not ordinarily associated with high adventure, but as Erskine later noted, William Maxwell Wood was "a forceful, intellectual, self made man" with "intellectual powers and powers of leadership beyond the ordinary. . . . Wherever he dropped down he became *the* force, the leader."[6] He forged a career for himself that went far beyond his regular duties.

In 1846 he undertook a dramatic mission that facilitated America's seizure of the California territory. He had just completed his tour of duty with the Pacific Fleet and was returning East by the overland route through Guadalajara when he overheard a conversation between Mexican officers (he was fluent in Spanish) that Mexican forces had ambushed Captain Thornton's command on the Rio Grande. Wood knew this information would be essential to Commodore John Sloat, who commanded the U.S. naval force along the Pacific Coast, for Sloat had been instructed to keep his forces in check until he received confirmation that the two nations were at war. It was rumored that the British fleet was eager to know if war had broken out—that they planned to seize California as a means of forcing Mexico to make good on its loans from British banks. With help from John Parrott, the American consul, Wood smuggled the information to Sloat at Mazatlan. Yet Sloat still hesitated. Wood placed himself in further peril by shedding his military uniform and crossing Mexico in plain clothes to inspect the fortifications of Mexico City and to gather more information about hostilities on the Rio Grande. His reconnaissance provided Sloat with the verification he needed to move into action. The following day Sloat sailed for Monterey, where, on July 7, he sent 250 men ashore to raise the American flag above the customhouse and claim possession of the territory for the United States.[7]

William Maxwell Wood wrote three books about his travels: sharply observed narratives that bristled with intelligence. Gracefully written, they displayed a frank, manly enthusiasm for life. Though his entire career was spent in the service of his country, he had no qualms about criticizing American arrogance. In *Fankwei* (Chinese for "white devil"), his finest book, he has this to say about gunboat diplomacy.

> An outrage is committed upon some Americans by a small body of individuals . . . perhaps, provoked by the abduction of some female . . . or by smuggling off pepper at night. Without inquiry, or the means of adjudicating the facts, a man-of-war comes along and batters down the town and the houses of some rajah and his people entirely innocent of the matter, and then goes away. . . .
>
> The eclat of vindicating American rights, by battering down some semi-barbarian town, may be brilliant in the home papers, but ten or twelve thousand miles' distance, and the absence of a press among the punished people, may prevent many contingencies appearing to tarnish that brilliancy.[8]

William Maxwell Wood's lively mind and forceful personality placed him on easy social terms with three American presidents. Following the Civil War, he was appointed the chief of the Bureau of Medicine and Surgery—the first surgeon general of the United

States Navy. But for all his energy, talent, and force of character, much of his influence on his son came from what he did not do. And what he did not do—or rather, what he only did irregularly—was live with his family.

When Erskine was three, his father left Erie and circumnavigated the globe with the Asiatic Squadron, passing through Madeira, Mauritius, Ceylon, Singapore, Siam, China, and Japan. He did not return home for three years. Erskine reacted to his father's absence with a rash of temper tantrums. "The whole family used to gather for one of my exhibitions," he recalled, "and stand around fearing I would (or would not) die. It took the form of beating everybody in sight with my baby fists and then probably chagrined at my impotence I would throw myself flat on the floor, kick, howl, hold my breath, get purple in the face and otherwise expend much valuable vitality."[9]

At that time, the family consisted of Erskine, his older brother Max, an infant brother, James, and two half-sisters from his father's first marriage, Elizabeth and Hannah, already in their twenties. (Wood's first wife, Hannah Moore Wood, died when their two girls were in their early teens; he remarried within a few years.) Later there would be two younger brothers, Thomas and David, and Roberta, his only full sister. None of his younger siblings figure much in Erskine's story: he went away to school while they were quite young, and in later years the family was scattered around the country. But Max, who bore the name of the father Erskine loved and resented, became the target of intense aggression. One time, Erskine flew at Max with a jackknife and cut his wrist open.[10] On another occasion, Erskine lost his temper and threw a hatchet at him.[11] In a sense, Max was a stand-in for Erskine's absent father—far less daunting than the real thing. As for Erskine's hysterical outbursts, when William Maxwell Wood returned home in 1858, he cured his son with a time-honored treatment: he heaved him in a tub of cold water.

From then until the outbreak of the Civil War, William Maxwell Wood was assigned to the steamer *Michigan,* a sidewheeler man-of-war that patrolled the Great Lakes. This allowed him to live at home and resume the guidance of his family. Erskine was an adventurous child, and his youthful transgressions rarely escaped his father's notice.

William Maxwell Wood never tired of giving his sons guidance on how to develop a proper manly character, as Erskine later remembered: "Love my mother and save her worry. Be diligent in my studies as education was power and my diligence could profit none but myself, my neglect of opportunity hurt none but myself—and Truth, Bravery, Courtesy to the weak made a gentleman, not money. That the absorbing pursuit of money was the most narrowing of vices."[12]

Years later, when William Maxwell Wood died, the family discovered a parchment coat of arms among his papers: a shield quartered, with oak trees in the two top sections and two smock-clad woodsmen, axes in hand, in the bottom sections. A clenched fist, gloved in mail, rested above the shield; and below, the motto: "DEFEND." Whether this was an authentic link to his ancestral past, or merely a symbol that appealed to his father, Erskine never determined. Nor was he able to verify the family legend that John Wood, an ancestor from the seventeenth century, was knighted for remaining loyal to the deposed monarch during Cromwell's Commonwealth.[13] In later years, Erskine joked about the possibility that he came from loyal, conservative forebearers, defenders of the faith; but there was no need to look back any further than his father. William Maxwell Wood despised aristocratic privilege, slavery, and the tyranny of concentrated wealth—evils Erskine would assail for much of his adult life. Yet along with these liberal views, William Maxwell Wood pressed upon his children what he believed to be the incontrovertible values on which justice, social order, and individual character must rest. His practice of ceaseless moral admonition smacks of the sturdy ax-wielding woodsmen, the mailed fist, the conservative commitment to "defend."

William Maxwell Wood loved his children. Whenever illness, injury, or injustice befell them, he ministered to them and did what was "good" for them. He was not lacking in affection, but a lifetime of military service led him to treat his children brusquely, with blunt dispatch. Intelligent, decisive, morally severe—William Maxwell Wood was a consummate example of the stern Victorian paterfamilias. To young Erskine he was more: distant, often wrathful, sometimes inaccessible, yet watchful, ready to intervene when most needed.

When Erskine was nine, William Maxwell Wood summoned his three eldest sons into his library. Erskine always felt the solemnity of these occasions. This time, however, his awe was compounded by fear that his father planned to interrogate him and Max about some missing cigars. But William Maxwell Wood had another purpose. On his desk lay a long official envelope with military orders: he had been appointed fleet surgeon of the North Atlantic Blockading Squadron; he was to report to the U.S. flagship *Minnesota* in Chesapeake Bay.

For months, Erskine had been feeling "a stir and excitement in the air" that worked its way into children's games of combat and military drill.[14] The year before he had witnessed the presidential campaign of 1860 and its torchlight processions of the Wide-Awake parades in shining black capes.[15] He had seen "the float representing Abe, the rail-splitter . . . a platform built upon a wagon. On this platform was a log and a man in a hickory shirt, sleeves rolled up above the elbows, was splitting the log with a wedge. The crowd hailed this float with terrific cheers and cried 'Honest old Abe! Abraham Lincoln. The man we want!' "[16]

Erskine caught a glimpse of Lincoln on February 6, 1861, when the president-elect spoke in Buffalo en route from Springfield to Washington DC. Erskine saw "a vast crowd and a very tall man wearing a black frock coat to his knees." For years, "the tall figure and the remarkable and unforgettable face" stayed with him as a "shining fact."[17]

During the first months of the Civil War, William Maxwell Wood supervised the physical examinations of recruits in the Lake Erie area. Everywhere recruitment posters declared, "We are coming, Father Abraham, five hundred thousand more."[18] Now, with the Union effort fully underway, Erskine's father left him again.

The Civil War brought important changes in Erskine's life. With his father gone, he began to see that his mother was an unhappy woman. William Maxwell Wood's absence increased the burdens on Rose Carson Wood, but there were other factors which Erskine sensed even if he was still too young to understand. Despite thirty years of distinguished military service, William Maxwell Wood had difficulty providing for his family. In part, this was due to the modest pay issued to officers. But Wood contributed to his own predicament. He was a connoisseur who insisted on the best of everything regardless of whether or not he could afford it: expensive provisions, fine wines, elegant furnishings, the most beautiful oriental rugs and pottery. "In spite of all his preaching of economy and honest effort to enforce it upon himself [he] was too much the Bohemian and reckless Naval officer to do so. He was eternally in debt, forever nagged of debt, and forever unable to really economize."[19] It was Rose's task to manage the household and keep up appearances in spite of the damage her husband's spending habits wrought on the family economy. Also, William Maxwell Wood was "a free drinker": his mahogany sideboard was stocked with several decanters of brandy and hard liquor, of which he partook liberally.[20]

Rose Wood suffered from her husband's excesses. She was "not strong willed or forceful against my forceful father who . . . dominated her life and the family—and I think often to the cause of her weeping. . . . She was one of those sad sacrifices to poverty and marital submission combined. . . . [She gave in to the joyless tyranny of] a man who was always an arrogant leader among men [who] would never dream of question or discussion in his own family."[21]

Though Erskine's mother was victim to her husband's willful behavior, she too imposed rigid restraints on Erskine's youthful nature. Rose Carson Wood was a deeply religious woman, a Scotch Presbyterian who traced her lineage back on her mother's line to Ralph and Ebenezer Erskine. In the eighteenth century, the Erskine brothers led Scotland's New Kirk movement, a radical assault on the stringent practices of Calvin and Knox that gained a wide following, including Rose Wood's favorite poet, Robert Burns. Whatever might have been the rebellious tendencies of his mother's forebearers, her own religious practice left Erskine feeling cruelly subjugated. "I loathed and hated Sunday," he recalled. "My dear gentle sweet mother added her share to the gloom and tyranny of our childhoods' home, not by her nature but as one of the many viceregents for the rigid and joy killing Calvin. . . . Many a time her gentle voice has interrupted me— 'Erskine, you forget what day this is. You must not whistle on the Sabbath.' So we must not take walks in the country nor read 'worldly books.' In fact Sunday meant a closed house—as if some one were dead. . . . A cold dinner. A colorless or black dismal day. To get up into the attic and play quietly was sin. To sing was sin unless it be psalms and hymns. . . . To walk in the country and scamper through the woods was sin. To laugh loud was sin. . . . In short it was the *Lord's* day out of seven."[22]

Not long after William Maxwell Wood left Erie to join the North Atlantic Blockade, Rose lightened her domestic ordeal by arranging for her two oldest boys to live away from home. She enrolled Max at Lawrenceville Academy in New Jersey, and she sent Erskine to live in Baltimore with her brother, Washington Carson, a successful coffee and sugar merchant. In Baltimore the war was close at hand: Antietam, Bull Run, and Fredericksburg were fought within eighty miles of the city; Richmond, the Confederate capital, was only 140 miles away. But for ten-year-old Erskine, the bloody conflict was little more than a vibrant backdrop to his life. War and adventure were part of his father's alluring world, while he strained against the yoke of his mother's Carson clan.

The Carson household was more severe than his mother's. Sabbath rituals were strictly enforced; even the games he played at school were censured by his aunt and uncle if, in their judgment, youthful sport appeared likely to encourage gambling. For Erskine, the one enjoyable bit of reading in the Carson library, ("the book case crammed with theology, theology, theology"), was "a fine old attack on the Catholic church written by some sour-visaged bigot," who described the rampant wickedness and sexual philandering that supposedly took place in nunneries.[23]

On March 9, William Maxwell Wood was stationed aboard the *Minnesota* when it and two consorts were attacked by the Confederate navy's frightening new war machine, the *Virginia* (remembered in history as the *Merrimac*, its name at the outbreak of the war). Union sailors saw a monstrous floating barn charging directly at their blockading vessels. Cannonballs bounced off its armor as it bore head-on into the *Congress* and the *Cumberland*, ripping them open with its iron ram. The following morning the Union ironclad, the *Monitor*, was pressed into action, and the *Virginia* was forced to withdraw for repairs. William Maxwell Wood had another extraordinary adventure to share with his son.

Several weeks after the historic battle of ironclads, Wood sent for Erskine to join him at Hampton Roads. The crew adopted the boy; he had free run of the ship and was permitted to explore the admiral's cabin at will. On one occasion, some crewmen took him ashore to explore the battleground at Norfolk, where he gathered bayonets and pistols as souvenirs. On another outing he accompanied the seining crew—a glorious afternoon running naked on the beach, splashing in the water, as the men hauled in their shining harvest of shad and sheepshead. Out in the harbor, the top masts of the *Cumberland* and *Congress* were still visible. Erskine rowed out to the sunken vessels and cut off bits of rope for souvenirs. At the holiday's end, William Maxwell Wood placed his son on a steamer that shuttled him across Chesapeake Bay, away from the realm of ships and sailors and heroic battles, back to mundane life at the Carsons' home.

It was a splendid vacation, a boy's dream come true. More than that, it was an impromptu rite in which the youth entered circles of power where his father commanded the utmost esteem. There had been other such moments in the past, but this episode came when Erskine was old enough to fully appreciate it. The nation was at war—and there he was, aboard the Union flagship. He had been welcomed into a world of great events, where his father moved with ease. It was as if he was being groomed to assume his father's mantle, encouraged to pursue his own heroic adventures—to sally forth as a child of privilege, shielded by the protective charm of his father's blessing.

Still, this radiant episode came and went with no change in William Maxwell Wood's authoritarian temper. In November of 1863 he wrote to Erskine from Hampton Roads, Virginia: "My dear boy—You have not, I am sorry to say, written me since I left home. You know that this is a disappointment to me, because I am always glad to hear from you, and annoyed if I do not. I am more sorry to find that your school reports, although better than formerly still contain what you should not allow to be written—'*Too late.*' That is entirely within your own control. . . . The boy who consents to be too late in a matter so entirely within his control, will most likely be behind hand in everything in life."[24]

This is the earliest letter that survives from William Maxwell Wood to his son. It is typical of what follows: didactic homilies, sharply critical, constantly citing universal principles of conduct which reveal the boy's shortcomings. Impersonal as the letter appears to be, it carries a poignant undertow of unexpressed love. William Maxwell Wood wanted his son to be healthy, happy, successful, and honorable;

he wanted to guide him into responsible manhood, but he lacked the instinct, the loving tone, to communicate those feelings.

What was Erskine to make of his father's admonishments for greater "control"? Here was a man who left his family as he pleased, whose lack of discipline reduced the family economy to shambles, and whose hard-drinking showed no self-restraint. Receiving his father's communications—with their uncompromising moral pronouncements, their cold minatory words, and an occasional trace of underlying love—Erskine must have experienced a baffling, painful mixture of emotions. Little wonder that the boy neglected to write.

In the early months of 1865, while the war was drawing to a close, William Maxwell Wood took advantage of deflated property values and bought a farm outside of Owings Mills, Maryland, about fourteen miles from Baltimore.[25] As soon as necessary preparations were completed, he moved his family into the brick colonial house that would be their home for the rest of Erskine's youth, the happiest years of his childhood.

Approaching the Wood house, one passed a vegetable garden of two or three acres and a picket fence with climbing roses. Then came the house itself, with its broad front porch. To the north lay rich pastures laced with streams; to the south chestnut and hickory trees and a thicket of young sassafras trees. Beyond the house was a peach orchard, an avenue of locust trees, and the busy life of the farm: fields of grain, wheat, rye, barley, and oats; pastures with cows, horses, and sheep; a duck pond, pigs, and a poultry yard with chickens and turkeys.[26] William Maxwell Wood dubbed his estate Rosewood Glen. Rose Wood was delighted with the home that bore her name.

In recognition of Wood's services during the Civil War, the U.S. Congress created the office of surgeon general and appointed him to the post. Wood's duties forced him to continue his residence in Washington. Rosewood Glen was less than an hour's journey by rail, and he visited his family frequently, but his separate life reenforced the distance and aura of paternal power that already existed. At his office in the nation's capital, Erskine's father remained a potent figure who mingled with America's leaders. Yet among his family he was a distressing presence: demanding, moralizing, emotionally remote.

With the family settled in their new home, Erskine was placed as a day scholar at St. Thomas School for Boys, a short walk from Rosewood Glen. The school advertised itself as being "in the most salubrious part of Baltimore County. . . . Boys will here be under the influence of a refined Christian home."[27] The task of imparting this constructive influence was given to "Old Murray," a sadistic drillmaster who conducted classes by rigorous rote learning. Erskine despised him. A rattan rod waited in the corner, to be liberally applied to any boy who drifted asleep or displayed signs of intellectual or moral laxity.

Rosewood Farm provided ample relief from the rigors of school. Erskine spent the summer of 1866 working side by side with his father's farmhands, gladly abandoning Old Murray's tutelage for that of Uncle Phil, the black gardener, a living repository of farming and hunting lore. Uncle Phil taught Erskine the art of "cradling" grain and the proper use of a scythe to cut hay. He taught him to milk cows, curry horses, and clip sheep. From Uncle Phil he learned how to set rabbit traps out by the sassafras thicket. And he followed the old man on his nighttime 'possum hunts, listening in wonder as Phil crooned to the treed animals, urging them to abandon their chilly perch for the comforts of the scalding bath he had prepared for them. Erskine became a "pagan" delighting in a world of animals, crops, hills, and streams, with illiterate freedmen as his companions and teachers. If his father and Old Murray set Erskine's intellectual development on course, it was Uncle Phil and other black farmhands who initiated him into the rich life of nature.

William Maxwell Wood soon became dissatisfied with St. Thomas School for Boys and enrolled Erskine at Baltimore City College, the high school of the Baltimore public school system. On a spring day in 1869, the school principal called Erskine to his office: an urgent telegram had arrived from his father summoning him immediately to Washington. Erskine made the hourlong train ride and hastened to the Navy Department, where an orderly escorted him into the surgeon general's office. William Maxwell Wood gave the orderly a series of instructions, and a dreamlike series of events ensued. The orderly delivered Erskine to the White House, where he was passed from one room to the next until he was ushered into the office of President Ulysses S. Grant. Wood later remembered "a short man, rather stout,

[he] had a black beard and was smoking a large cigar."[28] Grant called
Erskine's father a great man and cited his various achievements in
preserving the health of the navy and in overseeing the construction
of military hospitals. After a few minutes of chitchat, Grant rose from
his chair and told the boy he would not detain him any longer.

That evening William Maxwell Wood accompanied Erskine home
to Rosewood Glen to announce that President Grant intended to
nominate Erskine as a candidate for cadetship at West Point. Erskine
was never consulted. Wood withdrew his boy from Baltimore City
College and placed him in a special class designed to prepare candidates for their entrance examinations.[29] Soon afterwards, Erskine was
chosen by President Grant as one of eighteen "At Large" appointees
for candidacy to the United States Military Academy.[30]

Erskine reported to West Point on May 25, 1869. With 146 other
candidates he spent the next month studying for his entrance examinations.[31] William Maxwell Wood followed his son's studies with pride
and anxiety. "I think the continuous hard training of West Point is
the best making of a man," he wrote. "You will never forget my care
to educate you in one of the elements of work—early rising. If you
resolve to hop into the engineer corps you will do it, but it will
require your mental work to be kept up to the mark."[32]

The examinations were surprisingly easy. Candidates were asked
to name the principal battles of the War of 1812 and to name the
presidents who died during their respective terms of office. They
were asked to name the states that border the Chesapeake Bay; to
explain what a sea is; and to locate the Black Sea. They were asked
to parse sentences and to correct grammatical errors.[33] Nevertheless,
the general level of public education in America was so uneven—
especially in small towns and rural areas—that less than half of the
West Point candidates received passing grades. On June 27, the
anxious young men stood in formation while the names of those with
passing grades were read aloud in alphabetical order. As a "W,"
Erskine suffered an agonizing wait before he learned that he "was
one of the elect."[34]

Erskine had realized the first stage of his father's design for him.
Years later he claimed, with understandable relief, that he had passed
from under his father's discipline and control at an early age—that

his departure for West Point had brought an end to his boyhood.[35] Still later, however, when Erskine fancifully compared his education to the building of Noah's Ark, there was no question who he had in mind as the righteous seafaring patriarch, the source of both wonder and fear. As a child Erskine stiffened under William Maxwell Wood's authoritarian ways; he resented his father's extended absences and grieved for the tears his father cost his mother. Nevertheless, as he embarked upon his adult life at West Point, he realized that it was his father who had set him on that path. For all the strong antagonism Erskine felt, for all the differences between him and his father, he was very much the product of William Maxwell Wood's overbearing personality.

3. The Best Making of a Man

When Fourth Classman Wood settled in his barracks at summer training camp, the United States Military Academy at West Point was considerably different than the West Point of today. It was, of course, the place where the nation's military leaders were trained, but it was also one of America's leading institutions in civil engineering, mathematics, and natural philosophy. West Point graduates formed an elite corps of skilled personnel who were instrumental in building roads, canals, and railroads. Army engineers supervised the dredging of harbors; they constructed and maintained coastal batteries from Maine to Florida and along the Great Lakes. They explored and mapped the West. They collected scientific data; they built lighthouses; they even built the Washington Monument.[1] As engineers, West Point graduates were essential to America's economic development; as soldiers, they formed the leadership of both the Union and Confederate armies. In every sense, they were pillars of society.

After depositing his luggage in the barracks, Wood's first mission was to be fitted for "the coveted cadet grey." To be measured for the cadet uniform was to be measured for an influential role in American life. It was a rite of entitlement.

Wood was pleased with the dashing figure he cut. He bridled, though, at the abusive rituals of plebe life. "To be degraded in every way and compelled to do the menial and humiliating jobs of the camp"—that was the traditional ordeal for Fourth Classmen.[2] Plebes were driven through repetitive saluting, marching, and military drill, as well as humiliating commands meant to test the spirit and instill discipline. Having spent his childhood coping with his father's strict discipline, Wood was prepared to survive the brutal practices of hazing and to meet the severe requirements of the West Point code. But he did not enjoy it. He seethed under Academy discipline with the same rebellious resentment that he felt toward his father.

And his father continued to make his presence felt. William Maxwell Wood was concerned with every aspect of his son's life. He writes to ask where Erskine will store the toilet articles he has just sent him. And where does he keep his writing materials? A week later he sends Erskine more toilet articles, including "a razor and strap of French calf skin—the only kind which ought to be used." He goes on to offer detailed instructions on what Erskine must do to keep the razor at a fine edge. In William Maxwell Wood's eyes every activity, no matter how insignificant, had a moral ambience. Things must be done properly, with the right equipment, the right training, the right attitude, or else they were sure to be done in slapdash fashion, the sign of a slapdash life.[3]

It is comical and sad to see the limitless opportunities he finds to point out Erskine's flaws. With the boy gone from home, his father's criticism was no longer a matter of tyranny so much as a poignant, though oppressive, wish to offer guiding principles. Every letter was signed "Your affectionate father." Affection was clearly there; but he rarely dropped his hectoring, didactic tone. He was determined to give his son everything, even if he had to go into debt. But he could not give him one essential thing—not willingly, that is: his unconditional trust.

With summer camp over, Erskine encountered the daily pressure of West Point's grueling academic program. Faced with unrelieved routine, Erskine reacted the way he had done so often in his childhood: he got into trouble. The Register of Delinquencies shows him piling up all sorts of petty infractions: inattention at drill, not turning his head and eyes to the left, a soiled collar at guard mounting, shoes not properly blackened at reveille and inspection, swinging his arms as he marched from dinner. Then, on December 8, he was placed under arrest: charged with deserting his post and entering a room adjoining the post area. Erskine was cold and bored and fed up with unquestioning submission to rigorous routine, but that was hardly a compelling excuse. His offense might have led to a court martial, but he got off relatively lightly: he was confined to West Point for six months and forced to stand guard duty every alternate Saturday.[4] Still, it was hard for Erskine to take all this seriously. The week after his arrest, he earned more demerits for carving his name in the seat of a bench, a misdeed that was certain to be detected.

For a young cadet, deserting one's post was a serious violation of Academy rules. But to William Maxwell Wood it was a disgrace that would last indefinitely, taking from his life "what joy it has to a great degree":

> . . . To me it is no relief that you have escaped the penalty of your offence—the crime is not obliterated, it stands forever against you, and a stain upon your official career. . . . You say that the incident will be a useful lesson to you. It will not [for you are guilty of] . . . lying, deceit and trickery. . . .
>
> If you think I have written severely, reflection will show that I have written truly and you must bear in mind that in destroying or weakening my confidence in you, you have inflicted the greatest wound my happiness can receive. . . . I shall be ashamed to show myself at West Point again.[5]

The following summer was Yearling Camp, "a blitz-like sudden change" where survivors of Plebe Year were at last treated with courtesy and respect by upperclassmen.[6] Yearling Camp was an opportunity to relax. Along with practical instruction in field pieces, there were cavalry exercises, fencing lessons, and, as befit an officer and a gentleman, dancing lessons.

Wood's enthusiasm for the summer hops and balls accounts, in part, for his interest in Professor Robert Weir, his drawing teacher. At that time, drawing was a necessary adjunct to engineering, and Weir had been teaching drawing at the Academy for close to forty years. A West Point fixture, Weir was also an artist of national stature whose mural, *Embarkation of the Pilgrims*, graces the Capitol rotunda in Washington DC. The story is told how, in 1851, Weir had one student of particular brilliance who refused to let Weir alter his work. The boy finished first in all his drawing classes but proved mediocre in everything else. In 1853 Weir's gifted student was dismissed from West Point: like Edgar Allan Poe, another West Point failure, James McNeill Whistler was asked to leave the Academy.

Erskine enjoyed the opportunity Weir's classes gave him to visit his home and meet Weir's three daughters, who were in great demand at Academy social events. He also met their brother Julian just before he went off to Paris to study art. Several years later, when Julian settled in New York and began to establish himself as one of the eminent American painters of his generation, the two men would renew their acquaintance and become lifelong friends.

As a yearling, Erskine's insubordination brought him to the brink of dismissal from West Point. The Academy code specified that one hundred demerits automatically ranked a cadet as "deficient in discipline," thus putting his tenure at West Point in jeopardy. In the first six months of his second year, Erskine received ninety-five demerits. Several flagrant violations, such as whistling in the hall and being absent at mandatory events, showed that he did not much care if he got caught. By the end of the year his rank dropped to thirty-ninth in a dwindling class of forty-five.

The third year of cadet life began with summer furlough, which allowed Erskine to return to Rosewood Glen. To his delight, his neighbors, Wilson and Augusta Nicholas, invited Mrs. Nicholas's niece Fannie to spend the summer. Fannie and Erskine quickly became friends and riding companions. In July their pleasant country holiday was shaken by the appearance of Nannie Moale Smith, Fannie's cousin from Washington. Nannie arrived conspicuously—in a basket phaeton made up of bright woven willows. Her vehicle was equipped with a strong white horse with white reins; it was driven by a young black boy outfitted in a tailcoat with silver buttons, knee breeches, and a stovepipe hat. All this, and two greyhounds that loped along beside.[7] Nannie was beautiful, histrionic, and coquettish; she had thick chestnut hair that came down to her knees. Erskine was enthralled.

This captivating young woman lacked little in the way of clothes and comforts, but her personal life had been marked by loss and complicated emotional alliances. Nannie's father, a professor of surgery at the University of Maryland, died in 1860 when she was only five, and for much of the Civil War she lived in Baltimore with her mother's family in a large home teeming with aunts and uncles and cousins.

In 1866 Nannie's mother married Dr. Nathan Lincoln, her deceased husband's cousin. Their marriage offered a practical solution to the problem of providing for Nannie's well-being. Dr. Lincoln moved in Washington's highest social circles, and he was wealthy. Nannie never called Dr. Lincoln anything other than "Cousin Nathan," but he doted on her like the most indulgent father. She had "always wanted a shelf of fairy tales": when her mother remarried, her stepfather took it upon himself to make her every wish come true. Dr. Lincoln gave her a gold chain; he gave her a bedroom of her own; he sent her to Mme. Burr's private school where her classmates represented the cream of Washington society. Nannie might have easily imagined herself a penurious storybook princess restored to her rightful pleasures.

Nannie's mother, who had rarely been in good health, died in the summer of 1869. "Cousin Nathan" did everything he could to fill the bereaved child's life with pleasure. He gave her every advantage—singing, dancing, and music lessons—but she preferred to have "a gay time with the girls and boys." By her own admission, "I was nothing but the spoiled daughter of a lenient step-father."[8]

Spoiled she surely was, but the eighteen-year-old girl who burst into Erskine's life in her wondrous phaeton was beautiful and spirited, wholly alive. Erskine found her irresistible.

In March of 1873, the entire cadet corps crossed the frozen Hudson River and piled into railroad cars that took them to Washington to march at President Grant's second inauguration. In bitter zero-degree cold, they paraded without overcoats before immense cheering crowds; out of ranks they were treated "like young princes."[9] The corps was ordered to appear at the inaugural ball, but Nannie insisted on having a small dance at her house. Her family pulled the necessary strings so that Erskine and a few of his companions were given leave to attend. "Ah me!" Erskine wrote her a few years later, "how full of sweet memories are those two or three days. Can we ever forget them Nan? I know I went back to West Point the most miserable and the happiest of mortals. Do you remember our first kiss, pet? What a precious kiss that was to me. It made me happy on that cold and lonely journey back to West Point and it kept me true to you through all the days of my growing love."[10]

Several weeks later, Erskine began a journal of his feelings—an ongoing love letter to Nannie that he wrote before turning in each night: "Oh darling, I love you so dearly, so dearly. I cannot keep apart from you. I feel sometimes when alone and undisturbed that it is not so impossible to die for lack of the one we love and I do love you dear and I want you so much, I want to hold you and call you all mine."[11]

It is a peculiar thing, this journal. On the one hand, it is addressed to Nannie; on the other, it is a monologue directed to himself. He is drawn to Nannie, yet he barely knows her. The Nannie he writes to in his journal has few specific characteristics. She is "frail" and "precious," his "Petite," his "little darling" and "little Pet," his "little wife." "Love I have always loved you," he writes, "without myself knowing it." She is love itself—and, not infrequently, she becomes a mirror of his self-regard. "I know you love me darling," he writes, "because I love you so." In an effort at humility he expresses bafflement that she is drawn to him—and in the process he manages to pay himself several compliments. "What can my darling love me for?" he muses. "Love does not depend on anything so shallow and temporal as looks. Then what quality can I have that attracts one? . . . I used to think that I could have almost any woman I set to win. . . . I thought that I ought to wait and do something brilliant and dazzling and sell myself for a very high price. Ah you will know when I changed and found you a treasure."

Scattered amidst these romantic effusions are passages that dramatize what was, and would remain, a central issue in Erskine's life: a constant wish for money. With money he could marry Nannie; they could have "a cozy little cottage where we could live alone and undisturbed." Erskine's vision of domestic bliss was at odds with the low-paid life of a young army officer. "I seem to dream of happiness like a boy," he wrote, "and take no heed to the practical means of getting it."[12] Erskine could not bear the thought of waiting to take Nannie as his wife, and he hated to think of the strain rough army life would put on her.

That spring Erskine wrote to his father and made what he thought to be a very practical proposal: he would resign from the army to take up a literary career. That letter no longer exists, but we have William Maxwell Wood's scathing reply:

Thousands of men in mature age, of large literary ability, (I will not judge how their abilities compete with yours because you are not yet in the arena) are content to exist meagerly upon petty and uncertain clerkships which give them their daily food—and these men of education of mature years, even under more than ordinary success, will covet your position the day you graduate both on account of its honorable standing and substantial rewards. . . .

I think if you reflect upon this letter, you will be amused by your crazy notion that to be a literary man you must change a profession, or rather that your genius will be more fertile when you do not know where to get your breakfast than when it rests upon the comforts of that substantial meal. . . . I think you will see how easily a fellow can humbug himself.[13]

As if this was not enough, William Maxwell Wood somehow got wind of his son's "journal of feelings." In one more display of paternal despotism, he absolutely forbade his son from continuing it.

Throughout his last year at West Point, Erskine remained ambivalent, if not outright opposed, to pursuing an army career. Not surprisingly, he continued piling on disciplinary demerits. Once again, he stirred his father's wrath: "You seem determinedly resolved to deny to me and to your mother, ill able to contend with such griefs, the satisfaction of having a *well doing son*—I do not say a bright, brilliant and exceptional man, that, our parental ambition does not aspire to, and if it did, deserves that rebuke, which, it seems, you are determined to give it."[14]

Erskine had not wholly abandoned his dream of writing, but now two new possibilities attracted him. Dutifully, he shared his thoughts with his father: perhaps he would go off to serve as a mercenary in the Egyptian army; or maybe he would start an orange plantation in Florida. William Maxwell Wood ridiculed Erskine's dreams of "grasping fortune and fame directly . . . [as] field marshal in the service of the king of Dahomey, or some other barbarian. [Your proposal] gratifies a monomaniacal and boyish desire to change the routine of your first years of continuous mental and physical work. Such a letter might well have been written by academic cloistered school girls whose imaginations inflamed and perverted by fairy tales the Arabian

Nights and maudlin stories have destroyed all reasonable judgment and led them to feel sure that they have but to step from their school rooms to marry princes."[15]

Even when William Maxwell Wood spoke sense to his son, his tone was judgmental, sarcastic—a didactic broadside rather than an exercise in loving instruction. In this respect, his closing to this twenty-three page letter approached self-parody. "I do not wish in any way to control your decision of your avocation in life," he writes, "that is . . . your responsibility. I simply wish to show that you are not now in any condition of mental or moral fitness of any experience of life to make a sound judgment."

In spite of his father's judgment, Erskine thoroughly enjoyed himself at the Hundredth Night Celebration, a time of dinners, skits, games, theatrical entertainments, and noteworthy guest speakers— a celebration of the fact that only one hundred days remained until graduation. In these events he distinguished himself: he was funny, high-spirited, a natural extemporaneous speaker who his classmates selected to be valedictorian. Other than that, Erskine's claims to distinction were few. He graduated twenty-fourth in a class of forty-one. He stood apart from his classmates in only two areas: he was one of the top four or five students in drawing; and his four-year total of disciplinary demerits was surpassed by only three other cadets.

Erskine returned to Rosewood Glen for graduation furlough and made several upsetting discoveries. When he reached retirement age, William Maxwell Wood had been relieved of his office as surgeon general of the navy and appointed to serve as the navy's medical director, a post created for him. It soon became clear, however, that politics and bureaucratic confusion rendered the job meaningless. Along with this, Rosewood Glen was a financial fiasco. Like all William Maxwell Wood's treasured objects, the farm had been purchased impulsively—because it was beautiful, because he wanted it. But Rosewood Glen did not pay for itself. Faced with the pressures of increasing debt, and with no prospects of wielding his influence in Washington, William Maxwell Wood did what his father had done in similar circumstances: he turned to drinking. Each month when payday came around, he joined his old shipmates at the paymaster's office in Baltimore and went off on reckless drinking sprees. His career had been spent during "the age of hard drinking in the navy, and drinking bouts—when he who could remain off the floor longest was a hero."[16] But there was nothing heroic about buckling beneath the pressure of "debt and worries and declining strength of old age."[17] To see his father reduced to alcoholism, bitter and powerless, would have been bad enough. But Erskine also saw him abuse his mother with ferocious eruptions of temper. For years William Maxwell Wood had lectured his son on gentlemanly behavior, self-discipline, and the dangers of moral degradation. Now his behavior was "almost unbearable." There was nothing Erskine could do: "our home became a wretched place."

His main pleasure that summer was his campaign to hold Nannie's fickle affection. That August, Nannie's uncle, an accomplished horseman, challenged Erskine to ride bareback on an unbroken six-year-old horse. Eager to impress Nannie, Erskine caught the animal's mane in his hands and leaped onto his back. The spirited animal tossed him high into the air; Erskine fell heavily and broke his collar bone. It was, however, a fortunate fall. He was confined to Rosewood Glen for the month and placed under Nannie's daily care.

All that autumn, Erskine remained utterly infatuated with Nannie, a swooning Orlando ardently voicing every romantic cliché, discovered anew in the heat of churning emotion: "Just to think Nan of living together night and day without interruption for years. You will be good and sweet and kind to your boy who loves you so—won't you darling?"[18]

Erskine called on Dr. Lincoln and asked him for Nannie's hand. Dr. Lincoln reminded Lieutenant Wood that army pay of $115 per month could not support the pampered young woman he hoped to marry.[19] Dr. Lincoln prevailed on Nannie to wait.

In Washington, Erskine and Nannie bade goodbye. The lovers embraced and Nannie suppressed a sob or two. Faithfully observing the protocols of youthful romance, she pulled from her bosom a gold locket containing a photograph of herself and a lock of her hair which she gave to Erskine accompanied by more kisses and tears.[20]

A few days later, Wood was on his way West, untested by life, impatient to lay claim to his future.

4. A Glade in the Fir Forest

In August 1875 Lieutenant Wood's regiment docked at Fort Vancouver on the Columbia River, where they were met by a bustle of horses, wagons, and workmen assigned by the quartermaster's department to move the new arrivals to their quarters.

At the time of Erskine's arrival, Fort Vancouver had been under American sovereignty for less than thirty years. Before that it was a thriving British outpost for the lucrative fur trade established by the Hudson's Bay Company in the first decade of the nineteenth century. Back then, Fort Vancouver "was a fairy land to early travellers and settlers," a pocket of "civilized" life where British officers and their families shared the streets with Indians, mountain men, and New England merchants.[1] By 1859, when Oregon became a state, Portland, which lies just south of Fort Vancouver, had supplanted the army post as the principal town of the region. In just thirty years, trade from the fertile Willamette Valley propelled Portland from a struggling frontier settlement with tree stumps jutting in the streets to the second-largest city (after San Francisco) on the Pacific Coast.

At a time when much of America west of the Mississippi had not yet been divided into states, Portland served as administrative headquarters for the Department of the Columbia, a territory that covered what is now Washington, Idaho, and Alaska. Wood was delighted with his post. "The busy river traffic, . . . the booming commercial life of Portland, the concentration of officers and administrators (and, quite important to the young men, the presence of their daughters) all gave this post an air of relative gentility."[2] An attractive young officer who proved himself capable of rudimentary deportment was likely to be much in demand. Before long, he was a regular visitor to the home of General Oliver Otis Howard, commander of the Department of the Columbia. Not incidentally, Howard's daughter Grace had recently graduated from Vassar College and found her father's post grievously lacking in suitable companions.

For all their amenities, Fort Vancouver and Portland were isolated islands in an uncharted wilderness. "It was pretty much as when the First Dragoons received it from the Hudson Bay Company," Wood wrote, "just a glade in the fir forest with the broad Columbia in front and impenetrable miles of sunless fir forest at the rear. . . . This impassable and unexplored wilderness within a hundred feet of the back door inspired a feeling of awe."[3] What was "unexplored wilderness" to Lieutenant Wood was, in fact, the ancestral homeland for several groups of Native Americans. Beyond the virgin forests, eastward across the Cascade Range, lay the high desert plains and river valleys of eastern Oregon and Idaho, where the Modoc, Palouse, Cayuse, Paiute, Bannock, Nez Perce, and Flathead Indians struggled to keep their territory in the face of America's rush to reap profit from its western lands.

Letters from Nannie and William Maxwell Wood followed Wood to Vancouver Barracks. In the romantic tradition of her time, Nannie's letters were "cross-written." After penning sixteen pages in tight, precise script, she turned the note paper sideways and wrote another sixteen pages that crossed the previous lines at right angles. The completed letter, a puzzle of cross-hatched words, is virtually unreadable—except to her beloved. Nannie chides Erskine for some bit of mischief back at West Point. Has he hurt her? Is she playing the coquette? If, indeed, Nannie is truly uneasy, the length of the letter, the conspiratorial cross-writing, indicates their bond is strong; they will weather this lovers' storm. Or perhaps there is no storm at all, but only the episodes, real and fabricated, of two ardent young people forced to carry on their romance at a distance. Their minds (and bodies too, though they never mention them except as vessels for their feelings) are restless and eager.[4]

Erskine wrote regularly to Nannie—lengthy letters, almost comically conventional, gushing with the ardent spirit of young love: "My darling, darling, darling little girl how heartsick I am for you tonight.

Oh my sweetest one I have thought of you so much today, thought of you lovingly and longingly till it seemed as if my heart would break. My precious precious little girl my own dear treasure why are you not here to brighten my home and make me happy?"[5] On and on he goes, lost in his lover's world, with little mention of his active life.

As a child, Nannie could never quite pronounce her surname, Smith. "Sips" was the best she could do, and from that came "Sippy," Erskine's private term of endearment.[6] He hungered for every bit of news from his precious Sippy, new emblems of her affection. His father's letters moved him too, though they aroused complex, contradictory feelings. Soon after Erskine arrived at Fort Vancouver, he received a long letter from William Maxwell Wood bristling with the assured high-mindedness one might expect from a gentleman essayist of the eighteenth century. But this was not the Earl of Shaftesbury reflecting on the vicissitudes of human behavior: William Maxwell Wood's exercise in reasonable discourse was devoted to a financial crisis brought on by his own unreasonable behavior. He told his son that the failure of the farm to support his family was a matter of "a few stubborn facts." He remarked on the propensity of people to avoid admitting the true cause of their misery, yet he evaded the obvious fact that he had long been living beyond his means.[7]

There was nothing Erskine could do to relieve his father's burden. From time to time he sent money to Rosewood Glen, but this was only a palliative. When Erskine departed for the West, he was relieved to put an entire continent between himself and his domineering father, yet it pained him now to see his father rendered powerless by increasing debt. Erskine was also affected by his father's penchant for haughty self-justification. William Maxwell Wood needed to state his case in a manner that gave him "control" over his humbling situation. His inclination to transform personal difficulties into intriguing philosophical abstractions; his habit of substituting imperious didacticism for candid self-analysis—these evasive strategies made a lasting impression on his son.

At Fort Vancouver, Captain Robert Pollock made good use of Lieutenant Wood. The Department of the Columbia was responsible for maintaining civil order and for engaging in projects essential to the region's economic development. These activities often led to legal and jurisdictional disputes, as well as questions involving military discipline and criminal acts. To settle these issues, Pollock appointed Wood to serve as judge advocate of the Department.

In early 1877 Charles H. Taylor, a wealthy Chicago merchant, formed an expedition to explore the Alaska Territory and to climb Mount Saint Elias, one of a string of towering peaks that loom over the Gulf of Alaska at the point where southeastern Alaska connects to the great Alaskan land mass. When Taylor arrived in Portland with authorization from Washington to request a military officer to accompany him, General Howard selected Lieutenant Wood. On April 2, Wood was formally detached from active duty for the purpose of visiting Mount Saint Elias and gathering all military information of value.[8]

Just ten years before, in 1867, the United States had purchased the Alaska Territory from Russia. Several expeditions had undertaken preliminary exploration of the region, but most of this vast area had never been charted, or even seen, by anyone other than native Alaskans and a few Russian fur trappers. Erskine was elated at the opportunity to take part in the Taylor Expedition. At Sitka and other trading posts, he would find the kind of rough and tumble frontier life that was already passing from the American West. Farther north, he would be able to visit native cultures that were relatively untainted by encroaching "civilization." There would be a climb up the rugged mountain, the chance to prepare the first maps of vast unknown regions. Finally, and perhaps most important, the expedition would give Erskine an opportunity to pursue his dream of a literary career, for, in spite of his father's belittling reaction only a few years before, he had never relinquished his wish to become a writer. Now circumstances conspired to offer him this golden opportunity: leave from active military duty, and a journey into unknown parts of America's last great wilderness.

5. A Young Chief

In April 1877, the Taylor Expedition boarded the steamer *California* and headed north to the Straits of Fuca. In an account he wrote four years later, Wood's youthful enthusiasm shines through: "Our purpose was to climb Mount St. Elias, the highest peak in the world above the snow line, to explore the Mount St. Elias alps, and to acquire information about the unknown districts lying nearest the coast, with a view to future explorations. For less is known today of Central Alaska than of Central Africa."[1] He continued in a fanciful vein:

> As we entered the harbor of Sitka from the sea the general appearance of the place was tropical. . . . Everywhere below the snow-line the mountains were green with luxuriant growth. The harbor was protected against the sea by a curved line of reefs, on which grew firs and pines and cedars, with bare trunks and tufts of branches, making them look not unlike palms. The warm, moist atmosphere curtained all the middle distance with a film of blue, and, in the foreground, a fleet of very graceful canoes, filled with naked or half-naked Indians, completed the illusion.[2]

This "tropical" paradise is an "illusion," as Wood himself admitted, and rather strained as a piece of description. Perhaps this whimsical passage was a gesture at laying claim to his father's domain: not simply the exotic territory of William Maxwell Wood's Pacific exploits, but also the province of writing itself—the privileged role of imposing his personality, imagination, and voice on the world he encountered.

Sitka, as Wood quickly discovered, was the antithesis of a South

Seas idyll: it was a squalid frontier town of unadorned plank dwellings pressed close to the rocky shore. The snow-covered peak of Mount Edgecumbe loomed in the distance, an impressive sight; but the town itself offered little more than muddy streets. In Thlinkit, the Indian language of the region, "sitka" means "the best place"—and for the Russian and British traders who had made quick fortunes there, it certainly deserved its name. Sitka was, indeed, the best place to hunt sea otters: they swarmed by the tens of thousands in channels off the coast until, in the early years of the nineteenth century, hunters nearly obliterated them to satisfy the demand for their lovely pelts. With the sea otters gone, competition for the inland fur trade grew vicious. The rivalry was not simply between the two colonial powers, but also between the fur traders and local Indians who had no intention of surrendering their most valuable resource without getting something in return. It was an ugly situation that, over the years, corrupted everyone.[3] By the time of Wood's visit, Sitka was preeminent only as a breeding ground for dissolute living.

Taylor's days in Sitka were consumed by protracted negotiations with local chiefs and sub-chiefs who owned the canoes that would carry Taylor and his party north. As far as Wood was concerned, the whole lot of them were "grasping, shrewd, and unscrupulous," a bunch of "land-sharks."[4] Wood passed his time in Sitka gathering impressions of the crude community life. He must have been acquainted with Bret Harte's colorful anecdotal writing and that of young Mark Twain in *Life on the Mississippi* and *Roughing It*. The fragments that remain from his Sitka journal suggest that he wished to produce something similar: a humorous anecdotal account of frontier life, its roguish characters, and colorful speech. He was interested in stories of the "old times" under the Russian government, and he was struck by the "drunkenness, squalor, debauchery, prostitution, stagnation, filth, and . . . unreliability of the men for work" that prevailed in the present.[5]

Eventually, Taylor found a sturdy four-ton canoe and hired three Indians and a local prospector to serve as his crew. For several days the expedition paddled north through the channels, straits, and sounds that form an inland waterway through the Alexander Archipelago. With the mission underway, Wood's status as an army officer was almost beside the point. Here in Alaska he was an adventurous young writer discovering rich material. From Chatham Strait they paddled west against headwinds into Cross Sound, where the inland waterway opens onto the Gulf of Alaska. There they camped near Cape Spencer, within sight of Mount Crillon (12,700 ft.) and Mount Fairweather (15,300 ft.). At this point Tah-ah-nah-lekh, the boat's owner and spokesman for the crew, insisted that pushing on in open seas would mean death to all. Ahead lay turbulent waters with no landing places, only rocky cliffs. Continuing their journey was out of the question.

Taylor and his party remained near Cape Spencer for several days in hopes of persuading the crew to push on. Wood quickly fell in with Indian life. He lived in a hut where snow-shoes, nets, and fish hung from the rafters; where the walls were covered with traps, bows, spears, paddles, and skins of bear, sable, and silver fox. He observed women weaving baskets and sewing clothing. He sat with old men who spent their days smoking harsh tobacco and recounting tribal legends. He watched children play, and he interviewed the clan leader on matters of family inheritance, tribal law, and warfare. When a party of seal hunters set out for the icebergs and floating ice, Wood joined them "to learn the art."

With no hope of continuing north, Taylor decided to return to Chicago. Wood elected to stay on. He had already written Washington and requested a three-year leave of absence in order to explore the Alaska interior, "which was then but a blank paper." Rather than killing time in Sitka waiting for a reply, he mounted his own expedition and set out to locate the headwaters of the Yukon River. (Wood's hunch that the Chilkaht River would lead him to a point close to the source of the Yukon River was borne out by Lieutenant Frederick Schwatka, who led a reconnaissance of the Yukon Valley in 1883.)[6]

Things did not go as planned. Wood made his way to Glacier Bay, where he was welcomed by the chief of a village of Asonque Indians. He lived in the chief's cabin along with a bevy of the chief's wives. After several days in the Asonque settlement, Wood donned a belted squirrel-skin shirt, a conical fur headdress, and sealskin boots to join a camp of seal hunters perched on a ledge of rocks beside the icy waters. Even in these bleak surroundings, Wood found much to engage his interest. These people, who still used stone axes and knives, had never seen a white man. Their leader was a shaman named Coon-nah-nah-thkle, "the most thoughtful and entertaining

Thlinkit I had met." With the sound of icebergs crunching and grinding in the waters beneath the ledge, Coon-nah-nah-thkle captivated Wood with tribal legends recited "in low, musical intonations, almost like chanting."

Wood stayed with Coon-nah-nah-thkle longer than he had planned, though eventually he grew anxious to return to Sitka to see if permission for his extended leave had come through. On his way back to Sitka, near Hoonah at the head of Chatham Strait, an old head chief prevailed on Wood to come to his island and tend to his ailing son. Wood agreed to look at the boy but he was reluctant to do any doctoring. As he wryly observed, "the Thlinkit custom of killing the doctor in case his patient dies, is discouraging to the beginner." Nevertheless, Wood intervened. He prescribed hot baths to bring down the boy's fever, and he impressed everyone by administering a bubbling solution of seidlitz powder, a popular home remedy similar to today's Alka Seltzer. When the boy recovered, Wood was pressed into service to treat the aches and pains of the entire village. "During my stay I built up an extensive practice," he recalled. His breezy account of his brief career as a medical practitioner is in the same vein as that of Harry Morgan, Mark Twain's Connecticut Yankee, who ten years later found himself bringing the wonders of civilization to awestruck "primitives" at King Arthur's court.

As a stranger of rank, a veritable miracle worker, Wood was rewarded in the traditional way: the chief presented him with a young Indian woman, "the comeliest of her race"—a chief in her own right and the niece of a powerful Chilkaht leader. The plump, roundfaced woman welcomed him to her hut furnished with bear and seal skins strewn over the frozen earth, and there they lived together. In an article Wood wrote a few years later, he says she mended his clothes and sang chants for his pleasure. Out of chivalrous consideration for Nannie, Wood said nothing more about their relationship, but there is little doubt that he and his Chilkaht companion were sexually intimate. Fifty years later, long after a truthful confession could hurt anyone's feelings, Wood admitted to a friend that the young woman, "after the simple frank fashion of her sex among her people, made love to me."[7]

When Wood told his consort of his intention to search for the headwaters of the Chilkaht, she promised to mount the expedition herself, putting slaves and canoes at his disposal, and guaranteeing his safe passage through fur country where her uncle killed all intruders.[8] Wood explained that before setting out on his exploration he was obligated to return to Sitka. He promised to return. Still, in the Thlinkits' perilous environment every departure was a solemn occasion:

> In the gray dawn, as we were about to push from shore, the old chief came to us accompanied by two of his wives. My blanket was wrapped round him. He said I had a good heart. I was a young chief now, but some day I would be a great one. Among the Thlinkits, he said, when a friend was leaving on a long journey, they watched him out of sight, for he might never return. I was his friend. I was going away to my own land. He would never see me again. Therefore he had come to watch me out of sight. . . .
>
> The breeze was freshening. I wrapped my capote about me and stepped aboard. We paddled rapidly out to sea, and it was not long before the three figures were lost to view.[9]

6. A Crack at an Indian

When Wood arrived in Sitka in early June, he received word that the army had granted him the three-year leave he requested. However, there was also news that the Nez Perce Indians had attacked settlers in western Idaho. Information was fragmentary; the cause and extent of the conflict were unclear, but Wood learned that his Twenty-first Regiment had been called to the front. Had he chosen to do so, he might have ignored these tidings of war and headed north to chart the Alaskan interior. Instead, he caught the first steamer south.

At Fort Canby, on the mouth of the Columbia River, he received "stirring news" that all troops were ordered to the front. At Astoria, the old trading outpost, there was more news: reports that Captain David Perry and his men had been massacred. Everywhere was an air of excitement. "Go in and kill em boys!" civilians cheered. "Don't spare the bloody savages!" To which Wood reacted in his journal: "Confound these cusses! Wish they were going to fight them instead of standing on a wharf and pat[ting] us on the back."[1]

After an overnight stop in Portland, Wood boarded a Columbia River steamer headed east. With five companies of men and an ample supply of munitions, Gatling guns, and howitzers, he continued his journey to the strife-torn interior.

The Nez Perce outbreak, toward which Wood hurried so exuberantly, was one of the last times that Native Americans struck back at encroaching whites with armed resistance. The killing began when, nearly a year after Custer's crushing defeat at the Little Big Horn,

Nez Perce warriors inflicted heavy casualties on an army cavalry detachment at White Bird Canyon near the Salmon River in Idaho. As news of the "massacre" spread, the entire region rose up in a wave of vengeful anger, demanding that the Indians' "reign of terror" be crushed.[2]

The Nez Perce were one of the most respected western Indian nations. Centuries before the first white men crossed the Rockies, the Nez Perce hunted freely over an immense territory roughly defined by the Blue Mountains to the west and the Bitterroot Mountains to the east: an area that covered northeastern Oregon, southeastern Washington, and a broad belt of land across central Idaho. On buffalo hunts the Nez Perce ventured even farther—east along the treacherous Lolo Trail to the Montana plains, or south over the Continental Divide to the headwaters of the Missouri River. The Nez Perce lands were blessed with woods, fertile valleys, and camas prairies; rivers abundant with salmon; forests and valleys teeming with elk, deer, sheep, goats, antelope, rabbits, and gamebirds. When Lewis and Clark entered their territory in 1805, the Nez Perce provided the exhausted travelers with food and information, as well as guaranteeing them peaceful passage on their journey to the Pacific. In the years that followed, the Nez Perce cultivated good relations with whites. They received the first bands of settlers without rancor: there was land and bounty enough for all. They suffered the inevitable Christian missionaries with tolerance and curiosity—in some cases with unexpected fervor. As long as the incursion of whites was relatively meager, the Nez Perce accepted it with equanimity. Their resolute efforts to coexist led, in 1855, to an extraordinary gathering of northwestern tribes at which Governor Isaac Stevens negotiated an agreement guaranteeing Oregon's fertile Wallowa Valley as the Nez Perce's inviolable homeland. The United States Senate confirmed this treaty, which gave the Nez Perce legal title to an area larger than Massachusetts.

It did not take long before the U.S. government found itself unwilling to observe its written pledge. In the late 1850s gold was discovered in western Idaho; prospectors poured onto Indian lands by the thousands, along with bands of homesteaders eager to set up ranches and farms to provide horses, beef, and food supplies in exchange for gold. By the early 1860s close to twenty thousand whites were living illegally on Nez Perce territory. Pressured by demands from the tenacious settlers and by the possibility of extended economic development, the government foisted a new treaty on the Nez Perce in 1863, which cut the reservation boundaries by about four and one-half million acres. Tu-eka-kas (known to us by his missionary-given name, "Old Joseph"), White Bird, Looking Glass, Too-hul-hul-sote, and other Nez Perce leaders refused to sign the revised treaty, so government negotiators hatched a strategy to avoid them. They found new Indian leaders, most of whom were Christian converts, willing to sign away the Nez Perce's ancestral land and agree to provisions requiring the Nez Perce to move to the Lapwai Reservation in Idaho.

Over the next few years little was done to compel "non-treaty" Nez Perce to forsake their cherished Wallowa Valley. However, when homesteaders began arriving in greater numbers, many Nez Perce wanted to resist them with force. By now, Old Joseph was dead, but his son, Chief Joseph, was determined to press the Nez Perce's treaty claims without resorting to violence. Joseph often astonished listeners with his eloquence and reticent wit. One memorable exchange went like this:

"Do you want schools or houses on the Wallowa reservation?" they [an investigating commission] had asked him.

"No," he had answered. "We do not want schools or school houses on the Wallowa Reservation."

"Why do you not want schools?"

"They will teach us to have churches."

"Do you not want churches?"

"No, we do not want churches."

"Why do you not want churches."

"They will teach us to quarrel about God, as the Catholics and Protestants do on the Nez Perce reservation and at other places. We do not want to learn that. We may quarrel with men sometimes about things on this earth, but we never quarrel about God. We do not want to learn that."[3]

Joseph defended the Nez Perce homeland, guaranteed by the 1855 treaty, before the Bureau of Indian Affairs, a corrupt body that almost always supported white economic interests. The outcome was predictable. In 1875 the Department of the Interior permitted settlers to begin a wagon road into Joseph's valley, an invitation to further homesteading. This betrayal made it almost certain that sooner or later the Nez Perce would go to war. Joseph faced increasing pressure from non-treaty chiefs who favored armed resistance. Foreseeing the devastating outcome of confronting the army's vastly superior numbers, Joseph restrained his people and continued to petition government officials for honorable terms. Then, in September 1874, General Oliver Otis Howard was appointed commander of the Department of the Columbia.

With his thick black beard, high forehead, and thoughtful, brooding gaze, General Howard personified flinty New England piety. Known as "the Christian General," Howard served in the Union army and lost his arm at Seven Pines in the Battle of Fair Oaks. He returned to lead his Eleventh Corps in several major battles. With his empty right sleeve hooked to a button just above his belt, he cut an impressive figure. All in all, Howard was a fearless, competent commander— a humble man in a profession with more than its share of ambitious egoists.

At the close of the Civil War, Howard served as commissioner of the newly constituted Freedmen's Bureau, where he faced the imposing task of overseeing the welfare of four million freed slaves. It was Howard's job to set up appropriate instruments for famine relief, employment, and education, as well as to form initiatives to guarantee blacks' full legal rights as people rather than as chattel. His record was admirable. He encouraged education at all levels, well beyond mere token literacy. His advocacy of freedmen's education led to the founding of the black university which still bears his name. Howard gave five thousand dollars of his own money to Howard University, and he raised an additional ten thousand dollars to give its law department a firm financial base.[4]

It would seem that Howard was ideally suited for his assignment in the Pacific Northwest. In the Department of the Columbia his primary task would be to maintain good relations between white settlers and Indian tribes. Once again he could serve as a man of peace.

From the start, Howard was impressed with Joseph. On two occasions he authorized army officers to prepare reports on the legality of Joseph's claims. Both times he was told that the treaty of 1863 was invalid, that the government remained bound by its original obligations of 1855. But Howard had no means to alter Washington's policy. Nor was he inclined to try. He was a man of honor—this made him receptive to Joseph's character—but he had spent his life as a loyal soldier. Fifteen years before, Howard had fought to preserve the Union: whatever sympathy he felt for the Nez Perce, whatever injustice existed in the treaties and executive orders that expropriated Indian lands, "the Christian General" was duty-bound to uphold the United States government's authority.

Howard intended to deal with the Nez Perce firmly but without force. Joseph shared Howard's wish to settle matters peacefully, but his paramount duty was to keep his people on the land of their forefathers. If the Nez Perce fought to defend their lands, sooner or later they would be destroyed by the whites' superior numbers. But if they relinquished the Wallowa Valley, it would be a kind of suicide. Joseph had pledged to uphold his dying father's command: never to sell his home, never to lead his people from the resting place of their ancestors' bones.

In May 1877 matters came to a head. Howard met with the nontreaty Indians and bluntly declared they would be given thirty days to remove themselves to the Lapwai Reservation. Joseph urged his fellow leaders to accept Howard's proposal. It was an agonizing decision, for in acting to save his people's lives, he was counseling them to surrender the repository of their ancestors' souls.

In late May, the Nez Perce left their homeland. Joseph, Too-hul-hul-sote, White Bird, and other lesser chiefs led their people north, across the Snake River, then eastward into Idaho, where they joined the followers of Looking Glass and Koolkool Snehee. At Rocky Canyon the various bands of nontreaty Nez Perce assembled, six hundred people in all. There they held a ten-day council before moving on to the Lapwai Reservation, a day's journey away. Dispossessed, resentful, uncertain of their future, and extremely wary of the U.S. government's broken pledges, many of the younger Nez Perce clamored for war. For once, Joseph could not restrain them.

There were any number of causes for what happened next, but the immediate provocation was this: two years before, a white man had slain an Indian and his crime went unpunished. Now, spurred on by roiling emotions in the Rocky Canyon camp, the slain man's son vowed to avenge the disgrace. He went to the cabin of his father's murderer but did not find him—so he killed another white man who had often mistreated Indians. This led to sporadic killing and looting as small parties of Nez Perce took to settling old scores.

When word of these incidents reached General Howard, he sent Captain David Perry south from Fort Lapwai to protect settlers and to urge the Indians to hold to their promise to move peacefully to the Lapwai Reservation. On June 17, Perry led one hundred soldiers and a group of civilian volunteers after a band of sixty Nez Perce. They were met in White Bird Canyon by a party of Indians bearing a white flag of truce. A civilian volunteer opened fire. The Nez Perce returned fire from protected positions on the ridges and buttes, killing thirty-four of Perry's men. The soldiers panicked and scattered; many others might have been slaughtered but the Indians chose not to pursue them.

The bloodshed at White Bird Canyon was promptly labeled a "massacre," encouraging an alarmed nation to draw comparisons to the slaughter of General Custer and his men the year before. This was the "stirring news" that ended Lieutenant Wood's Alaskan adventures and sent him hurrying to the front.

During Wood's hasty journey from Sitka he felt mounting anticipation at the prospect of seeing his first combat. At White Bird Canyon, all this changed. He assisted in burning corpses that had lain exposed in rain and summer heat for ten days. "Terrible stench," he wrote, "arms and cheeks gone, bellies swollen, blackened faces, mutilations, heads gone." The regiment camped "[with] mutilated corpses and death in ghastly forms, strewn on every side."[5]

The days that followed brought bad weather, exhaustion, anxious boredom, a wish to get on with the inevitable: "Rain—eternal rain. . . . The advance, more rains, Indians speckling the hills like ants, firing, sudden feeling of anticipation on hearing the shots. Nervous eagerness for the fight. . . . Only want a crack at an Indian and feel no disposition to show any quarter."[6]

Howard's command of five hundred men trudged through mud and hail, moving pack mules and supplies twelve to fifteen miles per day, before resting at miserable camps. While Howard's cumbersome army pushed on in search of the Nez Perce warriors, Joseph guided a large body of women, children, and old men in an elaborate evasive action. The chiefs held several councils but they must have known they were merely choosing between different courses of self-destruction. They could surrender and settle on the unwanted Lapwai Reservation; they could flee, putting themselves still further from their homeland; or they could stand their ground and throw themselves into suicidal battle. Faced with these impossible choices, they chose to fight a limited defensive war. In many cases they avoided harming civilians. At the Slate Creek settlement, Nez Perce warriors gathered supplies and paid the astonished shopkeepers in full. For supposed savages on the warpath, such behavior was unprecedented.[7]

The Nez Perce marched east along the Cottonwood River, always keeping a day or so ahead of Howard's army. But by July 10, after they crossed the Clearwater River, Howard had closed to within six miles. That evening, Wood wrote in his journal about wild flowers and tulips. The following day he was huddled in a trench, fighting for his life.

The Battle of Clearwater, as it was called, was a near disaster. Howard's army advanced too rapidly; after initial success his men found themselves pinned on a plateau, with Indian sharpshooters firing at them from rocks and ravines. Howard's force outnumbered the Nez Perce five to one, but the Indians had thoroughly outmaneuvered them. Wood's first battle was very nearly his last. Howard's men were too well dug-in for the Nez Perce to overrun their defenses, but a protracted stalemate favored the Indians. Without water and supplies, with no hope of relief, Howard's army might have collapsed in a few days. But the Nez Perce chiefs were not out for slaughter. They understood that if they destroyed Howard's army, they could never hope to return to the Wallowa Valley and live in peace. After holding Howard at their mercy for close to a day, they withdrew.

At this point, Looking Glass persuaded his fellow chiefs to embark upon a bold and tragic trek. They could not fight their way back to the Wallowa Valley, he argued: it was time to think of survival. The Nez Perce chose to head east, along the Lolo Trail, a rugged 250-mile path that had been used for centuries by Nez Perce buffalo hunters. Farther east, they would cross the Bitterroot Mountains into

Montana and enter the great plains of Yellowstone Basin, where they hoped the Crows would welcome and assist them.

For the first time in the campaign, Howard seized prisoners: a band of local Nez Perce who had refused to take part in the rebellion. "Night with the prisoners," Wood reflected, "musings on the unhappy people and the fate before them. Thoughts on the Indian as a human being, a man and brother. His strange wisdom, inability to fuse with the white man." Wood was assigned to participate in a judicial charade in which he recorded the prisoners' alleged treaty violations, people he himself saw as "innocent captives." When they were sent off to confinement, Wood somberly reflected on their fate: "Night march, no shoes, no nothin[g] now."[8]

Howard did not take up immediate pursuit. The Lolo Trail was outside his jurisdiction. Protocol required that he await orders from General William Tecumseh Sherman, commanding general of the army. Before Howard resumed his chase, he promoted Wood to serve as his aide-de-camp. It would be Wood's duty to act as Howard's personal secretary: to write reports and orders, and to keep a formal record of daily events. Often, he sat up half the night writing orders and reports by the light of a candle stuck in a half of a raw potato.[9] Howard grew so fond of his devoted aide that he invited Wood to share his tent with him and his son Guy.

Howard's march through the Lolo Trail was a punishing ordeal. As General Sherman put it, "this is universally admitted by all who have travelled it—from Lewis and Clark to Captain Winter—as one of the worst *trails* for man and beast on this continent."[10] Nevertheless, the Nez Perce nation—some two hundred men and over five hundred women and children—completed the treacherous journey in only nine days, well ahead of their pursuers.

They entered Montana just below Missoula and cut south along the Bitterroot River. White communities in the region reacted with alarm. The Nez Perce astonished the frightened civilian population by explaining that they had no quarrel with them, no wish to settle on their land or seize their crops and livestock; they only sought safe passage on their eastward journey to Crow country. For a few days, an uneasy harmony prevailed. Joseph's people camped outside the town of Stevensville, where they traded for supplies with the townspeople. When isolated incidents of robbery took place, Indian leaders punished the offenders and made prompt restitution.[11]

Meanwhile, Howard stepped up his pursuit. On August 19, after days of strenuous travel, his army rested at a grassy campsite at Camas Meadow. The men welcomed the opportunity to relax. Wood joked with Howard's son that at last he could take his pants off at night, it was so safe a place.[12]

While the soldiers slept, Joseph led several Nez Perce past the picket posts into a meadow where the army's entire herd of mules was grazing. They cut the animals loose from their tethers and stampeded them. The startled troops staggered in the dark to find their camp in chaos: horses and mules galloping in terror, goaded on by Indians, shouting and crying, discharging their rifles into the night.[13] The Nez Perce failed to make off with the cavalry's horses, which had been kept close to camp. Yet by capturing much of the mule train, they stalled Howard's progress and gained valuable time. Howard marched his exhausted men to Henry Lake, where they bivouacked for a much-needed rest. Then, accompanied by Wood and a small detachment of men, he rushed north to Virginia City to telegraph for instructions. Howard believed it was unwise to push his exhausted men much further. He instructed Wood to telegraph General Sherman at Fort Shaw, Montana, to request fresh troops to take up the pursuit.

General Sherman issued a blistering reply: "I don't want to give orders . . . but that force of yours should pursue the Nez Perces to the death, lead where they may. . . . If you are tired, give the command to some young energetic officer, and let him follow them, go where they may, holding his men well in hand, subsisting them on beef gathered in the country, with coffee, sugar, and salt in packs. . . . No time should be lost.[14]

"You misunderstood me," Howard replied by telegraph. "I never flag. . . . You need not fear for the campaign."

"Glad to find you so plucky," Sherman answered. "Have every possible faith in your intense energy, but thought it probable you were worn out, and I sometimes think men of less age and rank are best for Indian warfare."[15]

Nevertheless, Howard remained under a cloud. Adding to Sherman's impatience, perhaps provoking it, was the way the nation's press had taken up the Nez Perce campaign and given it a new dimension.[16] Howard's frustrating chase was treated as proof that the army had bungled its mission to make the western territories safe for settlement and economic development. The campaign raised, once again, the issue of America's military readiness—a widely debated issue since Custer's devastating defeat. The eastward movement of the Nez Perce nation stirred alarmed speculation. What if the Nez Perce were to swing north toward the Canadian border? What if Sitting Bull and his hundreds of followers—the same warriors who had annihilated Custer and his command—were to swarm across the border to fight beside their Indian brothers? What if the Sioux, Cheyenne, and Dakota nations—only recently forced onto reservations—were lured by the Nez Perce into an alliance? A menacing Indian army might set out to destroy white civilization west of the Mississippi, turning the Great Plains into a bloody battleground.

The press portrayed Howard's dogged pursuit as totally inept. Why were his soldiers unable to keep pace with a horde of poorly provisioned Indians, two thirds of whom were women and children and old men too feeble to bear arms? The army came under increasing criticism, and Howard bore the brunt of it. It appeared the Nez Perce were leading him on a merry chase.

But there was no glory, no victory for anyone. The Nez Perce had "won" every battle of the campaign, but each victory forced them to trek further from their homeland. They had no appetite for war. Nor did Howard, really. He did not set out to win great victories and kill Indians. He had none of Custer's thirst for glory or Sherman's belief in genocidal slaughter; he merely wanted to return the Nez Perce to Lapwai Reservation. Following the skirmish at Camas Meadows it would be well over a month before Howard got his way, yet in all that time there was almost no fighting. The Nez Perce campaign was not a war so much as an epic exodus—1,320 miles in seventy-five days—with the Nez Perce avoiding battle whenever possible. Joseph and his chiefs understood that they were trapped in a war that they could not win and the United States could not lose. In truth, the government had already achieved its objective: the Nez Perce had evacuated their lands; white settlers were free to develop the disputed territory.

Though armed combat was all but over, the defiant diaspora of the

Nez Perce became an end in itself. From the Nez Perce's point of view their trek was hopeless, a journey to nowhere. There was talk of settling on the buffalo plains of Montana, but there was no place on earth that could replace their ancestral home. Still, they pushed on, for only in their tragic journey could they assert a measure of freedom. By exercising that choice, however absurd it might seem— by choosing a course of action that could not help but reduce them to a pitiful straggling band—they achieved tragic dignity.

Howard was bent on bringing the Nez Perce to justice. But there was no justice in any of this: there was only the overpowering self-interest of the United States government, which had unilaterally revised its treaty agreements in order to cast the Nez Perce from their land. The enemy against which young Wood went forth to do battle was no hostile military aggressor. It was a mass of retreating refugees: feeble elders, women, children, and a few hundred warriors whose leaders wanted nothing more than peace.

While Sherman telegraphed his harsh opinions and Howard gathered supplies for his men, the Nez Perce crossed the Continental Divide into the northwestern corner of Yellowstone National Park. The Nez Perce remained a few days ahead of Howard's army while to the east, alerted by telegraph messages from Howard, Colonel John Sturgis hurried his troops from Fort Lincoln and distributed them in a blockade of every known exit route from the park. With Howard closing on their rear and hundreds of troops blocking the canyon trails ahead, it appeared the Nez Perce could go no farther. But Nez Perce scouts found a narrow hunters' trail with overhanging walls that formed a natural tunnel: while a band of braves distracted Sturgis's troops, the Nez Perce caravan followed the hidden passage to safety. By the time Howard joined up with the baffled Sturgis, the Nez Perce were fifty miles away, marching north toward Canada.

In the sizable literature on the campaign, the Nez Perce's escapes and military victories have taken on legendary dimensions. One reads about Nez Perce valor, their brilliant strategies. But the larger truth, certainly the one that bore down on Joseph and his fellow chiefs, was the unrelieved futility of their journey. Their battles and extraordinary marches were desperate improvisations to forestall a fate of confinement and exile.

In the second week of September, after the Nez Perce had crossed the Yellowstone River near Billings, Crow and Bannock warriors began harassing them with periodic raids. It was a crushing blow to Nez Perce hopes: they could no longer sustain themselves with the expectation that the Plains Indians would come to their aid. Demoralized, they struggled on with little more than their own recalcitrance to sustain them. Though only two hundred miles separated them from British Columbia and freedom, they were defeated by the journey itself.

General Howard sent urgent messages to Fort Keogh, 150 miles to the east, calling for troops to intercept Joseph before he reached the Canadian border. On September 17, Colonel Nelson A. Miles, a "glory chaser" in the Custer mold, marched forth with 383 men under his command, along with forty wagons, a pack train with a month's provisions, and two pieces of heavy cannon.[17] Two weeks later, Miles's scouts found the bedraggled Nez Perce at the edge of Bear Paw Mountain, camped along Snake Creek, eight miles south of the Milk River. Miles was confident that a bold cavalry charge could vanquish the Nez Perce in a single blow. Joined by a band of Cheyenne scouts, Miles's Seventh Cavalry bore down on the camp. With gunfire everywhere and their herd scattered, the Indians scrambled to cover and fought back. Miles countered with repeated attacks, but the Nez Perce held their positions.

Though Miles failed to gain the decisive victory he sought, he succeeded in cutting off the Nez Perce's escape to Canada. Too-hul-hul-sote had been shot. Looking Glass had fallen. Ollokot, Joseph's brother, was dead. There was almost no food. That night, as the Nez Perce huddled in trenches, it began to snow. Miles had only to maintain the siege for a day or two before Chief Joseph would be forced to surrender.

Meanwhile, General Howard, Wood, and seventeen cavalry hastened across the frozen plain. On the evening of October 4, Howard's party entered Miles's camp. Wood was appalled by Miles's cold welcome. As he saw it, Miles was chagrined at the thought that Howard would reclaim his command, thus usurping the glory that Miles thought was rightfully his. But Howard had no such intention. He praised Miles and assured him that Joseph would surrender the following day. Then he spoke the words Miles longed to hear: not until Miles had received the surrender would Howard resume command. "Colonel Miles' entire manner changed," Wood observed, "he became cordial."[18]

Wood was upset by Howard's magnanimous gesture. He reminded Howard that the Articles of War specified that when two commands meet the senior officer is always in charge. Howard shrugged off Wood's argument, but Wood persisted. It was not right, he contended: the men under Howard's command had traveled far, under difficult conditions; they had faced hardship and peril; now they were camped only a day's march away—why should they be denied credit for the Nez Perce surrender? Howard assured Wood that, militarily speaking, his command was present, that their proximity added weight to the overwhelming arguments for Joseph's surrender, and that all reports of the proceedings would point this out.

"I do not trust Colonel Miles," Wood persisted. "I am sorry to say it, but I do not trust him."[19]

When Howard chivalrously shrugged off the honor of receiving Joseph's surrender, it may have touched the raw nerve of Wood's attachment to his father: how William Maxwell Wood's role in the Mexican War of 1846 had never been acknowledged. To young Wood, so eager to claim greatness for the man who had shaped his early life, General Howard's disarming modesty was as disturbing as Miles's apparent scheme to wrest all honor for himself.

But why all this concern for glory? In staunchly defending Howard's right to the Nez Perce surrender, and in faithfully arguing his grandiose interpretation of his father's role in the annexation of California, Wood was driven by the wish to place himself close to eminence, to be part of a great cause, to be the heir-apparent to the mantle of greatness.

On October 5, Howard and Joseph agreed on the terms of Joseph's surrender. The Indians would be taken to Fort Keogh, where the government would provide them with food and shelter; then they would be escorted to the Lapwai Reservation in Idaho, where they would be free to make their homes. Joseph accepted Howard's assurances that these terms would be honored by his government. That day, Wood was present when "Captain" John, an interpreter, arrived to convey Joseph's message of surrender. On his own initiative Wood recorded Joseph's words. "The speeches of Indians were not considered important," Wood later remarked. "I took it for my own benefit as a literary item."[20]

> About an hour or so before sunset there came from the ravine below, up to the knoll on which we were standing, a picturesque and pathetic little group. Joseph was the only one mounted. . . . Joseph threw himself off his horse, draped his blanket about him, and carrying his rifle in the hollow of his arm, changed from the stooped attitude in which he had been listening, held himself very erect, and with a quiet pride, not exactly defiance, advanced toward General Howard and held out his rifle in token of submission. . . . He said (Arthur Chapman interpreting):
> "Tell General Howard I know his heart. What he told me before—I have in my heart. I am tired of fighting. Too-hul-hil-sit is dead. Looking Glass is dead. He-who-led-the-young-men-in-battle is dead. The chiefs are all dead. It is the young men now who say 'yes' or 'no.' My little daughter has run away upon the prairie. I do not know where to find her—perhaps I shall find her too among the dead. It is cold and we have no fire; no blankets. Our little children are crying for food but we have none to give. Hear me, my chiefs. From where the sun now stands, Joseph will fight no more forever."[21]

Wood described this scene and recounted Joseph's eloquent speech on three different occasions—in 1877, 1884, and 1936. Though Wood's version of Joseph's words remained the same from one published account to the next, it now appears that Wood conflated two separate events in order to create the dramatic spectacle of the solitary chief delivering his words in person—a choice on Wood's part that made for good reading but bad history. In fact, Joseph remained at the Nez Perce camp and sent word ahead with an interpreter. Several hours later, Joseph arrived to present his rifle to General Howard.[22]

The struggle was over. In its aftermath came a succession of broken pledges. Despite Howard's and Miles's assurances to Joseph that the United States would honor the terms of the surrender, the Nez Perce were shuttled by riverboats to Fort Lincoln near Bismark, North Dakota. Later, they were moved by train to a malarial campsite outside Fort Leavenworth, Kansas—half a continent away from the Lapwai Reservation. Howard and Miles protested, but their arguments were overruled by Sherman and officials in Washington who backed him up. While Joseph argued his case for the Wallowa homeland before Congress and President Hayes, the Nez Perce were moved to the Indian Territory of Oklahoma. Years passed before the remaining Nez Perce were returned West, where they were divided between the Lapwai Reservation and Nespelem in eastern Washington.

After the Nez Perce surrender, Howard led his weary command to the mouth of the Musselshell River, where they boarded a steamer to begin their journey West. With Wood, Howard continued on to Fort Lincoln, where several officers came aboard with the Chicago daily papers. Howard scanned the news. "Suddenly, with a startlingly pale face, he came toward me," Wood remembered, "his empty sleeve jerking and waving on one side and the newspaper waving on the other. 'Look at this, Wood, look at this! I cannot believe it!' "[23] It was a report Miles had telegraphed to Chicago, which General Phillip H. Sheridan passed on to the press—the first news America received of the Nez Perce surrender: "We have had our usual success. We made a very direct and rapid march across country, and after a severe engagement and being kept under fire for three days, the hostile camp under Chief Joseph surrendered at two o'clock today."[24]

Miles's dispatch justified Wood's deep distrust: "Not a single word of Howard or his command . . . no more than if they were all in the moon. Yet undoubtedly Howard's arrival had produced the surrender—but not one word."[25] General Howard was "absolutely broken-hearted"—or so Wood chose to believe. He and Howard proceeded to St. Paul, and from there they traveled by train to Chicago. There, Wood prevailed upon Howard for permission to write a true account of Joseph's surrender. On October 25, his version of the final days of the campaign appeared in the Chicago Tribune under a dramatic heading: "The Pursuit and Battle: Semi-Official Report of a Staff Officer."

"It is in one sense an official report," the Tribune explained, "having been written by an officer of Gen. Howard's staff." It's unlikely, however, that many official reports were written with such élan:

> The earlier press dispatches, particularly that of the 14th to the New York *Herald*, are so full of blunders and errors that one unaccustomed to the cheerful and ready lying of most frontier scouts, and the wild stories of those who rush from a field of battle without waiting for a second look, would find it hard to account for so much deliberate representation. But all is accounted for in the explanation that they are rumors heard at the rear from scouts or fugitives who have hurried from a too close proximity to danger.

Since General Sheridan himself had released Miles's report to the press, Wood's references to "blunders and errors," "ready lying," and "wild stories" were surely calculated to raise Sheridan's hackles.

Wood's "semi-official report" emphasized Howard's essential role in defeating Joseph's people: "Sherman wrote to Howard: 'You are the pursuing force: no one expects you to overtake them. Only drive them with your infantry and others must head them off.' But some people knew better than Sherman what he wanted." Hell-bent on rebutting Miles's distorted report, Wood introduced his own questionable version of events. He cited General Sherman's benign comment—"no one expects you to overtake them"—yet conveniently neglected to quote Sherman's exasperated command to Howard at Fort Shaw that he "pursue the Nez Perces to the death, lead where they may."

In his account of Chief Joseph's surrender, Wood seized every opportunity to minimize Miles's role. "Joseph regarding Howard as Head Chief, had seemed reluctant to surrender to any but him," he wrote. Also, he argued that Miles's success depended upon the ability of Howard's command to decoy the Nez Perce. "Joseph said his attention was directed to Gen. Howard, and he never suspected that troops would be where Col. Miles was." Wood could not resist one last dig at Miles's conceit: he added that Joseph "had never heard of Col. Miles."[26]

Wood's account caused quite a stir at army headquarters. General Sheridan, Howard's division commander, was livid. Howard defended Wood, yet he refused to engage in accusations. It appears that Howard was far less interested in claiming credit for himself than in defending his young aide-de-camp. Sheridan had the power to destroy Wood's military career, but Howard gallantly intervened.

For many of the principal figures in the Nez Perce uprising— Howard, Miles, Sheridan, Joseph, and public officials in charge of Indian policy—the Nez Perce surrender began a new struggle to shape the narrative of what had happened. Wood was very much a part of this. His first military campaign ended with a war of words. In his *Chicago Tribune* article he had fought for Howard's (and thus his own) place in history. More important, by bringing Joseph's stirring surrender speech to public attention, he helped direct the admiration and sympathy of many Americans to the defeated leader, thereby assisting Joseph's continuing quest for justice.

Wood learned that our sense of history often depends on who tells the story, on what interests are served, and on how well the story is told. For an audacious young man with a yearning both for fame and a literary vocation, this was a valuable lesson.

Joseph, too, had come to a new view of the relation of language to power. For years, in spite of deep suspicions, he reasoned and negotiated with representatives of the United States government, seeking agreements that would permit his people to live in peace. He saw the United States ignore its written treaties. He saw his people driven from their lands and shuttled like livestock halfway across America. He saw his family die and disappear. Joseph learned that fine words mean nothing; words were powerless to compel the masters of the western empire to honorable action:

> I cannot understand how the Government sends a man out to fight us, as it did General Miles, and then breaks his word. Such a Government has something wrong about it. I cannot understand why so many chiefs are allowed to talk so many different ways, and promise so many different things. . . . They all say they are my friends, and that I shall have justice, but while their mouths all talk right I do not understand why nothing is done for my people. I have heard talk and talk, but nothing is done. Good words do not last long until they amount to something. Words do not pay for my dead people. They do not pay for my country, now overrun by white men. They do not

protect my father's grave. . . . Good words will not get my people a home where they can live in peace and take care of themselves. I am tired of talk that comes to nothing. It makes my heart sick when I remember all the good words and all the broken promises. There has been too much talking by men who had no right talk.[27]

7. Lights and Shadows

Nannie Moale Smith was in turmoil. All through her childhood, her stepfather had been at the center of her emotional life. Now, when the widowed Dr. Lincoln fell in love with a young acquaintance of Nannie's, she was mortified. Nannie regarded Jennie Gould as an unsuitable partner for her stepfather. When Jennie asked her to be a bridesmaid, Nannie could barely countenance it. "When I walked up the aisle with my head in the air," Nannie recalled, "people thought that Jennie was going to have a very disagreeable stepdaughter."[1]

Nannie exacted her measure of revenge, but she was hurt and confused. She reacted by throwing herself into a flurry of social activity, behaving as if she had set her mind on having every eligible young bachelor in Washington at her feet. A wealthy banker's son pursued her. There was a clerk in the State Department. After him, a young naval officer, and then a former classmate of Erskine's. Four love affairs! Nannie was everywhere at once, while her disagreeable stepmother could not even get herself invited into the better homes. As for Nannie's fiancé—well, she had not exactly forgotten about Erskine. But he was far from home, marching over deserts, paddling though Alaskan ice floes, being shot at by Indians—way too distant to give her the attention she required.

General Howard granted Wood a brief leave to enable him to visit with Nannie, but it did not go well. Nannie shuttled back and forth between Baltimore and Washington, playing the coquette, doing her best to juggle Erskine's amorous claims with those of her new suitors. Erskine pressed Nannie to take her engagement seriously; Nannie explained that her stepfather objected to her marrying out of the Roman Catholic faith. This was a sticking point—and it would continue to be—but quarreling over religion provided convenient cover for Nannie's flirtations. If she and Erskine could disagree over *this*, she might avoid an embarrassing discussion of whether she ought to curtail her amorous adventures.

Erskine returned to Portland in December, leaving matters between himself and Nannie unresolved. After Christmas he wrote to her at length about the importance of seizing her freedom:

> I wish your early education did not so very naturally and properly prejudice you in favor of Roman Catholicism because it is such an outgrowth of early darkness and superstition and even now is so firmly arrayed against investigation and education that to be a believer in and follower of its doctrines stamps the individual as narrow & contracted in mental calibre.
>
> ... The dogmas are to me such drivel, the talk of the priests out here so narrow mean and bigoted that [I] am almost becoming a bigot myself against the worm-eaten old institution.
>
> I hope I haven't hurt your feelings too much my heart's darling, I know I have *some*, but it was done in love dear. I love you exceedingly. I want to show you what has hold of these people who are persecuting you.[2]

All but gone are the lovestruck effusions Erskine wrote before going to war. He relished his role as knight errant of free thought, called upon to rescue a spellbound maiden held captive by the evil Church. His passion was fed by his family history. He loved his mother but despised the strict faith that governed her thoughts, that had spoiled his Sundays and suppressed the free play of his lively nature. By loving Nannie, he recreated the situation with his mother: loving the woman but hating the tyranny that possessed her. Courting Nannie became a crusade, an opportunity to resume the thwarted rebellion of his childhood against superstition and paternal authority.

As for his family, in the three years since Erskine had seen his father, William Maxwell Wood had become "a very old and battered man." Erskine spent several days at Rosewood Glen and came away shaken. His father was moody, nervous, subject to sudden outbursts of temper. All his life, Erskine knew his father as "a man strong in intellect and used to command and authority," yet now he had lost his grip on himself; he was "a different being." Exacerbating this transformation was his father's increasing dependency on whiskey and opium—taken, so his father said, to counteract the effects of hereditary heart disease. He fluctuated between extremes, "sometimes pleasant and sometimes almost a madman."[3]

Physical and mental infirmity loosened the powerful grip William Maxwell Wood had on his son. Yet in some ways Erskine remained in his thrall. Erskine had chosen to fall in love with a woman whose life was tangled in strict religious practice—not unlike the choice his father had made. And in Erskine's long letter to Nannie about her religion—in his didactic, argumentive tone—it appears that the broken man whose domineering counsel had shaped Erskine's life had found a disciple.

Soon after his letter to Nannie, Erskine broke off their correspondence. He had said all he had to say on the matter; he told Nannie she must not write to him until she came to a decision. Nannie was sick at heart. Her engagement to Erskine three years before had the unreality of an adolescent daydream. Now, with her home life turned inside out and her round of pleasant romances challenged by Erskine's threatened defection, she was forced to consider her life and future in a way she never had before. It was difficult for Nannie to share her confusion with Erskine, to ask his forgiveness. Beneath her coquettery was a vein of pride, a wish to enjoy life, to do what she wanted to do without apology. For a correct young woman of Nannie's day, there was not much opportunity to discover one's own nature; one had little freedom of movement or choice. Properly raised young women lived a mayfly existence, bursting from the chrysalis of adolescence into a gay, fluttering life of balls, teas, luncheons, cadets, beaus, escorts, callers, and courtship—a few years of lively possibility before entering the corsetted protocols of marriage, children, and domestic responsibility. Nannie's romantic dalliances were the outgrowth of her natural high spirits. Who can blame her if she welcomed all the pleasure she could? She was young, beautiful, fun-loving, hungry for affection. In her way, she was as eager for freedom and adventure as Wood himself.

At last, the young lovers renewed their engagement. Still, their lives had been touched by serious matters. Erskine's letters continued to record his lover's sighs and to describe his rites of adoring worship at the shrine of Nannie's photos, but his father's debts impressed on him the simple fact that lovers cannot live on love alone.

Back at Fort Vancouver, Erskine wrote a long letter to Nannie from General Howard's home, taking her on "a Voyage autour de ma chambre"—though he might more accurately have called it a tour of the shrine of love. He moved from one photo of Nannie to the next. In a purple velvet case was enshrined "a picture a Washington belle sent to me when I was at West Point. . . . I have polished the glass over the sweet mouth with my kisses for many weary years."[4]

Erskine saved his favorite picture for last: "a picture of strong lights and shadows." It was "a picture of a girl, a young woman in thought and feeling, and she is standing with hands clasped and is looking downward a little bit as if she were reflecting on all she saw in the years to come. This is a sad picture but I love it very dearly." Here, at least, he allowed some of the uncertainty and melancholy inwardness of the past few months to enter his adoring vision of Nannie. The passage is delicately put: Nannie was a girl, but the thoughts and feelings that passed during their estrangement carried her toward young womanhood—a transformation that was not without a certain sadness. The same was true of Erskine. He had fought for Nannie and given her up; and when she had come back to him, they were both chastened by what they had learned. Nannie had discovered that she could not indulge her wish for freedom without undermining her emotional security. Erskine had learned how his father's free-living, free-spending habits had brought him to ruin. For him and for Nannie, life had lost some of its youthful simplicity. Impulsive action, the kind of reckless living that had brought them close in their first summer together, was no longer possible if Nannie hoped to seal her engagement. Neither of these attractive young people was resigned to facing life, or one another, merely as solemn duty. Nevertheless, they had been shaken enough by their recent ordeal to take a more complex view of one another and their personal responsibilities—to see life as a matter of "strong lights and shadows."

8. The Old Broken Wheel

L t. C.E.S. Wood is at present engaged in painting a water color sketch representing a view on the Columbia River," the *Oregonian* reported in April of 1878. "He displays a degree of artistic skill and taste not at all discreditable."[1] Soon, however, the pages of the *Oregonian* were taken over by crucial affairs. In the summer of 1878, the Bannock Indians bolted from their reservation at Fort Hall in eastern Idaho and swept west toward Oregon. Lieutenant Wood set aside his water colors and hurried off to war again.

Unlike the Nez Perce uprising, which was essentially a defensive migration, the Bannocks sought to eradicate white civilization from the Northwest. Buffalo Horn, the Bannock leader, was well-known to Wood and General Howard. Only a year before, he and thirty of his men had assisted the army in their pursuit of the Nez Perce. In return, Buffalo Horn had been promised that the government would remove squatters and their cattle from the Camas Prairie where his people hunted—one more pledge the United States government failed to honor. "Friendly" Bannocks were treated shabbily, not much better than the "hostile" Nez Perce. An enraged Buffalo Horn led his people to war. He set out from Idaho with four hundred warriors. His plan was to sweep westward into Oregon, drawing the Piutes, Utes, Shoshones, Umatillas, Cayuses, Palouse, and Walla Wallas—all the Indian groups of the Northwest—into the conflict as he traveled. This powerful confederation would move on to the Washington Territory, prepared to do battle with whatever forces the army could muster.

The Nez Perce achieved little from their years of patient diplomacy, still less from their doomed exodus. If the Bannocks could win a few early victories and Bannock emissaries could persuade the various Indian groups to rebel, then the United States army would be unable to protect the scattered white population and at the same time wage war against hostile Indians.

"Here we are right in the thick of it," Erskine wrote to Nannie, "and it is always the most comfortable place, no more annoying summons and sensational stories we are right in the advance ourselves."[2] He sallied into this grave situation with the cocky enthusiasm of a young hero blessed with magical knowledge of his invulnerability. The journal he kept of those days is absolutely gay, as though Buffalo Horn's menacing strategy was no more than a call to adventure.

Wood accompanied General Howard on his urgent journey to Boise, the site of the territorial government. After a day of sending and receiving telegraph dispatches, they hurried off again. Howard was troubled by the latest news concerning Buffalo Horn's movements: the Bannocks had passed into southeastern Oregon and swept down on the Piutes at Malheur Reservation. Having suffered at the hands of squatters and the Indian agents assigned to look after their interests, many Piutes were inclined to join Buffalo Horn's uprising. Yet in spite of the indignities their people endured, some Piute leaders insisted that war would only hasten the destruction of their people; they argued that a strategy of peace, cooperation, and persistent moral pressure was their only hope for survival in the face of an expanding American nation. Chief Winnemucca was such a leader, as were his two children, Natchez and Sara.

The story of Sara Winnemucca deserves special attention. Throughout Sara's childhood her family had mingled with whites. In their early teens, Sara Winnemucca and her sister were "adopted" by white families for whom they did housework near Lake Tahoe. Then, in 1864, Chief Winnemucca and Sara created a stage presentation— "a series of tableaux vivants illustrative of Indian Life"—which they performed in Virginia City, the boom town of the Comstock mines, and later at the Metropolitan Theatre in San Francisco.[3] The tableaux included a war dance, five scenes representing the story of Pocahontas and Captain John Smith, and the "Scalping of an Emigrant Girl by a Bannock Scout." To some, the Winnemuccas' stage career was a lamentable example of self-exploitation: vaudeville Indians dramatiz-

ing exotic fantasies fostered by the very people who had usurped
their territory and all but destroyed their traditional culture. Certainly,
there was an element of this in the Winnemuccas' theatrical presenta-
tions. But Chief Winnemucca and his attractive twenty-year-old
daughter regarded themselves as propagandists for the Indian cause.
Mixed in with the sensationalism and sentimentality were affecting
appeals to the audience for Indian rights. Sara Winnemucca became
a celebrity. Along with predictable comments about her dark beauty
and child-of-nature allure, the San Francisco press expressed support
for the issues that Sara and her father addressed.

At about the time General Howard and Lieutenant Wood departed
from Boise, Oytes, a firebrand shaman, seized Chief Winnemucca
and held him prisoner at the Bannock camp in order to stifle his
objections to a Bannock-Piute alliance. Chief Egan, an aging Piute
leader, was also taken, though in his case there was reason for Oytes
to hope that sufficient pressure might convince him to take an active
part in leading the war plan. With Chief Winnemucca muzzled and
Chief Egan tempted by Oytes's arguments, the Piutes were drawn
into the rebellion.

Sara Winnemucca was determined to free her people from Oytes's
reckless scheme. She met with General Howard at Sheep Ranch, an
outpost in the southeast corner of Malheur County, and offered her
services. Howard told her she must contact her father and assure
him of government assistance if he could keep his people out of war.
Sara set off across desolate alkali flats, traveling one hundred miles
to the rebel stronghold in Steen's Mountains. She disguised herself
and infiltrated the Bannock camp; under cover of darkness, she led
her father and fifteen other Piutes to a concealed spot, where they
were able to hide undetected for several days. Then she hurried back
to Sheep Ranch to report to Howard—completing her dangerous two-
hundred-mile journey in just two days. Sara's feat made it possible
for Howard to subdue the Bannock renegades with few major engagements. With clear knowledge of where the Indian forces were concentrated, Howard was able to thwart the formation of a rebellious Indian
confederacy and compel negotiations without serious losses on either
side.

Only once in his lengthy notes on the Bannock-Piute uprising did

Wood address the cruel process in which he played a part. It came on June 22, after he and Howard had spent two days at the Malheur Agency. Because of the war emergency, Howard had little choice but to support the local Indian agent, W. W. Rinehart, in his severe treatment of reservation Indians. But Wood was sickened by the meager reservation lands, by the bullying way Indian agents treated peaceful Indians, and by the outright graft he saw. "The Reservation system is a good one for everyone but the Indians and the people," he wrote. "Linville's fraud and deception . . . Indians wards of the Nation one day, Independent sovereignties the next; treaties made with them, then broken. Then war (called no war), and so the old broken wheel hobbles around, breaking Army and Indians as it goes."[4]

With the Bannock-Piute uprising put to rest, Howard sent Wood to Washington. Over the next month and a half, from mid-October through November, Wood shuttled back and forth between the Indian Affairs Office and General Sherman's military command, advocating Howard's view that the destitute Piutes must be moved to safety. Howard knew that Wood would represent his views with enough persistence to overcome the self-interest and obtuseness that characterized the administration of Indian affairs.

But there was another reason why Howard chose Lieutenant Wood for this mission. After five years of courting Nannie Moale Smith, he planned to go East to bring her back with him as his wife.

9. A New Life

On November 26, 1879, Erskine and Nannie were married in Washington DC in the front parlor of Nannie's grandmother's house. A month later, with lavishly furnished baskets from the renowned Maryland Club to sustain them, they began their rail journey across the continent.

The trip provided Nannie with several startling glimpses of frontier life. Once, when the train stopped, she walked a little way ahead of the station and was attracted by the sound of a violin coming from a little shack. A man came out of the door for a little chat. She asked him if he lived alone and he replied that he had had a partner living with him, but a few days before, he had walked up the canyon and never returned. Eaten by coyotes, he concluded.[1]

Later on, there was a train collision and one of the passengers had his leg amputated. Farther west, the train came to an abrupt stop out on the prairie and a group of railroad officials and officers of the law filed through the honeymooners' car. A murderer had just been captured—he had killed a constable and his whole family, and the sheriff planned to hang him on the spot. The train fell to a hush as the doomed man was led through the train. Just opposite Nannie's window they threw a rope over a telegraph pole and hung him.[2]

Nannie was alarmed by the violence and uncouth manners she encountered, but the joys of married life more than offset the hardships of her journey. Erskine and Nannie lived extravagantly; they enjoyed the present moment with every certainty that the future would take care of itself. They began their transcontinental journey with lavishly stocked food hampers, but for the last two days they subsisted on a jar of anchovy paste.[3] The newlyweds reached the West Coast with nothing left but silver and napkins.

At Vancouver Barracks, Mrs. Wood stepped into the role of eastern sophisticate, dazzling the military post with lavish dinner parties done in "the very swellest style of diplomatic circles in Washington."[4] Surely, few military wives within a five-hundred-mile range would have thought to plan a banquet featuring "Little native oysters on the half shell; trout a la Meuniere, with Saratoga chips . . . roast grouse with bread crumb sauce and guava jelly; terrapin, Maryland Club style . . . and roast saddle of venison with sweet potatoes, [and] port wine sauce with currant jelly melted into it."[5]

On March 1, 1880, William Maxwell Wood died in his home at the age of seventy-two. Whatever memories Erskine held of his father's tyranny, he was determined to pay tribute to the public man. As a result, he wrote "An Unknown Turning-Point in the Destiny of the Republic," an account of his father's contribution to the annexation of California. "There are in the lives of all nations," he began, "certain pivotal points at which destiny seems to pause and rest the future in the hand of one man. Happy the nation which at such a moment finds at its service a man strong and true. . . . Mark how his hand gave an impulse to the whole Republic!" Wood's account assigned his father a pivotal role in the history of the Western Hemisphere. England was on the brink of seizing California, he insisted, but "Dr. William Maxwell Wood rebuffed Great Britain, and snatched the morsel from her mouth." By the time his article closed, it seemed that the fate of America hung in the balance: William Maxwell Wood was all that stood between Great Britain and California, the "coveted prize": "The port of San Francisco, controlling the Pacific, would have been British. Then the natural possibilities of our destiny loom up too vast to be discussed. The war with Mexico might have become a war with England. The war of the rebellion might have become the war of Southern independence."[6]

William Maxwell Wood was indeed a gifted man: he traveled more, risked more, lived more boldly, and left a more impressive record than most men of his time. But did he, like some latter-day Paul Revere, "save" our country? Six years later, in his magisterial *History of the Pacific States*, Hubert H. Bancroft played down the events in which Erskine assigned his father a heroic role. "The praise due Parrott [Wood's traveling companion] and the others for their service has been somewhat exaggerated," Bancroft wrote, "under the mistaken idea that their acts saved Cal. from being taken by England."[7] After reviewing the historical evidence, Bancroft concluded that "the danger of English intervention in any form was a mere bugbear."[8] To Erskine, Bancroft's dismissive judgment was an intellectual blunder, an insult to his father's memory that he vowed to one day rectify. As in Erskine's defence of General Howard's record, his determined effort to ensure his father's place in history seems driven by a wish to see himself in the heroic mold. He was a hero-to-be whose first trial was to defend the name and valiant deeds, and hence the "magic," of the exemplary titans from whom he derived his power. Wood's article was printed in the December 1880 number of the *Californian*, a monthly journal which had helped launch the careers of Bret Harte and Mark Twain.[9] Unlike the *Chicago Tribune*'s unsigned account of Chief Joseph's surrender, this piece bore the name "C.E.S. Wood." In praising his father, Wood assumed the role his father had forbidden: for the first time he saw his name in print as a published writer.

On April 6, 1880, a disturbing incident took place at the United States Military Academy at West Point. Johnson C. Whittaker, a black cadet from South Carolina, was found tied to his bed with serious head injuries. Whittaker claimed that three masked men bound him and inflicted the injuries; but from the start, officials at West Point suspected Whittaker of lying. After investigating his story, they claimed to have found evidence that Whittaker inflicted the wounds upon himself as a ruse to avoid examinations.

Since the Civil War, several blacks had been admitted to the Academy, but only one, Henry Ossian Flipper, managed to withstand the pressure of racism, physical assaults, and social ostracism—all this on top of the demanding workload—and survive to graduate. The Whittaker incident was widely reported in the press, placing a good deal of pressure on President Rutherford B. Hayes, whose Republican Party depended upon the black vote to remain in power. President Hayes did not relish the idea of approaching his black constituency with the repellant tale of a black man doing harm to his own body in order to "protect" himself from failure. Hayes acted to cut his losses: although he became convinced that Whittaker had staged his own beating, he criticized the findings of the investigation and for months refused to allow Major General J. M. Schofield, the superintendent of the Academy, to court-martial Whittaker on disciplinary grounds.[10] Schofield remained outspoken. To him, the Whittaker incident proved a larger point: that black people had not yet reached a point in civilization where they were suited for equal treatment.

President Hayes dismissed Schofield and chose General Howard, a man who had proven himself a friend to black people, to replace him as commandant of West Point. Howard brought with him the young man who had become indispensable as his aide and adjutant: Lieutenant C. E. S. Wood.

Howard handled the Whittaker case in a manner designed to give every impression of fair-mindedness. He met with President Hayes and advised him to grant Whittaker's request to have his trial moved from West Point, where prejudice against Whittaker made a fair trial impossible. This concession allowed the government to show a sympathetic face, while also removing unwelcome publicity from the Academy.

At his court martial in New York City, Whittaker was found guilty. He was sentenced and discharged from army service. But in a gesture calculated to put the troubling incident to rest, President Hayes allowed Whittaker to tender his resignation, after which he remitted Whittaker's sentence.[11]

What did Wood think about the Whittaker case? There is no mention of it in his papers, but as Howard's trusted adviser he certainly would have had a hand in it. This much is evident: many Americans who considered themselves open-minded on racial issues held views similar to those of Major General Schofield. They believed that it was possible, through the application of firm, paternalistic authority, to raise former slaves to a state of self-reliance, but that it was unreasonable to expect black people to perform as true equals to whites. The army's investigation of Whittaker's case was, at the very least, tainted by genteel attitudes of racial paternalism. At its worst—which is to say, at almost every stage of this disturbing incident—the case was marked by unthinking prejudice propped up by elitist assumptions about class and social order. There was no question of imposing social or intellectual parity on ill-prepared black people; such misplaced "kindness and indulgence" was certain to produce dire results. The Whittaker case was a prime example.

On special occasions Wood's home at West Point was used to put up visitors to the Academy. Such was the case when the Reverend Joseph Twichell of Hartford arrived to attend the graduation of one of his parishioners and to stay on for the June Ball. As he did so often in those days, Twichell traveled with his close friend from Hartford, Mark Twain. Wood was eager to please the famous author. In the attic room where Twichell and Twain were to spend the night, he decorated the sloping ceilings with quotations from Chaucer and Shakespeare, written in wriggling Gothic letters.

The following morning Wood sent a breakfast tray up to his guests' room. A short time later, Twichell came down alone and asked if he might have something to eat: Twain had been so absorbed in reading the painted quotations, Twichell explained, that he had inadvertently gobbled both their meals. Later, Twain told Wood "he had got a liberal education lying in bed—because having been a printer he could read upside-down lettering."[12]

Their discussion encouraged Twain to mention some farcical sketches he had written called *1601, or Social Conversation as it was by the fireside of Queen Elizabeth*. The piece is an overextended bit of puerile play in which Twain indulges his lifelong habit of ridiculing the pretensions of royalty. What makes *1601* unique is its bawdy language and scatological references—not the sort of work he could trust to public printers. Twain had printed four copies of his manuscript in 1880; but his chance meeting with Wood led to talk of running off a limited edition. The thought of using the Academy's printing press to turn out a prurient text surely appealed to Erskine's rebellious impulses: that he could pursue this scheme as the confederate of America's most famous writer made the plan irresistible.

The following April, Twain sent Erskine *1601* and gave him carte blanche to make any corrections he thought appropriate.[13] "I got a font of old style type," Wood recalled, "and had some special punches cut for the abbreviations of the day. . . . I had John Tucker Foreman of the printing shop stain with coffee some linen paper, and so we made a sort of a forgery of an antique relic. With Mark's permission,

I gave the obsolete Elizabethan spelling. . . . I forget how many copies I sent Clemens and how many I kept, but he was most enthusiastic and grateful and wrote me copies had gone to John Hay and our ambassador to China and to a well known Bishop—indeed all over the world."

Much as he was flattered by Twain's attention, Erskine thought little of the frivolous piece. "It is much fuss over a thing not worth it," he wrote, "for while a clever literary stunt with the coarse humour of those days exaggerated beyond limit, it is so obscene as to be repulsive to our own day. Mark had that streak in him, partly innate, partly because of his rude primitive frontier bringing up."[14]

Twain's visit, and Wood's role in bringing *1601* into print, initiated a friendship that continued until Twain's death.

In the autumn of 1881 Wood found a way out of the monotonous duties of Academy life. With Howard's approval he registered for courses at Columbia University, where he studied for a bachelor of philosophy degree.[15] Wood had a gift for friendship. During his years in New York he made several lifelong friends. One of these was Alexander Drake, a major figure in magazine illustrative art and a great art collector. Nine years older than Wood, Drake had already made a name for himself as art director for *Scribner's Monthly Magazine*, which in 1881 became the *Century Magazine*, one of America's most distinguished periodicals.

Through Drake and his circle of friends, Wood met Jimmy Inglis, an influential art dealer, as well as several talented young artists: George de Forest Brush, Olin Warner, J. Alden Weir, and the reclusive Albert Pinkham ("Pinky") Ryder, all of whom lived and worked at the Benedick Studios on Washington Square. Over the years, Wood became closest to Weir. But while he lived at Clinton Place he was drawn to Warner. Eight years older than Wood, Warner had worked for several years at a telegraph office in order to earn money for his first trip to Europe at age twenty-five. He arrived in Paris in 1870 in time to see the Second Empire fall, and he stood guard at the fortifications around Paris in solidarity with the Paris Commune. For several years after his return to America, Warner failed to make a dent in the New York art world. He eked out a living making bronze mantel ornaments and plated housewares, until Daniel Cottier, an influential British art dealer who had recently opened a gallery at 144 Fifth Avenue, recognized Warner's talent, exhibited his work, and offered him financial support. In 1877, Cottier urged Warner, Albert Pinkham Ryder, and several other relatively unknown New York artists to assemble an exhibition meant to challenge the conservative National Academy's stranglehold on standards of artistic merit. After that, Warner's career took off: he received a major commission to execute a statue of William Lloyd Garrison for the city of Boston; he created monumental busts representing the five races of man for the Philadelphia railroad station; and he produced a bust of President Hayes for the Union League Club.[16]

On one of Wood's first visits to Warner's studio, he was so taken by Warner's sculpture that he commissioned him to do a medallion of Nannie. Living on army pay with two infant children, Wood had no money to spare but, like his father, he refused to allow inconvenient reality to intrude on anything as important as his love of beauty. Wood could not afford a bronze medallion, but Warner kindly accommodated him by rendering Nannie in plaster.

In almost every respect, Wood was living the life he had imagined for himself. He was married to the woman he had desired for years, and she had given him two lively children; he was living in New York, mixing with artists and visiting their raffish haunts; he had published his first article in *Century Magazine* and there were prospects for a few more. Also, he was free from chafing authority—be it his father's overbearing attention or the rigid hierarchy of army life. The absence of an assured income or of a secure position for the future did not appear to trouble him. He was full of love and hope and playfulness, full of life—full of himself.

Wood's carefree sojourn in New York ended that spring when Columbia awarded him a bachelor of laws degree, cum laude.[17] For two years he had been able to pursue his studies with almost no interference. Now, following his final examinations at Columbia, he was assigned to company duty at Boise Barracks in Idaho. Compared to Portland, Boise City was drably provincial. Also, company duty gave Wood far less liberty than he had been accustomed to as a member of General Howard's staff. To make matters worse, during the three years that Wood spent at West Point, Colonel Miles had been promoted to the rank of general and given Howard's former command as head of the Department of the Columbia. Boise Barracks fell under Miles's jurisdiction, which gave him ample opportunity to make Lieutenant Wood pay for the debunking reports he had filed after Chief Joseph's surrender. But Boise and Miles were not the issue. There was no posting that could have satisfied Wood. He had had enough of the army. By June he was already exploring ways to support himself as a civilian.

Early on in his stay at Boise Barracks, Wood was plagued by chronic gastritis and other ailments. In August the post physician prescribed a regimen of sea baths, and Wood was granted a transfer to Fort Canby on the Oregon coast. Three months later, he applied for extended sick leave. When Miles got wind of this, he ordered Wood back to Boise. Wood retaliated by requesting reassignment at Fort Vancouver. Miles used the occasion to cast a cloud over Wood's career. "It has since been reported," Miles wrote to army headquarters, "on what appears to be good authority, that one object of Lieut. Wood's desire to go on sick leave of six months, was to enable him to enter upon active business in the city of Portland. . . . If officers were allowed to select stations where it would be agreeable, which they might think would be beneficial to them or promotion of their personal interests, and on certification of surgeons that their health would be benefited at particular posts obtain such stations, such a custom would soon result in serious embarrassment to the military service, and could not be permitted."[18]

Miles's suspicion was not misplaced. Nevertheless, Wood worked himself into high dudgeon over Miles's assault on his character. "If he [General Miles] means that under *cover* of a sick leave I intended to practice law he is worse than misinformed," Wood declared; "he has been told an absolute falsehood."[19]

Lieutenant Wood was way out of line. The U.S. Army does not countenance junior officers insolently accusing their commanders of lying. Miles demanded that Wood be court-martialed, but General Sherman, an old friend of William Maxwell Wood's, intervened. In spite of Wood's blustering indignation, in all likelihood he was relieved to have this blowup with Miles. In a short note he tendered his resignation as First Lieutenant in the Army of the United States. In March 1884 he painted a shingle; c.e.s. wood attorney and counselor at law, and hung it out in Portland.[20]

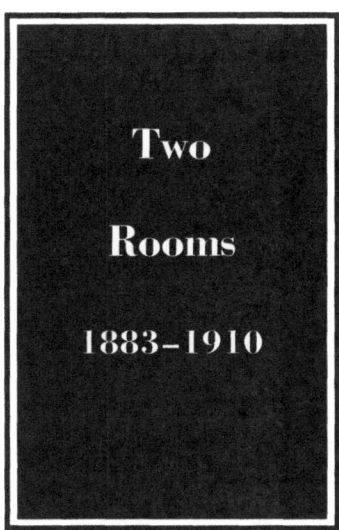

Two

Rooms

1883–1910

10. City of Destiny

On September 8, 1883, three hundred men representing the vested interests of America and Europe assembled at Gold Creek, Montana, to witness the driving of the last railroad spike of the Northern Pacific Railroad line. "THE IRON WEDDING," Portland's leading newspaper declared: "The Hammer Taps Echoed Half Way across the Continent—The Dream Railroad."[1] Two thousand Crow Indians in full war paint, led by Sitting Bull, the hated instrument of General Custer's destruction some six years before, were brought in to disport themselves before diplomats, a delegation of British jurists, European bankers, former President Ulysses S. Grant, and a congregation of politicians—all transported to that godforsaken spot to celebrate this marvel of economic optimism, public relations, engineering, hard labor, and untrustworthy financing. Progress and its presiding genius, capital investment, had conquered the forbidding western terrain.

Two days later, on the night of September 10, the distinguished assembly (minus the decorative Crows who were shunted back to their reservation) arrived in Portland, packed into four trains, for the city's "Last Spike Celebration." Twenty thousand gas jets illuminated Portland's prominent buildings. Banners, bunting, wreaths, and flags festooned the commercial establishments of First Street. Soldiers, bands, every able school child in the city, and the Knights of Pythias were mustered for a grand parade; they were joined by "a band of mounted Indians of the genuiner kind [local "savages" from the Warm Springs Reservation], painted and feathered and giving voice occasionally to war whoops of a blood-curdling character."[2] It was, as the *Oregonian* declared, "The Greatest Display Ever Witnessed in our City."[3]

No matter that Henry Villard's daring capital venture crashed into bankruptcy within a few months, or that the fortunes of several of Portland's merchant families were shaken by these reverses. The great deed was accomplished: Portland no longer depended solely on river routes or poorly maintained wagon roads to connect it to distant resources and markets. The railroad had come, and this vigorous frontier trading town was now "incorporated with the rest of the world."[4]

Only two years before, Wallis Nash, a traveler to the West, had described Portland as "juvenile but audacious," an oversized town that envisioned itself as "the commercial metropolis of the Northwest. To one who has seen real cities it is but a little place; but some of its twenty-one or twenty-two thousand inhabitants raise claims to greatness and even supremacy that make it difficult to suppress a smile."[5]

Nash was torn between admiration for Portland's remarkable growth and an impulse to deride the city's claims of eminence. He understood that Portland's wealth rested on the aggregate power, often ruthlessly applied, of a merchant class that controlled the flow of goods and money for the entire region. That such a class should establish itself at the confluence of the Columbia and Willamette Rivers was almost inevitable. The Willamette River runs through the region's most fertile valley, and the Columbia is the only western river to break the Cascade Range, making it a natural link between shipping on the Pacific Coast and the so-called "inland empire" of eastern Oregon, Washington, and Idaho.

Portland will be Wood's home for many years: where he will practice law and build a fine house; where Nannie will raise five children and tend her lavish garden, the envy and pride of the city's upper crust. It is where Wood will spend his most productive years; where he will acquire a public persona—"C. E. S. Wood" or "Col. Wood"; where he will be admired by some and reviled by many others. Portland will be the theater of his efforts to live well and to have some positive effect on his times. If we are to know him, we must know something of this young city that came into being virtually at the same time as Wood himself.

The hoopla surrounding the arrival of the transcontinental railroad revealed Portland's belief in its special destiny. Portland came by this conceit partly through the pride and ambition of its founders, but also through the rhetoric of America's westward expansion. In 1845, when President James Polk delivered his first annual message to Congress, he claimed that the Oregon Country, then jointly held by Great Britain and the United States, should no longer be subject to the whims of a distant European government. The territory of North America was meant solely for the North American people. The notion of a unique American destiny is explicit in tracts and declarations dating back to John Smith and the pilgrim colonists, but several months before Polk's address John L. O'Sullivan, editor and founder of the *United States Magazine and Democratic Review*, an expansionist journal, wrote of "our *manifest destiny* to overspread the continent allotted by Providence for the free development of our yearly multi-plying millions."[6] Soon, "manifest destiny" became a rallying cry in a national debate over Oregon.

In 1846 the Polk administration resolved a territorial dispute with Britain, and within a year three thousand settlers poured into the Oregon Country to lay claim to their share of the American dream. The settlers who consolidated control over this new land rarely doubted the rightness of their undertaking. Indian populations were driven onto reservations; treaties were broken; Indian agents betrayed their charges. Chinese workers, whose cheap labor built the railroads and seaports of the West, were treated like vermin. Blacks in this slave-free territory were legally cast into separate, unequal schools. Yet these wrongs appeared relatively minor even to people of conscience. For the pioneers who flocked to Oregon were driven by a sense of high purpose—or rather they conjured lofty justifications for their quest for land and wealth: they were instruments of history, coura-geously and providentially helping America realize its manifest des-tiny.

The colonization of Oregon was greatly accelerated when, in Janu-ary of 1848, gold was discovered in California. Using Portland as a base from which to supply California prospectors, Portland merchants realized 100-percent markups. These favorable circumstances attracted a wave of easterners determined to make their fortune in this volatile, expanding market. In 1851, the year before Wood's birth, William S. Ladd and Henry W. Corbett arrived in Portland within a month of one another. Both were in their early twenties and both received financial backing from wealthy investors in the East. Josiah Failing, another of the city fathers, also arrived in 1851 to sell goods for a New York commission house.

When Ladd, Corbett, and Failing arrived in Portland, the city had barely gotten used to its name. Just seven years before, in 1844, Francis Pettygrove of Maine flipped a coin with Asa Lovejoy of Massachusetts to determine whether their newly formed trading site should be called "Boston" or "Portland," after their respective New England cities.

In the freewheeling spirit of the times, merchants cornered the market on basic goods: turpentine, molasses, nails—anything they could get their hands on; then they boosted the resale price to whatever the market would bear. Henry Corbett extended credit to customers and charged them up to 3 percent interest per month, well above the legal rate of 10 percent per annum.[7]

During these years of rapid expansion, what was good for Portland's first families was generally good for the prosperity of the city itself. Lumber mills, agriculture, banks, railroads, real estate, river transport, meat packing, construction—the power of these few families extended into every aspect of commerce. Plutocratic governance was not unique to Portland. Across America ambitious men had a relatively free hand in shaping the nation's development. One can respect their energy and their impulse to build, as well as their personal identification with the fate of their communities, their regions, and with the fate of America itself. Yet their attitudes and methods were often reprehensible. The Indian Ring, the Whiskey Ring, Robber Barons, city bosses, crooked Washington lobbies—this is part of their legacy. In Portland as in the rest of the nation, the decades following the Civil War were a time of scandal and corruption, of private monopolies exploiting public trusts, and of ruthless business practices unrestrained by effective laws and regulatory codes.

Portland's prosperous elite founded clubs, churches, school and library subscriptions; they threw lavish parties and built new homes. Though proud of their status and self-made fortunes, they were practical men with little sense of refined living. As westerners they masked their awkwardness with the kind of cocky, joking brashness that Mark

Twain so often expressed in his laconic public persona; yet their
efforts to acquire the accoutrements of culture often produced unhappy
results. Portland's plutocrats flocked to Europe in the 1870s and
1880s, returning home with costly art works and furnishings of dubi-
ous value which nonetheless proclaimed their conviction that wealth
and refinement somehow went hand in hand.[8] In truth, the men who
willed Portland into being had only the most conventional notions of
how to spend their fortunes for comfort and pleasure. They expressed
themselves most truly, not in their homes and furnishings, but in the
city they controlled.

Pictures and photos from those times give a vivid sense of the
character of this energetic new city. In Olof Grafstrom's canvas, *View
of Portland*, painted about the time of the Last Spike celebration,
we view the city from afar. At first glance, it is a familiar Romantic
composition: two observers in the foreground, perched on a high bluff
from which they contemplate the landscape. But there are unusual
details. The clearing on which they stand is littered with felled trees.
The two observers peer out over a stretch of dark spruce at the
sprawling river town below: white homes on a symmetrical grid of
carefully parcelled lots; a bustling port with steamships and sailboats
moving up and down the river. On the far side of the Willamette,
smoke rises from a thriving lumber mill.

It is not a pretty sight. There are skeletal trunks of ruined trees,
a new town of no particular beauty. Grafstrom's image exists as a
somber variant of Friedrich's Rhine River canvasses and Thomas
Cole's splendid Hudson River panoramas. It is not the "Sublime"
that Grafstrom has rendered but its opposite, or rather the forces
leading to its elimination: settlement, development, man's destruction
of the wilderness.[9]

Let us enter the city and take a closer look. Over there is Park
Avenue: block after block of barren earth, neatly staked out by white
markers that protrude like little teeth to keep the city at bay. Each
plot is bordered with rows of newly planted saplings. In years to
come, the simple homes that surround the park will give way to
stately structures erected as testaments to Portland's civic pride: the
Arlington Club, the Masonic Temple, the Portland Auditorium, the
Portland Art Museum.[10]

Nearby, at Sixth and Yamhill two handsome three-story mansions tower above newly planted trees. The properties are bordered by freshly painted picket fences and white plank sidewalks that extend across the dirt road as well. These were the years when Portland's great families built their dream houses: evidence that not only they, but their city too, had "arrived" and could well afford to show it.

The first of these grand mansions belongs to Henry Corbett. Built in 1870, it is designed in Victorian Italianate style, with an imposing array of columns, porches, balconies, and architectural refinements. The interior presents a conspicuous display of cluttered mantels and table tops littered with costly bric-a-brac. An expensive crystal chandelier hangs in the main sitting room, where classical marble figures preside from their pedestals. These rooms are not for family life. They are formal settings in which Corbett could continue his busy public life at home. Thick curtains cover the windows. The furniture is heavy, solidly constructed out of the finest woods. Delicate lace antimacassars grace the sofas. In the sitting room, six paintings, all ornately framed, crowd one cluttered corner. To the modern eye it is a hodgepodge of conspicuous consumption, but by the standards of Henry Corbett's time it is impeccably correct, all the good taste his substantial fortune could buy.[11]

Henry Failing's prominent dwelling, built just three years after Corbett's, is one block away. The Failing mansion is done in Italianate Mansard style—a handsome spacious structure with high-ceilinged rooms. His interiors are less crowded, with fewer signs of cultural shopping sprees than Corbett's. Mr. Failing is even content to live with occasional patches of bare wall. His taste is nothing if not serendipitous: in his entrance hallway you are greeted by the sculpted figure of a young Roman man, along with his unlikely companions— a mounted elk's head and a lugubrious moose.[12]

Step outside again and, with the help of another photograph and a bit of imagination, walk one block east. At Seventh and Yamhill, where more of Portland's wealthy families have raised their homes, all is white, immaculate, brand new. Houses sit in empty yards. In this town that will soon call itself "the City of Roses," there are no shrubs, no gardens: an air of unsettling isolation, of eerie emptiness, prevails. It is difficult to shake the feeling that there is something tentative, insecure even, about life in this isolated commercial town. Portland emerged from its frontier past in a position to dominate the entire Pacific Northwest; it boasted a record of rapid economic growth and physical expansion; and it had a core of hard-working conservative leaders who regarded it as their duty to band together and guide the city toward its manifest destiny. It had these assets and many more, but its character was yet to be established.

As a city, Portland was young and full of promise, determined to have its way in the world. In choosing Portland as his new home, Charles Erskine Scott Wood must have realized he'd found a city commensurate to his own yearning nature, the very place to put down roots and begin his new life.

11. The Sculptor and the King

When Wood began his new life in Portland in 1884, he was already well connected there. During his tour of duty at Fort Vancouver, a time when he was accepted as a member of General Howard's family circle, he had met and favorably impressed many of the city's most influential people. And back in 1880, the year Nannie had spent with him in Oregon, the attractive young couple had been welcomed in the homes of Portland's leading families.

Cicero H. Lewis, one of Portland's merchant princes, was particularly fond of young Wood. Following Wood's resignation from the army, Lewis invited him and his family to live as guests in his spacious home. For Wood, who was practically penniless, Lewis's invitation placed him at the center of Portland's ruling circle.

By the time Wood and Nannie settled in at the Lewis home, Lewis's wife had given him eleven children.[1] But living space was no problem. Lewis had recently completed construction of a mansion that he copied from the floor plan of Henry Failing's imposing dwelling. On a double-size block, between Northwest Ninteenth and Twentieth Streets, his stately home was graced by wide lawns, a stable and greenhouse, and a long sweeping driveway bordered by "carefully placed trees and flowering bushes."[2]

Through Lewis and other acquaintances, Wood picked up his first clients. Soon he was able to move to his own house on the corner of King and Salmon Streets. By now, there were four Wood children, and the King Street house, with woods all about, delighted them. Nannie ordered furniture shipped from the East and, in spite of his limited means, Wood hired a man who served as cook, gardener, and companion to the children.

All was well in the Wood household. Wood and Nannie were "young, joyous and popular."[3] They did a good deal more entertaining than their budget could support. Lacking the resources of their wealthy friends, they relied on ingenuity and the bright impression they made to carry them through. When the Failings threw a fancy-dress ball, Nannie had no dress to wear and Wood had no money to buy her one, so Nannie took down her muslin curtains and fashioned her own costume. Since they had no carriage, Wood took a box and fastened it to his son Erskine's sled. He lined the box with furs he had saved from his Alaska explorations; then he placed Nannie in it, a makeshift Cinderella, and hauled her through the snow to the doorstep of Failing's elegant mansion.[4]

In May of 1884, the *Century Monthly* published Wood's article "Chief Joseph, The Nez-Perce." Wood's piece is particularly blunt in its criticism of the U.S. government's cynical strategy of negotiating treaty agreements with christianized Indians whose voice had little weight among their own people: "It was false and absurd. With them [the Nez Perce] . . . the decision of a majority is not regarded as binding the minority; this principle is unknown. . . . If there be but one man who dissents, his right to depart from the action of the others is unquestioned."[5]

For those few families of Portland who subscribed to this esteemed literary monthly, it must have been a source of pride to see the name of their new neighbor, this multitalented young attorney, appear beside the likes of Julian Hawthorne, Henry James, George Washington Cable, Austin Dobson, Christina Rossetti, and Andrew Lang. Neither they nor Wood himself could have imagined how the Nez Perce's tolerance of dissent would take root in Wood's own life: how in years to come this gifted young attorney would become so committed to dissenting voices that he himself would be identified with enemies of law.

The *Century Monthly* article was one more indication of Wood's abhorrence of authority. Yet in February of 1886 he accepted an appointment as lieutenant colonel in the Oregon State Militia.[6] For the rest of his life the title "Colonel Wood" stayed with him. He often ridiculed his inflated rank, but in the era following the Civil

War elevated military titles were common: it was useful to be "Colonel Wood," especially at political and civic functions where he was frequently called upon to speak.

In that same year, the passing of two of Portland's most successful citizens drew Wood further into the exclusive circle of power. In March, Morris Fechheimer, a gifted attorney, died of stomach cancer. At forty-one he was just eight years older than Wood, yet he had already built a flourishing legal practice. During Wood's first years in Portland, Fechheimer had taken an immediate liking to him and passed several cases his way. Then, in 1886, Fechheimer became ill. On his death bed, in a gesture of immense generosity, he brought Wood together with his young associate, Henry Ach, as a full partner in his law practice.[7] Wood and Ach moved quickly to strengthen their prospects: they invited Judge George H. Williams to join them as a full partner, and the firm of Williams, Ach, and Wood set up their practice in the First National Bank building on the corner of First and Washington Streets.[8]

George H. Williams brought distinction and political muscle to the new firm. He was probably the best-known Oregonian in America, though much of his fame rested on the notoriety, well-deserved, that came to him during President Grant's scandal-ridden administration. At first it might appear that a wheeler-dealer of Williams's prominence had nothing to gain by entering into partnership with Wood, who commanded little influence in the powerful circles where money was to be made. But Williams had no formal legal training: though he proved immensely useful to the firm by reassuring prospective clients that they could count on his unquestioned clout as a consummate backroom politician, he needed someone of Wood's ability to take care of actual legal matters. As for Wood, he chose to disregard Williams's tainted past and to view his partner as a colorful political insider. Though Williams's machinations rankled Wood, he understood that a partnership with the old judge was sure to bring him credibility, acceptability, and very lucrative clients.

That the offices of Williams, Ach, and Wood should be in the First National Bank building was as good an indication as any of how closely Wood's legal practice was tied to Portland's elite. The First National was founded in 1869 when Henry Corbett and Henry Failing had followed the example of their friend William Ladd and bought themselves a bank. On several occasions Wood was able to enhance his standing without setting foot outside the building. One day, Wood was sitting in his office when he received a message from Failing in the bank below, requesting him to come to his private office. Failing had been called upon to execute a provision left in the will of Steven Skidmore, who for twenty years had prospered as the city's leading druggist. Skidmore left a bequest of five thousand dollars "for the erection of a drinking fountain, to be placed in the business part of the city, for men, horses and dogs."[9] Failing told Wood that he wanted Skidmore's fountain to be a focal point for civic pride. He asked Wood to invite the best sculptors in America to design the fountain. Wood agreed to help; he wrote to both Olin Warner and Augustus Saint-Gaudens to see if either was interested. Saint-Gaudens, the most renowned American sculptor of his day, had a backlog of commissions, so Wood offered the work to Warner, his old friend.[10]

Warner was amused and challenged by Skidmore's insistence that the fountain serve men and animals. In May 1887, he signed a formal agreement to create the fountain, and by the following summer the Portland papers were issuing daily reports on the fountain's passage across America. A fence went up at the fountain site on First and Ankeny in the heart of the business district. From the middle of August until the third week of September, Warner supervised the installation. With the unveiling ceremony only days away, Henry Weinhard, the city's venerable brewer, dropped in to speak with Wood: "When we were alone [he] unbosomed himself of the proposition that he himself would bear the expense of whatever hose was necessary, in addition to the fire hose of the city, to connect his largest lager tank with the fountain, and have the fountain spout free beer."[11]

Failing and the fountain committee vetoed Weinhard's tempting offer. They had invested several thousand dollars of their own money to supplement Skidmore's bequest. Enhancing their city's cultural life did not come cheap, they learned, and the prospect of a beer-sodden unveiling, with drunken horses and soused dogs, did not present itself as the most fitting note to strike for the occasion.

When the great day arrived, Wood was called upon to deliver a dedicatory address. Thousands of people spilled into the area. The city's finest families gathered in front of the speaker's platform to hear Wood speak of Skidmore's self-made success and his generous gift to the city he loved. Since the coming of the Northern Pacific five years before, no single event had so galvanized the city. William S. Ladd, a crusty old New Englander, listened to Wood's speech and wept.[12]

In four years Wood had emerged as an eloquent voice for Portland's vision of its destined greatness. He was the spokesman, the living symbol, of new initiatives to add learning, beauty, and culture to the prosperous town. The creation of Skidmore Fountain was the most visible evidence of Wood's role, but there were other instances as well. In August of 1886, Wood was elected to fill Morris Fechheimer's post as director of the Library Association of Portland. Under Wood's leadership, the Association constructed its own two-story stone building. Corbett, Reed, Failing, Lewis—most of the city's leadership—joined together in this project, which was completed five years later.

In 1888, the same group founded the Portland Art Association. Corbett and Failing served as the guiding lights, but Wood, who occupied a unique place in the select group of city leaders, played an essential role in getting the project off the ground. He was a good twenty years younger than the first generation of wealthy merchants, yet he was older and more experienced than any of their sons, several of whom were beginning to take on their fathers' responsibilities. None of the older men had gone to college; none had had the time or the training to absorb much in the way of fine arts. They sent their sons to college—Amherst, Harvard, the best that money could buy. But Wood was not merely college-educated: his writing appeared in the *Century Monthly*; he was a talented amateur painter; he could amuse his stolid Arlington Club companions with lively anecdotes of youthful high jinks among New York's leading artists; and, as his participation in the Skidmore Fountain project had proven, he was able to bring their work to Portland.

Given his interests, aptitudes, and personal connections, Wood could not have arrived in Portland at a better time. The energetic men who had made their fortunes and built their grand mansions now regarded the shaping of the city as their paramount project. They understood, without ever explicitly stating it, that along with investment, expansion, capitalizing transportation, development, irrigation projects, settlement plans, and the like, Portland's future also depended on its acquiring an air of culture and refinement. As if in answer to that call, Charles Erskine Scott Wood arrived to make Portland his home. As the city's leaders saw him, Wood had impeccable family origins, a West Point education, and a military career devoted largely to bringing peace—hence, prosperity—to Oregon. Wood carried himself well; he had culture, wit, a sparkling wife. And style. More than any one quality, he communicated a sense that he knew *how* to live. For this, the elite families of Portland valued him. They had money, more than they knew how to spend. But Wood had taste and charm; he was familiar with literature, art, the daunting cities of the East and their enviable refinements. If Portland did not yet have these things for itself, Portland now had Wood. He would enliven their dinner parties and Arlington Club lunches with stories of wilderness adventures, of Civil War generals, Chief Joseph, his father's travels, of New York, Washington, and Baltimore, of Warner, Weir, Ryder, and all his artist friends—their nights in Bowery dives eating macaroni and drinking chianti till dawn. Yes, Portland valued Wood. And Wood, who had no family fortune, could only hope that as he enriched their lives, his proximity to money and power would eventually enrich his own.

In 1887 Nannie gave birth to a fifth child, Berwick Bruce Wood, and Wood turned thirty-five. By life expectancy figures of his time he was well into middle age; and that very year happened to press reflections of mortality upon him. In the autumn he was called to eastern Oregon to see to important business. The United States government was taking testimony to forfeit the land grant of the Willamette Valley and Cascade Mountain Military Wagon Road Company, which had passed by purchase into the hands of Messrs. Lazard Freres. As their Portland attorney and manager of the grant, Wood accompanied the government's representatives, taking testimony at various points along the grant.[13] This particular mission was marked by misfortune. In Prineville the U.S. commission's stenographer dropped dead, prompting Wood to gloomy speculation about his own fragile existence. A few days later, Wood was thrown from a horse and broke his leg; not long after that he received word that his infant son, Berwick, was dangerously ill. In time, Berwick recovered and

Wood's leg healed enough for him to make the trip home. Yet he remained shaken by his brush with death and began to feel disenchanted with straightlaced Portland society. Writing to his friend, Alexander Drake, the art director at the *Century Monthly*, he commented: "Everybody seems to me nowadays small in the human figure, small in manner, or in prettiness, just prettiness. I hate prettiness. Why can't they be more like the great men & make beauty & ugliness both poetical & both strong. . . . I wish I could sit on a cloud and contemplate the world's progress and gradual death, forever."[14]

Wood's impatience with the world he moved in was offset by a deep desire to live well. In 1888 he bought property for a home he intended to build on the corner of Main and Ford (now Vista), up the hill that borders West Portland, somewhat removed from the wealthy neighborhoods where his social life took place. Though Wood could not afford to build his dream house, he consoled himself by ordering shrubs and trees to plant in anticipation of future prosperity. He wrote to Erwanger & Barry Florists of Rochester, New York, requesting "enough La France roses . . . for a hedge 150 feet long" as well as Sweetbrier, Eloiri de Dijon, and sweet scented violets.[15] A month later, he inquired about 250 feet of Japanese Quince for another hedge, and he wanted to know which fruit trees were most adaptable for training on a trellis.[16]

All this was costly for a man with a family of five, but Wood knew only one way to live. William Maxwell Wood, with his exquisite eye, his insistence on the best, the finest, the most beautiful, had shown him the way. To Messrs. Jacques & Marcus in New York, he wrote: "I am very much pleased with the studs. They meet my anticipations as to workmanship and surpass them as to beauty of the stones used. The only disappointment; you have no concern with, is they pale somewhat and look somewhat glassy upon a starched linen shirt front and are, if not *inappropriate* to the surrounding at least not at the *best* upon dark tones (especially non-lustrous). They are exceedingly beautiful, and my conclusion is that nothing could surpass an opal arrangement for ladies wear, but had I to repeat the experiment I think for studs I would try rubies, garnets or turquoise. It is not with me a matter of intrinsic value but of artistic value."[17]

What jeweler would not be delighted with such a customer—a man of obvious refinement, to whom money was apparently no object, and for whom rubies, garnets, and turquoise were of "artistic value" only? Those studs, along with the La France roses, the Eloiri de Dijon, and the 250 feet of Japanese Quince were prizes Wood had to have. Given his rapid ascendence in Portland, his reputation as a man of taste, he might even persuade himself that acquisitions of this nature were expected of him. Wood might further impress his friends by pronouncing his roses' French names with easy fluency. And though his wealthy Arlington Club brethren could afford studs far costlier than Wood's, how many of them were acquainted with New York's finest jewelers?

This and all the other expenses needed to maintain Wood's high style put a severe burden on his finances. In May he wrote to his friend, the artist George de Forest Brush: "I only regret that my needs seem to keep pace with my prosperity and taking the heavy burden of debt with which I started, I am not as flush as I might be."[18] It may be that Wood assumed part of his father's debts after his death. Also, he made regular payments to help his younger brothers through school and to help support his stepsister, Hannah. But none of this deterred him from living well: from purchasing art and rare books; from ordering French wine and cheeses shipped from San Francisco; from buying jewelry, an expensive watch, fine clothing, property, a yearling colt for little Nan—whatever his vision of graceful living required.

When Olin Warner came to Portland to supervise the installation of Skidmore Fountain, Wood asked him to do a bust of him, and Warner obliged. Warner's sculpture is three-quarters life-size. The head is handsome, with good features and a large nose, but the image is not very compelling. There is no life in the eyes; Wood's mouth is hidden under a mustache and beard. The piece reveals little. It is not Wood, but rather the head of a young Roman senator. Perhaps, in that sense, the piece *is* revealing—an image of the wealth and status to which Wood aspired.

During Warner's stay, Wood arranged for Chief Joseph—recently settled at the Colville Reservation—to visit along with seven other tribal chiefs. Wood invited them to lunch, an event his children bruited up and down Flanders Street. Neighbors hung out their windows hoping to catch a glimpse of Indians in their war paint marching up the street. "I was a bit taken aback," Nannie recalled, "to go down to my parlor and see them lounging about on my divan and pillows."[19]

Wood valued his infrequent meetings with Joseph, and he thoroughly enjoyed the opportunity to startle the good citizens of Portland. But this time he had an additional motive in mind: to persuade Warner to do medallions of Joseph and several other Indian leaders. They were a dying generation whose deeds were as great and worthy of sculpted monuments as the mounted generals that presided over town squares across the land. Given his intense political beliefs, Warner did not need to be persuaded. The following year he returned to Portland and executed a fine medallion of Joseph in profile.

Wood also promoted the work of another artist from his New York days: George de Forest Brush. With Wood's encouragement, Henry Failing purchased *The Sculptor and the King*, a large piece for which Brush had recently been awarded the first Hallgarten Prize from the National Academy of Design.[20] The "sculptor" of the title is a barechested Indian in a loincloth. In his right hand he holds a chisel. The "king" is festooned with a great pink plume, dark green cape, yellow leggings, and a gold armlet. They meet in an improbable Mayan/Aztec setting: a majestic stone palace, empty except for a rumpled carpet, a huge clay vessel on which the young artist rests his knee, and the sculpture itself—a mythic god-king.

It is Brush's rendering of an Indian Golden Age: a Mayan Medici bestowing his blessing on a Michelango in loincloth. As allegory its meaning is clear: Creative Youth pays homage to Manhood and Authority; Art and Power stand side by side—an apt and flattering theme for Failing, himself a king of commerce, and now a patron of the arts.

There would be little point in describing this hyperbolic piece were it not for Wood's reaction to it. After his first glimpse of *The Sculptor and the King*, Wood wrote Brush an eleven page letter praising it as a masterpiece, one of the great paintings of its time. To Wood, *The Sculptor and the King* seemed almost Shakespearean in scope and achievement. He praised his friend for creating a moment of high drama in which the power, prosperity, and authority of the king is played against "the sculptor's expression of conscious pride and certainty of approval mingled with suspense till the verdict be given."[21]

Among his artist friends Wood was known for his unerring judgment. In time, he acquired a fine collection of works by Weir, Hassam, Warner, and Corot, as well as *Jonah*, one of Ryder's most admired canvasses. Yet never did he wax as enthusiastically about any of these fine works as he did about Brush's allegory. What happened to skewer Wood's judgment? Perhaps Brush's painting gave Wood an idealized version of his own life drama: that of the gifted young man seeking approval from his kingly superior, hoping for a gesture of royal largesse, perhaps even a share of his power. How many times had Wood himself felt the sculptor's "conscious pride and certainty of approval mingled with suspense till the verdict be given"? In his dealings with General Howard, Twain, Morris Fechheimer, Judge Williams, and Portland's prosperous old men—most of all in his relationship with William Maxwell Wood, his sovereign father—Wood cast himself repeatedly in the role of Brush's sculptor: talented, respectful, proud, and determined to wrest approval, glory, and prosperity from the potent, expressionless king in his magnificent, insurmountable palace.

12. The Magic Pearl

My dear Mr. Meyer: It is getting so that I cannot attend to your business and the law business and live. I am about played out. It is too much for one man."[1] Eugene Meyer, the man to whom Wood shared his exasperation, was Wood's most prized client, a resident partner of the powerful banking house of Lazard Freres, in charge of their West Coast affairs.

In the decades following the Civil War, German, British, and French interests invested heavily in America's capital growth. Among this group of adventurous bankers was the house of Alexander and Simon Lazard, who held a vast tract of land in Oregon. At least, that was their claim. Eight hundred thousand acres of land granted by the United States government to the Willamette Valley and Cascade Mountain Wagon Road Company had subsequently been purchased by buyers associated with Lazard Freres. However, the old road company and many other land-grant enterprises had a tangled history of broken promises, bribes, and financial chicanery. By the early 1880s, a reform movement spearheaded by Secretary of the Interior Carl Schurz prompted Congress to challenge land grant holders in court. As a result, Lazard Freres was forced to defend its title to the Oregon lands. A vast fortune was at stake: with Eugene Meyer keeping a watchful eye on his every move, Wood devoted great effort to representing Lazard Freres's interests.

The Wagon Road Land Grant and its critical legal requirements remained with Wood, in one form or another, for thirty years. Like the nightmare fantasy of *Jarndyce v. Jarndyce*—the legal dispute that engenders the gloomy fog of Charles Dickens's *Bleak House*—

the land grant issue tested the lives of those who became involved with it, revealing much about their hopes, their professional ethics, and their character.

The Willamette Valley and Cascade Mountain Wagon Road Company came into existence in 1864 when a group of wealthy merchants guaranteed a thirty-thousand-dollar investment to create a toll road from Albany in western Oregon, over the Cascade Mountains and across the grasslands of eastern Oregon to the Idaho border. In 1866, unable to meet their financial obligations, the company directors sought a federal land grant to avoid bankruptcy. Land grants were essential to the economic development of the West. Between 1860 and 1890, eighty million acres of the public domain, mostly west of the Mississippi, were given away to railroad and wagon road companies to spur construction of transportation networks and the settlement of western lands. In their simplest form, land grants ceded a checkered band of alternate sections of land on either side of the projected road or railroad, in exchange for which the company was obligated to construct their road. Since the Willamette Valley and Cascade Mountain Wagon Road was to extend hundreds of miles across the timbered Cascades and through extensive grazing land in eastern Oregon, the land grant acreage had enormous potential value.

With eight hundred thousand acres suddenly placed in their hands, the road company's owners became less interested in fulfilling their obligation to construct a toll road. They had access to a fortune in land; all they needed to do was meet the minimum terms of their federal grant. They constructed a slipshod trail and called it quits. As soon as they received their land grant windfall, they were inundated by suits from settlers who had built homes on the land. While some suits questioned whether the company had satisfied the terms of the grant, others challenged whether the toll road even existed.

As lawsuits piled up, the directors and shareholders became increasingly eager to turn the land holdings over for immediate profit. In August 1871 the company was sold to a group of men who instituted sharper strategies of eastern banking and investment practices, and in 1879 representatives of Lazard Freres gained control of the company.

Meanwhile, the ongoing clamor over unresolved lawsuits captured the attention of Carl Schurz, secretary of the interior and an energetic member of the reform wing of the Republican Party. He sent W. F.

Prosser of Seattle to investigate the road. Prosser personally traveled
the road and recorded his detailed observations. He concluded that
the wagon road was a fraud: that "legal measures be taken," and that
those responsible for the fraud be "severely punished."[2]

Prosser's indignation is easy to understand. But where did this
leave Lazard Freres? The banking house insisted that they were
"innocent purchasers"; they could not be held responsible for failures
and contract violations of their predecessors. Powerful business interests were threatened by Prosser's report, and they used their considerable resources to sway congressional opinion. It was hardly surprising
that, in 1881, the House Committee on Military Affairs advised
against government efforts to annul the wagon road grant and reclaim
the land as public domain. There was a narrow legal justification for
the decision, but beyond matters of law, it reflected the laissez faire
spirit of the national economy: the conviction that America's interests
were best served by giving private capital a free hand.

The favorable government ruling in 1881 did not close the issue.
In the years that followed, Congress engaged in a stream of debates
and investigations concerning land grant forfeiture, all of which had
a direct bearing on the Lazard Freres properties. Finally, in 1888
President Grover Cleveland pressed Congress and the judiciary to
begin suits of forfeiture against delinquent road companies.[3] Once
again, Lazard Freres was forced to defend its title to the Oregon land.
With Morris Fechheimer gone, they relied upon the legal services
of Judge Williams and Charles Erskine Scott Wood. While Williams
used his powerful connections to place Lazard Freres's position in
a favorable light, Wood took on increasing amounts of research and
preparation for the courtroom fight.

Wood set about the grueling task of traveling along the old wagon
road route in order to gather testimony to counter the government's
case. Wood needed his commission, he needed to win the case, but
at times he became fed up with the whole thing. "Damn the land
grant!" he wrote Meyer. "There! That's my feeling today and I know
you must often echo the sentiment."[4]

In spite of the pressure Wood faced in the land grant case and
from his own financial straits, he continued to live and spend extravagantly. His desire for the good life, purchased in expectation of an
affluence certain to come, threw his personal finances into disarray.

His crisis coincided with the strained state of the national economy. The 1880s were marked by long stretches of depression brought on by ruined speculative ventures and bank failures. Periods of recovery fueled the rapacious spirit of reckless investment.

Economic pressures notwithstanding, Wood was determined to enjoy himself in style. On October 11, 1890, he and several friends arranged a private "Whist Dinner" at the Arlington Club. Their meal was a classic display of the jovial gluttony that characterized festive gatherings of well-to-do men in the Gilded Age: oysters, sherry and bitters, consommé royal, Chateau Yquem, broiled trout, deviled crawfish, Chateau Lafitte, broiled snipe, champagne-frappe, saddle of mutton, peach sherbet, grapes, pears, peaches, plums, coffee, cigars, and cognac. The printed menu ended with a celebratory poem: "Six of us and a boy and a darkey; / The tricks of us and our joy, now hark ye."[5] At the top of the "Bill of Fare," in gothic type, is the boast: "No damned crowned head in Europe ever / Sat down to a meal like this."

One year before, in 1889, Mark Twain's *Connecticut Yankee in King Arthur's Court* appeared in print. Surely, Wood must have read his friend's latest novel: the cocky, chauvinistic tone of the bill of fare epigraph is precisely that of Hank Morgan, Twain's zealous American time-traveler. Wood must have realized the satiric intent in Twain's devastating vision of self-righteous American optimism. But whatever his insights, Wood's life, like Twain's, was caught up in ironies not unlike those that give *Connecticut Yankee* its disquieting moral energy. Wood believed that America was the most promising nation on earth. He despised the class-ridden feudalism of Europe's past, its history of tyrants and terrible wars. He gloried in the inventions and buildings and progress he saw around him. He enjoyed his comforts, his art, good meals, the feast of life that America placed before him.

Wood thrived on hard work and high living, but Nannie's health buckled under the strain of five pregnancies and five childbirths. In 1889 she suffered from typhoid fever.[6] Two years later, her sixth child died in infancy, and the following year she came down with consumption. During this time, and in the years to come, she spent several months a year apart from Wood at a spa in Colorado Springs.

In the midst of all this, Wood sent his oldest son off on an extraordinary adventure. In July of 1892, he gave Erskine over to Chief Joseph, and for the next six months the boy lived with Joseph and his two wives in his tepee on the Nespelem Agency in northeastern Washington. Joseph made no concession to Erskine's youth or his "civilized" needs. The twelve-year-old boy hunted and fished with the Nez Perce men; he shared their food and shelter, the rhythm of their daily lives. In every respect, he lived with Joseph as a son. It is touching to think of Wood, who pursued Joseph on his heroic exodus, placing his eldest boy in Joseph's keeping. It is even more moving to think of Joseph, his tribe shattered, his family destroyed by U.S. army forces, welcoming this soldier's child into his life. One wonders if Wood ever paused to reflect that while his son hunted, ate, and slept in the home of the great leader of the displaced Nez Perce nation, Wood devoted his energy and intelligence to a courtroom struggle in which his clients held claim to considerable portions of the Nez Perce homeland—land they themselves had never even seen.

On December 16, 1892, Judge W. B. Gilbert of the U.S. Circuit Court dismissed the U.S. government's case against Lazard Freres. Wood had his day of triumph and Lazard Freres had clear title to 790,000 acres of land. It was a sweet victory for Wood—singularly important to his financial future. In the years that followed he collected substantial fees and commissions as Lazard Freres's company agent. More significantly, Lazard Freres was now free to sell its land. Meyer and the company officers in New York knew that when they found a proper buyer they had, in Wood, an attorney of proven mettle who could take on their large and profitable project.

All this happened in Wood's fortieth year. He was a strikingly handsome man, with black wavy hair parted just to the left of center, a curly black beard and mustache, and thick dark eyebrows—all of which drew attention to his eyes. Photographs from these years display a direct gaze. He is confident, forthright, a man who is right there, ready to get the job done. But there are other photos where Wood seems to look out past the camera—if not toward a distant object, then perhaps in search of one. Yet it is not yearning his countenance reveals so much as a hint of wistful irresolution, a traveler's gaze as his vehicle hurtles through some enticing landscape. It may be he has always wanted to rest and loaf there, to throw off the speed and cares of his journey, to luxuriate, however briefly, in an alternate existence where he is unknown, unencumbered with the demands of adult life, free to experiment with latent selves, free to act foolishly if need be, but free, above all else, free.

Wood's son Erskine remembers storytelling sessions from this time. The five children would gather in the parlor around their father, a fire glowing in the hearth:

> One of his stories I remember was "The Magic Pearl." It went on endlessly night after night for weeks and was entirely extemporaneous. He made it up as he went along, without a hitch or a break or a letdown in the suspense. The central theme was that the possessor of the Magic Pearl could do anything. He could make himself invisible at will. He could cross the oceans in the wink of an eye. Of course he could fly. He fought battles against savages or wild beasts. He rescued beautiful princesses, made himself a king, thwarted the plans of evil magicians. His adventures and his powers were endless and as fanciful as my father's imagination.[7]

To Wood's adoring children it must have sometimes seemed that their own father, the teller of the tale, held that precious charm himself. Had he not lived in the wilderness, traveled through the desert fastness, fought and befriended Indians, lived with Eskimos, seen the great rivers and mountains and cities of America, and won the heart of their beautiful mother? Had he not given them a warm and comfortable home, filled with art and surprising visitors? His powers seemed endless; he could do anything.

In just eight years Wood had established himself as a prominent figure in Portland's select social and cultural circles. He had a lovely wife, five vivacious children, a good home, and, with the land grant case successfully resolved, his prospects were excellent. What did he need, what could he possibly want, that he might not reasonably expect to attain in the next few years?

Still, one wonders what Wood felt as he spun out the saga of the magic pearl to his enchanted children. After blessing his hero with endless powers and sending him forth on wondrous adventures, what did Wood dream of at night? What did he want from his life? To all appearances he was a contented man. If there appears to be a suggestion in a few old photographs of something else—well, who can say what photographs really tell? And just because the story of the magic pearl comes to him readily, fluently, in a never ending series of fantasies, is that any reason to speculate whether or not Wood might have felt confined by the life he lived, cut off from his youthful dream of writing and seeking his fortune in faraway lands? It is all conjecture. The magic pearl is a bedtime story, nothing more. Wood was forty: old enough to know there was no magic in his life.

13. A Labor of Love

Portland in the 1890s is a changed place from the town in which Wood and Nannie settled in 1884. At the city's commercial center along Front and First, new office buildings vaunt ornately detailed portals. Buildings and whole blocks bear the names of Wood's prosperous friends. Telephone lines stretch along every street. Portland has become substantial, stolid. Like many of its most successful citizens, the city has accumulated girth, an air of portly well-being.

An oil painting of Portland done in 1897 by one Thaddeus Welch offers almost the same view of Gustafson's canvass: but strangely, "correctly," the despoiled clearing in the foreground of Gustafson's image has been supplanted by a bucolic scene. A narrow country road winds gently uphill past a trio of contented cows grazing peacefully on the grassy slope. In the distance, the city of Portland exudes streams of smoke with the lazy self-satisfaction of a hardworking papa enjoying his Sunday pipe after a week of industrious effort.[1]

In the spring of 1893 Wood departed from Portland on the Western Pacific Railroad to join Nannie in Colorado Springs, where she was still recovering from tuberculosis. On the station platform he noticed a young woman bidding goodbye to her husband: "Her weeping over the husband, who I suppose goes somewhere and has a cigar and a toddy with his friends, reminds me of Sippy weeping over my worthless carcass. I should think she'd be glad to be rid of it sometimes."[2] Sullen thoughts for a man about to embark with his wife on their first extended vacation together.

A few days later, Wood and Nannie were on their way to Mexico. As their train crossed the Rio Grande Valley, Wood reflected on the desolate desert scene: "One cannot feel these grand relentless immensities from a saloon train. The sense of isolation and of danger is lost. You feel comfortable. Water is at hand. The rails and the wires lead to civilization. But to face the desert with a weary horse and a canteen of warm water, a saddle bag of hard tack. . . . That is to feel the power and the charm of the desert."[3]

Wood's travel notes are laced with restless yearning. He feels cut off from "the power and charm" of the "grand relentless immensities." He resents the saloon car that conveys him—comfortable, civilized, married—on his passive journey while the true desert passage, at least the more alluring one, lies outside, to be undertaken in a solitude he can only dream of.

Their route took them to "ragged, straggling" El Paso, where they took a stroll. Their walk was interrupted by a paralytic, "who with the egoism of misery thinks we know all about him." The man started to weep "with that painful inability to control the emotions common to paralytics." Then he seized Wood's hand and addressed him as "brother." Wood found him repugnant. "Hope I won't be paralyzed some day," he wrote. "Rather die."[4]

Wood's sharp reaction suggests tensions in his own life which he could not yet fully acknowledge. He felt threatened by a kind of spiritual paralysis: his life was becoming fixed, responsible, predictable—or so he feared. And he would not, could not, share his apprehension with Nannie. As upsetting as the paralytic's physical affliction was, Wood was equally disturbed by the man's failure to control his emotions, his "egoism of misery." What's worse, the pathetic paralytic seized Wood's hand and called him "brother." It was like a bad dream.

Later that day, having resumed their journey to Mexico City, Wood listened to a man tell him how he missed his big chance to get rich. "How horrible it must be to look back on life and see a row of 'ifs,' " Wood reflected.[5] This journey jarred something loose in Wood. He did not speak about it, nor would he even write about it freely in his private journal—but during the next three weeks in Mexico, his travel notes were packed with anguished observations.

In Mexico City, Wood and Nannie explored the streets and visited churches, markets, and outlying villages. Wood appreciated the "thick block-like houses" that illustrated "the fitness of a country's natural styles to the country itself."[6] Later, Wood recorded "a pathetic sight":

[A poor peon] was struggling down the dusty road bent beneath the weight of a cheap coarse coffin. *He was bound to it or it to him with ropes typical of the death fastened upon us all*—and he stopped, leaning against a tree, while the sweat made little mud drops at his feet. He wiped his brow with his cracked and calloused hand—and then took his way down the road, the large black coffin obliterating his body. Only his thin brown legs shown beneath so that he seemed some gigantic beetle grotesquely prome-nading, the weariness and melancholy of his face, the solemnity of the hour and the wretched poverty of the sufferer took away all feeling for the grotesque and left only the thought: *Here is a labor of love, of Love and Death, two immortals* (italics mine).[7]

In the margin, Wood sketched that grotesque "gigantic beetle": a coffin with feet—the grim image of a man "obliterated" by his "labor of love." How this scene reflected the shrouded sphere of his personal unrest is painfully clear. He was appalled by the submissive spirit foisted on Mexico's peasants by Catholicism, Nannie's religion. For two years Nannie had been ill, and for several difficult months, Wood had feared she might die. Now, in Mexico, he beheld repeated images that released those apprehensions and others. Nannie's name rarely appears in Wood's passages on Mexico, yet her presence is inescap-able. His Mexico notes are a wrenching string of guarded reflections on his life, particularly his marriage—circuitous, obscure, unwittingly encoded in his travel observations. Though Wood was incapable of saying it, his journal reveals that his marriage was becoming a burden, that his labor of love weighed heavily on him, that duty to Nannie threatened to obliterate his freedom. Instead he flailed out at what he saw: tyrannous Catholicism, peasants crawling submissively, a helpless peon buckling beneath his labor of love.

Wood saw one thing to prize in Mexico. He wrote how the burro, "buried in burdens," hauls crushing loads with stoical resignation, yet still manages to break forth with a "bold . . . triumphant" sound. "Would that I had the unbroken spirit of a donkey," Wood mused.[8]

When the Mexican visit ended, Wood returned to Portland and Nannie journeyed to Colorado Springs for the summer. Back in Portland, Wood addressed a Memorial Day audience on the subject of "national

morals and national responsibility, as they are to-day reflected from
the great lessons of the Civil War." With elaborate rhetorical embel-
lishments, he argued that the morals of the nation ought not be any
different from the morals of individual citizens: "See to it then, that
rather than wealth, or fame or power you treasure the truth. . . . If
there shall be such breeding as that, then we are safe; but if it shall
be that all our men sacrifice their personal independence, their
personal integrity, their personal convictions for the cold tampering
with policy and profit, then I say, let us beware! Or no! Let us now
beware for if ever that time shall come we shall be utterly lost."

It is possible that his call for truth was unconsciously directed at
himself. He went on to extol the virtues of those who fight for what
they believe.

> It may seem to you a harsh thing to say, but it seems to be the
> teaching of history that wars are stimulating. . . . It seems to
> have been the edict of history that the nation, sunk in intermina-
> ble peace, thinks too much of ease, too much of luxury, becomes
> too effeminate, and the moral fiber, strange to say, becomes too
> weak, and then comes war; and if there be anything left of the
> moral fiber, war, like the thunder-storm, clears the air, and on
> every leaf the dew shines brighter and the flowers rear their
> heads sweeter and stronger than before.[9]

For Wood, who challenged militarism throughout his adult life,
this passage is a striking anomaly. His praise of purging, masculine
combat as an antidote to the feminizing effects of "interminable
peace" is indistinguishable from Teddy Roosevelt's cheerful jingoism
of a few years hence.[10] But to truly understand Wood's words, it is
useful to keep in mind the concerns about his personal life that he
was unable to utter. As with his impressions of Mexico, Wood's
Memorial Day address gave voice to inner turmoil. Substitute his life
for that of "the nation" and his remarks on war become a challenge
to himself to overthrow the domestic peace (his marriage) which has
become "interminable."

At the close of his speech, to great applause, Wood hears the
silent voices of America's war dead rising from graveyards across
the land, calling "Power! Freedom! Order! Union!" And later, pulling
"the stops of the organ Time" he hears "the grand diapason of Liberty

and Equality, Freedom without Anarchy, Law, Order and Power." It is unlikely that many in the audience knew what a diapason was, or were conversant with Commodus, Hannibal, Pericles, Augustus, or Charlemagne—all alluded to by Wood—but they seemed to appreciate this bit of decorative erudition as a deserved reward for being American. Wood gave his Memorial Day audience the same rewarding performance he had been giving Portland's plutocrats for years: his wit and learning and easy rhetoric, his very presence, gave their lives a trace of culture, worldliness, and elegance.

After the troubled reflections of Wood's Mexican journal, his Memorial Day address seems disingenuous. How could he call out for people and nations to live truthfully while he himself shunned his truest feelings? He admonished his fellow citizens that "we shall be utterly lost" if personal convictions are sacrificed to "cold tampering with policy and profit." Yet this gifted, idealistic, indulgent man often compromised his deepest beliefs in order to keep his life afloat. And at what cost? Would he ever be worthy of his eloquent principles?

That July, Wood's essay, "Famous Indians: Portraits of Some Indian Chiefs" appeared in the *Century Monthly*. Wood's ostensible subject was Olin Warner's seven medallions of western Indians, but he used the occasion to offer a scathing vision of the winning of the West:

> The Indian always esteemed bravery, virtue, and truth, so I believe he has gained little or nothing from the white civilization, and has lost everything. He has lost the fine flavor of the wilderness, much of the simplicity and integrity of natural life, or "savagery," and has readily absorbed the pleasant vices of civilization. With drunkenness, disease, dependence upon a paternal government which is not paternal, and the annihilation of his environment, it has become as impossible for the Indian to exist as for the buffalo.[11]

Wood's elevated tone and angry, ironic attack were reminiscent of the hectoring letters his father wrote him at West Point. It is as if, in search of moral authority, Wood instinctively adopted the voice that commanded his own obeisance throughout his youth. Wood's ringing attack depicted the same warring forces of self and society as in the first part of his Memorial Day speech. In the earlier speech

Wood had argued that personal integrity must preserve itself against society's temptations of "wealth, or fame, or power." Here he drew a picture of what can happen when "the pleasant vices of civilization" triumph. The Indians' ethic of "bravery, virtue, truth," "the fine flavor of the wilderness," the "integrity of natural life"—all this is gone. Wood was rattling the bars of his own cage.

His final portrait was of Yatiniawitz, the Cayuse chief who captured and slew Chief Egan (called "E-He-Gant" by Wood) during the Bannock-Piute uprising and brought his severed hand to General Howard as evidence of his death: "He is truly the embodiment of the wilderness, a creation of nature, and it would be as impossible for him to cultivate the lands allotted to him in severalty . . . as it would be for a cougar to turn sheep-dog. He still keeps to the simple wants of the savage, still lives as he has always lived, accepting the good and evil of his life with fortitude, and above all things insists that a man needs only two virtues—bravery and truth."[12]

One thinks of Wood, just four months before, peering out at the savage desert from his saloon car—feeling fettered by his comforts, his work, his domestic life, his success—daydreaming of facing the wilderness head on, being *in* it once again to test his bravery and fortitude. What Wood yearned for in his own life, he found in the lives of the Indians he most admired. In that sense, his sketches of Indian leaders were displaced expressions of his longing for freedom.

In July Vice President Adlai Stevenson passed through Portland. Wood wrote in his journal that Stevenson "brought out all the fools in town in procession. Asses beating sheepskins and more noise, disturbance and waste of time and money. . . . And Adlai and the Mayor waving to right and left. Pah! Man is still a monkey."[13]

These were private thoughts. But how much indignation could Wood suppress before he spoke out and jeopardized his standing with Portland's conservative establishment? And how much longer could he keep his silence with Nannie? They were caught up in something inexpressibly sad. Each of them knew it and communicated it in separate ways. Nannie wrote to her husband in early September, a letter filled with wifely concern about changing weather and its effect on his and her health. "My dear one, keep warm and dress properly," she wrote. "Don't catch cold. Remember I am not there to warm you—and how I wished I was last night."[14] Couched within her solicitous comments about snow and cold and the salutary effects of sulfur hot springs and proper diet, a pulsing apprehension cuts deeper than all her concern about changing weather. Even as she writes to Wood, a long letter from him is on the way: "I went up to our room, a thing I dread when you are away. It is like going where someone you loved has died. It gives me that empty hearted homesick feeling to see your clothes, your hairpins—your little odds and ends— our bed, and if I could conjure you back out of the air to rush into my arms how quickly I would do it."[15]

Wood's attempt to put words to his feelings—the sense of his and Nannie's bedroom as a place "where someone you loved has died"— strains his self-control to the breaking point. He tells Nannie how he wishes she would rush into his arms, but the unspoken truth was quite the opposite: Nannie would not return to his eager arms, for he and she were divided by more than the plains and mountains that separated them. It has been twenty years since they first met and shared that romantic summer at Rosewood Glen; twenty years since Grant's inauguration and Nannie Moale Smith's memorable party. There have been five children, their blossoming life in Portland, shifts from one house to another, Wood's growing discontent with the spirit of the age, and with it, a gnawing sense of confinement. So much has happened, so much has changed. Wood's passion for Nannie has been all but lost in time.

But how could he say this to her? He loved her still. He could not bear the thought of hurting his wife. And Nannie was not well: all those stays at hot springs, spas, and rest hotels—she had become a pilgrim on a perpetual grand tour for the permanently frail. How could he possibly add to her distress?

Wood filled his letter with cheery reports of various social encounters, descriptions of friends they had known for years. Yet the tension was almost tangible. He was holding back, fighting off some deeper truth, hoping to appease Nannie with assurances of his love. Then he breaks out:

> I am sorry to say you have demoralized me so that when you are absent I fear to mention certain people to you for fear of giving you pain.

To conceal anything from you is beneath me, and there is nothing to conceal, and yet I shrink from telling you so trivial a thing as that I lunched with another woman in a distant city or that I am to dine with the Wilsons today. I hate myself for the timid distrustful feeling, and I cannot even bear to tell you how I love you and others are nothing to me for it seems instead of love words to be defenses and apologies—yet I know all I am writing and all your resolves will not change your nature, which ever fears you are not as necessary to me as I to you. Ah, if you could but see—if you could only know as indeed I think you ought to know, that the world is empty without you.[16]

Nannie was the one and only woman in his life. Of what was she jealous then? "To conceal anything from you is beneath me, and there is nothing to conceal," he insisted. But Nannie knew Wood intimately; she knew him well enough to realize he was struggling to balance his life against new thoughts and feelings that troubled him. Was he having an affair? Perhaps. But quite apart from that, her husband had a secret life that he concealed from her—urges, ideas, and fantasies that he worried would hurt her. Despite his recent speeches celebrating truth and courage, he could not find a way to share his discontent or his confusion with his wife.

14. Closet Drama

In 1894 the Woods moved into their new home at Ford and Main Streets. The interior of the home was dark, opulent, sensuous. Heavy damask curtains with dense floral patterns gave the rooms a cloistered, spellbound air. Handsome Persian carpets covered dark wood floors. Chairs, sofas, and cushions were upholstered with boldly contrasting fabrics. The rooms were filled with vases, porcelains, figurines, Greek statues, and woven Indian baskets. Wood's treasured paintings hung on the walls. Warner's bronze of the children held a prominent place, along with handsome bookshelves packed with rare editions and Grolier Society printings of the classics. A faded photograph shows little Nan sitting on the porch steps: just behind her, identical castings of Olin Warner's bronze bust of her father pose face to face, stationed like tutelary gods. Vines cover the porch columns and railing, furthering the impression that Wood's house was an enchanted bower, a world unto itself.

That November, Wood traveled to New York to collect information for a forthcoming case.[1] He stepped easily into New York life, filling his evenings with dinner parties, visits to the opera, and reunions with friends. Corinne Roosevelt Robinson was especially delighted to have him in town. A member of one of Manhattan's preeminent families—vigorously represented by her brother, the bumptious Teddy—Corinne married into old upper Hudson River money in the person of Douglas Robinson, Jr., a boorish real estate salesman who Wood constantly twitted. Just how Wood and Corinne met, and when, is unclear—their acquaintance may have gone back as far as Wood's law school days—but Wood rarely came to New York without seeing her. For years they carried on a confidential, discretely daring, correspondence in which she addressed him as "my dear Laureate," and he anointed her his "Sappho." Their letters are laced with intimations of romance, but Corinne Roosevelt Robinson was a very proper lady and her infidelities were almost certainly incorporeal.

That first week in New York, Wood saw *Faust, Otello*, and *Lohengrin* at the opera, where his old pal Jimmie (John) Inglis, now a successful art dealer, had a private box.[2] With his dandiacal flair Wood sometimes found himself a part of the spectacle. There is a story he loved to tell of how he defied the fashion of the time. In those days, gentlemen attended the opera in identical formal dress: tails, a vest, black tie, and a starched white shirt. Wood, however, did not think much of starched shirts. One evening he went to the opera wearing a soft silk shirt with opal studs. Heads turned as he entered the grand lobby. His breach of proper taste left Douglas Robinson, his companion, feeling ill at ease. Wood reassured him: "All right, Douglas. Wait, you'll see." He shifted to an affected British accent: *"I went with the Prince down to Cannes—wish you had been there, Douglas. Asked to the Prince's shooting lodge. Couldn't. Engaged to be with the Duke of Marlborough."*

Wood's performance attracted notice. Within a few days Manhattan's finest haberdashers began displaying unstarched silk shirts in shop windows. "Can't keep up with our orders," a salesman told Wood. All New York, it seems, was clamoring for soft shirts, in emulation of the well-connected British nobleman who had appeared at the opera.[3]

Men's fashion aside, what Wood most valued during his days in New York were the times he spent with old companions: Olin Warner, Pinky Ryder, Alexander Drake, J. Alden Weir, and Inglis. He saw Warner and Inglis often, the three of them trading stories from their youth: memories of eccentric roommates and crazy pranks, raffish hangouts and underworld characters they had known. These gatherings revived in Wood a spirit of heady freedom, the chance to feel fully alive in a way that seemed impossible in Portland.

Returning home after another business trip to New York, Wood overheard a young mother say to an old lady, "I didn't have any care or trouble at all till I got married—now it's all worry."[4] Wood's journals record many such moments when he observed or overheard snippets that mirrored his own unspoken sentiments. What caught his attention so often were variations on the same theme: the ordeal of marriage and parenthood; fatigued adults turned martyrs or cynics by overwhelming responsibilities. "Scene for a play," he writes; "divorced husband bidding farewell to his children and reading them the lesson of his fault while enjoining their love loyalty to their mother whom he still loves. She overhears this, and her forgiveness of him and her love comes too late."[5] Wood never wrote the play, nor is it likely he ever expected to. Nonetheless, his notes reveal a looming personal crisis: a play of longing and fantasy within the shut closet of his psyche.

15. Two Rooms

On July 7, 1896, the Democratic National Convention met in Chicago, a gathering dominated by William Jennings Bryan and the free silver movement. Just thirty-six, Bryan had already captured national interest as an electrifying speaker in Congress and on Chautauqua lecture tours. The Democratic Party platform, pushed through by Bryan's faction, condemned trusts and monopolies as well as high protective tariffs and court injunctions against organized labor. Most notable, however, was its call for free and unlimited coinage of silver at a 16–1 ratio—a demand that was first set forth by the People's (or Populist) Party in 1892.[1]

The free silver debate gave Bryan an opportunity to exploit deeply rooted antagonisms toward the eastern establishment. Around the central issue of bimetalism he pieced together a populist platform calculated to appeal to farm states, labor, and mining states. Then, on July 9, he delivered his famous "Cross of Gold" speech and walked off with the Democratic nomination.

Not all Democrats were pleased with this turn of events. The "gold Democrats," mostly representatives of the eastern states, believed that bimetalism would drive the economy into catastrophic depression. The flight of foreign capital, the failure of banking establishments, the decline in wholesale prices, and widespread unemployment—all this, insisted gold Democrats, would come to pass if free silver carried the day. Simply put, Bryan was unacceptable. The gold Democrats bolted from the convention to form the National Democratic Party.

For several years, Wood had followed Bryan's career with interest.

He respected Bryan's conviction that the common man deserved a fair share of the economy, yet he mistrusted Bryan's character. Bryan's platform seemed more a gleaning of convenient attitudes than a coherent program—a demagogic appeal to an alienated electorate rather than a systematic approach to real change. Also, Wood regarded bimetalism as pure folly: "Not all the Nations of the earth nor God Almighty could create and sustain a true bi-metalism."[2] Wood refused to join the Bryan bandwagon. His opposition quickly drew the attention of the new National Democratic Party: they urged him to attend their national committee meeting at Indianapolis.

Wood left Portland, via Union Pacific, on August 3. The committee was already in session when he hurried into their room. He was greeted by a storm of applause. Wood addressed the evening session and argued that it was pointless to form a true third party. Since either Bryan or McKinley was certain to be elected, it was better to support one of these men while preserving a platform from which to negotiate and hope to gain influence in the future. His remarks "fell very flat and evidently on uncongenial soil."

Wood left the meeting feeling uneasy about the coming election. He saw that "the great danger in this campaign will be . . . that every man in debt or discouraged or discontented, envious of the rich and the colossal fortunes of the few, feeling an instinctive and proper dread of these enormous fortunes and of corporations, will vote for Bryan because Silver promises better times . . . a '*change*.' There lies the danger, the reckless and desperate desire for a change."[3]

Meanwhile, Olin Warner lay unconscious in a New York hospital. While riding his bicycle through Central Park, Warner had suffered a stroke; he tumbled from his bike and fell under a horse-drawn cab, which inflicted a severe concussion. When Wood received word of his friend's crisis, he hurried to New York. Warner's brain was swollen—black and engorged with blood, it pressed against the skull. An operation provided only temporary relief: Warner rallied, then slowly sank.[4]

Wood and a handful of Warner's friends gathered in his home at 467 Central Park West for a simple funeral service. Afterwards Wood, Ryder, Inglis, Drake, and a few others visited Warner's Washington Square studio to view an unfinished figure that was to have been his crowning achievement: massive bronze doors for the new Library of Congress, representing "The Oral Tradition" and "Writing."

Ryder was particularly shaken by Warner's death, and Wood saw him several times over the next two weeks. Ryder told him of his wish to transform the medium of his art, "to get my paint less painty looking than any man who went before me."[5] Wood saw in his friend "another gentle, dreaming genius, not so robust and commanding as Warner. A timid man, whose soul shrinks from offending any one— cafe waiter or street walker—as his face would shrink from a blow, yet silently obstinate to his own gait in art."[6]

Wood returned to Portland and put aside all thoughts of the renegade National Democratic Party. At their September convention, the new party nominated John M. Palmer of Illinois as their presidential candidate. In the November election, William McKinley, the Republican candidate, won with 7,035,638 votes to Bryan's 6,467,946. Palmer captured a mere 131,529 votes.

Though the land grant forfeiture case was out of the way, Wood's ongoing duties for Lazard Freres required much work—so much so that he rented space in the Chamber of Commerce building to use as his private office. From room 418 Wood administered the huge Oregon land grant under the supervision of Charles Altschul at the Lazard Freres office in New York. But Wood's new office had two rooms: room 418 connected with room 419, which became Wood's private domain: an inner sanctum, providing a measure of freedom from the decorum of his firm's main office in the Spalding building. He bought a fine old writing table and a comfortable couch; he brought in favorite books and works of art. Outside, he might be an attorney, civic leader, club member, curmudgeonly Democrat, husband, father, or Colonel C. E. S. Wood. But room 419 was his retreat.

Wood hired Kathryn Seaman Beck as his personal secretary. "Kitty," as Wood called her, had recently extricated herself from a disastrous marriage to the scion of one of Seattle's pioneer families. In those days divorce was uncommon, a desperate measure frowned upon by the courts and polite society. In conservative Portland a broken marriage was a grievous blot on a woman's social standing. Kitty Beck was young and emotionally fragile. Her situation moved

Wood; he was eager to help. She, in turn, was touched by his kindness; she took to her work with youthful enthusiasm, determined to please him. She saw Wood daily, just the two of them, alone in his private rooms where he felt most truly himself. It was not long before she discovered Wood's hidden anguish: the frustration he felt living out his years in Portland's corseted society; his increasing discontent with American political life; his anxiety about money; his thwarted wish to give himself to poetry and writing. And she sensed his estrangement from Nannie, his need to be loved.

When their affair began is unclear, nor is it clear how long it lasted. No more than a few months, perhaps. But over the years they renewed their sexual relationship intermittently. This much is certain: Kitty's caring presence became absolutely essential to Wood. She was his confidant, his most intimate companion, the one person who could pass at will into room 419.

In all likelihood, Kitty was not Wood's first extramarital lover. Later, in the summer of 1899, he wrote a series of sonnets describing a passionate, ill-fated romance with a woman who wanted to bear his child. It did not help matters that this new lover was one of Portland's most visible women. Not only was she beautiful, but, as her name declared, Helen Ladd Corbett combined the fortunes of two of Portland's wealthiest families. Her father, William S. Ladd, founded the great bank that bore his name. The man she married, Henry J. Corbett, was old Henry W. Corbett's son. In a city that fostered family mergers, the Ladd-Corbett marriage was one of Portland society's brightest achievements. Then in 1895, Mrs. Corbett's husband dropped dead at the age of thirty-five. What was this rich and handsome widow to do? Remarriage was out of the question; it would jar the exquisite family equilibrium that made her one of the best-set women in the city. Yet Helen Ladd Corbett was too young, too haughty, too hungry for life to accept her widow's role with equanimity. In many ways she epitomized Portland's conservatism, its snobbery and self-absorption. Yet she was determined to seize pleasure where she found it. And she found it in the arms of Charles Erskine Scott Wood.

Wood's divided life gave him a taste of freedom, yet he remained very much a part of the straitlaced society against which he rebelled. He served on boards and committees, spoke at public events, dined at the Arlington Club with Portland's plutocrats, and each night came home to Nannie. At times, the strain of living in "two rooms" overwhelmed him. He felt hypocritical, confused, hungry for greater freedom.

Nannie could hardly overlook his change of affection. The thought of her unhappiness made Wood feel guilty, helplessly cruel. He loved her still, but that love had changed, a transformation he could not even attempt to explain without undermining Nannie's entire existence.

For her birthday that year he wrote a poem:

> Dear mother who hath nursed us
>   shielded our helplessness.
> Who for us thy life hast given
> And for self hath thought never.[7]

He continued in this vein—all from the point of view of her children. Nannie is not the object of *his* passion; she is not even his wife here. She is the revered mother—mother of his children, of course; but within the poem, she is also Wood's mother: devoted, selfless, the antithesis of her husband's restless impulses.

Wood had given Nannie and the children everything they could possibly want; he had given his life for them. Yet now, by claiming his share of pleasure, by dividing his life between two rooms, he embarked on a course that was certain to plunge Nannie into despair. Feelings he once held for his mother—pity mingled with love—now gathered about his wife. Their marriage struggled on.

16. I Must Unite with Myself

In the bright illumination of a photography studio, he poses in a heavy melton overcoat. His face is pale. His hair is longer now, still parted down the center, flecked with grey, as is his beard. He peers straight into the camera, fine sharp eyes lost in thought; an inward gaze of ineffable world-weariness. Ennui, one is tempted to say; and indeed, there is a fin-de-siècle aura to his composed countenance: sensitive, intelligent, ineffably sad. His right hand rests gently on a fur robe draped across his lap, delicate white fingers settled on luxurious thick folds. He could be a character limned by one of his European contemporaries: Chekhov or Huysmans, even Wilde.

With his mien of dandiacal finesse, the dreaming melancholy of a waning class—it must be said, the figure he presents approaches self-parody. One suspects he may be too much a "character," too much his own creation. Sitting there, comforted by that fine warm fur, he is a study in self-conscious egoism, a man of paradox: knowing, yet confused; willful, yet oddly passive; an actor of some talent, bored by the role that has become second nature to him; fated, it seems, to strut and fret across his narrow stage—denied the larger life he can imagine but which he fears he will never claim as his own.[1]

In 1898 the United States annexed the Hawaiian Islands and went to war to liberate Cuba and the Philippines from Spanish domination. Debate over imperialism divided the country. The spirit of bellicose territorial expansion found its most rousing advocate in Albert S. Beveridge, a young Republican who trotted out the old rhetoric of manifest destiny from fifty years past to exhort America to seize its God-given Pacific empire. "Have we no mission to perform," Beveridge asked, "no duty to discharge to our fellow-man?"

Hawaii is ours; Porto Rico is to be ours; at the prayer of her people Cuba finally will be ours; in the islands of the East, even to the gates of Asia, coaling stations are to be ours at the very least; the flag of a liberal government is to float over the Philippines, and may it be the banner that Taylor unfurled in Texas and Fremont carried to the coast.

The march of the flag! . . . The infidels to the gospel of liberty raved, but the flag swept on! . . . The ocean does not separate us from lands of our duty and desire—the oceans join us, rivers never to be dredged, canals never to be repaired. Steam joins us; electricity joins us—the very elements are in league with our destiny. Cuba not contiguous! Porto Rico not contiguous! Hawaii and the Philippines not contiguous! The oceans make them contiguous. And our navy will make them contiguous.[2]

Wood, who was forty-six at the time, volunteered his services for the war in Cuba. Both the secretary of war and the governor of Oregon respectfully declined his offer. "I was delighted not to go," he admitted. "It would have been at great personal sacrifice. Nor did I wholly approve of the war; but the country once involved, my duty seemed clear."[3]

If Wood did not "wholly approve" of the war over Cuba, he thoroughly disapproved of the muddled Philippine conflict. President McKinley's administration supported Cuban independence, yet it chose to keep control of the Philippines as a strategic foothold in the western Pacific. At the start of hostilities with Spain, the United States encouraged Emilio Aguinaldo to bring dissident Filipinos together in a rebel army. Spurred on by assurances of American support, he formed a provisional government and declared independence from Spain. However, when the United States negotiated the Treaty of Paris with Spain, it claimed a military and administrative presence in the Philippines until the Filipinos were "ready" for self-government. Understandably, Aguinaldo felt betrayed. On February 4, 1899, he led his people in armed revolt against the American occupation.

Just how strongly American imperialism disturbed Wood became clear when he addressed the Oregon Democratic Party at its annual Jefferson Birthday Dinner, a gathering dedicated to party unity.

Wood's audience was divided on America's role in the Philippines. Those in favor of America's presence in the Pacific believed in the nation's civilizing mission abroad and welcomed the extraordinary opportunity the Philippines offered to advance American security and economic interests in one bold stroke. However, anti-imperialist Democrats were not at all sanguine about America assuming responsibility for an island populated by non-Caucasians. Their opposition had as much to do with race and America's tradition of isolationism as it did with high moral principle. No matter what position Wood's listeners held, his speech on "Imperialism v. Democracy" was calculated to startle them.

Wood told his audience that economic and military expansion abroad was certain to centralize economic and military power at home. He insisted that imperialism was utterly inconsistent with democratic values. "It is said our age is different," he continued, "the spirit of our age makes long liberty possible. That seems to me the song of the fool soothing himself with his folly. . . . Has the spirit of our age . . . swept away all corruption, all selfishness and tyranny— Has it? I call the miners of Pennsylvania and Illinois to witness. I call to witness the Standard Oil Company, the Pennsylvania Railroad, the Sugar Trust, the legislatures of Pennsylvania, Utah, Ohio, Washington, California, Oregon and the United States senate, and lastly I call to witness the 'rebel' Filipinos. Where the rebel Filipinos are to-day, under the armed heel, your descendants may be an hundred years hence."[4]

"So I am opposed to this imperialism," Wood continued, "because I believe it is opposed to every element of our natural life, and is but the first step on the old, old race for glory, gain and power—the path by which a few have risen, but the people have gone down."[5]

Wood reminded his listeners of the simple principle of the Declaration of Independence.

> . . . We were born to carry freedom, not fetters. Our boast has been not that we can subdue the feeble nations to an easy vassalage, but that all men are created equal, and there is no just law under heaven, save by consent of the governed. I had rather this young republic of the free never stretched her borders one foot beyond her sea-grit shores and chose the boundaries,

than that she became mistress of the world by treason to her noble creed. Better that she conquer her own spirit than that she subdue to a sordid harvest the distant savage praying for freedom. . . .

The argument that we mean well is nothing; so did the Spanish inquisition. The Filipinos have a right to a government of their own making, though we could give them a better one. Little by little the mask is being slipped aside and the cry for expansion is sounding more and more in one note. Business! Commerce! Trade![6]

In closing, Wood insisted that it was impossible to impose America's noble principles on a foreign people without violating those very ideals:

. . . Is it true, or is it not true, gentlemen, that men have a right to life, liberty and happiness; to pursue their own life in their own way, and to have some voice in the law to which they yield obedience? Is it true, or is it not? If it be true, then the savage has an unalienable right to live in a palm-thatched hut and eat raw fish if he finds there greater happiness, rather than be well housed and fed in the rice fields of the tax gatherer.

. . . Were I a Filipino and thought upon my long struggle against the Spaniard, the dawn of hope in my breast as I watched coming from the East across the sea, the strong, Young Giant of the West, the bitterness to find he came with hammer and sword, not to strike off my shackles, but to rivet them faster, I would in my despair put my young ones and their mother in the cane, and I would fight, fight, fight till the sun was blotted from my eyes.[7]

Wood's assessment of American policy distanced him from all but the most radical voices. Rather than merely criticize President McKinley's aggressive foreign policy, Wood portrayed a nation driven by corruption and economic expediency—a nation whose huge appetite for power violated the founding principles that gave its people their one claim to greatness. Wood's far-reaching vision of this American dilemma was not likely to win friends at a partisan political gathering where so many careers were based on caution, compromise, opportunism, and, of course, the distribution of money and favors. But Wood was never much of a politician. His splendid speech was not going to change the world, but it did define the role he would play in coming years: that of an establishment figure who was driven by moral outrage to criticize the society in which he lived so comfortably.

As for Wood's comfortable life, it had become way too costly. There was the new house to pay for; spas and physicians for Nannie's delicate health; Erskine's tuition at Harvard; a constant flow of money for food, clothes, fine art, household help, a gardener; and the expense of entertaining Portland's first families. Wood's legal practice did well, but not nearly well enough to support his lavish spending. He had come to Portland at a time of seemingly unlimited possibilities; it must have seemed to Wood that it was only a matter of time before his active presence in that new and energetic town would join him to that dream. So he spent his fortune freely, even before it was his. Reality would have to shape itself to his will.

But it did not. Wood's investments were primarily in land, and land values depended on irrigation projects, railway construction, new roads, an influx of settlers with money to purchase the land. However, from the mid-1880s until the first decade of the new century, these essential components for growth were hindered by the general volatility of the American economy. Some people did get rich, but Wood never realized his great expectations.

To a certain extent, Wood's financial difficulties ran in tandem with his changing view of American life. As a young man he was imbued with the optimism of his times. He had tied his future to a city that saw itself as the epitome of that hope. Yet over the years that promised prosperity continued to elude him. He did not blame America for his predicament, but his failure to gain a fortune may have prompted him to look more critically at a nation that buoyed itself with visions of ceaseless development and valiant expansion, mandated by providential approval.

It *was* a dream: Wood was coming to realize this. A dream for people like himself—a nightmare for the Nez Perce, Filipinos, and underpaid workers in sweatshops, Pullman cars, packinghouses, mines, and steel mills. Yet even with his new readiness to speak out against the established order, Wood felt bound to remain within that system to meet his financial obligations. He placed his hopes in

Lazard Freres's enormous land holdings: if he could negotiate a sale
and put together the complex legal agreements, he would stand to
make a large sum on his commission. In his Jefferson Day speech
he railed against "lust of power or love of wealth and luxury." But
in his urgent pursuit of money, Wood did what he had been doing
since he first came to Portland: he joined his dreams to the fortunes
of the rich and powerful.

In 1901, at the end of young Erskine's senior year at Harvard, he
came down with tuberculosis. Wood and Nannie's efforts to restore
their son's health placed new burdens on their finances and marriage.
In spite of vows of frugality, Wood always insisted on the best. When
Erskine's physicians recommended that he take up residence at a
sanitarium in Germany, Wood sent him and Nannie abroad. Two of
the children, Lisa and Max, joined Nannie for various intervals; but
Wood himself was unable to come. Expenses related to Erskine's
illness and sanitarium cure enlarged Wood's debt. in July 1902, he
wrote his friend J. Alden Weir that he was "more in debt than ever.
Bills on all sides of me. . . . I am so hopelessly involved I can never
win out unless I sell the [Lazard Freres] grant. You see I really owe
between seventy five and a hundred thousand."[8]

On Washington's birthday, Wood attended a dinner given by the
Manhattan Democratic Club. Like the Jefferson birthday banquet
three years before, the object of the dinner was to bring warring
factions of the Democratic Party back to the fold. All too often,
appeals for harmony were thinly veiled attempts to silence criticism
and to urge party members to unite behind the status quo, but Wood
seized the occasion to challenge Democrats to discard rhetoric and
look honestly at their own hypocrisy. "All sorts of Democrats went
to the Manhattan Club last evening," a New York newspaper reported,
"and all sorts of Democracy were preached to them. Most of the
speakers had nothing new to suggest, and all of them said that the
thing needed was harmony—that is, all of them except Col. C. E. S.
Wood of Oregon, who provided the sensation of the evening."[9]

Even before he spoke, Wood attracted attention:

At the guest table sat a stranger of singular personal appearance,
who had been noticed by some of the curious. His head covered

with clustering curls, and on his breast a frilled shirt bosom supported by a white waistcoat the cut of which would have defied description, he might have taken the grand prize at a nineteenth century fashion show. He was evidently a man of means, accustomed to refined society, and, as his speech proved, he had command of a cultured and effective style of oratory. But while he sat at the guest table during the dinner he looked like some rare human exotic. Had he not spoken, his striking personality might have been remembered with an impression that he was probably a French poet or an Oriental prince traveling incognito.[10]

Wood called his speech "Democratic Democracy":

In the seven or eight minutes allotted to me I have a message for you from the West—that land of vast deserts which reach to the rim of the sky, and gigantic mountains whose snow peaks pierce even up to the silence of God. The solitude of the desert and of the mountain begets brooding, and from brooding comes truth. In the breezes of the vast desert there is no taint of restraint, but it whispers thoughts of liberty. The civilization of the West is founded on the lawlessness of the mining camp, and I think it a good foundation. In the West a man has the lawful right to drink when and where he pleases, and the saloon and the theater are as open on Sunday as the church and the school. Each one is permitted to decide for himself whether he will attend the church or the theater. We believe that man has an inalienable right to go to hell and be damned, if he pleases.

I have listened with interest to the speech of one who has made classical the words: "I am a Democrat," and have heard him and every other speaker urge harmony in the Democratic party.

As for myself I do not know whether I am a Democrat or not. I was on the stump in 1896 for Mr. McKinley, and in 1900 for Mr. Bryan, and if these opposite factions of the Democratic party are to unite, then I must unite with myself.

"I must unite with myself." It is a striking phrase, bearing meanings no one in that room could have possibly known. It touched on Wood's personal anguish, his contradictory impulses, the lies brought on by his affairs, the divided life he kept in his two rooms in the Commerce building. He was unable to unite with himself: to bring his public and private selves together; to live truthfully, rather than tactically; to do what he wanted to do instead of what life required of him. Wood did not offer the phrase as a personal confession; he uttered it in the context of comments on party unity. But the fact that it cut so close to his own struggle indicates what this speech and several of his other public addresses from this period meant to him. He had not become the person he wanted to be. Debt, family responsibility, and his own deep ambivalence about what he might and might not do made it impossible for him to act freely, with the undivided purpose he yearned for. Even so, he gained access to public forums where, for a short span of time, he could claim his freedom, uniting intellect, style, artistic temperament, and deep conviction.

As Wood spoke, he jibed at his listeners' charade of unified purpose; he challenged them to examine their slogans and unexamined political premises. Still, his speech was interrupted several times by applause and laughter.

> It has been said here to-night that the fundamental principle of the Democratic party is equal opportunity for all, and special privilege to none. I agree with all that has been said against Imperialism and in favor of tariff reform. But let me remind you that the Democratic party went into power on that same platform of Tariff Reform, and with a Democratic President in the chair and Democratic control of both houses, showed itself as much the subservient tool of the vested and protected interests as was the Republican party.

Wood introduced questions that reached well beyond conventional politics: what use do ordinary people have for party unity and political platforms if all this merely serves the interests of a privileged class? How could there ever be true liberty, true democracy, while so much property remained in the hands of so few people?

> Everyone seems to recognize that the concentration of such enormous wealth in the hands of very few is a menace to popular liberty, and from it will naturally evolve an oligarchy. . . .

I think, looking to the far future, seeking for the living idea which is to make the Democratic party truly the party of the common people, we must finally face this question of property rights and economic reform. . . .

In conclusion, let me say, that no one echoes more fervently than I the battle cry of Democracy, "That government is best which governs least; equal opportunity for all; special privilege for none;" but I want to understand, and I want to know what you mean, by privilege; and precisely what you are going to do about it; and this is the question which I think the people will want to know.[11]

The force of Wood's personal style, his urgent message, his obvious impatience with the clichés of political discussion—all "provided the sensation of the evening."[12] For the eight minutes he spoke, Wood fulfilled his own imperative: he united with himself.

17. The Most Beautiful Theory

In March of 1902, not long after his speech on "Democratic Democracy," Wood discussed the theoretical foundations of his thinking in a long letter to the *Public*, which he titled, "Socialism or Individualism—The Trend of the Centuries."[1]

Wood began his piece by describing a grave crisis in the American system: the concentration of wealth and power had come to a point where democracy itself was doomed unless the nation corrected its course.

Wood had said much the same thing in "Democratic Democracy," but here he did more than examine current conditions—he proposed an ideal solution: philosophical anarchism:

> [It] seeks to bring about absolute personal liberty, in which law, order, government, or whatever you choose to term it, shall be evolved wholly from the voluntary association of individuals, and not by any compulsory idea, as statute law or other law enforced upon a minority of peaceful citizens by a majority of peaceful citizens. . . .
>
> It is the most beautiful [theory] . . . the right of every one to do as seems best to him, so long as he does not invade the rights of his fellow men; and the right of every one freely to associate himself with those of his own way of thinking and to live as they voluntarily elect to live as free beings, so long as they do not invade the rights of any other associate or community or individual.

In contrast to this, socialism proposed to rectify the ills of privilege and inequality by advocating "government control of all industries—

everything is monopolized by government." And therein lay its failure. To operate perfectly, socialism "requires the surrender of the liberty of every individual in the state to the state." But was there any reason to place such faith in an all-powerful state? "If you have more government with greater powers," Wood continued, "I believe the same selfish desires and political practices which have put a few men in power and in control of the 'welfare' of the country under our present system, will put just such men in control of the still more highly-organized machinery of socialistic government."[2]

In advocating anarchism Wood knew he was using a word that inspired fear and contempt. In three indelible incidents over the previous sixteen years, anarchism had become associated in the public eye with revolutionary violence. On May 4, 1886, anarcho-communists held a meeting at Haymarket Square in Chicago. When police moved to break up the rally, a bomb exploded in their front ranks, leaving seven policemen dead and wounding sixty others. Though the identity of the actual bomb thrower was never established, seven anarchist leaders were sentenced to death and four of them were executed.

In 1892, Alexander Berkman, a Russian-born anarchist, assaulted Henry Clay Frick for his part in organizing a brutal Pinkerton raid on workers locked out of the Carnegie Steel Plant in Homestead, Pennsylvania. Berkman broke in on Frick and stabbed and shot him in a desperate assassination attempt he had planned with Emma Goldman. Berkman was sentenced to twenty-one years in prison.

Nine years later, President McKinley was assassinated at the Pan-American Exposition in Buffalo by Leon Czolgosz, a mentally unstable Polish-American. The assassination came at a time when America was busy driving Spain out of Cuba and the Philippines, and when it had alienated other foreign interests by supporting England in the Boer War. Czolgosz was vigorously interrogated to determine which of America's enemies had put him up to his crime. The only "conspiracy" security officers uncovered was that Czolgosz admitted to attending speeches by Emma Goldman in which she advocated self-government. Attempts to implicate Goldman in an assassination plot failed and she went free. Nevertheless, anarchism was demonized in the popular press and the public imagination: alien forces were afoot, armed with guns, dynamite, and dangerous arguments calculated to foster unrest in America's labor force.

Quite apart from these sensational events, there was a second line of anarchist thought from which Wood drew his essential ideas: a homespun utopian tradition originating with Anne Hutchinson and Henry David Thoreau and extending to Josiah Warren and Benjamin Tucker. In the 1630s, when Anne Hutchinson rebuked the Massachusetts Bay Colony as a "covenant of works" and advocated "a covenant of grace" based on one's personal experience of God's will, she was, in a sense, advocating philosophical anarchism. If God spoke "by the voice of his own Spirit to my soul," then governing bodies had no authority to command her to act against her will.[3] And there was Thoreau's eloquent argument in "On Civil Disobedience": that "the only obligation which I have a right to assume is to do at any time what I think right. . . . Any man more right than his neighbors constitutes a majority of one. . . . I was not born to be forced. I will breathe after my own fashion."[4]

If Hutchinson and Thoreau were revered ancestors of American anarchism, Josiah Warren was its founding father. In 1833 Warren set forth his views in a newspaper called the *Peaceful Revolutionist*, and for many years he lectured extensively on his philosophy of absolute individual sovereignty. Warren's lectures and writings stirred others to follow his course. In 1872 Benjamin R. Tucker, a well-to-do student at MIT, heard Warren speak at a meeting of the New England Labor Reform League. Within a year he had become "a convinced anarchist." Supported by ample financial resources, Tucker founded *Liberty*, an anarchist newspaper, which he published from 1881 to 1908. From *Liberty*, Wood derived the basic tenets of his own anarchist principles. Writings by John Stuart Mill, Herbert Spencer, and William Graham Sumner all fed Tucker's belief that "the powers of any state, however limited, were crimes against individual liberty." In place of government as it now existed there would be voluntary associations. In place of law—or most law—there would be voluntary contracts between individuals. Instead of the coercive force of police, nonviolent social sanctions, such as boycott and ostracism from community life (what Warren had called "a complete system of noninterference"), would be used to discipline antisocial behavior.[5]

To some, Tucker's philosophical anarchism truly was "the most beautiful theory." His vision of individual sovereignty found its largest following among academics, journalists, and professionals—people whose economic situation was already relatively good. But how could the disappearance of government benefit an unskilled immigrant worker, crammed with his family in some shabby urban tenement? Neither Tucker nor Wood was so naive as to imagine that anarchism was feasible in their own time. Even so, anarchism gave Wood a useful instrument with which to assess the current system. What freedoms had Americans unknowingly surrendered? In what ways did the economic system impose tyranny? How did government and the courts betray democratic ideals? To explore these issues, it helped to begin with a vision of perfect social order.

But philosophical anarchism held another attraction for Wood: it spoke directly to his personal needs. What was marriage but a legal intrusion upon what ought to be a personal agreement between two people? What was wrong with Wood's free decision to make love to Kitty, to Mrs. Corbett, or anyone else he might choose? Had he in any way invaded the rights of Nannie? Could exercising one's free will be bad if the alternative was repression, hypocrisy, unhappiness? In anarchism Wood found a political philosophy that supported his vision of social justice, and that also endorsed his "pagan" commitment to personal freedom and guiltless pleasure. What's more, anarchism gave him a new means to challenge and shock his peers, to bite the hand that fed him (though never so hard as to force that bountiful hand to withdraw completely).

Though he was drawn to anarchist theory, Wood remained active in the practical politics of reform. In early 1902, he helped W. S. U'Ren organize the People's Power League. The league's program stemmed from that of the People's Party convention in Omaha ten years before: a platform of "direct government" that became a mainstay of populist and progressive policy. Behind the movement for direct government was the widespread belief that legislative assemblies were unresponsive to the people who voted them into office—that elected representatives were either too removed from public opinion, or too readily influenced by special interests, or both. For the first 137 years of America's existence, U.S. senators were elected by state legislatures which, all too often, were controlled by politcal machines and special interests. In 1892, the People's Party had endorsed a three-fold program of voting reform:

1. The initiative: permitting voters the right to propose and directly enact legislation over the heads of representatives.
2. The referendum: giving voters veto power over the actions of the legislature.
3. Direct primary election (popular election) of United States senators.

Though Wood's deepest wish was for revolutionary change, he understood that voting reform, though modest in relation to this larger vision, was still a meaningful step toward individual freedom. The immediate goal of the People's Power League was to win voter approval for an amendment to the state constitution that would give the people of Oregon the powerful electoral leverage of initiative and referendum. Once the initiative was passed, it was hoped that voters would go on to endorse legislation supporting popular election of U.S. senators. Several powerful figures in Portland's ruling circle supported the amendment for direct government, not because of any longing for progressive reform, but rather for the political opportunities these changes promised to bring. As a trusted friend of both the progressive reformers and the well-heeled power brokers, Wood was useful in keeping the unusual coalition together. The group organized a persuasive campaign: that June, Oregonians approved the amendment by a vote of 62,024 to 4,668, and the so-called "Oregon System" of direct government became the prototype for progressive election reform across the country.[6]

Along with philosophical anarchism and electoral reform, Wood also promoted the ideas of Henry George. George's thinking defied easy labels. He was more a socialist than an anarchist, but his greatest impact was inspirational. His book, *Progress and Poverty* (1879), proposed specific measures that he promised would eliminate economic and social inequality. It was, perhaps, the most influential book of its time. In sales, it surpassed the most popular romances, and by 1905 some five million copies were in print.[7] The heart of

George's argument appears in the very center of his book, in his chapter, "The persistence of poverty amid advancing wealth":

> In all our long investigation we have been advancing to this simple truth: That . . . everywhere, in all times, among all peoples, the possession of land is the base of aristocracy, the foundation of great fortunes, the source of power. . . .
>
> What I, therefore, propose, as the simple yet sovereign remedy, which will raise wages, increase the earnings of capital, extirpate pauperism, abolish poverty, give remunerative employment to whoever wishes it, afford free scope to human powers, lessen crime, elevate morals, and taste, and intelligence purify government and carry civilization to yet nobler heights, is—*to appropriate rent by taxation.*
>
> In this way the State may become the universal landlord without calling herself so, and without assuming a single new function.[8]

In conjunction with the taxation of rent, George proposed *"to abolish all taxation save that upon land values."*[9] George predicted that the single tax would "readjust the very foundation of society" by necessitating the "simplification and abrogation of the present functions of government."[10]

George went on to argue for the reduction of judges, laws, and public officials, and the elimination of military forces, the diplomatic corps, and welfare. But unlike the anarchists' stateless society, George's utopian state would continue to exist to provide essential social services. For this reason, Wood regarded George's program as "a remedy, but not the most philosophical and root-reaching one"— a means of transition from the current system to "the most beautiful" vision of anarchist society.[11]

Wood spoke out on these new ideas with passion. Yet this only underscores an obvious question: how could Wood believe what he professed and yet continue to live his life as he did? He accepted arguments to eliminate or vastly reduce the body of law and the practice of law, yet for eighteen years he had been earning his living as an attorney. Wood railed against the timidity and corruption of both political parties, yet in 1902 he agreed to be the Democratic Party's senatorial candidate and was defeated in a nonbinding preferential popular vote. Wood actively supported the single-tax movement based on Henry George's principles, yet in the entire Northwest region there was no more glaring example of land speculation than the vast Lazard Freres holdings that Wood was urgently attempting to sell. How could Wood harbor these contradictions?

The answer is both simple and complex. Wood was trapped in his life; stuck in increasing debt; bound by emotional ties that could not be easily dissolved. All this made him receptive to ideas that spoke to his wish for freedom. Still, he coveted the fruits of the inequality he criticized. He had enjoyed the benefits of privilege throughout his childhood, in his presidential appointment to West Point, and, for years, in his association with Portland's prosperous families. His material circumstances joined him to the world he castigated. As for his public speeches and writings, they became for him an expression of hope: his link to the truth he believed men must live by. His words were often contradicted by how he lived, but they defined the life he longed for. And though his radical utterances called attention to his inconsistencies, in a more personal way they resolved them and allowed him, in the midst of his divided life, to be whole. Wood's "most beautiful theory" drew him deeper into the politics of his time and gave him a clear beacon in his lonely course toward liberty.

18. Westward the Course of
Empire Takes Its Way

Portland had seen nothing like it in over twenty years, not since that memorable September day in 1883 when the Northern Pacific Railroad pulled into town on its maiden journey. On June 1, 1905, the Lewis and Clark Exposition, commemorating the one hundredth anniversary of the legendary explorers' arrival in the Oregon Country, opened its gates to summer visitors. A great parade assembled at Sixth and Montgomery and proceeded to Twenty-eighth Street and on through a grand entrance to the Lewis and Clark Exposition grounds. There, one speaker after another paid tribute to the glowing economic future of the Pacific Coast in general and Portland in particular. "Westward the course of empire takes its way" was the exposition motto and every speaker drove home the theme.

Portland's business community had been considering an exposition for several years: to renew the city's sense of purpose and to create a means to lift the city out of its recent economic depression.[1] (The masthead of the *Oregon Booster*, the exposition's promotional weekly, depicted a horse-drawn wagon labeled "Business," its wheels sunk deep into a furrowed street. Two men labor earnestly to get the vehicle rolling. "Put your shoulder to the wheel," the masthead declared, "and get out of the rut.")

When Harvey Scott, editor of the *Oregonian*, became chairman of the exposition project in 1903, he joined the historical mission of Lewis and Clark to the new vision of American imperialism. Portland, he argued, was strategically placed to benefit from the coming era of expanded Pacific commerce. "That future is begun already," Scott declared. "It is manifest, it presses, and it remains for us of America to seize it, to bear our part of it. We propose our exposition both as an incident and as an agent of this coming greatness."[2] The exposition featured several reminders of America's growing involvement in the Pacific. Ships from Admiral Dewey's conquering Philippine fleet sailed down the Willamette River to tie up at the exposition site. In early August, exposition visitors were treated to "the biggest and most realistic sham naval battle ever projected"—a small-scale reenactment of the Battle of Manila Bay.[3]

The exposition also reveled in technological developments that promised to transform everyday life. Oldsmobile sponsored the first transcontinental auto race: a forty-four day journey from Broadway and Fifty-ninth Street in New York to the exposition grounds in Portland. The exposition-goers also had their chance to marvel at the wonders of flight when Lincoln Beachey, an eighteen-year-old balloonist, circled over Portland and landed on the roof of the Chamber of Commerce building.[4]

These crowd-pleasing reminders of America's military and technological achievements were subsumed by the exposition's theme—the taming of the West: the great undertaking that had absorbed much of the nation's resourcefulness and energy in the one hundred years following Lewis and Clark's journey of discovery.

Just twenty-five years had passed since young Lieutenant Wood had encountered the raw, unruly West in his first posting at Camp Bidwell. Yet already the "wild West" had become the stuff of nostalgia, folklore, and banal representation. Scattered over the exposition grounds, melodramatic outdoor sculptures evoked such western subjects as "Cowboy at Rest," "The Blizzard," "Sacajawea," "The Indian Buffalo Dance," "Cow Attacked by Mountain Lion," and Fredrick Remington's "Shooting Up the Town." Along with this, the exposition presented the paramount western spectacle: "a counterfeit presentment of the Custer massacre" in which several hundred Native Americans from Oregon's Umatilla reservation took the part of Sitting Bull and his Sioux warriors, while members of the Oregon National Guard served as General Custer's doomed soldiers.

Had the exposition come fifteen years earlier, Wood would almost certainly have played a major role in bringing it about. By 1905, however, he was less inclined to present himself as spokesman for the city fathers. Nevertheless, he took part in some of the exposition's most notable events. From June 28 to July 5, the thirty-seventh annual convention of the National American Woman's Suffrage Association convened at the exposition. Propelled by the crusading efforts of Elizabeth Cady Stanton and Susan B. Anthony, this organization had mounted a succession of state by state suffrage campaigns in the West. At eighty-five, Susan B. Anthony remained honorary president, but effective leadership had passed to two successors: Carrie Chapman Catt, who built the association into a powerful national movement; and Anna Howard Shaw, the current president and the group's most eloquent speaker.

The convention chose Portland for its meeting largely because of the single-minded efforts of one woman: Abigail Scott Duniway. For over twenty-five years, the suffrage movement in Oregon had been spurred by the remarkable Mrs. Duniway, who managed to support six children and a handicapped husband while turning out the *New Northwest*, a provocative feminist weekly. At the invitation of Mrs. Duniway, Wood addressed the convention on "Injustice of Majority Rule." In Duniway's opinion, it was an "eloquent and logical" speech.[5]

Wood began with a display of collusive charm: "I confess to some internal trepidation as to the impression I shall make. If I were speaking to an assemblage of men, I would feel sure of myself, for men are stupid. . . . I do not mean that the masses of men are stupid— even men know that—but from the woman's point of view *all* men, the best and the ablest, are in some things stupid. . . . Do not judge me too severely. Remember I am only a man."

In glowing, ethereal language Wood summarized the suffrage movement's "craving for Justice." Then he challenged his listeners to consider what a women's vote would mean on a practical political level: "When women vote justice will be done according to present institutions, but the result then will be much the same as now. We cannot assume that all the women will always vote the same way, and unless they do, I cannot see much chance for a practical result different from now. . . . The average voter is a mere stuffed image."

Wood went on to say that majority rule, presumably the cornerstone of democratic government, is "crude and foolish," fundamentally unjust, a form of tyranny. Then he outlined his vision of the ideal social contract—anarchism: "The function of government would be merely to keep the peace and all the sources of graft and all the meddling with the morals of others would fall to the ground. . . . All special privileges and inequalities are the creatures of law. The law is the creature of the majority. The majority is the creature of the governing few—and its edicts are tyranny."[6]

It was a brazen performance. Having assured his women listeners that men are stupid, Wood warned them that the vote they sought was not likely to make much of a difference—unless, of course, they agreed to adhere to his political agenda.

That summer Portland welcomed a stream of notable visitors to its exposition. On August 7, E. H. Harriman arrived in splendor on board a "palatial train" bearing his family, his sons' tutor, three maids, and a personal valet.[7] The city welcomed him with a grand banquet at the New York pavilion. Few financiers of the age showed greater brilliance, greater ambition, or more sheer arrogance in pursuit of wealth and power than E. H. Harriman. Just four years before, Harriman had embarked on a memorable attempt to punish James J. Hill for gaining control of the Chicago, Burlington & Quincy Railroad, a midwest line that Harriman coveted. Secretly, Harriman attempted to buy Northern Pacific out from under Hill. In one of the great financial battles of the era, J. P. Morgan placed his vast resources behind Hill and the market went crazy. As competition reached its height, Northern Pacific stock jumped from $110 to $1000 a share. Financial markets across Europe reeled in confusion until a peace conference in New York brought an uneasy resolution to the Northern Pacific Panic. Harriman won several concessions, Hill kept control of his railroad empire, and the two men continued to scheme at ways to break one another's territorial powers. Since 1898, when Harriman's Union Pacific Railroad purchased the Oregon Short Line and gained control of the Oregon Railroad & Navigation Company, the development of Oregon's agricultural heartland rested in his hands.

Harriman's intentions in Oregon were of no small interest to Wood. Wood's hope of financial freedom rested on his efforts to dispose of Lazard Freres's land grant, and two things were certain to make the close to eight hundred thousand acres more commercially attractive: increased irrigation and access to railroad transport for its produce. Harriman had it in his power to turn the Lazard Freres holdings into a bonanza, but he was preoccupied with other projects. Wood despised Harriman, whom he regarded as utterly devoid of social responsibility. Nonetheless, he dutifully attended the banquet in Harriman's honor.

Harriman's vanity and power made him virtually immune to the pomp and flattery that Portland lavished on him. If he were ever to choose to extend his empire into central Oregon, it would more likely be as a result of pressure from his old rival, James Hill. All through the early months of 1905 there had been rumors and intimations that their competition might flare up again. At first it was said, with no evidence, that Harriman planned to begin construction of a trunk line to bring central Oregon into his rail system. Then in March the *Oregonian* reported that "the fight between the Hill and the Harriman interests may result any day in abrogation of the compact entered into two years ago between them whereby each agreed to keep off the grass of the other."[8] Rumor had it that Hill had sent surveyors into central Oregon to search for an easy grade to permit economically feasible rail access to the untapped natural resources east of the Cascade Range, especially the rich pine belt along the Deschuttes River.

With these reports afloat, Portland welcomed James J. Hill, the "empire builder," as its potential savior. His appearance at the Lewis and Clark Exposition inspired an even more lavish reception than the one for Harriman—the grandest banquet in the city's history. On the evening of October 2, somewhere between five hundred and six hundred guests assembled at the American Inn, a huge hall on the exposition grounds whose pillars were covered for the occasion with Oregon grapes, fir boughs, roses, sweet peas, and autumn foliage. The dais ran two hundred feet, the length of the entire room. On a table in front of Hill's seat stood a railway locomotive wrought of violets and other blossoms. The tender bore the letters "G.N.R.R." (for Hill's Great Northern Railroad). It was, declared the *Oregonian*, "the most enthusiastic and influential [gathering] ever assembled in Portland."

Basking in Portland's welcome, Hill gave a good-natured speech full of praise for Oregon and loaded with promises of regional development. He would build a railway along the northern bank of the Columbia River—a Spokane-Portland-Seattle line that would link Portland to the Northern Pacific and Great Northern lines and to the vast markets Hill controlled in the Midwest and the East. He would construct a larger railroad terminal for Portland. Portland's harbor would be deepened to make it competitive with port facilities in San Francisco and Seattle. Hill added a proposal that must have been music to Wood's ears: he would set to work developing a system of trunk lines to join central and eastern Oregon to his transcontinental system. Each of these assurances was met by rousing ovations.

Prominent citizens took turns praising their benificent guest. Then Wood, the last speaker on the toastmaster's program, brought matters to a lively conclusion, speaking of the city's much-anticipated economic renaissance. Harriman had made promises, Wood observed, but his railroad lines had never come. Now, all this was about to change. At last, striding across the continent, a freight car under one arm and a pullman under the other, came Sunny Jim Hill. "Mr. Hill," Wood continued, "it has been written that a city set on a hill cannot be lost, and Portland is stuck on you."[9] After the applause subsided, Hill congratulated Wood on delivering the greatest after dinner speech he had ever heard.[10]

Wood, who railed against plutocratic economic domination, who vigorously criticized the new imperialism, was nonetheless attracted to Hill's expansive vision. Unlike Harriman, Hill saw himself as an innovative steward of the public interest, a person willing to use his vast resources to improve the lives of his fellow men. But like Harriman, Hill was more than willing to be a law unto himself, and he, too, was driven by the conviction that he could do a better job of running things than anybody else. Wood might quarrel with him, but he was still captivated by Hill's grandiose plans to colonize unsettled stretches of the Northwest, including eastern Oregon; by his efforts to spur immigration by distributing promotional flyers across Europe; by Hill's agricultural demonstration trains that brought innovative farming methods to isolated areas; and by Hill's generous distribution of prize English bulls along the Great Northern railroad route.

At the Lewis and Clark Exposition the city of Portland cast its lot with America's ongoing venture of economic and geographic expansion. Whether Wood liked it or not, his freedom rested with these same forces: with James Hill, the empire builder; and with the quintessential example of opportunistic economic policy in the West, the Lazard Freres land grant.

19. I Glory in Being a Rebel
and a Fanatic

In late August of 1905, Wood wrote a lengthy entry in his journal which he titled "Rebellion."

> I rebel against the suppression of the individual, the lack of freedom and the falsity, the hypocrisy of the smooth successful life. I rebel against all the ideas of sex that it is wicked, low, vulgar, that it is to be suppressed and made little and base. . . . I rebel against the praise of submission to authority and I preach the gospel of rebellion. There has not been one step in the eternal evolution and progress except by discontent and rebellion against authority. Had rebellion stopped a thousand years ago we all would be walking about with iron collars on our necks, absolute and besotted slaves to a few.
>
> I deify Rebellion. I glory in being a rebel and a fanatic. These are only other names for mind progress and earnestness.[1]

However much Wood might celebrate rebellion, these notes were written for his private journal. This and other journal entries were experiments with his "self," attempts to find a voice by expressing his true feelings privately: a process that, in time, might bring him from solitary reflection to greater integration in his personal and public life—the unity of thought, feeling, and action he longed for.

With increasing frequency, Wood did glory in being a rebel. Often he used mischievous humor. At a party given to raise money for charity, Wood invited Portland's respectable citizens to the gaming tables with a sign urging them to "Gamble for God's sake."[2] At a pre-

Christmas charity event, Wood was invited to preside as chairman, to "sit up there and look solemn." Instead, he surprised his audience with a speech reminding them of uncharitable forms Christianity had taken: "Filled with love and mercy as was Christ, there never has been so merciless a persecutor as his church—the rack, the boot, the thumbscrew, the fires of the Inquisition, thirty and a hundred years of bloody war, conversion at the point of the sword or the faggot, literature wiped out, the Dark Ages and the earth running with blood all in the name of the meek and lowly king . . . whose whole creed was love, forgiveness, toleration."[3]

Wood's penchant for challenging conventional thought left him open to savage, and sometimes incisive, attacks. "It is a habit with Mr. C.E.S. Wood to boast that he is 'an anarchist,' " an editorial in the *Oregonian* began. "That is for stage effect, when he meets 'the masses,' at socialist meetings, or at the people's forum. Mr. Wood is, however, exceedingly fond of the rich among whom his select associations lie. No moth flies more industriously about the arc lights." Wood, the *Oregonian* continued, was no less than a latter-day avatar of Gaius Petronius, author of the *Satyricon* and director of the pleasures of Nero's imperial court:

> Mr. Wood plainly aspires to be, and surely is, the Petronius, the arbiter elegantiarum, of our local plutocracy. . . . His decision "goes" on all affairs in which our "upper classes" are interested,—on duds, music, painting, poetry, quantities, metres, scansions and accents; on architecture, law, hair dressing, perfumes, latest fads in furniture, Browning, literature (Shakespeare and Milton omitted), face powders, chafing-dish specialties, and what not. People who know nothing themselves, who merely have their inherited wealth and nothing else, look to the Colonel. He has a veneer and a smatter that will suffice them. From it and through it he lives, in all the beauty and glory and social advantages of elegant life. But he has side issues, in which he shines also;—as anarchy, socialism, free love, impatience under restraints of law and government.[4]

It was easy enough to attack Wood for inconstancy toward both his social class and the causes he espoused. Yet his social criticism was becoming increasingly frank. Despite the daily obligations of his legal practice, he was remarkably productive, a gadfly who brought his views before the public in all kinds of literary forums. In "Impressions," a column for the *Pacific Monthly*, he spoke out forcefully on numerous issues, including voting reform, woman suffrage, and anarchism. In late 1906 he stepped up his criticism by submitting didactic fiction and lively opinion pieces to Benjamen Tucker's *Liberty: The Pioneer Organ of Anarchism*. If this was not enough, he also wrote occasional pieces for *Mother Earth*, a radical journal edited by America's most demonized champion of radical causes, Emma Goldman.

When Lincoln Steffens came to Portland in March of 1907, it was inevitable that the two men would meet. Steffens was researching an article on Oregon's timber frauds: a far-reaching scandal in which lumber companies paid off state and federal officials, who then smoothed the way for the companies' false claims on the federal government's huge domain of valuable forest. Steffens remained in Portland for less than two weeks, but it was enough time for him and Wood to begin a friendship which flourished in later years.

When Steffens's piece, "The Taming of the West," appeared in the October number of the *American Magazine*, it raised issues close to Wood's heart—and to Wood's efforts on behalf of the Lazard Freres land grant. "The map of Oregon to-day is streaked up and down all around by zigzags of 'military road grants,' " Steffens began, "which show no roads but which do show fortunes in timber. And so with the railroads. They also got land from the government to help them finance their schemes for the development of the state. They also turned grafter. But that is not all. . . . To get their grafts, and keep them and get more, the grafters have to go into politics and corrupt the government."[5]

A month before "The Taming of the West" appeared in print, a piece by Wood, "On the Looting of the Public Domain," appeared in his "Impressions" column in the *Pacific Monthly*. "The public domain has seemed a great treasure house with the doors wide open," Wood observed, "and for a generation or more thieves have been carrying off all the valuable lands." Wood's short piece anticipated Steffens's article, but it cut even closer to home: "One man can carry away half the forest lands in Oregon in an inside pocket if he can get a patent or a deed to these lands. And even though he has got the deed by fraud, if he sells to another who has no knowledge of the fraud, that other will hold the title."[6]

Wood's remarks are an apt description of how Lazard Freres gained title to 790,000 acres bought from private developers whose claim to the public land rested on construction of a wagon road they never built.

Though Wood chafed at his life in Portland, he found creative ways to keep his days from sliding into prosaic routine. In 1908 Childe Hassam came to live with him. Hassam spent close to a year as Wood's houseguest, during which time he drank heavily and chased after Portland's women with unbridled enthusiasm. Wood commissioned his friend to execute a group of paintings for his library: "a lot of naked ladies bathing on rocks at the sea," is how Nannie described them. Wood proudly displayed Hassam's work to his dinner guests. The paintings were "admired by some," Nannie tactfully conceded, "but the majority of people do not care for them."[7] Obviously, Nannie did not care for *him*. "He led us a merry dance," she said, "and sometimes I had a hard time keeping things right in the house." In what was surely a gross understatement, Nannie added: "He was not very dependable." Nannie recalled a dinner Wood gave for several judges and their wives from San Francisco. "He begged Mr. Hassam to come home sober from dinner; and later, to his horror, he looked up and saw Mr. Hassam lolling on the shoulder of Mrs. Ross."[8]

Whatever hazard Hassam might have presented to Nannie's nicely managed household, his presence raised Wood's spirits. That May, Wood took him out to Harney County, to the clear air and brilliant, blazing light of the high desert plateau that always seemed to restore his spirits. There Hassam painted a series of canvases, almost improvisations, charged with light and delicate desert hues. A photo shows Wood and Hassam out in the middle of the desert expanse: easels propped amidst tufts of rabbit brush and sage brush, both men busy at their painting. There is a touch of absurdity at the sight of two grown men pursuing their artistic work in the middle of nowhere, dressed in nothing but Skivvies. Hassam is bare-chested, thickset, bearing down on his canvas. Wood works a few steps behind him, a broad hat shading his face; but he is smiling, relishing this brief opportunity to live on his own terms.

Had Wood become the "rebel and fanatic" that he wished to be, he would have lost his unique access to the parlors, clubs, and assemblies of the very interests he depended upon for his livelihood. Instead, he exploited his divided life, using his links to the rich and powerful as a means of bringing new ideas to the enemy camp. One of the most memorable of these occasions was Emma Goldman's lecture series in Portland in May of 1908.

Goldman arrived in America in 1887, when she was eighteen: a Russian Jew, with no money. She made her way to Rochester where she worked sixty-three hours a week in a clothing factory for which she was paid $2.50.[9] Not surprisingly, her greatest differences with the genteel anarchism advocated by Wood and others stemmed from her rage at the abuses perpetrated on working people by business and industry—torments she had experienced first hand. She was not a reformer; she wanted the current system overthrown. Had she devoted her life solely to advocating revolution, Emma Goldman might be relatively unknown today. However, she spoke passionately on many issues: racial and sexual equality, birth control, and the absolute right of free speech. On her frequent lecture tours, she was constantly harassed. The First Amendment was disregarded when "red Emma" came to town. Her right to speak itself became an issue, attracting wide support from less radical, "respectable" elements.[10]

In Portland, the outcry against her was overwhelming. When the YMCA and the Arion Society reneged on contracts to rent her halls in which to speak, Wood promptly took up Goldman's cause. He welcomed her to Portland and arranged for her to stay with Kitty Beck at her home on Harrison Street. In a letter to the *Oregonian*, Wood denounced the YMCA and took the press to task for misrepresenting her as an advocate of guns and bombs and violence.[11] He set to work rounding up support among his influential friends, insisting to all who would listen that anarchism was not the issue: the Portland community had violated Goldman's First Amendment rights to free speech—a far greater threat to democracy than the supposed danger presented by her lectures.

"Do not be alarmed," Goldman told a reporter, "I have no dynamite in my pocket. . . . Education is the only bomb sanctioned by true anarchism, which stands for freedom in the truest and highest sense."

Goldman went on to express her admiration for America's fundamental ideals and to assert her right to criticize her adopted country's faults. "Anarchism as we teach it does not advocate or tolerate violence, but it does declare for the right of rebellion—a provision widely incorporated in the constitution of this country. When the Government becomes too oppressive to a people, they are entitled to rise up and overthrow it."[12]

Wood's public efforts on Goldman's behalf aroused widespread resentment, but neither his family nor anyone else could pressure Wood to back down. He found Emma Goldman a lecture hall, and at her opening lecture he introduced her. Here is Goldman's account:

[Wood] was a fine looking man of gracious personality, and a libertarian in the truest sense. He had been instrumental in securing the two halls, and he was very much distressed that the owners should have backed out. He tried to console me with the assurance that the Arion Society could be held legally responsible, because they had signed a contract for the rental of their hall. When I told him that I never invoked the law against anyone, although the law had often been invoked against me, Mr. Wood exclaimed: "So that's the kind of dangerous anarchist you are! Now that I have found you out, I shall have to take others into my confidence. I shall have to ask them to meet the real Emma Goldman." Within a few days he not only introduced various persons to me, but he also inspired Mr. Chapman, one of the editors of the *Oregonian*, to write about my lectures, and the Reverend Doctor Elliot, a Unitarian minister, to offer me his church. He induced a considerable number of prominent men and women of the city to declare themselves publicly in favor of my right to be heard.

After this it was easy sailing. A hall was secured, and the meetings were attended by large and representative audiences. Mr. Wood presided at my first lecture and delivered a brilliant introductory speech.[13]

The introductory speech that Goldman speaks of was one of Wood's finest moments. He began by telling his audience of a prince born in India who left his royal estate to labor for the good of the common man. This prince, who we know as Buddha, was met by "the insolence of prosperity and the bigotry of those who were in comfort." Wood went on to say that Buddha, toward the end of his life declared: "The field that I plow is Ignorance and the weeds thereof are Error. The plow that I use is the Truth, and Self-Combat is the fertilizing rain."

Wood proceeded to recount Emma Goldman's difficulties in securing a suitable lecture hall. The Arion Society, a German cultural group, had forbidden her the use of their hall. Wood questioned how a group that cherished Germany's struggle for liberty in 1848 could, in Goldman's case, submit to "that illiberal and bigoted ignorance which judges before it has heard, or, worse than all, which deliberately refuses to hear and still judges."

As for the YMCA, they had given Goldman a contract but withdrew it in fear of public controversy. Wood attributed their actions to "bourgeois and comfortable ignorance; an ignorance of the facts of Anarchism and an ignorance of what Miss Goldman has actually said and what she stands for." He suggested that "those gentlemen who raise that storm owe it to their name as the Christian Association to leave their golf games, their amusements, their comfortable and pleasant places, and come here now and hear for themselves what Miss Goldman has to say."

Wood's taunt drew cheers from his audience. He went on to observe that "Christianity is easy. It costs nothing to-day to say you are a Christian. I very much doubt if these same comfortable gentlemen would have been Christians in that day when to be a Christian meant to take your place on the Roman fagot pile, to be hunted into the catacombs, and to be racked and tortured by power and authority because you professed the name of the great Anarchist, Jesus Christ."

He informed his listeners that a lawyer he knew had told him Emma Goldman "is a damned Anarchist and she ought to be hung." What would people say, Wood wondered, if Emma Goldman suggested that Rockefeller be hung? She would be condemned as an apostle of violence. Freedom of speech, Wood reminded his listeners, ought not to depend on whether or not we like what the speaker has to say: "I stand here to-day to put myself on record as saying that Miss Goldman and her doctrines and her opinions are not the point; are not the important question. The important question is the right of every American to utter freely his opinion on any subject whatever, and I stand here to-day to put myself on record as determined, cost what it may, to defend free speech and human liberty."[14]

In his journal, Wood congratulated himself for standing apart from the respectable attitudes of Portland society: "I am now 56 years old and nearing the close of my life and I can truly say I have never been popular and seldom respectable. . . . Faugh God, deliver me from your smooth-shaven flabby-cheeked human octopus, the rich respectable man—I'd rather live on greens from the fence rows and be myself and die a man such as I chose to be than a stuffed figure of respectability."[15]

Though Wood wished to be delivered from "the rich respectable man," he continued to depend on rich respectable men to shield him from bankruptcy. Once again, he shared his fears with Weir: "I am desperate. I cannot sell this infernal land grant, and it is my only hope. The law does not pay expenses, taxes, life insurance and interest on my indebtedness now over $100,000—the losses and accumulated debts of 12 years."[16]

Wood was at the mercy of the Ladd & Tilton Bank, whose lenient treatment of his debt allowed him to survive, and Lazard Freres—particularly Charles Altschul in New York—who trusted him to sell the Oregon land grant. In Wood's efforts to sell those 790,000 acres, his fate rested on the designs of two extraordinary men, both of whom had shaped the development of entire regions of the western lands. Without the economic resources, the influence, and personal trust of William Hanley and James J. Hill, this self-declared "rebel and fanatic" had little hope of gaining his liberty.

20. A Versatile Citizen

If Wood was ever to find a way out of his crushing debt, much depended on his friend of many years, William Hanley. Hanley was a cattleman in eastern Oregon, perhaps the most powerful Oregonian east of the Cascades. His realm was the same high desert country that Wood had criss-crossed as a young soldier; where he fished and camped with his boys; where he returned summer after summer to renew himself.

Hanley knew this country as well as any man alive. Fifty years before, as a boy of sixteen, he had left his father's farm in southwest Oregon, leading a small herd of cattle across the Cascades for the open plains of the Harney Desert, four hundred miles east. Just south of Malheur Lake, on pastureland bounded by the two prongs of the Silvies River, Hanley set up his cattle ranch. The nearest railroad depot was at Winnemucca, Nevada, three hundred miles to the south.[1] Young Hanley survived the challenges of nature as well as battles between cattlemen and settlers for legal title to the land. As his land holdings grew, Hanley became the most influential man in the region and an avid spokesman for economic development. Early on in Hanley's career, grueling three-hundred-mile cattle drives to the Winnemucca railroad depot impressed upon him the importance of railroads. The Columbia River and the rivers and roadways of western Oregon created a "rim of transportation" for eastern Oregon, but rail systems stopped well short of Oregon's eastern and southern borders. Hanley saw that the economic future for his section of the state depended upon having a railroad line to spur settlement and facilitate the shipping of produce to and from the area.[2] Hanley took it upon himself to bring this about. He was respected by businessmen and bankers across the West; he knew all the great railroad entrepreneurs, whose empires were economically linked to the cattle industry. He was determined to bring a railroad trunk line into his land for the good of everyone—and ample profit for himself.

Hanley was a colorful figure: unaffected, blunt, generous, idealistic. Now, with Wood seeking to find a buyer for Lazard Freres's landholdings, the two men realized that they had much to gain by working together. Hanley used his extensive contacts throughout the West to tout the Lazard Freres property. Also, he included Wood in land acquisitions that promised to soar in value with the construction of a railroad trunk line.

When Hanley set out to get his railroad, he enlisted Wood in a strategy that revived the fierce rivalry between E. H. Harriman and James Hill. Like many Oregonians, Hanley resented the fact that the public good depended so heavily on the whims of monopolistic capitalists. With this in mind, he sought Wood's support in lobbying the Oregon legislature to pass an amendment that would allow the state to issue bonds to build its own railroad connecting eastern Oregon to the national network.

Riding the publicity of this plan, Hanley contacted James J. Hill and told him the time was ripe to pour his resources into Oregon.[3] Hill had a double motive for considering a railroad line into central Oregon. To begin with, the line would expand his market in the Pacific Northwest. One year earlier, Hill had broken E. H. Harriman's grip on Portland by completing a line along the northern bank of the Columbia River, which linked Portland to Hill's Northern Pacific line at Wallula, Washington. If Hanley's glowing vision was accurate, a Deschuttes River line would add immensely to the reach of his empire. But wealth and power were not Hill's only motives. Hill saw an opportunity to strike back at Harriman for his intransigence ten years before, when Harriman refused to give Hill fair rental rates on the Oregon Short Line (controlled by Harriman's Union Pacific)—the vital rail link between Portland and Hill's Northern Pacific terminus in Spokane. Over the past four years Harriman had been using every resource at his disposal to obstruct Hill's Spokane, Portland & Seattle line: from lawsuits to dummy construction projects to physical assaults on Hill's work crews. Now, with Hanley and Wood egging him on,

Hill considered a daring incursion into Harriman's own territory. With a Deschuttes River line in place, Hill might extend it south, constructing an inland route all the way to San Francisco, thus breaking Harriman's control of California's riches.

Hill couldn't resist the challenge. He began a link to his Portland-Wallula line, from the Columbia River south along the Deschuttes River. Harriman responded by rushing his own crews to the site. Soon the two titans were locked in madcap competition, with crews at work on opposite sides of the narrow river canyon. Oregonians were treated to the spectacle of two fabulously wealthy capitalists engaged in identical railroad construction projects when only one line made any sense. It was an absurd display of waste and raw egoism. As the great race proceeded, Hill sent his son Louis on an auto tour of the Oregon interior, the first time a motor vehicle had braved those taxing roads. Under Hanley's guidance Louis bounced hundreds of miles over rutted wagon tracks, while the state press gave the event its hopeful attention. Hill was seen as the savior of the region, the key to the economic future of the state.

Eventually, Hill and Harriman cut a deal that gave Hill right of way from Ontario, Idaho (on the Snake River), to Burns, the largest town in Hanley's region. Hill now had a foothold in the region, but he was in no hurry to build his railroad until Wood found a buyer for the Lazard Freres land grant. Hill insisted that he was simply a railroad man: he had no interest in purchasing land for settlement projects. Nevertheless, Wood's search for a buyer turned to St. Paul, Hill's center of operations.

Selling the land grant preoccupied Wood, yet he showed an increasing willingness to identify with the enemies of capitalism and conventional morals. By now, his private office in the Commerce building had become an informal legal aid center where proponents of all kinds of unpopular causes came to beseech Wood for legal and financial support. Reformers, agnostics, drunks, labor organizers, birth control advocates, would-be revolutionaries, suffragists—all came to room 419. Wood did what he could: he provided pocket money, bail, pro bonum legal aid, and he continued to speak out from public platforms.

That November Wood delivered a courageous defense of IWW members' freedom of speech. Wicked as Emma Goldman may have appeared to upstanding citizens, the Industrial Workers of the World existed as yet a greater evil. Four years earlier, left-wing labor forces had gathered in Chicago with the intention of creating "One Big Union" to supersede Samuel Gompers's American Federation of Labor and keep the workers' movement on an aggressive, radical course. Led by Eugene Debs and William "Big Bill" Haywood of the militant Western Federation of Miners, the Industrial Workers of the World was founded. "The aims and objects of this organization," Haywood said, "shall be to put the working class in possession of the economic power, the means of life, and control of the machinery of production and distribution, without regard to capitalist masters. We are the Continental Congress of the Working Class." The IWW, or "Wobblies" as they were often called, made a dedicated effort to educate workers about the nature of their exploitation and to encourage them to fight back with militant strikes—measures that invited brutal responses from industrial management and law enforcement officials. One such confrontation occurred in Spokane in the summer of 1909: when IWW members attempted to hold an open air rally, they were rounded up and thrown in jail on charges of attempting to incite a riot. Wood did not approve of the IWW's inflammatory rhetoric about meeting violence with violence, but he supported the Wobblies' radical program, and he deplored the way civil authority supported industry's brutal campaign to destroy the union. The Wobblies had the constitutional right to assemble and speak freely. This is what he told his cheering audience in Merrill's Hall:

Citizens have as much right to use the streets to talk in as to walk in. . . .

It is not free speech if a man must first obtain consent of his ruler. That condition exists in Russia. If you are willing only that the man who speaks your way should have an audience, you do not deserve free speech. The raggedest imbecile, if you please, has the right to give to his fellow men the thoughts the Creator put in his brain. You do not know but that in the glacial movement of the ages his thoughts may turn out to be truth, and yours the lie.

Are you a Socialist? There was a time when Karl Marx stood

alone. Are you an Anarchist? There was a time when Prudhomme stood alone. Are you a reformer? Martin Luther once stood alone. Are you a Christian? Christ once stood alone. . . .

[Wood then argued that discontent was good because it moved the world] . . . I work with the Democratic party because it is nearer my ideals than others. Yet that party would be the first to deny to me the title of Democrat. I don't want it. I am an Anarchist. That's my ideal [Great applause and yells].[4]

For a man whose future depended on the trust of powerful capitalists, Wood took an extraordinary risk in declaring himself an anarchist before a volatile assembly of IWW members—and a hostile press. "Wood is Anarchist"; "Portland Lawyer Puts Freedom Ahead of Morality"; "I.W.W. Members Cheer": the *Oregonian* had a field day. "Imbeciles' Rights Defended," was their creative summary of Wood's defense of tolerance.[5] The following day, the newspaper assailed Wood in an editorial.

A VERSATILE CITIZEN

Mr. C.E.S. Wood stirred the enthusiasm of I.W.W. members in a Portland meeting last Sunday by declaring himself an Anarchist for which he was rewarded with loud applause and yells. . . .

The Colonel—such he is sometimes called—is lithe in adjusting himself to varying degrees of wealth and social status. As attorney for one of the biggest land monopolies in the West— a wagon road company in Eastern Oregon—he stands champion of a land system far more monopolistic than that which he denounced amid cheers last Sunday. As attorney for the gas monopoly in Portland, he stands defender of special and capitalistic privilege that enrages the Industrial Workers of the World. As counselor of big banks and rich estates and as frequenter of aristocratic, exclusive social strata, the Colonel might seem disqualified from being the boon companion of rowdy, fetid Have-nots of the street, who howl for free anarchy, free land and free speech.

All of which shows Colonel Wood an unusually elastic, versatile man. It is a rare make-up of person that can flatter such far-flung elements of the social body all at the same time. The question, "Whose man is he?" is out of order each time asked,

either in high or low places. The Industrial Workers of the
World regard the question unimportant and if they are satisfied,
nothing more is needed to make happiness complete—except
anarchy.[6]

The *Oregonian* editorial highlighted Wood's hypocricies—and
with some justification. But it had also taken moral courage to step
forward as Wood did to speak from his heart. His life *was* contradictory; he could not claim otherwise. Still, he refused to allow this to
immobilize him. Instead of keeping his convictions to himself and
living a life of unquestioning respectability, he spoke out—though
doing so meant exposing his inconsistencies to the public eye.

Wood's mixed allegiances were there for all to see; he made no
apologies for them. He had the force of character to bear his contradictions in a manner that commanded respect from many quarters.
Wood's creditors had the power to ruin him, yet they held back.
Hanley, Altschul, and Hill had no reason to risk their millions on a
man they did not trust. Radical leaders sought his support. Emma
Goldman, the enemy of the rich, became his lifelong friend. All saw
him as a man of integrity. He was indeed a versatile citizen.

On April 2, 1910, Wood announced that W. P. Davidson and a
syndicate of Minnesota capitalists had paid one hundred thousand
dollars for an option to purchase the Lazard Freres land grant. In
his public statement Wood emphasized that the purchasers were not
acting for James J. Hill of the Great Northern Railroad. Nevertheless,
it was obvious to everyone that this immense transaction was conducted with Hill's blessings and his behind-the-scenes supervision.

Six weeks later, Lazard Freres transferred its 790,000 acre grant
to the new owners. It was the largest sale of privately owned real
estate in the history of the United States. The *Oregonian* rightly
described the original land grant as "a princely gift."[7] The land grant
included 660,000 acres of land suitable (after future irrigation) for
agriculture, and 140,000 acres of timbered hills (with perhaps four
and one-half billion timbered feet).

The St. Paul investors announced that plans had been made for
a massive colonization project to be put into effect immediately. To
nobody's surprise, they promised to join James J. Hill in his mission

to educate all America about the advantages of settling in Oregon, and to "send that news all over the world. . . . The people are coming to Oregon."[8]

Lazard Freres, Hill, the colonization company, Hanley—all the participants in the land grant sale acted entirely within the law. Nevertheless, given the views that Wood publicly espoused, the land grant sale represented much that he condemned. Absentee ownership of land; a few wealthy capitalists controlling vast natural resources; the power of moneyed interests to influence government policy (for now Wood would be called upon to serve as a lobbyist to drum up federal support for irrigation projects for the region)—all this he had spoken against, and all this he tacitly supported in his faithful service to Lazard Freres. Simply put, Wood could not afford to do otherwise.

That July, Nannie took a cruise to Alaska. In a letter to Wood she worried about how the heat wave in Portland would affect him. She sent him wildflowers that she found growing among the mountain rocks "like a kiss." She told him: "you will [feel] my lips touched them for you. I wish I could know that you & the boys are all quite well."

Love remained, but the true sphere of their marriage was one of separation and worry. "My dear heart," Nannie wrote, "further and further away I go from you & that is not to my liking."[9]

Her premonition was sadly accurate. A few months later, Wood embarked on a phase of his life that placed him still further from his loving, unhappy wife. It began in October: Wood was working in his office when Clarence Darrow burst in.[10] "Wood," he said, "I have a friend out here that I want you to know. She's just come out and I want you to meet her. She's very lonely. She needs contact with the more liberal elements, if there be such a thing in Portland, and I'd like you to be my guest at dinner tonight."

"I can't, Darrow," Wood replied. "I'm taking my wife to a dinner at the Portland Hotel."

"Well, can't you get out of it?"

"I don't know. . . ."

Darrow gave him a wry, skeptical look. "Why don't you just lie to her? I find that's the easiest way out."

Wood was surprised by Darrow's persistence. "Who is this person?" he asked.

"Well, her name is Mrs. Ehrgott and she's a minister's wife."

Wood was flabbergasted. He knew Darrow was as much an agnostic as himself. "What have I got to do with a minister's wife? Darrow, you know we wouldn't have anything in common at all."

Darrow leaned over and said, "Listen, she's one of us."[11]

Love

and

Anarchy

1910–1918

21. A Deeper Gladness of Soul

Had she been at all vain about her appearance, Sara Ehrgott, the woman whom Darrow insisted that Wood meet, would have had no trouble drawing attention to her physical attractions. At twenty-seven, she was slender, with full lips, round cheeks, and clear, brown eyes that promised a direct, unaffected nature. But Sara was a minister's wife; she had no money to spend on clothes and personal luxuries. She also had no inclination to do so: she was a serious young woman whose main concern outside her husband and two children was social reform and her own intellectual growth.

Wood dined with Darrow and his party at the Hofbrau, a popular bohemian restaurant, where Darrow made a point of seating Sara by Wood's side. Her fluent grasp of ideas impressed Wood. Here was a woman who seemed driven by the conviction that social issues and one's personal life were inseparable. Wood was taken aback. How different she seemed from Nannie, who reflected the rigid habits of mind that characterized her Portland circle; from Helen Ladd Corbett, with her potent vanity and love of luxury; and from Kitty, so fragile and self-effacing, who accompanied him that evening.

Sara's husband, the Reverend Albert Ehrgott, was Wood's age, with black hair, black piercing eyes, and a black assertive mustache heightened in effect by very white teeth.[1] In spite of Wood's disdain for organized religion, Ehrgott was not undeserving of respect. Nine years before, he had traveled to Burma with Sara, then only eighteen, to serve as minister of a Eurasian church in Rangoon. When medical necessity forced Sara to return to America, Ehrgott accepted a pastorate in a poor neighborhood church in Cleveland, where he played an active part in the reform movement inspired by Mayor Tom Johnson. Ehrgott was articulate, well-read in philosophical literature, and a great lover of classical music, especially Wagner. But something was "off" about this somber man. No one could doubt that he approached his public and private responsibilities with tireless energy, yet he never quite succeeded at his undertakings. Both as a minister and as a husband, he lacked warmth.

With dinner over, Darrow proposed that everyone move on to Wood's private office. The Reverend Ehrgott had a meeting to attend; he made his apologies and went on his way. The rest of the dinner group accompanied Wood back to room 419 in the Chamber of Commerce building. While Darrow read aloud from a volume of Galsworthy, Sara took in the beauty of Wood's office: oriental rugs, a fine Old English desk, objets d'art everywhere. And there was Wood himself—his curly gray hair and youthful complexion; the keenest and kindest eyes she had ever seen—so much a part of that wonderful setting.

Several months passed before Sara heard from Darrow. "I'm sure you and Wood have become good friends," he wrote. But the Ehrgotts had not seen Wood since that spring night at the Hofbrau. Prompted by Darrow's note, Sara invited Wood to her house for dinner. Wood came alone and was served roast beef, burnt to a crisp by the Ehrgotts' flustered maid. Wood pronounced the meat delicious and offered a brief disquisition on how charcoal crust enhances the taste of good meat.

Some time later, Wood invited the Ehrgotts to his home for dinner. There was no sign, no mention of Mrs. Wood. Except for their initial meeting when Wood brought Kitty along, he had been alone each time Sara had seen him. After dinner, Wood invited Sara to his private study, where he showed her his rare books and some of the treasured pieces he had collected over the years. Their talk turned to the idea of free love. Wood picked up a book and read Sara a chapter. It was impossible to promise stable love, the book argued; anyone who guaranteed to love another person till their dying day was saying something that was beyond human control. Sara reflected on her own domestic situation. She was living through the rituals of married life in order to keep a home intact for her children; yet she no longer actively loved her husband. She realized that no matter how she attempted to conceal it, the growing difference between herself and Ehrgott could not help but strain the domestic arrangement she was trying to preserve. The idea began to crystallize in her mind: by living honestly and breaking free of her marriage, she would also be preparing a freer and better life for her children.[2]

Sara's longing for freedom would soon join itself to Wood's, forcing the issue in ways that cast both their lives into disarray. Without Sara it is likely Wood would have persisted in trying to hold his contradictory impulses in an improvised equilibrium that pleased no one. But Sara changed his life; or rather, she revealed his life to him by disrupting the stasis in which he lived. She challenged him to view himself honestly and, though he often resisted, she impelled him toward growth and freedom. Their friendship quickened to an urgent love affair that drove them to practice deceit, something they both hated. It led to painful confrontations with their families, and with one another. It led to scandal, loneliness, despair, exasperation, shattered health, extreme tests of faith—until, often, all that sustained the two lovers was their desperate yearning for relief from their suffering. The ordeal almost killed Sara. In a sense, it ruined Wood's life—for he could not possibly free himself from his emotional suspension until he confronted his elaborate evasions, convenient romantic arrangements, self-pity, and the deeply rooted contradictions that had become the tenor of his existence. All this lay ahead for him. In the years to come, his life and Sara's became enmeshed—so much so, that to tell his story one must tell hers as well.

Early in 1911, the Reverend Ehrgott dropped by Wood's office. He explained that income from his ministry at the East Side Baptist Church allowed for only a meager living, and Sara was eager to work. Was there any chance, he inquired, that Wood might help Sara earn something with her pen? Wood promised to speak with his friends at the *Pacific Monthly* and the *Oregonian* on Sara's behalf. In the meantime, he needed someone to help him gather and edit his poetry: he hired Sara to be his assistant.

Sara's first assignment was to read galley proofs of *Maia*, a collection of sonnets Wood had just completed that gave voice to his ideas about free love and his "pagan" creed of living in accordance with nature. Sara responded candidly. Read as a group, the sonnets were monotonous, she told him: they appeared to be randomly organized, and too many of them repeated the same themes. She suggested eliminating a number of poems and arranging the remainder according to the sequence of seasons, allowing nature's cycle to mark the evolving growth of two archetypal lovers.

All through his years in Portland, Wood had undertaken his creative work in isolation. Even when the *Pacific Monthly* and *Liberty* began to print his poems and stories, his artistic solitude continued. Wood's writing, for which he refused any payment, helped keep these magazines afloat; as a result, his submissions were accepted and printed without much editorial intervention. In Sara, Wood found a reader who was at once sympathetic and unflinchingly honest. Though Wood's sonnets were not very good, Sara was moved by the "large and ample and spacious and all-inclusive" spirit that animated the man who had written them.[3] By taking his work seriously, she gave him the artistic companionship he longed for, and by showing him how his random poetic sentiments contained within them the story of an ideal love that he himself longed for, she revealed the "deeper gladness of . . . soul" that he despaired of ever finding.

Nannie sensed Wood and Sara's growing intimacy before they acknowledged it themselves. On one of Sara's visits, Nannie entered Wood's study and discovered him examining a book with her—an innocent moment, but Nannie blanched with apprehension. She stepped out of the room and fainted dead away.[4]

Though she was unable to admit it, Sara was being drawn into a new dimension of feeling. Wood's presence nourished her, which only exacerbated her troubled thoughts about her empty marriage. She lost weight; she tired easily; she did not look well. On one of her visits to Wood's office, he suggested that she might have tuberculosis. He told her to have X-rays and a thorough medical examination, that he would take care of her bills.

Sara walked over to the window and stood looking out. "No, I don't think I have tuberculosis," she said. What made her ill, she felt, was a haunting feeling that up to now she had fought to suppress. "I'm troubled about my home life," she said, "and how any departure from it, breaking up the marriage—which is no longer a real marriage—

how it would affect the children." Like a flash, the whole thing broke. "I'm in love with you!"

Wood quickly echoed her sentiments.

"And there we were," Sara later recalled, "knowing at last that this was a matter so vital that we were willing to make almost any sacrifice on earth to establish a life together."[5]

Although they spoke of love, they were not yet lovers. Wood remained tangled in his responsibilities, and Sara was not yet prepared to act on her feelings. Then, in June, Sara's health broke down. She underwent surgery and was confined to a hospital bed for several weeks. Wood visited her almost daily, showering her with books, flowers, appetizing dishes—and finally with caresses. In Sara's words, they shared, "that flowing together of two souls and two bodies meeting in a great unspeakable realm of understanding after the long long want of all the Past."[6]

Sara's passion streamed forth with agitated vitality, whereas Wood often slipped into a circumspect tone, his wish for freedom held in check by financial worries, jumbled emotional commitments, and guilty concern for Nannie. Even so, it was a time of hope. In Sara, he had at last found a companion to share his creative work, a kindred spirit who promised to free him from the deep solitude of his Portland life.

That May Wood found another source of hope when New Jersey's newly elected governor visited Portland on a speaking tour designed to establish him as a national political figure. Addressing the Portland Press Club, Governor Woodrow Wilson declared that "honesty is all that is needed in politics, honesty and some knowledge of the game the other fellows play."[7] After spending several hours with Wilson, Wood concluded he would make a great president. He saw Wilson as a man of determination who had an exceptional grasp of theories and the history of government—a man who felt deep sympathy for the common man and who understood the economic falsities of present conditions. Wood was impressed by Wilson's clear intellectual vision founded on the principle that society ought not and does not exist for a favored few, that the common mass was entitled to a full voice in government.

Wood was especially struck by Wilson's remarkable deftness as a public speaker. "Thought is the only moving force," Wood observed in his "Impressions" column, "and Governor Wilson threw out to the people thoughts so matured that they could be called truths, and expressed in language so clear none need lose them. Crisp, clean and definite they came, new-minted from the lips. . . . He makes the best combination of reformer: scholar and practical politician (in its highest sense) I have seen."[8]

A year later, during his presidential campaign, Wilson articulated his vision to the American people with an intellect and grace that seemed to elevate the entire political process. "The truth is, we are all caught in a great economic system which is heartless," he told audiences.[9] "American industry is not free, as once it was free; American enterprise is not free. . . . Why? Because the laws of this country do not prevent the strong from crushing the weak. . . . The strong dominate the industry and the economic life of this country."[10] He went on to declare that "an invisible empire has been set up above the [form] of democracy."[11] Not only Wood, but labor leaders, radical journalists, intellectuals, and many others who had little faith in conventional party politics were won over by Wilson's criticism of the American system and by his zealous advocacy of reforms calculated to return the nation to its people.

Wilson supported Thomas Jefferson's contention that the government which governs best, governs least, but he added that "complicated circumstances" of modern life required government intervention to insure "fair play" for the individual. In language that spoke directly to Wood's anarchistic principles, Wilson stated that "it is still intolerable for the government to interfere with our individual activities except where it is necessary to interfere with them in order to free them."[12] Wilson seemed to share Wood's belief that liberty and growth are the great forces of life—that the great purpose of government is to insure their uninhibited activity. "Anything that depresses," Wilson said, "anything that makes the organization greater then the man, anything that blocks, discourages, dismays the humble man, is against all the principles of progress."[13] It even appeared that Wilson embraced the kind of political dissent that so many others sought to crush or control. "The so-called radicalism of our times," he proclaimed, "is simply the effort of nature to release the generous energies of our people."[14]

Wood was thrilled to hear all this from a presidential candidate.

He must have felt an affinity with what one historian has called Wilson's "contagious self-righteousness,"[15] a quality that he himself displayed in great abundance. He became an active Wilson supporter and remained so long after Wilson's actions contradicted his eloquent words.

Through the summer of 1911, Wood and Sara continued their affair. Though Wood railed against the "great falsities" of his world, he adhered to his old habit of allowing himself occasional deviations from complete truthfulness. Sara's emergence in his life did not end intimate relations with Kitty Beck; nonetheless, he told Sara that his attachment to Kitty was a thing of the past. But the truth was not so simple. Wood's feelings had been divided for so long that he could not easily concentrate his emotional life on one person.

Sara was well aware of Wood's divided sympathies. Responding to a letter from him, she wrote that she "had great difficulty in making out who you were most interested in." By way of illustration, she appended a list of persons mentioned in his letter along with the number of times their names appeared. "Mrs. Wood" appeared four times, "God" three times, "Sister" three times, and, "C.E.S.W. in connection with lunches, too many times to mention." As for herself, she appeared just once—an ignominious last place she shared with Teddy Roosevelt. "I could not quite make out who you were most interested in," she teased, "but finally decided it was C.E.S.W and the lunches, which shows great introspective power on my part and understanding of the non-understandable *man*."[16]

As August drew to a close, Wood prepared for his summer camping trip at Bill Hanley's ranch in Harney Valley. Before leaving, he and Sara met in room 419 for a lovers' farewell. The following day, Sara wrote to "my lover-Husband":

> How I love the atmosphere of this room. It is all the home I have, the real true home made by the things unseen and untouched that flow from the soul. I sat here and sang "home, sweet home" to myself, laughing happily like a young bride just coming into her love nest. . . . I gave myself up to the rapture of last night's memories. . . . The night! The night! My soul goes singing up and down.[17]

"We are mated," Wood wrote from his camp in the high desert. "We fit into each other. . . . Love is above analysis. . . . It simply is. . . . I love you, you have buried yourself deep into me."[18]

These sentiments did nothing to dispel Wood's reluctance to hurt Nannie. "Nothing will eliminate the dread of hurting others," he wrote. For fear of hurting her, he was willing to endure "a voluntary bondage and even degrading hypocrisy. . . . I cannot stand the joy of life blotted out from others by my act."[19] For the time being, there was no need to confront Nannie. Mary Field, Sara's older sister, was on her way to Los Angeles to cover the forthcoming McNamara trial for the *American Magazine*, and she persuaded Sara to join her. Bright, assertive, and rebellious, Mary had often blazed a trail for Sara. When Sara was still a high school student living under the strict control of her tyrannical father, Mary defied him and built an independent life for herself. After attending the University of Michigan, she moved to Chicago where she directed a settlement house and moved freely in the city's intellectual community. Theodore Dreiser promised to find work for her as a journalist, and Clarence Darrow became her lover.[20] To Sara, Mary was living proof that women with intelligence and courage need not submit to a secondary position—that it was possible to set aside conventional expectations and forge a productive, free life commensurate with one's talents.

The McNamara trial offered a suitable opportunity for Sara to try her hand at journalism. Wood spoke to his friends at the *Oregon Journal*, and they agreed to take her on as their special correspondent. On October 5, Wood said goodbye to Sara. She boarded the steamer *Rose City* in Astoria and set sail for San Francisco.

EDITOR'S ACKNOWLEDGEMENTS

Thanks to:

Sudeshna Shome Ghosh: for always countering my meltdowns with grace and good cheer.

Radhika Shenoy: for yor keeen editorial eye & ur infnite payteince... --- ##

The authors in this book: for trusting me with your strange and beautiful words/images. You guys are the best.

Yamini: for reading, for believing, and for being.

22. The Great Cause

For years, General Harrison Gray Otis, publisher of the *Los Angeles Times*, had wielded his considerable influence to keep the city free of union organizing. Then, in 1910, with the city facing a general strike, dynamite rocked the *Times* building, taking the lives of twenty employees. General Otis vowed to pursue the murderers and bring them to justice. He hired a squad of detectives from the Burns Agency and, after months of intensive investigation, James and John McNamara were arrested and charged with setting off the deadly explosion.

Eugene Debs spoke for many on the left when he insisted that the only conspiracy to be found in Los Angeles was entrenched capital's determined efforts to crush labor. The McNamara brothers were dedicated members of the militant International Association of Bridge and Structural Workers in Indianapolis. Rank and file labor had complete faith in their innocence. Given General Otis's proven hostility to the union movement, there was even suspicion that he had devised the dynamiting himself.[1]

Organized labor was on trial. Samuel Gompers, president of the American Federation of Labor, raised a huge defense fund and set out to enlist Clarence Darrow. He offered Darrow a $50,000 retainer plus an additional $200,000 for expenses. Darrow turned the money down, insisting he was in poor health. He was not well, it is true; but he had also been warned that the Burns detectives had gathered incriminating evidence against the McNamaras.[2] He confided to Ernest Stout of the United Press that he would not take the case because he thought the McNamaras were guilty.[3] Gompers kept up the pressure on Darrow: flattering him, pleading with him, berating him, imploring him to give the McNamaras the first-rate defense they would need to offset Otis's heavily financed vendetta against labor. Reluctantly, almost with a sense of foreboding, Darrow agreed to be the McNamaras' attorney.

Darrow asked Wood to join the defense team, but Wood refused. Wood told Darrow that his law partners, with their conservative clientele, disapproved of his taking part in this controversial event: he felt duty-bound to respect the concerns of men he had worked with for so many years. But there were other reasons for Wood's decision. For one, Wood was not at all convinced of the McNamaras' innocence. He knew that some labor militants took the idea of class warfare at face value: they had few qualms about using violence to advance their cause. Yet even if the McNamaras did dynamite the *Los Angeles Times* building, they were entitled to the best possible defense: a defense, moreover, that would give a public forum to their belief, and Wood's, that capitalism itself was a form of violence—institutionalized brutality that left far more casualties than the *Times* explosion. There remained, however, the underlying reason why Wood refused Darrow's offer: he did not trust Darrow's professional ethics. In fact, he believed Darrow would stop at nothing to win his case. Several years before, after Darrow's brilliant success defending Bill Haywood and his associates at the Moyer Pettibone trial in Boise, Darrow had intimated to him that his clients were guilty as charged and that he had tampered with the jury to gain an acquittal.[4] Now, in the hubbub preceding the McNamara trial, Wood saw that events were likely to get out of hand. With immense pressure on Darrow to gain an acquittal, with Darrow's ample ego conspicuously exposed, Wood knew Darrow would carry the struggle outside the courtroom. Driven by necessity, Darrow would obstruct justice in any way that might contribute to a satisfactory outcome. Wood detested what he took to be Darrow's rationale: that, for a just cause, the end justified the means. With this in mind, he steered clear of Los Angeles.

As the trial approached, organized labor held demonstrations across the nation. On Sunday, October 8, 1911, three days before the trial began, six thousand men and women representing forty trade unions marched through Portland four abreast, a procession that stretched for fifteen blocks, demanding justice for the McNamaras. An equal number lined the streets and cheered their support.[5]

At Park and Madison, Wood addressed the volatile throng:

> We are not warring against individuals but against institutions. We are not battling for individuals but for institutions. The more we permit ourselves to become irritated by a man like Harrison Gray Otis, the more blind we become to the real issue which is neither Otis nor McNamara but the emancipation of labor and the triumph of Right. If this demonstration means a human sympathy with men who are in trouble and who are by law presumed to be innocent, it is a righteous demonstration. If it means that the ranks of labor demand a fair trial and evenhanded justice and protest against a vindictive railroading to the gallows . . . then it is a righteous demonstration. But if it shall be twisted into meaning, as I have heard it will be, that Labor comes to the rescue of the McNamaras because they belong to the laboring class and demands their acquittal, innocent or guilty, then I think Labor will have received a deadly blow. . . .
>
> I stand here to say, better that the McNamaras should die, innocent martyrs to a great cause, than that being guilty they should be acquitted by the combined force of the laboring classes demanding their acquittal . . . better that they die innocent, than that the great cause be discredited with violence and tainted with falsity. There is only one way to win your battle my friends that is by the eternal way of Truth. . . .
>
> I do not wish my words warped into any intimation that these men in peril of their lives are guilty. Whether they be guilty or innocent I do not know . . . but if guilty . . . these men are not malicious murders. If they have done this thing, the reason is the fearful injustices, the fearful sufferings of men, women, and children, slaves to an iniquitous system. This is the real question at trial.[6]

There is an element of patrician detachment in Wood's speech. At times, one hears the haughty moralizing voice of his father, stubbornly advocating exalted principles in an era when neither institutions nor individuals could bear up under scrutiny based on absolute standards of moral conduct. But Wood would not yield on this one idea: that great causes must reject violence and avoid the taint of falsity, that truth itself is the most powerful weapon for revolutionary change. Believing as he did in the justice of labor's demands, he also believed that labor must act justly.

Wood's doubts about Darrow were quickly confirmed. Less than a week after Sara arrived in Los Angeles, she was alarmed by Darrow's conduct. "He's sure playing a queer game," she wrote Wood, "first with Mary, which is a personal grievance, and second with the Cause which is an impersonal but greater grievance." Darrow met Mary and Sara regularly: they dined together, and he spent hours alone with Mary in their apartment. On one occasion he made a pass at Sara in the kitchen: "hugging me like an old grizzly to my unspeakable discomfort. I told him I was 'not eligible' whereupon he made the rather strange remark that if I were out of funds to come to him anytime."[7]

The trial was weeks away—protracted jury selection had just begun—yet Darrow confessed to Mary that he believed the McNamaras were "guilty as hell" and that he hadn't "the shadow of a chance to win." Sara wondered how Darrow was able to keep up the farce.

But Darrow had little choice. He had become the instrument of Gompers and Debs and all those who believed the McNamaras were innocent. Perhaps he should have shared his fears with Gompers and other labor officials before things got out of hand, but he did not. He lived under enormous pressure: he became snappish, almost paranoid, when people questioned his decisions. "Everyone who does not take his position is a 'damn fool' or a 'damn idiot,' " Sara told Wood. "[He] seems to take it as a personal grievance that everyone who is radical at all is not 'with him.' "[8]

Sara's letter confirmed Wood's worst fears. He wrote her a thirty-page reply, roundly condemning the man whom many considered to be the most brilliant lawyer of his time:

If you get a key to a person's nature and it is the universal pass key, you know in advance what they are going to do. Darrow is above all things selfish—with a not necessary adjunct to *selfishness*, vanity—and a side development, avarice. . . .

Now for prediction. When he is sated [with Mary] he will

treat her like a sucked orange. . . . A woman's body is nothing more to Darrow than to the Sultan—a delicious morsel to be taken everywhere found, and forgotten. A woman's mind is nothing to him except that the adoration of a brainy woman is more subtle flattery. But he'd take flattery from a chorus girl. . . .

[Darrow] is not making this fight for the Cause of Labor, nor for the McNamaras—but for C. Darrow, and in this he is like the most of us lawyers. We prate of our fight for justice, we are fighting for our own glory and profit. Darrow's glory and Darrow's pocket is what he is fighting for. Of course these can only be served by McNamaras' defense, and indeed acquittal. *That* is why he is unscrupulous to win. He knows as well as I do that true devotion to the great cause would be to lend his great influence to teach Labor that only by a *repudiation* of such methods can it ever hope to win. . . . He is undermining, not building up. . . . He will use bribery where safe. Perjury where safe.[9]

As Wood foresaw, Darrow did his best to circumvent the law. With labor's two-hundred-thousand-dollar fund at his disposal, Darrow combatted Otis's team of Burns detectives with investigators of his own. Soon Darrow was spying on the prosecution and the prosecution was spying on Darrow. Agents were bribed, allegiances shifted, secret files were stolen, false information was planted—till it seemed no one could be trusted. Yet one essential truth emerged: as jury selection dragged on, Darrow's investigators uncovered overwhelming evidence that the McNamara brothers were guilty of the charges against them— and much more.

Darrow's defense team adopted a desperate strategy. Jim Harrington, one of Darrow's associates, disbursed sizable amounts of money for highly secret activities. Bert Franklin, one of Darrow's investigators, attempted to bribe a juror and sought to buy the vote of a man on the venire list. Though no one could prove that Darrow actually knew of these schemes, even many of his friends came to believe that, at the very least, he condoned them by allowing himself to be conveniently ignorant of what some of his staff were up to.

Darrow's situation was hopeless. He was ready to try almost anything. Then Lincoln Steffens proposed an outlandish compromise.

Steffens, who had come to Los Angeles to cover the trial for his syndicated column, quickly grasped that the McNamaras were guilty. After several difficult talks with Darrow, he persuaded his despondent friend to undertake a remarkable course of action: if Darrow was prepared to give up a losing courtroom fight, Steffens would intercede with representatives of the Los Angeles business establishment and negotiate a settlement. Steffens planned to impress upon them the ruinous effect that a bitter trial would have on the city's image. He would tell them that Darrow was willing to change the McNamaras' plea to "Guilty," if they, in a charitable gesture, would urge the judge to spare the young men's lives.

With characteristic zeal, Steffens placed his plan before the McNamara brothers. The young men refused. If they admitted their guilt, they told him, it would implicate the entire labor movement. They preferred to die as martyrs. But Steffens won James over by assuring him that if they pleaded guilty, John, who was barely involved in the bombing, would be given a light sentence. Through November, Steffens pursued his scheme while Darrow, knowing full well that labor faced a crushing defeat, struggled to maintain a positive public image. It was all very much as Wood had predicted from the start.

Meanwhile, Wood was shaken by an unexpected turn of events. In late November, Kitty hastily married Dr. Lloyd Irvine, a rough, hard-drinking man she did not really love. Wood felt desolate, bereaved, abandoned. Though he would not admit it, he felt betrayed. To Sara he insisted that he and Kitty were "just father and daughter chums," yet he couldn't conceal his jealousy.[10] Kitty's defection obsessed him. The following day he wrote Sara a forty-four page letter rife with tangled emotions. Kitty's sexual union with another man aroused Wood's fear that Sara, too, might leave him for a younger lover. "I thought myself long dead," he writes, "and you have really resurrected my youth by your spiritual fire and my great love for you. But how long will I last? Oh, it is so sweet with you. I cannot bear to lose it, and if I do, shall I lose you to another?"[11]

But passion was not the primary reason for Kitty's rash decision. Kitty's sister Sissy told Wood what he must have already suspected: that Kitty's marriage to Irvine was an impulsive attempt to pull away from the only man she truly loved. Several times in the past she had begged Wood to let her take her own life, and each time Wood managed to steady her.[12] The attention he lavished on Kitty, along with his constant need for her devotion, had held her life together for over ten years—until Sara appeared. Now Kitty felt cut off from her only reliable support. Her doomed marriage to Irvine marked a return to morbid fatalism. In its way, it *was* suicidal.

Kitty's reckless action had one further effect on Wood. It sharpened his appetite for freedom. "I feel tempted to be bold," he wrote Sara, "to throw sympathy to the winds and defy the world, hurt all hearts that we may live our own lives."[13] This was easier said than done. He went on to make bold promises he was not prepared to keep. "When you are ready for the splendid life so am I. I will spare no one. I will defy everything."[14]

Sara matched her lover promise for promise. Her sexual and emotional awakening kindled a gritty resourcefulness that surprised even her. Toward the end of November, Steffens invited Sara and Mary to a banquet given by the Los Angeles press for the out-of-town correspondents working on the McNamara trial: 150 men in all—plus Sara and Mary.

Steffens made a fine speech. Then Darrow addressed the group. While he was speaking, the chairman approached Sara and asked her if she would follow Darrow with a few words on "Woman's Sphere in Journalism." Sara was at a loss to formulate all the things she wanted to say, but she was too game to refuse the opportunity. With no preparation, she rose and told the roomful of men that, in every sphere of life, women were ready to enlarge and correct accepted reality by contributing valuable insights, earned through hard experience that, in the past, had customarily been ignored. "It was a good move," Sara admitted. "It has given me a public introduction to the Press."[15] Indeed, it had. Steffens became a lifelong friend; and George West, a gifted young journalist, seems to have fallen in love with her on the spot.

On December 1, the McNamaras appeared in court and changed their plea to guilty. The courtroom was stunned. Across America, labor supporters felt bitterly betrayed—more by Darrow than by the McNamaras themselves. Four days later, Judge Bordwell censured Darrow and Steffens from the bench for trying to cut a deal outside the courtroom. It was for the court to determine sentencing—not the Los Angeles business community, not Steffens, not Darrow. With that, he sentenced James McNamara to life imprisonment and his brother John to fifteen years hard labor. If this was not enough, Darrow was indicted on charges of attempted bribery.

At his trial, months later, Darrow mesmerized the jury by insisting that he was being persecuted because of his love for the poor and his support of oppressed labor.[16] He was vindicated, but Wood and Sara continued to believe that, driven by egotism and zeal, Darrow had actively schemed to subvert the judicial process. (In spite of his contempt for Darrow's conduct, Wood supported his friend throughout the ordeal. To help pay for Darrow's costly defense, Wood sent him a handsome check—a kindness that Darrow never forgot.) At the summation in his own trial, Darrow called the McNamara bombing "a terrible moral accident." The same can be said of Darrow's desperate machinations.

The trial's shattering conclusion preyed on Sara's thoughts, setting loose a chain of gloomy speculation: "This sudden ending of the McNamara case involving, as it has, such deceit, such shaken confidence, such ill will, such betrayed trusts and social disorder and disaster; Kitty's tragedy. . . . Mary's heart-rending situation, her loyal tho misplaced faith, her hopeless love and . . . you my darling to whom I may not come save as a stranger—all this fills my heart with unutterable anguish to-night and I feel that life is not good."[17]

Wood, however, was convinced that life was very good—or would be, as soon as he broke off from Nannie. "O Sara," he wrote, "I cannot trifle. I know it means heartache, wreckage—your home and mine, but for the first time in my life I say I *must* have her. I will give up all for her. I will do anything to spend my last years with her. She is a *necessity* to me. I must have her." Just rehearsing this daring speech gave Wood a certain satisfaction, as if anticipating freedom was tantamount to having it. "I am consumed—at my age I can firmly decide I will leave the wife of thirty three years, the children, all all for you. I am as incapable of reason as any school girl, insane with love. It is insanity, but blessed insanity. I am glad I did not die till I knew it."[18]

Sara knew they faced difficult times. "The steamer nears *you*," she wrote on her journey home. "Coldly the thought of other arms and other lips presses upon my sensitive soul. Shrinking, I feel the old burden of deceit and pretence settle in its accustomed place upon my back. I write, I pray the gods to take him from my path, to painlessly remove him that I may not have myself to inflict the blow or, on the other hand, bear the touch that I now have come to loathe. How desperate I feel!"[19]

23. All Our Nights Are Bridal Nights

In early April, Wood went to San Francisco to settle business
matters following the death of Eugene Meyer, his old friend from
the Lazard Freres land-grant case. His visit allowed him to spend
time with Darrow and a handful of friends who had gathered to piece
things together after the McNamara debacle: Anton Johannsen and
Olaf Tvietmoe, two militant labor organizers, and Fremont Older, the
crusading editor of the *San Francisco Call.*

Darrow was due to appear in court in a few months, to defend
himself against bribery charges. If convicted, he would be ruined
and labor would suffer another blow to its public image. Though
Tvietmoe and Johannsen publicly supported Darrow, Johannsen
admitted to Wood that he believed Darrow had betrayed them. As
Johannsen saw it, Darrow had known he was about to be charged
with bribery: hoping to make the idea of jury tampering appear
absurd, he had prevailed upon the McNamaras to plead guilty before
he was indicted. Like so many of their labor brethren, the McNamaras
revered Darrow: they changed their plea to save his neck.

Johannsen went on to say that Darrow's claim of financial hardship
was a lie: labor had given Darrow two hundred thousand dollars, and
Darrow "couldn't have spent more than half at the outside." The
whole thing was a fiasco. Darrow "departed on a piratical course and
was too flabby to be a pirate."[1]

Johannsen's version of these events may be true, but the full extent
of what Darrow did remains a matter of conjecture. Johannsen was
far too involved in these events to be a reliable informant. He seems
to have known the McNamaras were guilty well before Darrow and

Steffens suspected it. Quite possibly, he had a hand in supplying them with the dynamite. From what he told Wood, it appears that he was not at all surprised to learn of the McNamaras' guilt. What disturbed him was their decision to confess their crime and drop their plea of "innocent." Most likely, Johannsen hoped to have it both ways—a dynamite attack on labor's enemy, General Otis, and two martyrs to flaunt before a sympathetic public.

Johannsen's willingness to deceive the rank-and-file is what troubled Wood about radical labor: the very issue he had addressed at the Portland rally on the eve of the McNamara trial. Still, he did not want to dissociate himself from Johannsen and Tvietmoe completely. So long as he showed himself to be a loyal friend of labor, it gave him a measure of influence, a chance to have his say among men who controlled one of the largest labor followings on the West Coast.

That autumn, at the request of Woodrow Wilson's campaign headquarters, Wood criss-crossed the state on behalf of the Democratic Party. The Democratic platform was a far cry from Wood's anarchist vision; even a reform-minded president was unlikely to depose the entrenched interest groups whose power undermined, or rather redefined, the American system. Still, Wood believed that if Wilson came to power it would be beneficial for labor, beneficial for voting rights, beneficial for free speech, and beneficial for individual liberty. His election would be a useful step toward Wood's goal of dismantling overreaching government.

For much of October, to the dismay of Tvietmoe and Johannsen, Wood behaved like a loyal Democrat. He campaigned in Hood River, Baker, Weiser, Ontario, Twin Falls, Ashland, Medford, and on into Washington and Idaho—a schedule that would have exhausted a man half his age. He neglected his legal practice, his family, and his writing to speak in behalf of the only presidential candidate he had truly admired since he had reached voting age some forty years before.

It would be hard to exaggerate the influence Sara had on this burst of activity. She had barely returned from Los Angeles, when she was off again, barnstorming through the Oregon boondocks to speak on woman suffrage. The campaign was sponsored by the College Equal Suffrage League, a group of young women determined to build upon the courageous efforts of Abigail Scott Duniway to bring about a pro-suffrage amendment in the state constitution. As chief organizer of the Portland branch of the College League, Sara sent speakers across the city in open automobiles: wherever suffrage workers found small groups, they stopped their vehicles and delivered their case from the fender of their cars.[2] In an age when proper ladies rarely expressed political views in private, much less on street corners, the suffrage campaign was, in itself, a bold demonstration of what the "new woman" might be. Through the winter and early spring, Sara traveled by train and car from one rural town to the next. She brought the suffrage cause to dusty streets, speaking to indifferent passers-by until enough curiosity-seekers gathered round to form an impromptu audience. She visited church socials and small gatherings in private homes; she spoke wherever and whenever she could find people who would listen; she drove herself to the brink of physical collapse yet still managed to push on to the next speaking engagement. Woman suffrage galvanized her; it took precedence over her health, her marriage, her children, over everything, even her affair with Wood. The Reverend Ehrgott could hardly ignore what was happening: Sara's efforts for woman's suffrage had upset their domestic equilibrium, and she seemed intent on claiming even greater liberty.

Wood was deeply affected. He saw in Sara a feminine complement to himself, a companion who shared his vision of radical change, who shared, too, the overriding wish to bring his personal life into harmony with his political ideals. It upset him to see her drive herself into a nervous fever; it bothered him that her campaign travels limited their chances to be together. But more than anything, he admired her courage and unshakable belief that her existence had little value unless she gave herself to the struggle for a larger life, not merely for herself but for all women.

Sara's courage gave Wood the impetus to pursue his dream of freedom. That summer, he corresponded with Fremont Older about creating an anarchist commune in Los Gatos, "exactly 49 miles from the Fairmont Hotel"—a retreat Wood and Older planned to develop along with Steffens, Darrow, and Helen Todd, all of whom had already expressed interest in the project.[3]

Wood sent Older a three-thousand-dollar deposit, along with his reflections on how the commune should be organized:

I don't see any better arrangement for these commonly owned properties than the present country-club idea,—a voluntary association of people under certain rules and regulations and subject to certain assessments. . . . At my age, I hardly expect to run a redlight district or a harem, but if I should be attracted to a woman and desire her as a companion I should not hesitate to put her under my roof, and whether she was my literary companion, my secretary, my cook, my mistress, or all these together, I would consider my own affair.[4]

Wood realized, however, that Darrow's wife, Ruby, was not likely to go along with a free-love community that endorsed her husband's philandering. Clearly, it would not be easy to transform the commune idea to concrete reality. Plans for the colony continued into the following year until they foundered on Cora Older's preoccupation with protecting her share of the property from communistic joint ownership. The collapse of the anarchist "country club" was a disappointment, but Wood did not relinquish his hopes for creating "a restful and joyful retreat" where he and Sara could begin their life together.

In the course of the suffrage campaign, Sara's spirits swung from rapturous joy to near-suicidal despair. It would be easy to say she had an unstable personality, but this ignores a deeper reality. In a relatively brief period, the hard shell of her life with Reverend Ehrgott had been cracked open by the unshakable conviction that Wood was the key to her soul's satisfaction. She was a married woman, the wife of a Baptist minister who had given her no cause to leave him. What right had she to claim a new life for herself? Her sensitive nature was overtaxed. No wonder her thoughts turned so often to her own extinction.

All this was exacerbated by the need for Wood and Sara to conceal their affair. In his effort to make Sara's life more comfortable, Wood befriended Ehrgott and offered to loan him money. In June, Ehrgott sent Wood a promissory note for a $350 loan, addressed to "My dear true friend" and closing with "let my much love and esteem flow to you."[5] The money was sorely needed, but Sara felt sickened by "the whole sordid, mocking perversion or reversion of what is right." She realized she had to speak with her husband, but she could not bring herself to do it.[6] By mid-July, "soul numbness" took over, accompanied by "torrents of grief." Once again, Sara felt miserable. She confided to Kitty that she had thought the matter out: for her children and Ehrgott's future, and for Wood too, she believed that the best solution was to slip out of the way. She asked Kitty if her husband, Dr. Irvine, would get her some cyanide.[7] Kitty refused, and Sara's ordeal continued.

In late July, in the midst of the suffrage campaign, Sara pulled herself together and told Ehrgott the truth. She wrote that she no longer loved him, that she had lied to him with respect to her feeling for Wood. She told him she was on the brink of chronic invalidism, perhaps even death. She begged for his understanding and asked him to release her so that she might pursue a life with Wood.[8]

In spite of Sara's blunt declaration, Ehrgott hoped to win her back. "You are the victim of a false philosophy," he insisted, "the prey of a fatal code of ethics." Wood, the anarchist free-lover, had his impressionable wife "in the grip of an hallucination."[9]

By the time the suffrage campaign reached its final weeks, Sara had become one of its most effective speakers. In September she departed on a two-week lecture tour of eastern Oregon—Hood River, the Dalles, Biggs, Arlington, Condon, Hepner, La Grande, Baker City, and Pendleton. Her weight dropped below one hundred pounds. Yet when she spoke, her fragility added to her riveting presence. People saw Sara as the living image of the goals for which she campaigned: the "new woman," a positive example of what her sex might aspire to. In town after town, she was sought after by whatever liberal or intellectual element existed. People wanted to dine with her, talk with her, assist her, spend time with her. A lead article in the *Morning Democrat* of Baker, Oregon, captures the excitement of her tour:

STREET CORNER SPEAKER WINS MANY FRIENDS

UNUSUAL SIGHT IN BAKER

FEMININE ORATORS, SUCH AS MRS. EHRGOTT

WILL CERTAINLY MAKE FRIENDS NO MATTER

WHAT VIEWS OF THE SUFFRAGE QUESTION THEIR HEARERS HOLD

While the first thought to the spectator was that the speaker was out of place in making a street corner address, still after listening to her for a few moments and noting her interest and enthusiasm for her cause, the feeling of idle curiosity changed to admiration for the little woman, who as a last resort for the suffrage cause is bravely facing street crowds in advocacy. . . .

Until hearing her it is doubtful if many, even those favoring suffrage, would have favored the appearance of a lady in a street corner speech. The most refined person in her audience, however, could not find the least grounds for criticism of a street meeting such as conducted by Mrs. Ehrgott, and whether or not her arguments changed the views of her hearers, they certainly admired her bravery in going to such extremes to advance her cause.[10]

A week later, Wood joined her at Hood River. That night he led Sara to the outskirts of town, out into the woods. Beneath an arching oak, he pledged that "all our nights are bridal nights." Sara promised Wood that whatever might come—infirmity, impotency, age, helplessness, and weakness—nothing could diminish the grip of love that joined them. From that night on they regarded one another as husband and wife.[11]

Not long after this "pagan" wedding, the Reverend Ehrgott called upon Wood and forbade him from visiting his home. He told Wood that due to overwork, nervous excitement, and various physical ailments, Sara was not in her right mind. Wood replied that what Ehrgott called insanity was Sara's growth of mind, but Ehrgott cut him short. If Sara did not love him, if she was willing to abandon her home, then she was surely insane. What's more, if she left him he would explain her insane behavior and her immoral actions in court: he would demand custody of their children.[12]

For a few weeks more, the suffrage campaign kept Sara out of Portland. On those occasions when speaking engagements brought Wood and Sara to the same town, they sometimes addressed the audience together, with Wood departing from his basic pro-Wilson speech to make his own appeal for woman suffrage. Wood and Sara formed a remarkable team, the likes of which those isolated towns had never seen. Elegant and strikingly handsome, Wood dazzled his listeners with an eclectic speaking style that mixed folksy anecdotes, the rich experience of his youth, and erudite references to classical literature, ancient history, and the philosophic principles of the Founding Fathers. In contrast, there was Sara: primly dressed, unadorned, frail yet radiant, given over completely to her cause. Her determination to reveal the moral necessity of woman suffrage transformed her. Her words, forged from personal ordeal, were intimate, poetic, yet intellectually rigorous. She was electrifying. Wood took pride in being an impressive speaker, but invariably it was Sara who drew the loudest applause.

The suffrage campaign reached its high point on August 11, when twenty-five thousand people gathered at the Oaks Amusement Park in Portland, the largest suffrage assembly in the history of the state. Members of the College Equal Suffrage League, dressed in mortar boards and academic gowns, flooded the park with yellow decorations (the official suffrage color), with leaflets, posters, cartoons, mottoes, and badges. "Vast Audience Tearful," the *Oregonian* reported:

> Mrs. Sarah Bard Field Ehrgott delved down yesterday at Oaks Amusement Park into the sensibilities of one of the biggest equal suffrage gatherings ever seen in Oregon with incidents of the hardships and woes of women and children for which she claimed that suffrage was the sole panacea. She literally forced her way through skepticism. With pitiful tales that brought to tears many in that audience.
>
> Then, with cold logic and brilliant argument, C.E.S. Wood healed the wounds she had made. Each was the foil for the other. The meeting might have been a Gipsy Smith revival meeting from the number of "converts" made.[13]

When Election Day came round, Teddy Roosevelt's renegade Bull Moose Party divided the Republican vote, thus ruining the chances of the incumbent president, William Howard Taft. As a result, Woodrow Wilson won a huge electoral majority. As for Sara's suffrage campaign, Oregon voters joined Arizona and Kansas as the seventh, eighth, and ninth states to grant women the right to vote. (The first six states to ratify woman suffrage were Wyoming [1869], Utah [1870], Colorado [1893], Idaho [1896], Washington [1910], and California [1911]).

With the campaign over, Sara returned to Ehrgott and the children she had neglected. It was everything she dreaded. After months of tasting a new and larger life, she was welcomed home by a husband who believed her to be insane, the unknowing victim of Wood's brainwashing. She longed for freedom; she wished for an impossible rescue. She beseeched Wood to "pick me up amidst all the world's clamor and dismay and place me at your side."[14]

But Wood could not forsake his tangled commitments—not even now, when he had finally found his ideal companion. The restful and joyful retreat he planned with Older was still a distant dream. Sara had no way out: if she wanted to see her children, she would have to live with Ehrgott. For three weeks she submitted to the impossible situation: she couldn't sleep, her weight dropped, she ran a fever. Then she began spitting up blood. As Wood had feared, Sara had tuberculosis.

24. An Awful Awakening

Sara's breakdown brought an end to her domestic life with Ehrgott. With his wife's health at stake, and with no financial resources of his own, Ehrgott did not object when Wood sent her to San Francisco to rest and regain her health, a move that was absolutely necessary for her survival.

Sara's absence worried Wood. She had torn herself loose from an impossible domestic situation, but her health was shattered, and by separating from Ehrgott she had taken herself out of his life as well. Wood and Sara exchanged letters several times a week. Medical news, expressions of love, surges of anxiety, amusing anecdotes, gossip, reflections on life, literature, and politics—whatever came to mind found its way into their correspondence. They were determined to share the shifting currents of their lives, every thought and feeling, with the greatest candor; yet the nature of letter writing altered their romance. Personal events were censored, simplified, and compressed; the random flow of thoughts and impressions gave in to the orderly flow of letter-writing; thwarted desire worked its way into urgent testaments of love. None of this was false, yet everything was transformed. The stream of correspondence continued month after month: ten- or twenty-page letters several times a week; hundreds, thousands of pages. At times, it must have seemed to Wood that he existed only in words, or at least that his truest life, his only hope for happiness and peace, came when he sat down to write to Sara.

When Sara arrived in San Francisco, her doctors told her she was close to nervous prostration brought on by overwork and mental strain.

Not only did she have a tubercular condition, but very likely she suffered heart trouble.

Sara returned to her room to find a letter from Ehrgott, full of hopeful sentiments about their reconciliation. "What have I done?" she wrote to Wood, "allowed him to kiss me good-bye—passively kissed his cheek—refrained from constant reference to my desire for freedom. And he has taken this as a 'providential triumph of truth and love.' " The thought of ever going back to him repelled her— she saw it as nothing less than her soul's extinction—yet the enormity of actually telling him their marriage was over incapacitated her. "I don't know what to do," she wrote, "I feel like a suffocating person crying for air, air."[1]

In 1912 the forces arrayed against divorce were enough to make any woman balk. Divorce was viewed as an act of desperation, a scandalous reflection on the moral character of the parties involved. What's more, the legal system reflected this. In many states, marital infidelity was punishable by law: if Ehrgott produced evidence of Wood's affair with Sara, he could destroy Wood's career. It was even possible that Wood could be tried and sent to prison. If this was not daunting enough, few states accepted "incompatibility" as grounds for divorce. For most people, there was no resolution to marital unhappiness, except resignation to continued misery.[2]

By conventional standards, Ehrgott was in the right. He was a man of God, a model husband who honored the forms of holy matrimony. He saw it as his duty to restore Sara to her true self—as his obedient wife. He refused to believe Sara was lost: dogged perseverance would bring her back to him.

Sara's spirits were bolstered when Emma Wold came to San Francisco to look after her. A founder of the College Equal Suffrage League, Emma had grown fond of Sara during the Oregon suffrage campaign. Years later, she would move to Washington DC and begin an outstanding career in public affairs—but as a young woman she was painfully self-effacing, an adoring satellite to Sara. Emma was the first of many people who found themselves drawn irresistibly to Wood and Sara's struggle for freedom. She was with Sara every day, looking after her health and serving as her companion in exile. She corresponded with Ehrgott and persuaded him to give Sara some breathing room; she kept Wood posted on every new development;

and when Sara placed herself in La Cresta Sanitarium in Los Angeles, Emma went with her.

With Sara settled in a sanitarium, with doctors and Emma keeping a watchful eye on her, and with Ehrgott temporarily out of the way, Wood had reason to hope that Sara would start to mend. Then she informed him she was pregnant.

Given Sara's fragile condition, neither she nor the embryo was likely to survive a full-term pregnancy. Wood wished they could bring their own "soul-created child" into the world, but he could not bear to let Sara take a risk that might cost her her life.[3] He urged her to have an abortion at once, when blood loss and the shock to her system were likely to be less. Sara required prompt attention, but she dreaded disclosing her condition to the medical staff for fear that Ehrgott would discover that Wood had made her pregnant. But before Sara could decide on a course of action, it was over. A fit of tubercular coughing induced a miscarriage.

Meanwhile, Ehrgott continued his campaign to win her back. To Emma, he confided, "My wife is so under spell of Mr. C.E.S. Wood's personality that she is fairly enslaved, as if by hypnotism, by him." He foresaw "an awful awakening—I pray for Sara that she may be fortified for it."[4]

When Wood heard of the letter, he wrote Ehrgott a long, closely reasoned reply. It was pointless for Wood to argue his case with Ehrgott, but the situation held an irresistible attraction for him. His effort to free Sara from Ehrgott's power paralleled the two great rivalries of his youth: his efforts to protect his mother from William Maxwell Wood's despotic rages; and his determined battle to pry Nannie loose from Dr. Lincoln and what he saw as her thralldom to Catholicism. These trials had aroused Wood's vital emotional and rhetorical energies. Now, Ehrgott emerged as a new adversary—one whose capacity to obstruct Wood's happiness provoked him to retaliate with cold moral fury.

There was another way in which Wood's battle with Ehrgott recapitulated his past. In rising to confront Ehrgott, Wood assumed the haughty, didactic voice that William Maxwell Wood once directed at his rebellious son. Wood's letters to Ehrgott read like pages torn from his father's scalding correspondence. Like his father, Wood was disposed to view personal matters in terms of overriding moral principles and to do battle on that elevated plane. William Maxwell Wood had taught his son to despise the old abuses of feudalism, yet there was a thread of chivalric idealism in the habit both he and his son shared of transforming personal ordeals into moral crusades. All that mattered was truth and justice: both father and son stubbornly persisted in the illusion that they were able to set emotional issues aside. Both believed that they acted, not from blind impulse, but from unassailable reason, compassion, and unflinching allegiance to eternal moral verities.

Wood regarded Ehrgott as a zealot, an egoist, a hypocritical proponent of Christian charity. But Ehrgott was not the fool Wood made him out to be; he was a canny rival who had seen enough of Wood to form vivid impressions. What he had to say was tainted by pain and anger, but there was more truth in his attacks than Wood or Sara were willing to accept. When Ehrgott maintained that Sara had fallen under the spell of Wood's personality—that she was virtually enslaved, as if by hypnotism—Wood and Sara scoffed at the lurid notion of Wood as Svengali, wickedly mesmerizing Sara to do his bidding. But Ehrgott was speaking figuratively, and many of Sara's love letters added substance to what he said. Sara was not Wood's love slave; she was not hypnotized; but passion casts its own spell. "There's not a throbbing atom of my body," Sara wrote, "as it welcomes you into its home, that is not shot through and through with a spiritual essence that hallows and purifies and ennobles the whole wondrous intermingling."[5] Desire had shattered her life. Ehrgott was not entirely wrong when he warned of dire consequences.

Hoping to intercede on behalf of his two friends, Darrow tried to mediate with Ehrgott. Ehrgott respected Darrow, whom he had known since his days in Cleveland, but no one could dissuade him from fighting to preserve his marriage. After speaking with Ehrgott, Darrow visited Sara in Los Angeles to report to her. It seems, however, that Darrow was unable to address an attractive woman without resorting to an amorous proposition. He told Sara that Wood would never manage to change the habits of a lifetime and break away from his marriage. Then he made a pass at her. "It is disgusting to me," Sara wrote to Wood, "how he tries to make love to me every chance he gets." After this, Sara made a point of having Emma in the room whenever Darrow dropped in. Within a short time, his visits tailed off.[6]

Back in Portland, Wood attended a gathering of two thousand workers who came to Gipsy Smith Auditorium to hear Big Bill Haywood speak. Labor turns the wheels of the world, Haywood explained, and if it turns them, it can stop them. To do this, labor had to dedicate itself to one big union free from discrimination based on race, color, or sex. Capital seems all-powerful, but in reality it is no more than stored labor. A general strike by all working people would force capital to capitulate to labor's demands and virtually abolish conventional politics.

Haywood was a stunning speaker who mixed humor and illustrative anecdotes with "forceful vital thought clothed in forceful vital words." Even so, Wood had qualms. When a young member of the Socialist Labor Party in the audience stood up to challenge Haywood, he was hooted down. Wood felt Haywood should have taken the lead in assuring the man a chance to say what he had to say. Wood worried that Haywood showed "the spirit usually shown by labor—'Now *we* are on top we'll be as intolerant as others have always been to us.' "

But all in all, Wood admired Haywood. "He is a proper leader," Wood noted. "Knows his people, his task, his adversaries, and has clearly got the mental concept of what Anarchism has been preaching so long—Solidarity of action, by all the disinherited without distinction or discrimination among themselves. Direct action instead of Political. Voluntary co-operation instead of Government. From his enunciation of their program I would say the IWW's are anarchists."[7]

"In this man and his like I can see the beginning of the end of the present order of things," Wood observed.[8] But one thing continued to trouble him about Haywood: his flirtation with violence seemed as much a part of his philosophy as physical courage seemed a part of the man himself: "He then spoke of '*force*' and '*violence*' saying they advocated the *force* of solidarity, the force of strikes, the force of sabotage, not the violence of dynamite etc. Yet I thought all the way through I detected a covert sympathy with an innuendo favoring violence. I would like to talk to him on this.[9]

At the start of February, Wood put Portland life aside in order to join Sara in California for three weeks. Sara was full of feverish anxiety: "all mind," he observed, ". . . all tension, all aquiver."[10] She left the sanitarium to spend two weeks with Wood in San Francisco and Larkspur in Marin County—a sojourn that elevated her spirits and partially restored her health.

Wood returned to Portland with a case of the flu. Nannie fussed over him, exaggerating the severity of his illness for the pleasure of having him at home. Wood promised Sara he would not let pity get in the way; he was determined to go through with his plan to tell Nannie about his wish to leave her. A week passed, and still Wood said nothing to her. Then, on March 3, he propped himself up to get out of bed and the whole universe seemed to turn over. He tumbled back, unable to keep his balance.

Waiting for the doctor to arrive, Wood had ample time to diagnose his condition. He feared he had suffered a stroke, that his health was permanently impaired. His hopes for a life with Sara receded. He had forestalled too long on his dream of a quiet retreat, of devoting his last years to poetry. He was sixty-one years old, and in all likelihood he was dying.

25. I Will Sing a Dirge unto Civilization

What Wood imagined to be a stroke was diagnosed as vertigo brought on by an infection of his inner ear. He was confined to his bed for several days until the infection passed and his equilibrium was restored. Though it was not the crisis Wood had imagined, from this time on he treated every cold and fever as a medical emergency. For a man his age, this made perfect sense: influenza and pneumonia could kill as readily as a stroke.

Wood's quickened feeling of his own mortality made him all the more anxious to pursue his creative work. For years, he had been in the habit of scribbling observations, ideas, and drafts of poems in pocket notebooks. Room 419, his private office, was filled with diaries, correspondence, manuscripts of stories, poems, and magazine articles he had filed away haphazardly. Now he planned to gather up his work and put the written fragments of his past in order.

Two weeks after his vertigo attack, Wood mailed Sara a packet of autobiographical reminiscences, an undertaking that over the next few months grew to eleven segments, 145 pages in all. "These tedious biographic sheets," he called them.[1] In fact, in the opening pages his voice is pedagogic, ill-at-ease. But after a shaky start, he allowed his childhood memories to speak for themselves. For the most part, Wood kept didactic commentary out of his narrative, but as he wrote his story in 1913, the boy he once was merged with the anarchist he now wanted to be. Young Erskine resists dogma; he defies authority; force angers him. At all costs, he is determined to preserve his liberty, be it sexual freedom, the freedom to speak his mind, or the impulse to flee school and spend a fine spring day fishing or playing pirate and camping under the stars.

Wood proudly described his father's circumnavigation of the globe, and he recalled the efforts of his parents to raise their children properly in a rough, new society. Many of Wood's liveliest memories covered his education and how the attractions of the great outdoors spoke to him more profoundly than any teacher. His narrative ended just before he left home for West Point. Had he continued he might have produced a memorable document. But he did not have time to see his project through. His reminiscences appear to have been written hurriedly, each segment scrawled off in a single sitting. Yet his prose was graceful, endowed with a writer's intangible gift— "voice."

In March, Sara devoted herself to reading *Paradise Lost* and *Faust*. The times cried out, she wrote to Wood, for "a world poem on the 20th Century view of the struggle between good and evil." She urged him to write it.[2] Wood agreed that a great epic to dramatize the spirit of the age would be a wonderful achievement, but he did not see himself undertaking such a lofty design. Nevertheless, Sara's suggestion took root. Within a few weeks, Wood embarked on what he believed would be his one great work.

Six months before, during a vacation at Hanley's ranch, Wood wrote several pages of a philosophical poem called *Civilization*. As he later explained, "I was full of my lifelong meditations that this is a world distorted by man and founded on injustice, and with little thought of art I expressed my soul."[3] Like so many of Wood's writing projects, *Civilization* was abandoned. But when Sara began organizing his papers, she discovered his notes for *Civilization* and encouraged him to write more.

In the four months it took Wood to write his first draft of *Civilization*, several important developments brought him closer to his dream of financial freedom. In early March, he received word that in two months he would receive the first of two $100,000 payments for his commission on the land grant sale. The initial $200,000 would be just enough to settle his financial obligations.

"I am so rich I can't remember things," he wrote to Sara. "There will still come to me commissions on timber and further land sales of the grant in which the Linthicum estate [his former law partner] has no interest. They are all mine and will be very considerable. . . . I would estimate them as a quarter of a million to fall in within five years."[4] For the first time in his adult life, Wood could look forward to a future free from financial anxiety. Not only would he be out of debt, but he would be in a position to guarantee a substantial sum for his children's security as well as leaving Nannie handsomely provided for. Enough money would remain to secure for himself and Sara a quiet retreat to begin their life together.

Meanwhile, Sara made it clear to Ehrgott that she would stop at nothing to win her freedom. For several weeks, Darrow had been making inquiries on Sara's behalf, seeking out a favorable venue in Nevada, where liberal laws permitted anyone to sue for divorce after establishing a six-month residency. By the end of April he had settled on Goldfield, where the local magistrate, Judge Summers, was a great admirer of Darrow's.[5] That May, Sara left Los Angeles with her daughter Kay to establish legal residence in Goldfield and sue for divorce.

As its name suggests, Goldfield owed its existence to the gold rush. During its days as a boom town in the 1860s, Goldfield boasted a number of saloons and whorehouses: new buildings went up so fast that carpenters earned an exorbitant $12.50 per day. Once the gold veins were depleted, prospectors and businesses quickly abandoned the place. Goldfield was "desolate, forsaken, dying," Sara wrote to her sister Mary. "This town is like a body in which a hot fever once burned, but now the fever is gone, and with it, the vitality. It lies limp and pale and weak, with only here and there the faster beat of a pulse to show there is still life."[6] Sara might well have been describing her own tubercular symptoms.

Sara struggled to keep up her spirits in Goldfield, but she felt overcome by isolation and thoughts of the long struggle ahead. Wood deluged her with a steady flow of letters, telegrams, and parcels, but nothing could alleviate the tedious daily reality of her exile.

Sara's life in Goldfield fed Wood's vision of the great desert as a bulwark of liberty. After all, was it not "civilization," with its unjust application of law and religion, its feudal notion of people as property, that had driven Sara into the Nevada desert? And was it not in that very desert that she hoped to reclaim her freedom? Just after Sara departed for Nevada, Wood jotted in his journal: "Write S. who goes to Goldfield in search of her lost soul."[7] Seen in this light, Sara's undertaking is not unlike the Poet's quest in Wood's poem.

On June 8th, Wood had finished a draft of his poem. To Sara he wrote: "Burst the bombshell, fire the gun, / Civilization is done! done! done!!!"

Civilization begins with a "Poet," alone in the infinite desert solitude:

> I have entered into the desolate places of the Earth.
> I have come into the bare and solemn Desert;
> The stricken and defiant land which fears not God.
> The Desert is athirst as my soul is athirst.
> We are athirst for the waters which make beautiful the path.
> . . . .
> Nature spreads her garment, beautiful beyond estimation.
> She embroiders continually her mantle
> But Man spreads poverty, and out of poverty
> Cometh all crime; all degradation; all ugliness.
> . . . .
> . . . I will lie like a mourner
> Upon a bare and barren bosom of the great Mother
> And I will chant a dirge unto Civilization.[8]

These bombastic lines set the tone for what follows. The Poet is joined by Truth who, conveniently, turns out to be a righteous anarchist:

> Forever there have been the poor.
> Because forever there have been the enforced laws.
> The Laws make rich the ones who make the Laws,
> And these made rich do make the Laws.
> . . . .
> Abolish Privilege and ye abolish Poverty.
> The State is a dragon whose breath is Force,
> Whose claws are Soldiers and Police.
> It robs the Weak and serves the Strong;
> It chokes the brave.
> The wise.
> It hates the voice of Liberty.[9]

The Poet and Truth carry on their exchange about the fallen state of America through twenty-six sections, just over one hundred pages, addressing one another in free verse that falls somewhere between the rich cadences of the King James Bible and the fixed line of regular blank verse. In their lengthy dialogue the Poet and Truth cover all the issues that preoccupied Wood in his public and private life. At one point Truth declaims: "Nature hath named Love holy, / But man hath named his mumbled marriage / Holier than Love. / Lies! Lies! Everywhere lies!"

In response, the Poet admits his own participation in society's charade: "And I have consented. / In degrading ye, I have degraded myself." To which Truth replies: "And whoever consents to the Things that Are / Is guilty."

In this exchange Wood expressed the underlying ambivalence of his own life. He criticized the status quo: party politics, economic interests, the hypocrisy of marriage, and the voices of public morality. Yet in both his career and in his struggling marriage he had given tacit consent to "the Things that Are."

Civilization was Wood's attempt to write the "world poem" Sara had urged him to write. It embodied his wish to withdraw from the turmoil of life, to pursue poetry, to bring his life in harmony with truth—and with Sara. But for all his excitement, Wood suspected that Sara might be displeased. He warned her that his poem had "lost the free impromptu style and character of the first writing in the desert, the words hot from the mind." He added that there was a great deal of repetition "of man's oppressions and the anarchistic counter-thought" in order to strengthen the proselytizing effect of his argument.[10] Wood was right on both counts. He was wrong, however, in his hope that by pointing out these features he might turn *Civilization*'s liabilities into assets.

Noble concepts and good intentions are insufficient in themselves to produce a work of art. The greatest flaw in Wood's poem is the language itself. His reliance on archaic idioms like "ye," "hath," "cometh," "skyey," and "brethren" (presumably to give his diction resonance and a tone of moral gravity) is in marked contrast to the direct, vernacular eloquence of Whitman's *Leaves of Grass*. Regrettably, Wood was blind to this glaring fault. He admired Whitman's remarkable poem; yet in setting forth his anarchist vision, Wood chose a poetic language that was, in its way, reactionary. Years before, on his visit to Mexico, he had admired the "thick block-like houses" that illustrated "the fitness of a country's natural styles to the country itself."[11] Yet Wood's poem is constructed in a language which is wholly unnatural, utterly alien to the country of which he writes.

For all his deep sympathy for human suffering, Wood's poem is unaffecting except for isolated passages. There is no poetic stance more likely to fail than that of the bardic observer, the epic singer, declaiming the life of his people. Vision, voice, and character must all come together or the great song is likely to fall flat. Wood undertook *Civilization* with a compelling vision of how government and social institutions betray both man and nature, but his Poet's observations are too abstract and philosophical. His outrage is stagy, an anemic simulation of biblical prophecy. Just seven years later, Ezra Pound would describe a failed poet, Hugh Selwyn Mauberly, with lines that address Wood's flawed project with uncanny accuracy:

> He strove to resuscitate the dead art
> Of poetry; to maintain "the sublime"
> In the old sense. Wrong from the start—

The excesses of Wood's grandiloquent Poet are not unlike those habits of mind that the journalist Herbert Croly attributed to President Wilson in an acid essay describing his "other-worldliness:"

> [He] seems to be one of those people who shuffle off their mortal coil as soon as they take pen in hand. They become tremendously noble. They write as monuments of great men might write. They write only upon brass, and for nothing shorter than a millennium. They utter nothing which might sound trivial at the Last Judgment, or embarrass them in the most august company.
>
> [He makes] even the most concrete things seem like abstractions. . . . His mind is like a light which destroys the outlines of what it plays upon; there is much illumination, but you see very little.[12]

In time, Sara drove most of these criticisms home. Wood listened, resisted, yielded, revised, changed the title to *The Poet in the Desert*,

and revised it all again. But *Civilization*'s few virtues were overshad-
owed by its glaring shortcomings.

As a writer, Wood's greatest potential lay in his complex encounter
with America. There is nothing he set down in his poem that might
not have been more compellingly presented through the specific
experiences of his autobiography. But Wood was less interested in
the "prose" of his past than in the "poetry" of visionary philosophical
reflection—a vision that included his longing for Sara and their
dream of creative retreat. Not even Sara, with her clear understanding
of Wood's shortcomings as a poet, had the heart to persist in enumerat-
ing the errors that weakened *Civilization* at its very core.

26. A Day in Paradise

Wood had barely completed his poem when he was drawn back into the system of wealth and privilege he had just condemned. "The infernal Land Grant is in a snarl again," he told Sara. Davidson and his backers in St. Paul were threatening to exercise their legal right to pull out of the contract unless Altschul extended their payment period to 1921, a concession Altschul refused to make.[1] If he failed to get the two parties to reach an agreement, Wood stood to lose $750,000 in commission fees. In mid-June, he hurried East to try to save his fortune.

Wood arrived in New York on June 20, accompanied by Bill Hanley. Hanley, who'd been friends with Davidson for many years, had been instrumental in bringing him into the land grant deal. Now, Wood counted on Hanley to keep Davidson at the bargaining table when things got rough. This would allow Wood to work on Altschul and make the case that, in spite of Davidson's annoying demands, it was in Altschul's interest to humor him.

Negotiations quickly came to a standstill. Davidson rejected Altschul's offers and returned to St. Paul to confer with James J. Hill. Wood hurried off to Washington for a series of hasty meetings with Secretary of State William Jennings Bryan and other high officials in the Wilson administration. If he could persuade them to back irrigation projects in eastern Oregon, this would spur land development which, in turn, would sway Davidson to hold onto his land-grant purchase.

Wood went on to St. Paul to confer with Hill. Then he returned to Washington to consult again with Bryan, Secretary of the Treasury

W. G. McAdoo, and Secretary of the Interior F. K. Lane. The pace of negotiations grew frantic. In New York, Altschul remained obdurate, forcing Wood to hurry back to St. Paul on a second visit to thrash out a new proposition with Davidson and Hill's son, Louis. After a day in St. Paul, Wood was back on the Twentieth Century for New York and a visit to Henderson House, the family estate of Douglas Robinson, Corinne Roosevelt's husband.[2]

"I sit in the seats of the mighty," he reported to Sara, "and motor in their cars and ride their horses. I am so cared for I am unhappy. I have lost control over my shoes and clothes. They are taken from me by stealth by a valet who does not speak English and who returns them when *he* thinks a gentleman ought to rise and then hangs 'round to dress me, helps me into my trousers as if I were a paralytic and disturbs my modesty."[3] Wood's days with the Robinsons were a far cry from his ringing denunciation of wealth in *Civilization*.

> I have eaten at the tables of the rich,
> And I have dwelt with them in their palaces.
> Their palaces are of marble, and of bronze,
> The hearts of the prosperous are hard
> With the hardness of those who say It is the will of God.
> Though they have neither created, nor earned,
> They are sure that their wealth is the
> Award of God, and is just.[4]

"These are not the 'idle rich'," he assured Sara. As evidence, he recounted how Corinne castigated Jack Astor, who had just perished in the *Titanic* disaster, as "the basest of men" who had "not the slightest sense of his great stewardship—no sympathy with the poor and as arrogantly assuming his wealth was *his*."[5] In Wood's eyes, *his* rich friends were largely exempt from criticism because they accepted the great social responsibility that came with great wealth. Perhaps they did, but "stewardship" is a far cry from anarchism.[6]

In late August, Altschul finally consented to Davidson's proposal. With business out of the way, Wood shook himself loose from his circle of bankers and bluebloods to host a dinner at the Hotel Astor for Max Eastman, John Sloan, Art Young, and assorted staff members of their radical magazine, the *Masses*.

This was Wood's first meeting with Eastman and his associates, but their magazine was well-known to him, and he was known to them. John Reed, a leading contributor to the *Masses*, had attended Portland Academy with Wood's sons. He admired Wood and corresponded with him while he was at Harvard. But it was Mary, Sara's sister, who engineered the gathering. She had been friends with Ida Rauh, Eastman's wife, since 1909 when they shared a flat in Greenwich Village. Mary sent a note to Eastman telling him that Wood was a kindred spirit: she encouraged the two men to seek one another out.

The story of the *Masses* has been told often and well by Eastman, Art Young, Rebecca Zurier, and others. Six months before Wood's meeting with Eastman and his friends, John Reed and Eastman published the new magazine's statement of purpose:

This magazine is owned and published co-operatively by its editors. It has no dividends to pay, and nobody is trying to make any money out of it. A revolutionary and not a reform magazine; a magazine with a sense of humor and no respect for the respectable; frank, arrogant, impertinent, searching for the true causes; a magazine directed against rigidity and dogma wherever it is found; printing what is too naked or true for a money-making press; a magazine whose final policy is to do what it pleases and conciliate nobody, not even its readers.

Wood felt an instant affinity with Eastman. He admired the lively anarchistic spirit with which Eastman and his associates ran their magazine—or tried to. With its constant financial crises, its heated intramural political squabbles, and its head-on collision with government censors, the *Masses* sometimes seemed more involved in its struggle to survive than in the class struggle it hoped to encourage. Nevertheless, the *Masses* deserved its legendary status—not simply for its radical politics (some contributors had little to do with its radical agenda), but for its innovative layout and the high quality of its writing and its art. Carl Sandburg, Sherwood Anderson, Djuna Barnes, Mabel Dodge, Vachel Lindsay, Amy Lowell, William Carlos Williams, Romain Rolland, Bertrand Russell, and Maxim Gorky all published in the *Masses*. John Sloan, George Bellows, Stuart Davis, and Art Young contributed illustrations and political cartoons that are as notable for their execution as for their frequent indignation.

Wood's dinner with Eastman established personal ties that provided an important outlet for his writing. After their meeting there was nothing to keep him in New York. With his land grant commission secure, he hurried home.

Wood promised Sara he was preparing to live his own life, but apprehension about hurting Nannie stopped him dead in his tracks. "I have thought deeply and much on the problem," he wrote, "and one thing still bothers me—how bold and open ought I to be . . . or how tactful and secretive to spare Mrs. Wood suffering. Of course cowardice chooses the life of least resistance, and says be tactful, and the difficulty is to find out is it cowardice or good judgment dictates the course?"[7] It would be wise, Wood reasoned, for Sara to settle into a house near San Francisco, where he could visit under the pretext of collaborating on artistic projects. For the time being, Wood preferred gentle lies to the "premature cruelty" of telling Nannie his real intentions.

Sara recognized that Wood's behavior stemmed from "the claims of many affections," his deep-rooted need to please those who loved him, even when his efforts left him at cross-purposes likely to satisfy no one. "The pity," Sara realized, "is that, all unconsciously, you are misleading her by your silence and by your actions, by no attempt at getting to an understanding of your real life-purpose."[8] The issues Sara raised were deeply fixed in Wood's nature, especially his habit of drawing women into his life—then allowing himself to be manipulated by the anguish he kindled.

Sara sensed, meanwhile, that Wood was becoming romantically involved with Frances Burke, a talented pianist and longtime friend. Wood denied it emphatically: he assured her that there were enough claims to his affections without adding Mrs. Burke. Why did Sara work herself up over nothing? "It is all absurd," he told her. "We'll not take time over it."[9]

Soon Helen Corbett was making jealous overtures to win Wood's attention—or at least to make him pay, literally, for their long affair. A stunning set of reversals had left her bankrupt. She asked Wood for three thousand dollars, reminding him of the lavish gifts she had pressed on him in years past.[10]

Wood found it difficult to acknowledge that there might be some-

thing in his own conduct that drew him into these jams. But Sara
knew that, even when he was not consciously flirting, Wood invited
women's attention, which he received all too readily. His generous
nature and reflexive sympathy inspired affection and a certain romantic daring in women. But as Nannie and Kitty already knew, and as
Sara was rapidly learning, his habit of returning the tenderness he
invited often led to situations that hurt the women who loved him.
Wood found it nearly impossible to understand this. He wanted to
please, to protect, to provide, to ameliorate suffering—but his emotional entanglements put him at odds with his intentions.

Back in July, in one of his letters to Sara, Wood rehearsed what
he planned to write Corinne Roosevelt Robinson about free love. He
would tell her that he and Sara had found "the universe in each
other. . . . Body, soul, mind—all satisfied by each to each. . . . The
great boon of freedom will be to banish lying, hypocrisy, jealousy,
and murder for love—and teaching couples to plunge madly into the
mad joy, knowing if it should pass they can part loving friends saying,
'We have had each other for a day in Paradise'."[11] But how was Wood
to possess his vision if he could not tell Nannie that—body, soul,
and mind—he was Sara's? How could he ever expect to enjoy "the
great boon of freedom" if he devoted himself to futile efforts to soothe
Nannie's sorrow? Did he imagine he could banish lying and hypocrisy
through half-truths and vacillation? Could he secure his freedom
through an irresolute rebellion that prolonged the very anguish he
longed to prevent? He yearned for "a day in paradise," but he
remained encumbered by the emotional ties of a lifetime. He knew
what he needed to do to unsnarl his life; similarly, he recognized
the rightness of Sara's cogent criticism of his poetry. Yet he held
back. As he told her, "my mind agrees but my soul rebels."[12]

27. The Old Man of the Sea

The outcome of Sara's divorce case was never really in doubt. Judge Summers, the magistrate who would hear the case, admired her principle and integrity. He assured her that she could depend on receiving a favorable decision from his court.[1] Nevertheless, Ehrgott's determined efforts to reclaim her left Sara anxious, exhausted, "bowed down with grief" for the suffering she had caused. "I do wish we could get rid of this nightmare," Wood wrote to her. "[Ehrgott] is an Old Man of the Sea who rides on my neck too."[2]

In February of 1914, Wood had *Civilization* printed in a small private edition; but Sara still urged him to make sweeping eliminations. Yet, in spite of repeated revisions, Wood never realized his dream of a revolutionary poetic masterpiece—a visionary poem that even the common reader might appreciate. In a sense, he wanted to reinvent Whitman's *Leaves of Grass* for his own didactic purposes. But as Whitman remarked in the closing paragraph of his preface to *Leaves of Grass*, "poems distilled from other poems will probably pass away."

Meanwhile, Sara found a new ally in her divorce case. At the Goldfield Hotel, she ran into an influential young lawyer who knew of her work in the Oregon suffrage campaign. When he learned that her divorce case was dragging, he intervened on her behalf and worked out an agreement with Ehrgott whereby Ehrgott would have custody of the children and Sara would have unrestricted rights of visitation as well as regular visits from them. Finally, in March the court issued a decree in favor of divorce.

Sara had suffered illness, loneliness, and wrenching guilt in order to win her right to begin a new life with Wood, but the relief she felt at clearing away all these obstacles was short-lived. In spite of the land grant sale, Wood remained mired in his Portland life. And now that Ehrgott had lost his capacity to govern Sara's life, Wood could no longer locate the cause of his unhappiness in an obstinate rival.

Wood had only himself to blame, yet the origin of his dilemma can be found in his distant past. In a sense, Wood intuited the source of his problem in his letter to Sara, when he compared the Reverend Ehrgott to the Old Man of the Sea. Wood's allusion is to one of the best-known adventures of Sinbad the Sailor: an old man persuades Sinbad to carry him on his shoulders; then he locks his legs around Sinbad, holding the young hero captive until he devises a way to dislodge the old man. Wood chose to imagine the Reverend Ehrgott tenaciously clutching him like the old man in the tale, but surely the first and most inflexible old man of the sea in Wood's life was his seafaring father. All through Wood's youth, William Maxwell Wood had ridden him with severe moral instruction followed by hectoring letters to West Point. Wood claimed that he threw off his father after he graduated from West Point and headed West; but William Maxwell Wood's hold on his son was tighter than he ever realized. The troubles that still vexed Wood were proof of his father's influence: he carried the old man with him through life. Like his father, Wood indulged himself on fine things. Good food, rare books, fine clothing and accessories, a beautiful home with handsome furnishings and valuable art—all this he regarded as his by birthright, whether he could afford it or not. He lived way beyond his means, and, like his father, when debts mounted he attributed his predicament to uncontrollable external forces. Now Sara was free, telling him "I am all yours." But like his father, he was saddled with financial obligations of his own creation.

After her divorce decree came through, Sara moved to San Francisco and rented a flat at 1623 Lake Street, where she began a life of her own. After months of separation, she was thrilled to see her son, Albert, again. More than anything, she looked forward to being with Wood. Wood planned to come to San Francisco in early April and spend several weeks with her. Then at the last minute he wired Sara to tell her Nannie insisted on traveling with him.

During the three weeks he spent in San Francisco, Wood saw Sara several times a week but always with the distracting awareness that he must attend to Nannie. Wood explained to Sara that there was no reason to tell Nannie the full truth until he had the money to make his break. But Sara turned his excuses back on him. If money problems were what kept him in Portland, then why did he continue to live so indulgently? "The reform lies with me," he said. But that reform never came. Instead, he placed his hope in the dream that had brought so many people West: that the land itself would release its bounty, providing him with wealth, freedom, and happiness. "If only Eastern Oregon Lands would move," he told Sara, "I'd blossom out rich."[3]

Sara saw how thoroughly tangled Wood had become in his muddled personal affairs. It depressed her terribly, a reaction that further undermined her health. She was "morbidly self-depreciative," Wood told her; her failure to take better care of herself threatened *his* future happiness. Sara would have none of it. The greatest danger to her spirit and her physical well-being, she replied, was his behavior. Sara challenged Wood's habits of a lifetime. She insisted that he acknowledge his own nature, that he truly see himself in order to overturn the hypocritical patterns that were the real cause of his captivity. It was more than Wood could handle. He disavowed Sara's criticism, but he could not quite dismiss it from his thoughts. She was right—right about his lack of honesty, right about his lack of constancy—and certainly she was right about the wearying effect this had on her spirit. He responded, as he did so often in similar situations, with enthusiastic assurances that he was turning over a new leaf. "I have discovered my love for you, my real need of you," he told Sara, "and I am willing to do anything; for hard and cold in my heart is the sense of justice. *I*, too, have a right to live my own life."[4] Wood told Sara what he felt, what he wished for. But when it came time to act upon his bold resolutions, they proved to be passionate fictions.

When Emma Goldman passed through San Francisco on a speaking tour, Sara was invited to her birthday party. Like Wood, Sara admired Goldman's fervent love of justice, her courage and the vital force of

William Maxwell Wood,
Fleet Surgeon, c. 1845.
This item is reproduced
by permission of The
Huntington Library, San
Marino, California.

Second Lieutenant Wood,
c. 1875. Reproduced by
permission of The Hun-
tington Library.

Chief Joseph of the Nez Perce,
November 1877. Photograph by
F. Jay Haynes. (Original photo-
graph probably by O. S. Goff.)
Courtesy of Haynes Foundation
Collection, Montana Historical
Society.

Nanny Moale Smith Wood, c.
1880. Reproduced by permission of The Huntington Library.

An attorney of proven mettle,"
c. 1890. Courtesy of Oregon
Historical Society (OrHi
50232).

With his mien of dandiacal
finesse," c. 1900. Reproduced
by permission of The Hun-
tington Library.

"Literarily Yours—Sara Bard Field Ehrgott," c. 1912.
Reproduced by permission of The Huntington Library.

Emma Goldman, 1906.
Courtesy of Chicago His-
torical Society (DN-3882).

Clarence Darrow, 1912.
Courtesy of Herald Exam-
iner Collection, Los Angeles Public Library.

"A youthful old man,"
1920. Photograph by Will-
iam S. Dassonville. Cour-
tesy of Oregon Historical
Society (OrHi 021696)

Sara, c. 1925. Reproduced
by permission of The Hun-
tington Library.

Fiesole, 1924. Left to right: Lincoln Steffens, Ella "Peter" Winter, Wood,
Sara. Reproduced by permission of The Huntington Library.

"Zeus as bohemian guru"—Wood at The Cats, c. 1936.
Reproduced by permission of The Huntington Library.

"A living link to . . . the Old West," c. 1936. Courtesy of Oregon
Historical Society (OrHi 35936).

her character, but she was put off by the rancorous revolutionary talk that surrounded her. "Such a weird looking group. Such talk! Such smoke! Such drinking. . . . There was the same discussion of isms. . . . Futile, useless themes!"[5] Emma's uneven learning, her high-strung arguments, and her contempt for anything that hinted of genteel behavior rubbed Sara the wrong way. Emma was capable of brilliant flashes of insight, but Sara questioned whether she had the steady fire of penetrating intellectual analysis. In Sara's eyes, Goldman was effective in arousing indignation and demands for change, but she had little impact in overturning the conditions she criticized. Sara found greater merit in the suffrage movement, where women engaged in practical political action.

A month later, Emma Goldman arrived in Portland to deliver a series of lectures. As usual, she showed up with no money. She counted on Wood to look after her, to pay the advance on her hall rental, to pay for advertising flyers, and to use his influence to publicize her talks. Emma *expected* Wood's indulgence. Wood understood. Though she sometimes irritated him, he continued to support her with affectionate loyalty and bemused forbearance.

On July 21, she spoke to a large audience at the Central Library on "Intellectual Proletarians."[6] "She had some satirical words for the Intellectual Proletarians," Wood wrote, "who like Mrs. Belmont furnished bail to striking girls, Jack London who stood in a bread line to get 'copy'—the rich intellectuals who furnished champagne when the right to earn bread was in question, who in good clothes drove in autos to be dilettantes in the field, and drove back to their comfortable Fifth Avenue homes. When (I forget whom she said) had said if you are going into the revolution put [on] old clothes they will surely be torn."

Wood was delighted by Emma's "dauntless uncompromising spirit" even when she aimed her barbs directly at him. Later in her speech she encouraged her audience to subscribe to her magazine, *Mother Earth.* "Mr. Wood is a contributor," she told them, "—*sometimes* not as often as I would like. I suppose he finds himself too *busy*." She placed a subtle shade of emphasis on "too busy." Wood could not fail to get her point: Goldman was including him among the elite intellectual proletarians who were "too busy with their moneymaking, and their respectability, and comforts, and the friendship of their swell friends."[7]

Emma's moral stature made Wood tolerant of her criticism. But she was an exception. In March, Sara had written to him from San Francisco of a young radical who charged Wood with dilettantism. The criticism was, in essence, no different than Emma Goldman's, but Wood conceded nothing:

> Most people casually glance at two patent facts. He has a big law practice and wealthy clients. His protestations of anarchy if taken seriously would deprive him of this support—ergo, he is merely a joke, and in a practical sense they are right. Lots of my clients who continue with me in spite of my verbal utterances would desert me if I went down into the procession and incited riot. There is no doubt they refuse to take me seriously, and there is no doubt the way to make them take me seriously would be to hurt them in their idolatry of property. They do not fear my "mere theories."
>
> But my conduct is deliberate. There are enough in the ranks suffering and serving. I cannot see that I would add anything to the cause of being one more to be harried contemptuously from jail to jail. . . .
>
> It is true I have eaten better, slept better and generally lived better than if in jail or on a braketeam . . . but there are so many of these reformers who . . . have criticized me who are really parasites themselves on such as I who keep our jobs to give them their sustenance.
>
> No, No, every movement has to have its more or less temporizing or wily supporters. From Christ down, no rebellion has been able to do without its "respectable" and "wealthy" sympathizers. No one can say I ever kept my mouth shut when it should have spoken or ever denied the truth.[8]

In his rebuttal to the charge of dilettantism Wood depicted himself as a kind of anarchist Robin Hood—earning from the rich to support revolutionary change; mingling with the elite in order to bring his subversive message to a respectable audience with little patience for professional radicals. In reality, he demonstrated a kind of oscillating integrity that permitted him to sustain his dual commitments. He was not a hypocrite; he was not a dilettante; even Emma Goldman's more accurate conceit of "intellectual proletarian" does not quite account for Wood's ambivalence. Forty years before, young Wood had tried to overturn his father's expectations and leap recklessly into life. That wish had been thwarted by William Maxwell Wood's sharp call "to abandon all feverish and restless desire after change with all its probabilities of disappointment" and to apply himself to "the claims and obligations of the present around you—and of the place and position to which you are called."[9] Wood submitted to his father's will, yet he never relinquished what William Maxwell Wood saw as a "feverish and restless desire after change." Those contending forces captured Wood as surely as the Old Man of the Sea clutched Sinbad in his vise-like grip. Wood took pride in his achievements. He could make a case in his own behalf, and he often did, but he could not make peace with himself.

28. The Portland Experiment

In August 1914, Wood broke away from Portland to join Sara at Corte Madera in Marin County where, for two weeks, they stayed in a hilltop cabin, living out their dream of sharing an idyllic refuge, a day in Paradise. It was probably during this visit that Wood tossed off a brief satiric sketch ridiculing the spectacle of Christian nations piously preparing for the slaughter of World War I. "A Heavenly Dialogue" begins with God looking down upon Europe on the brink of war and exclaiming, "Jesus, those little animals of yours seem to be mad. They are running about in circles."

Taken aback by God's detachment, Jesus asks, "Father, don't you take any interest in men?"

"Not the least," God replies, "that is one of their superstitions."

And so it goes. When belligerent nations send their appeals heavenward, Jesus cries, "Look out, Father. Here comes a prayer."

Before long, God tells Jesus he must face the fact that he is a "perfect failure":

For two thousand years you have preached brotherly love and there has never been a day of it. Not a day.

For two thousand years you have taught that color of the skin and nationality are nothing but that all men are brethren, and there has never been an hour of it. Not an hour.

For two thousand years you have declared, "Blessed are the meek. Blessed are the peacemakers," and have promised "Peace on earth. Good will to men." There has never been a minute of it. Not a minute. Look down there now. You know what is going to happen. See the poor common people. See the oppressed. See the whole wretched squirming mass of poverty stricken puppets, patient, obedient, suffering. They have piled up the strength of war by their labor and their bodies are the sacrifice to battle. They carry their gilded oppressors on their backs. They work for them in peace and now they are going to die for them. . . . All the time your temples will be hypocritically snarling of peace and brotherhood and love. I shall be made sick with stale incense. Prayers will arise from each ant hill asking that I help it to devour the others. Then, indeed, will come peace—the peace of exhaustion; the peace of the charnel house. The workers will take up their dreary round more stooped than ever. No my Son, your experiment of two thousand years has been rather a failure.[1]

Almost twenty-five years before, Wood had shared a moment of disenchantment with "dear old Drakey"—Alexander Drake, art director at *Century Monthly.* "Damn the world," Wood wrote, "the times are out of joint, and when we die all ends. I wish I could sit on a cloud and contemplate the world's progress and gradual death, forever."[2] This is precisely the role of Wood's cantankerous God. The times are out of joint, and the world has earned the contempt of its creator who sits on a cloud from which he offers blasphemous commentary on the damned human race.

Wood's piece owes something to Mark Twain's last published work, "Captain Stormfield's Visit to Heaven," sections of which appeared in *Harper's Magazine* in 1908. Like Wood, Twain created an agnostic's heaven in order to criticize human folly, but Twain's piece is little more than an unfinished anecdotal yarn. Wood's satire is more pointed, more philosophical, more provocative—and funnier. What the two works share is the same debunking spirit, the same principle of divine common sense scoring repeatedly against the twisted, often dangerous, constructions of contemporary American life.

Sara sent Wood's "Heavenly Dialogue" to Max Eastman, who published it in the October number of the *Masses.* At first, Wood seems to have had no intention of writing a sequel; but over the next three years he wrote six more pieces for the *Masses* under the running title "Heavenly Discourse." (A seventh appeared under its own title: "Billy Sunday in Heaven.")

Wood's God marvels at man's vain assumption that he is uniquely sanctioned by his Creator. The human race is an experiment run amok; God has little impulse to tinker with it, let alone to "redeem" it. Still, it's the only game in town. Wood's God cannot help but inject a note of indignation into the folly He witnesses. He even convenes occasional colloquies that pit sensible rebels against representatives of the gang who have made such a mess of things: prominent spokesmen for religious orthodoxy, imperialism, puritanism, and censorship.

Wood did not regard his satiric improvisations as anything special. "It is not literature," he wrote years later, "but it is, I think, propaganda. Of course like all propaganda it is not read by those hostile, but it somehow gives the already converted courage and spreads the doctrines."[3] Wood's evaluation is accurate, yet in retrospect it appears too modest. Back in 1914, he could never, in his wildest dreams, have imagined the improbable outcome of his project. In 1927 his "Heavenly Discourse" pieces were published as a book and sold an astonishing 75,000 copies!

Quite by chance, Wood was writing a bestseller.

Buoyed by his days with Sara, Wood returned to Portland to speak before the Industrial Relations Commission, a panel created by President Wilson to investigate the causes of antagonism between labor and management. With Frank P. Walsh, an aggressive reformer, serving as the commission chairman, radical organizers envisioned the Industrial Relations hearings as a rare opportunity to attract public attention to their views. With great zest Wood attacked the legally sanctioned system of land monopolies that permitted four railroad companies to dominate the nation's economy through its ownership of the anthracite coal fields. Title to land and valuable resources should depend on beneficial use, Wood argued, not on concentrated wealth. It was no wonder that labor rebelled at such conditions. Wood admitted that he did not approve of closed shops and pressures against internal dissent—labor's own infringements on personal liberty—but these evils, he pointed out, were made necessary by the greater evil of the unions of capital. "Capital rests on law-granted monopolies," he explained, "draining from labor its share of its own product. . . . Capital wants all these false monopolies but wants Labor, the other factor in the production of wealth, to be wholly unprotected in cutthroat competition. . . . [It wants] no limit to the production of labor . . . but a monopolistic limit to the opportunities for labor."[4] When asked if he was a single-taxer or a socialist, Wood replied that he was neither—that he would "get into any conveyance that I found going my way."

When asked if he could suggest laws that would remedy the situation, Wood replied that he did not believe in laws. "I am an Anarchist!" he said to loud applause and scattered laughter. "I want to atrophy the State, minimize it and make all effort depend on voluntary, not enforced, co-operation."

"Do you think it can be made to work?" he was asked.

Wood challenged the committee to tell him if Christianity had ever been "made to work." After all, he explained, "Christ really was an anarchist" who believed that "no man shall by force control the life of a peaceable man."[5]

Wood presented a formidable public persona—cultivated, eloquent, and brazenly self-assured—yet in his dealings with Sara he still failed to bring words and feelings in line with his behavior. Back in San Francisco, Sara had challenged Wood to tell her the complete truth about his supposedly innocent friendship with Frances Burke. There was nothing to it, he maintained. Sara understood Wood's loneliness, his need to be loved, the way he doted on women's affection. But no explanation could remove her apprehensions. "There remains the horrid tendency," she told him, "to discount what you say, by what has passed between us."[6]

All this made Sara exceedingly suspicious of his resolutions to break free of Portland. Wood conceded her point, but he insisted that it was impossible for him to close his Portland business in the immediate future. Their only way to be together, he explained, was for Sara to come to Portland. He knew their life would be complicated by Nannie and his family and by the hard scrutiny of Portland society, but he preferred a half-life with Sara to nothing at all.

It was a wrenching time for both, further complicated by Bill Hanley's decision to mount a campaign for U.S. senator. Hanley knew, or believed he knew, what programs were good for Oregon's future; but he understood little about practical politics. As was his way, Hanley abruptly made up his mind and lurched into action. He told Wood he was running and insisted that he manage his campaign. Wood agreed. To Sara he complained that he had no choice, that loyalty forced him to stand by his friend. But surely there were other considerations as well. With Hanley in Washington the possibilities of gaining government aid to irrigate eastern Oregon would be greatly improved—and with it, the chance to turn a handsome profit on his own land holdings.

Whatever Wood's excuses, Sara was fed up. When the opportunity arose for her to assist Anne Martin and the Nevada Equal Franchise Society in their campaign for a state suffrage amendment, she promptly signed on.

Wood worried that Sara's rigorous campaign schedule might undermine her health; he felt panicky at the thought of losing her. Ignoring his objections, she threw herself into the campaign. In small towns like Fallon and Hazen, Sara addressed raucous crowds that taunted her with catcalls. More often than not, she prevailed. As the Nevada campaign continued, she began to realize that the ailments that had plagued her since meeting Wood were exacerbated by the rest cures prescribed by Wood and the various physicians who backed him up. Isolation and passivity only intensified her physical and mental duress, whereas her active work on behalf of women's freedom made her feel alive and whole.[7] What made Sara's speeches so effective was her instinctive ability to infuse the issue of women's rights with the emotional intensity of her own struggle.

Anne Martin was not the only suffrage leader who recognized Sara's gift. Mabel Vernon, an organizer for the newly formed Congressional Union, was also struck by Sara's galvanizing impact as a public speaker. The Congressional Union, led by Alice Paul, was driven by a bold plan: rather than fighting for woman suffrage amendments state by state—the current strategy in the western states—they set their sights on a federal amendment (the so-called "Susan B. Anthony Amendment") that would guarantee universal suffrage once and for all.[8] Mabel Vernon, who had been close to Alice Paul since their college days at Swarthmore, brought Sara to the attention of the national committee: before the Nevada campaign ended, Sara was invited to come East as a salaried organizer for the Congressional Union. For Sara, the thought of supporting herself made the offer particularly attractive. "I know you never take me seriously," she told Wood, "but I am growing more earnest about the idea of getting a position which would pay enough to let you give yourself up to literature. If you can look after the provision for Mrs. Wood, I truly believe I am going to be capable of making an income for you and me."[9]

Sara's offer confounded Wood. Here she was, physically fragile and absolutely impoverished, offering to support him! He could not bear the thought of Sara putting an entire continent between them. He begged her to abandon her outlandish plan and to come to Portland where he could take care of her.

Wood's campaign work proved far less fruitful than Sara's. On Election Day, the voters of Nevada supported the suffrage amendment, while in Oregon Hanley received less than 11 percent of the vote and finished a weak third to George Chamberlain, the Democratic candidate.

With the campaign out of the way, Wood renewed pressure on Sara to join him in Portland. But to Sara the "Portland Experiment," as she called it, was doomed. She refused to come until he told Nannie and Frances Burke that he loved her and planned to live with her. If he failed to do this, Sara warned, he would only add to the unhappiness of those he loved. Wood promised Sara that he would be truthful, no matter how much it hurt, yet he still doubted whether he could overcome the habits of a lifetime. "I never as a boy could stand sorrow in others," he wrote, "and lied then to try and comfort them. When a woman breaks down, breaks through all the long hard conventions, and throws herself wretched and heartbroken upon me and sobs—O pity me, pity me, I love you so—I just can't help soothing her and kissing her and telling her I love her."[10]

Wood finally managed to tell Frances Burke that he loved Sara. A few days later, he forced himself to speak with Nannie. He told her that his friendship with Sara was based on understanding, congenial temperament, and Sara's ability to stimulate his poetic production. But there were things Wood could not bring himself to say. "I am too old for the sex question to come in," he told Nannie. He told her that he loved Sara as he loved his daughter Lisa—not quite the same as saying that he was her lover.

Wood was heartened by his performance. "No growth without breaking and bursting," he wrote Sara, "no birth without pain. I know

I am right to live my life. I know I am right to stand by truth."[11] He reserved a room for her at the Multonomah Hotel: she booked passage on a steamer, and for the next two months they were together in Portland.

Neither Wood nor Sara left a record of her visit to Portland. There is good reason, however, to suppose that it was tense and unsatisfactory, spoiled by Wood's efforts to juggle his various obligations.

The clearest indication of Sara's lingering doubts about Wood's efforts to extricate himself from Portland came in a letter she wrote to him just after her return to San Francisco. Ruth Draper, the innovative actress, had just arrived in San Francisco to give a series of performances, and Wood asked Sara to look after her and introduce her to their friends. Sara met with Draper once and was put off by how quickly she fell in with the upper echelons of San Francisco society (due in large part to a list of names Wood had given her). "I think she liked me," Sara observed, "and wanted to see more of me but she is a tool in the hands of these rich folk who exploit her talents and ability because of their own mental poverty. It is a shame. I would eat slugs before I'd sell myself, my time, my liberty, my intellectual outreach to a bunch of vapid plutocrats."[12] Given all Wood had put Sara through, it is hard not to see her reaction to Draper as a criticism of Wood as well.

Back in Portland, Jack Matthews, an old friend of Wood's, lay dying in the hospital with cancer. Wood was prompted to reflect: "What a miserably ordered world it is with its death and denials and suffering. Why not a happy life till Pop!—suddenly it is all over." He left the hospital with Kitty and walked up the terraced streets of Portland Heights. It was a dreamy opalescent day, and Wood planted himself beneath an old fir tree to take in the view of the city in which he had lived for close to thirty-five years. "How beautiful it all was," he wrote to Sara, "the city spread before us like a toy for gods, the steam and smoke from their tall chimneys pearly against the lazy blue sky."[13]

More and more, Wood looked upon his life in Portland as he did that day—as something distant, almost make-believe. He wanted to rise above the miserably ordered world, separate himself from its death and denials and suffering, yet he could not turn away from Portland. Whatever joys he and Sara may have shared during the two months of their "Portland Experiment," with Sara gone Wood felt alone and constantly harried, afraid for his future. As he did so often under similar conditions, he sought relief by taking measures that would only complicate his life. He fell in love again.

29. The Golden Bars of Your Cage

Two weeks after Sara returned to San Francisco, she rented the second floor of a house at 1601 Taylor Street, high up on Russian Hill. "The Eyrie," as she called it, was to be her home with Wood. Wood shared her excitement. "When I get there to your arms," he told her, "I don't care what furniture is there except a bed and sheets as poor young peasants begin life."[1] But no peasant ever lived in Wood's style. All that month, he gathered furniture, valuable pottery, oriental rugs, and fine bedding for their home. He could not help but laugh at his conspicuous consumption.

For Wood, it was every bit as important to live beautifully as it was to pursue anarchism and free love. When Ben Reitman, Emma Goldman's lover, spoke in Portland in early May, Wood was put off by Reitman's use of profanity. "To speak offensively like Ben Reitman merely to show your independence is just as anarchistic and considerate and useful as to urinate over your hosts' carpet at the dinner table. . . . [Goldman and Reitman] violate my two points of creed— they are un-anarchistic in its finer sense—uselessly invasive tho' not by force. They are un-aesthetic, unbeautiful."[2]

In Wood's eyes, Reitman's failure, which Emma shared to some degree, was that not only did he attack the status quo, but he also violated its customs and manners—he behaved "improperly." This irritated Wood. An anarchist society made up of people behaving like Reitman would quickly fall into chaos. If coercive institutions were to be dispensed with, it was up to each individual to exercise constant self-restraint in order to avoid being "uselessly invasive"; which is to say, there would be more necessity than ever for good manners and intelligent standards of public speech. The only way an anarchist utopia of the sort Wood envisioned could exist would be if all people acted with exquisite sensitivity to one another— perhaps something like the colony he had hoped to start with Fremont Older: a "country club" of genteel anarchists.[3]

Wood's dedication to aesthetic living was obvious in his revised version of *Civilization: The Poet in the Desert*. In April, the printer, F. W. Baltes, completed production of one thousand copies of Wood's poem: nine hundred printed on commercial stock, the remaining hundred printed on handmade Italian paper. Wood reserved this elegant limited edition for radical acquaintances, old friends, and loyal business associates. Portland's wealthy elite must have marvelled that the man who had served their interests so well could find time to write such a long poem condemning them. There was an obvious incongruity between the poem's theme and the deluxe edition in which he presented it. What had happened to Wood's initial intention to write his poem for the laboring masses? It took Emma Goldman—who admired his poem—to point out that he had made his work inaccessible to the very audience who would have most appreciated it.[4]

If Wood's deluxe edition of *The Poet in the Desert* jarred with the poem's condemnation of wealth, his flurry of indecision about whether or not to distribute his book publicly jarred with the poem's vision of defiant rebellion. Wood worried that if he put his nine hundred copies up for sale he could be prosecuted for obscenity, which would embarrass his law firm and further complicate his financial predicament.[5] Wood found himself stuck in a predicament that young John Reed had posed the year before in a bit of clever doggerel:

> How can an artist create his Utopia
> With his best eye on the World's cornucopia?[6]

Wood finally overcame his qualms. "I begin to feel," he wrote to Sara, "I ought to launch the ship and let the resulting splash shower where it might."[7]

In the spring of 1915, Wood placed himself under the care of Dr. Constance Janina Klecan, a specialist in immunology who believed she could alleviate his painful rheumatism through a series of vaccine injections. Though she was a gifted physician, her personal life was in disarray. A marriage in Poland ended so badly that she rarely mentioned it. She immigrated to Portland in 1912 and soon afterwards entered into an intermittent affair with a doctor whom she did not really love. She was intelligent, outspoken, and sympathetic—all qualities Wood admired. She was also lonely and intense: in spite of her apparent self-sufficiency, she was immensely needy—a quality that Wood found irresistible. When Sara met her, she sensed immediately that Janina was likely to appeal to Wood.

Wood welcomed the opportunity to show Sara how he had grown. "I've told her how bright you are," he wrote Sara, "how sympathetic we are, how I miss you, how we work together and that I love you. . . . If it comes ever to a situation to be faced, I shall tell her so frankly, so sincerely, the whole truth and that never never could it be possible for me to love her, or anyone but you."[8]

Having eliminated any chance for misunderstanding, Wood felt free to offer himself to Janina as a sympathetic friend. Janina reciprocated, telling Wood that she felt great affection for him but that she had no interest in sex and all the discord it brings.[9] Wood shared all this with Sara, determined to show her he had nothing to hide. "You don't need to have sex," Sara observed, "to have a love affair with this woman."

Sara reacted as she did so often when her chances for a life with Wood seemed to recede: she gave herself over to woman suffrage. Soon she was working as a "hostess" at the Congressional Union's booth at the Panama-Pacific Exposition. The booth's walls displayed photographs and literature, as well as a large banner proclaiming the suffrage slogan: "We Demand an Amendment to the United States Constitution Enfranchising Women." The space itself was done up as a sitting room—with wicker rocking chairs, a carpet, and potted ferns—where exposition-goers could visit a domestic setting to discuss the suffrage cause with Congressional Union "hostesses." In spite of bad health, Sara worked at the booth through the spring and early summer.

In early August, the National Council of Women Voters held a widely publicized assembly at the exposition that featured William Jennings Bryan as a guest speaker. Just one month before, Bryan had resigned as secretary of state because he believed that President

Wilson was preparing to violate his pledge of neutrality and take measures that might draw America into World War I. In an act of political conscience, Bryan severed all ties with Wilson's administration. In his speech before the National Council of Women Voters, Bryan told his audience that women could exert real influence in protesting America's drift to war. World suffrage could bring about world peace, he told them—then added that women should be patient in pressing for the vote. Sara and a deputation of Congressional Union members confronted Bryan as he left the civic auditorium to ask him to clarify his position. Did his call for women's participation in the antiwar effort mean that he would be willing to support universal suffrage and give his backing to the Congressional Union?

"No," said Bryan, "I will speak for no organization that fought the Democratic Party."

"Why not?" Sara responded. "The Democratic Party fought suffrage by both sinister silence and willful refusal to heed its claims."

"The Democratic Party," said Bryan, "is concerned with the two paramount issues before the American public—tariff and currency."

"Not according to your speech just delivered," Sara shot back. "You said War was the great issue and that you believed women could stop it and when we take the quickest and surest method to get the weapon to express our influence you get mad."

Bryan smiled blandly, "The Lord does not ask you to do the impossible."

"O, yes, your Lord does," Sara said. "The God of your Bible is always asking Abrahams to lay their Isaacs on the altars and little Davids to go out to fight Goliaths and little Gideons bands to take mighty cities."

"I see you know your Bible." Mr. Bryan snapped. He turned upon her and asked, "How much money did the Republican Party pay you for fighting the Democrats?"

Sara was furious. "Don't charge us with the low-down, old party political methods of campaigning," she replied. "You know as well as I that we never got a cent from any party. You know as well as I that if you did not have the vote as a man today you would forget tariff and currency and fight for that fundamental and inalienable right in just the way we are doing it."[10]

Sara's run-in with Bryan took place in full view of the press. The story was picked up by the news services and carried in newspapers across the nation. Sara cared little for the publicity, except as it helped attract attention to the suffrage campaign. But the excitement she generated prompted suffrage leaders to renew their request that she participate more actively in the upcoming phase of their national campaign.

In mid-July, Wood returned to Portland from eastern Oregon and fell right into the sort of confused emotional drama that had hurt Sara repeatedly in the past. Kitty advised him that it was time to break off from Janina, that he had nothing to gain and Janina had much to lose. "I see the force of all that," he wrote to Sara, "yet it does also seem hard to rob a hungry, lonely woman of a little joy in life in just, fine, understanding friendship."[11]

"You amaze me," Sara replied. She told Wood that she had agreed to go on salary with the Congressional Union and to speak wherever her services were required. "As soon as I am getting this money," she told him, "I want you to feel released from my support."[12] How could she continue to keep her life free for him when he seemed helplessly bent on finding duties and distractions that kept him from her? "There is the undercurrent to your letters that fills me with a melancholy yearning," she explained, "—the rebellion against your false life; the beating on the golden bars of your cage; the longing for rest and the free air in which to 'grow a soul.' "[13]

Sara described the essence of Wood's dilemma. His debt, the land in eastern Oregon he was unable to sell, pressures from his law partners, his wish to make Nannie happy even as he broke her heart— all this kept him from his dream of living with Sara in artistic solitude. None of these obstacles came from fate, or bad luck, or uncontrollable circumstances: they were the outgrowth of Wood's actions, his personal choices. For close to thirty years he had felt the strain of his divided life, yet he had chosen inadequate solutions—borrowing more money, investing in new ventures, having love affairs—that allowed him to carry on in Portland without risking the essential changes that would set him free. The cage in which he found himself was his own creation; and though he did rebel against his confinement, he had also come to depend upon it.

As Sara understood, Wood prolonged his unhappiness by beating at the golden bars of his cage. Had he been less enamored of the pleasures of his captivity, he might have discovered that his cage had never been locked. To cast off a subjection of his own devising, he had only to repudiate his false life—not merely in words, but in deeds worthy of his deepest longings—and he could leave Portland a free man.

30. I Also Am a Wage Slave

During one of Wood's visits to San Francisco, Anton Johannsen and Olaf Tvietmoe asked him to speak with two young men who faced trial in Los Angeles for their role in the McNamara bombing of the *Times* building. There was no question that Mathew Schmidt and David Caplan had taken part in the McNamaras' scheme. The nitrogelatin used for the explosion was purchased at the Hercules Powder Plant on San Francisco Bay by three "businessmen" who said they intended to blast boulders and tree stumps. These men were later identified as James McNamara, Schmidt, and Caplan. A skilled engineer, Schmidt accompanied the McNamaras for months prior to the bombing incident, using his know-how to assemble time bombs for McNamara to plant. Caplan, an associate of Johannsen and Tvietmoe, owned the cart used to carry the explosives to a house where Schmidt fashioned his bomb. By the time of the McNamara trial, Schmidt and Caplan had gone into hiding. (The radical-bohemian community rallied to support Schmidt and Caplan's fugitive existence. In her memoirs, Mabel Dodge recalls giving a dinner party for "Schmitty" and his lawyer, along with Hutchins Hapgood and his wife, Neith Boyce: "We sat there in peaceful secrecy and security while Schmitty entertained us all with interesting talk, and was safe under a pseudonym.")[1]

The capture of Schmidt and Caplan put California's militant labor leaders on the defensive once again. By pleading guilty five years before, they deprived the prosecution of an opportunity to introduce damning proof of militant labor conspiracies into the public record. Now the prosecution had a second chance: in presenting evidence against Schmidt and Caplan, they could haul out their McNamara material and reveal Johannsen and Tvietmoe's clandestine activities.

Schmidt and Caplan did not deny their involvement in the bombing. They impressed Wood as brave young radicals who had succumbed to a misguided creed of revolutionary violence. Wood abhorred what they had done, but he did not want to see the young men's lives ruined by a sloppy defense. He was prepared to represent Schmidt and Caplan, but he proceeded cautiously. After the debacle brought on by Darrow's desperate actions four years before, Wood wanted to make certain that, if he were to participate in the defense, it would be conducted according to his standards. He left it to the defense committee to fix a fee, but he demanded assurance that he would be designated chief counsel—that he would have full control of the defense strategy, of publicity, and of the disbursement of cash. Tvietmoe and Johannsen respected Wood's courtroom skill, but they were reluctant to give him free rein: Wood disapproved of sabotage and violence; he was not working class; he was not one of them.

In July negotiations broke down over Wood's fee. The defense committee thought that Wood had waived any consideration of fee, but Wood insisted he had simply left it to them to offer fair payment for his services. Sara was dismayed. She had hoped that the Schmidt-Caplan trial would give Wood large expression for his legal ability, a chance to instruct a vast public forum on the class struggle.[2] She did not want him to lose this opportunity because of a quarrel over money.

Wood explained to Sara that the defense committee had wasted valuable time. Now he was caught up in a lawsuit brought by Bill Hanley to secure irrigation rights to their land in eastern Oregon. Wood insisted that he could not desert his friend's case "just because it is *property* and another is *human freedom*." His professional honor was at stake, he argued: Hanley was a client as well as a friend. Besides, he added, "Hanley thinks *his* case is human freedom. He says we are trying to break down a great California monopoly which seeks to keep this a cattle range, and we are trying to get water on to the desert to make homes for families." Attributing noble purpose to Hanley's case did not make it so. Hanley wanted to put families on the land so that he could reap an immense profit. Furthermore, Hanley was not only Wood's client and friend: he was also Wood's business partner. Wood's talk about professional honor could hardly conceal the fact that his own vital interests were at stake. He was unwilling to "desert Hanley in his extremity" because it meant sacrificing a crucial opportunity to increase the value of his land in eastern Oregon. "I am sorry," he told Sara, "but I am *not* free. . . . I also am a wage slave."[3]

A week later, he reiterated his argument in a letter to Schmidt and Caplan. "I, also, am a wage-slave of only a little greater freedom," he told them. He could not work for nothing, he explained, because he was obligated to give 70 percent of every fee to his law firm. His own 30 percent he had always intended to contribute to the defense fund, but this did not mean he could waive a fee altogether. "Under my own conditions of economic slavery, I have gone just as far as possible."[4]

Sara pleaded with Wood to change his mind, and by the end of July it was settled: he wired Sara that we was prepared to enter the Schmidt-Caplan defense without reservation.

As quickly as Wood's reversal came about, he began to undermine it. He reiterated his demand to be designated chief counsel and to have full control of the case. When the defense committee invited him to come to San Francisco to discuss a satisfactory arrangement, Wood insisted he was too busy. After hearing nothing from the committee for several days, Wood wrote to Tvietmoe that he assumed his demands were too great an obstacle, and he withdrew from the defense.[5]

"They lie like a shadow on my heart," Wood said of Schmidt and Caplan.[6] Still, at the very time when he might have placed his legal skills in the service of his radical ideals, he chose to work for Hanley's water rights.

The first week in August, Emma Goldman and Ben Reitman returned to Portland on their annual lecture tour. On the evening of August 6, Wood introduced Emma to her audience at Turne Halle where she spoke on "Birth Control: How and Why Small Families Are Best." As she began her talk, a patrolman in plain clothes came to the stage with a warrant for her arrest. Emma was charged with distributing immoral circulars at her lecture the night before: information on

"Family Limitation," a topic specifically banned by the Portland City Council in a legislative order calculated to curtail her activities.

Wood presented himself as her attorney and insisted the officer read the warrant aloud to the audience. Then Emma surrendered to the officer, descending from the stage to a rousing cheer from the crowd.[7]

The following day, Goldman and Reitman were charged in municipal court with distributing "literature of an illegal character." Wood put several doctors on the witness stand who testified that the information in Emma's forbidden pamphlet was readily available in respected medical texts. Furthermore, it was sanctioned by the American Medical Association and by the governments of Holland, Sweden, and Denmark. Nevertheless, Goldman and Reitman were found guilty and fined one hundred dollars each.

Wood set aside his other work to carry their appeal in circuit court. On August 13, he took up Emma's case in a courtroom crowded with spectators. Under his cross-examination, Mrs. Josephine De Vore Johnson, who filed the complaint, admitted that she did not see the banned circulars until the following day, when one was given to her by somebody in confidence.

Wood pressed her to reveal the name, but she refused. Judge Glatens ordered her to answer. Once again she refused, though she admitted having been asked to sign the complaint by parties connected with the mayor's office.

That exchange set the tone for the trial. Judge Glatens ruled in Goldman's favor. "The trouble with our people today," he observed, "is that there is too much prudery. . . . We are all shocked by many things publicly stated that we know privately to ourselves, but we haven't got the nerve to get up and admit it."[8]

While Wood looked after his work in Portland, Sara was besieged with opportunities to open up her life. When the fabulously wealthy Mrs. O. H. P. Belmont, an avid supporter of woman's suffrage, visited the Congressional Union booth that summer, she was sufficiently impressed by Sara to propose that she return East to assist her in writing her autobiography. Sara was tempted by the opportunity to support herself, but she was reluctant to put so much distance between herself and Wood.

Sara was more intrigued by another offer. Alice Paul devised a bold plan to dramatize the call for women's voting rights: a delegation representing the enfranchised western states was to drive cross-country from San Francisco bearing a gigantic petition demanding universal suffrage to present at the opening of the Sixty-fourth Congress. En route, they would deliver speeches, gather more signatures to the petition, and, whenever possible, present their case before the press. Alice Paul selected three women for this extraordinary piece of political theater: Mabel Vernon, Francis Joliffe, and Sara. Mabel Vernon, the Congressional Union's chief organizer for the Southwest, was to travel ahead of the suffrage car by train to arrange publicity, public meetings, and accommodations. Francis and Sara were entrusted with the Congressional Union's petition, listing half a million names, which they were to carry through the American heartland along with the suffrage message.

On September 14, the Congressional Union held a convention at the Illinois building at the Panama-Pacific Exposition grounds. The gathering welcomed women from all over America, but its purpose was to emphasize the political importance of women who already had the right to vote: some four million enfranchised women in twelve western states. A "glittering and wonderful and packed convention, wildly enthusiastic," cheered Sara and her companions at an evening rally.[9] Ten thousand women gathered at a farewell spectacle where a chorus of five hundred women clad in robes of white, purple, and gold—the Congressional Union colors—sang Sara's lyrics, "The Song of the Free Women," to the tune of the *Marseillaise*.

> We are women clad in new power
> We see the weak. We hear their plea
> We march to set our sisters free
> Lo! Has rung the chime from Freedom's tower
> We come. We come at last.
> Night's portal we have past.
> We come. We come. Trust thou our might.
> Thou, too, shall walk in Light.[10]

The next morning the suffrage car departed for Sacramento. Sara and Frances Joliffe traveled in a brand new Overland roadster, driven by two grim-faced Swedish feminists from Rhode Island. Frances

Joliffe was a bright, attractive socialite whose skill at hobnobbing with the great and near-great had proven immensely useful in the Congressional Union's efforts to enlarge their support at the exposition. Sara was not enamored of her. "She has just returned from abroad," Sara observed, "with her heart full of sympathy for the dying proletairs and her trunk full of wonderful clothes for the living Frances. Paris seems to be able to turn out its usual gown creations in spite of the chaos of war."[11]

When the suffrage car arrived in Sacramento, Frances abandoned the tour and went home. To Sara it appeared that Frances was spoiled—that she had felt too inconvenienced by her one day of automobile travel, as well as by the prospects of traveling three thousand miles with the two Swedish women who bored her to tears. But Frances, who died of cancer a few years later, may have sensed that her health could not hold up on the demanding cross-country journey. Her defection left Sara to carry out the mission on her own.

In 1915, at a time when a Sunday drive was likely to be a memorable adventure, cross-country automobile travel was virtually unheard of. There was nothing that remotely resembled an interstate highway system; roads were inadequately marked and poorly maintained. As for the spectacle of three women making the trip on their own—it was simply not done.

Festooned with banners and slogans, the suffrage car carried Sara to Salt Lake City, Cheyenne, Denver, Colorado Springs, and on to Kansas City and Chicago. At every stop, mayors, governors, and U.S. senators praised the suffrage movement and added their names to the petition. Everywhere her arrival was the occasion for receptions, interviews, and huge rallies where thousands of people sang her lyrics: "The Song of the Free Women."

Sara's relentless schedule exhausted her. In Des Moines, a doctor told her she suffered from high nervous tension caused by an aggravated goiter condition. But she pressed on, delivering speeches with quick intelligence and extemporaneous eloquence that inspired men and women alike. She refused to spare herself. For the two months of her cross-country journey, Sara was the outstanding spokesperson, the living embodiment, of one of the most important American political movements of the twentieth century.

Wood sent letters and telegrams to every stop along her route.

Sara wrote to him almost daily to describe her latest adventures. From Dodge City, Kansas, he received a harrowing telegram: "Bad day yesterday car thrown into ditch by slippery road pitching me forward unconscious for few moments."[12] Two days later, there was more disturbing news: "Stuck in mud half Monday night walked through water and mud a mile to farm house for assistance."

The incident happened in Kansas, where heavy rains turned the dirt road into a slough. The suffrage car plowed on until it sank to a stop. Sara's Swedish companions were unwilling to leave the vehicle, so she went off on her own to look for assistance. She waded through mud that splashed up to her waist, slogging two hours in the dark until she stumbled to an isolated farmhouse. The astonished farmer used a truck and team of horses to drag the car to solid ground, and the following morning Sara walked into the Emporia Hotel covered in mud. When William Allen White, the renowned editor of the *Emporia Gazette*, got wind of the story, he hurried to the hotel, where he found Sara shivering in bed. "He was both highly amused and extremely awed by the whole project," Sara recalled.[13] "He is the only good thing in Kansas," she wrote to Wood. ". . . He strangles in a spiritual vacuum . . . of mediocrity and prohibition. . . . He sits down to the table with sanctimonious mutts. . . . White said the movement of women was the greatest thing in the history of the world."[14] As Sara left Emporia, "White was almost childish in his begging of me to remain 'if only for a few hours.' "[15]

By the time Sara arrived in Chicago, she had become a celebrity. Mayor Thompson signed the Congressional Union petition on the steps of the Art Institute before an immense crowd. Newsreel crews persuaded the women to perform in a trumped-up scene of "tire trouble": Sara and the two Swedes jacked up the car and waved cheerfully to movie audiences who would soon see them in hundreds of theaters. The New York Lyceum Bureau offered to put Sara on a lecture tour. "It is all so funny to me," she wrote Wood. "I feel like a person moving in a drama and yet being outside of it."[16]

In Chicago, a reporter for one of the local papers interviewed Sara. Unlike so many of the journalists she patiently endured, this man showed an independence of mind that impressed her. "There was none of the claptrap or ordinary questions," she recalled; "there were interesting and different ones expressed in a very original manner."

In every way, the encounter proved refreshing. "He had a strange old-young look about him," she said of the thirty-seven-year-old man, "an idiom of his own that delighted me." Then she discovered that Carl Sandburg had recently published a volume of poetry (*Chicago Poems*, 1914): "We found each other more than just interviewer and interviewee. We really began to feel that we had started a friendship."[17]

During her stay in Chicago, Sara met with Darrow. He praised Wood as a great man, then rued that she had not found a younger partner. Sara burst into tears—she spoke so movingly of Wood that soon Darrow was crying too. Then, true to form, Darrow proposed a tryst with Sara in New York.[18]

Before she left Chicago, Sara made one more attempt to jar Wood free. "Do the big, brave heroic thing," she wrote to him, "and step out of that strangling environment before it is too late. . . . I am getting frightened about you. I realize more each day what delay means."[19]

For a year and a half, Sara had been urging Wood to do what she herself had done: to be truthful and to act upon that truth. She asked no more of him than what she asked of herself, but Wood remained snared in the life he had made for himself in Portland. As Sara began the final leg of her journey East, borne along by the momentum of her burning mission, it seemed that she and Wood had never been farther apart.

31. Love and Anarchy

Sara's blouse is open at the throat, her hat pushed back on her head. She stands with her left hand cocked on her hip in a feisty stance that recalls the famous frontispiece of Walt Whitman on the 1855 edition of Leaves of Grass. *Sara looks right back at the camera: relaxed, at home in her body, a countenance that is not merely confident, but ironic, suggesting the detachment and easy self-assurance of someone who has grown accustomed to living in the public eye.*[1]

In New York, suffrage supporters welcomed Sara with a grand pageant. The suffrage car led a parade that originated at Eighty-third Street and Fifth Avenue and proceeded south to Sherry's at Forty-fourth Street, where Sara addressed the crowd.

> I held that rather tired and wholly blase audience spellbound as I blazed before them this newer, more militant aspect of suffrage. . . . One paper called me "a dot of a woman with a giant's power." People literally swarmed up. "A born orator." "The most wonderful suffrage speech ever given."[2]

Everyone wanted a piece of Sara: suffrage organizers and special interest groups, senators and representatives. Henry Ford invited her to join the contingent he was gathering for his "Peace Ship" to Europe. Mrs. Belmont offered her a suite of rooms in her mansion, complete with "lackeys and limousines and maids"; she also renewed her offer to Sara that she co-author her autobiography. Sara rejected Mrs. Belmont's offer and took a dreary three-dollar room at the Hotel Astor. She felt similar misgivings toward Alice Paul, the suffrage movement's leader. "I dread Alice's coming," she told Wood. ". . . She loves society and splendor and pomp. I hate it more and more. She adores Respectability. I fling my scorn at it. You can see we are not very chummy. She is very elegant, stylish and dull!"[3]

Sara felt more at home with Ida Rauh and Max Eastman. They invited her to join them for a Sunday outing at the "House Barn and Acre Club," a cottage in Croton-on-the-Hudson that they shared with Doris Stevens, Max's sister Crystal, and several other friends. That evening, Sara read to them from *The Poet in the Desert*, but Eastman did not think much of Wood's poem. He felt the abstract figures of Truth and the Poet were archaic in concept, that their presence obstructed Wood's urgent message. It was hopeless, Eastman argued, to expound modern, revolutionary ideas through Wood's "peculiar classicism," the manner of a long-past age. Sara defended the poem, but, in truth, Eastman had given voice to her own misgivings.

Sara's weekend with Ida and Max was one of the few respites she had had since leaving San Francisco some ten weeks before. From New York, she headed off to Washington and the Congressional Union's long-awaited meeting with President Wilson. On December 6, in raw winter wind, the suffrage car—battered and worn and bulging with baggage—led a great parade through Washington. The front grill bore a sign declaring "On to Congress." A banner wrapped over the rear fender displayed the Congressional Union slogan: "We Demand an Amendment to the United States Constitution Enfranchising Women." Sara, Mabel Vernon, and Frances Joliffe sat in the open vehicle as it rolled down East Capitol Street. They were escorted by twelve women on horseback, representing the twelve enfranchised western states, followed by decorated cars and throngs of marchers waving purple, white, and gold banners.

The parade paused at the Capitol to cheer Sara and Frances as they delivered their demands to Congress. Then the great march proceeded to the White House, where President Wilson received three hundred representatives of the suffrage movement in the East Room. After Frances delivered a formal speech, Sara invited the President to examine the petition. Wilson advanced and perused the document with a proper show of presidential interest. Then Sara delivered a forceful appeal:

Mr. Wilson, all great men have had the quality of mind which
permitted Truth to write new records on it week by week. You
have changed your mind on many matters since you became
President. Some of us have watched with sorrow, others with
assent to your change on the subject of preparedness. Changed
circumstances in this nation have altered your judgment. We
suffragists claim that there are changed circumstances regarding
the suffrage question which might now convince you it has
become a national issue. . . . Four million women of the West
cry out for national action on this question.[4]

Stirring words were unlikely to alter Wilson's position. Were he
to support the suffrage amendment it would divide the Democratic
Party and diminish his support at a time of impending war. He
complimented the women on their plea for suffrage, but he made no
promises.

"I wonder what the year will bring to me," Wood wrote on the first
day of 1916.[5] Sara, too, was caught up in uncertainty. She moved in
with Ida Rauh at her flat at 118 Waverly Place just as Ida's marriage
to Eastman was drawing to a messy end. With cheerful self-absorption,
Max sprang into sexual adventures whenever it suited him, with little
regard for Ida's feelings. Ida was distraught, eager to open her heart
to someone—and Sara was right there. "She battled against her
faults," Sara wrote Wood, "and Max excused and gave way to his.
He was as he was and didn't care to be different for his own sake or
Ida's." In Ida's ruined marriage, Sara saw "the cruelty of Nature in
fashioning women to want so much and get so little return from men."[6]

Sara was also a valuable friend and counselor to Louise Bryant
who, in the last days of December 1915, abandoned her husband in
Portland and hurried to New York to live with John Reed, whom she
had met only a few weeks before. In early January, Bryant moved in
with Reed at 43 Washington Square, just down the street from Sara.

Sara and Louise had known one another since 1912 when Bryant
was living in Portland as the wife of Dr. Paul Trullinger. Back then,
Sara had brought Louise into the suffrage campaign, and the two
women had become friends. Just three years younger than Sara,
Louise looked up to her as a mentor. Now, after her scandalous flight

from Portland, Louise was relieved to find Sara close by at Washington Square. During her first weeks in New York, Louise spoke with Sara often. She knew, of course, the story of Sara's fight to end her marriage to the Reverend Ehrgott. For those who advocated free love—which is to say, a substantial portion of the Greenwich Village intelligentsia with whom Sara and Louise mingled—the drama of a determined suffragist breaking away from a tyrannous Baptist minister in order to love a man married to a Roman Catholic woman dead-set against divorce was looked upon as an exemplary tale.

Ida Rauh's home was hardly the calmest setting for Sara to reflect upon her uncertain future with Wood. "My heart *is* full of many conflicting—no, not conflicting, but mixed emotions," she confessed to Wood. "I have come to believe that a vein of insincerity *has* developed in me."[7] What Sara could not quite bring herself to say was that George West—a diffident young journalist with strong ties to the labor movement—had fallen in love with her and proposed marriage. At the McNamara trial, where West met Sara, he had taken it upon himself to give her a crash course in trial reporting. Now, he had become Frank Walsh's secretary on the Industrial Relations Commission and editor of the Commission newsletter. Since mid-December, when Sara arrived in Washington, West sought her out at every opportunity, revealing his feelings in lovestruck letters.

In early January, Mathew Schmidt was found guilty. Wood wrote a long letter to Olaf Tvietmoe condemning labor for its disunity and lack of revolutionary fervor:

> Labor politicians, like other politicians, carry water on both shoulders as long as they can and when they must decide they always decide to preserve their status as respectable citizens. When some individual, maddened by cruel conditions, resorts to force and violence as a protest, Labor and Labor leaders hasten to explain that it is a mistake; he did not do it at all. It was an accident. The bitter facts are hurried out of sight and all exclaim they are law-abiding citizens and nothing is wrong anywhere except the unjust suspicions of Capital against Labor and the prejudiced courts. Labor is quite as jealous of being law-abiding as Capital. . . .

The world never was moved by law-abiding citizens and never can be moved without breaking the law, for the law stands for past traditions. . . . Personally, I believe the only value of force or violence is as it promotes an idea, and if you deny to the act of force and violence all the idea and responsibility back of it, what good has been done? The doer becomes a mere criminal and the idea is repudiated and smothered out of sight.[8]

On January 22, these same arguments appeared in "What Is the Matter with Labor," an article Wood wrote for Alexander Berkman's new radical magazine, *Blast*, whose first number appeared the week before. Berkman was indignant at what he saw as labor's timid defense of a courageous revolutionary worker. He felt that Schmidt's lawyers should have abandoned futile efforts to prove his innocence. Radical labor should have taken the offensive with nationwide agitation, making the case that capital was guilty of far more terrible crimes— that actions such as Schmidt's and the McNamara brothers' ought to be understood as retaliatory violence, provoked and morally justified by the savagery of the capitalist system.

Wood agreed with Berkman. Had he defended Schmidt, he would have used the widely publicized trial to make a case for the moral imperatives of radical action. If his correspondence and articles are any indication, he would have reminded the court that Jesus, Galileo, America's Founding Fathers, and John Brown all broke the law in the interest of revolutionary truth, that their crimes led to enlightenment, freedom, democracy—that these men would not have been "criminals" if wealth and power had not resided in the hands of a privileged few determined to protect their interests.

In February 1916, a few days before his sixty-fourth birthday, Wood was operated on for a rectal fistula. Sara canceled all her speaking engagements in the East and hurried to join him in Portland. When they met she told him she was thinking of marrying George West. She made it clear that she was not in love with West, but that there were several practical considerations that marrying him would serve. At a time when Wood worried constantly about gaining his freedom, Sara's marriage would relieve Wood of the financial burden of supporting her. Of course, she still intended to see Wood: they would continue their friendship and literary work—but their time together would no longer be fraught with worry, tortured explanations, and looming separation. As Mrs. West, Sara would have a respectable position: when she came to see Wood in Portland there would be none of the air of scandal which had poisoned every visit for her.

Within a few days, Sara decided she could never go through with it. But whatever suffering she may have caused Wood, he more than returned it when he admitted that he had become Janina Klecan's lover. It was the story of Kitty all over again. Wood's sympathetic nature and his need for adoration had attracted the desperate affection of an unhappy woman whose torment eventually laid claim to his feelings. Janina dramatized her despondency with tearful scenes and hints of possible suicide. Once again Wood had stepped into an emotional drama he might have averted and which he now felt a guilty responsibility to resolve.

Wood condemned himself for "the inexpressible soul torture" he caused Sara and Janina. As in the past, he claimed to discover in his crisis a rebirth of truth, a steadier faith in love. "I at 64 have grown as a boy might; out of this agony I have found my own soul and truth."[9] But Sara was hardly disposed to accept Wood's convenient discovery of a new self. She left Portland for San Francisco, and though Wood accompanied her and spent a month with her at the Eyrie, Sara was too wounded to grant more than probationary trust.

As Sara pondered her next move, her health became increasingly erratic. At first it seemed to be the outcome of overwork and mental duress brought on by Wood's liaison with Janina. However, it soon became clear that her discomfort was distinctly physical. "I have a secret to tell you," she wrote Wood. Once again she was pregnant.[10]

In mid-May, Sara returned to Portland, where Janina performed an abortion. Given Sara's fragile health, Wood's advanced years, and the distressing fact of their continuing separation, there were many reasons for Sara to terminate her pregnancy. It is difficult, however, to understand why either of them would turn to Janina for help. There was no question about Janina's professional skill, but in light of her brittle emotional state and her ongoing affair with Wood, there was every reason to regard her as an inappropriate choice. For weeks after her abortion, Sara was troubled by regular bleeding that increased until she was forced to go to a hospital. There, she learned that portions of fetal matter had decayed and infected her uterus, causing acute inflammation. Fortunately, the infection passed after doctors administered a curettage—the simple procedure Janina had neglected to perform.

Sara left Portland at the end of May, sapped of hope and energy, fed up with trying to accommodate her life to Wood's. In reaction to all this, she resumed her suffrage work. In a few days Congressional Union members would gather in Chicago to reconstitute their organization as a political party, and Sara planned to be there.

Before leaving for Chicago, Sara challenged Wood to straighten out his life: "*All I ask* is for you to know the truth and make yourself and me free with it."[11]

32. Sexual Politics

O n the evening of June 5, Congressional Union delegates from all over the country convened at the Blackstone Theatre in Chicago, where they reconstituted themselves as "The National Woman's Party," an independent political party whose specific purpose was "unceasing opposition to all who oppose the Amendment."[1] The National Woman's Party's first course of action was to send delegations to the national Democratic and Republican party conventions to demand platforms supporting a suffrage amendment to the Constitution.

Sara played an active role in all this. She delivered a speech on opening night at the Chicago convention and joined Alice Paul in St. Louis, where preparations for the Democratic convention were underway. In spite of the Woman's Party's efforts, the Democratic Platform Committee stood by President Wilson's position: the committee recommended the extension of voting privileges to women, but left it as a matter for individual states to determine as they saw fit. Angry Woman's Party members disrupted the convention with cries of "Shame! Shame!"[2] From that point on, they set out to punish Wilson and his party. "He kept us out of war" was Wilson's campaign slogan; the Woman's Party countered that with "He kept us out of suffrage."[3]

While the Woman's Party condemned Wilson for playing politics with woman suffrage, others rose against him for abandoning his policy of strict neutrality. The nation remained at peace, but for months Wilson's administration had been directing a vast and costly military buildup that made war a near certainty. Across America, city administrations and various civic organizations staged Preparedness parades. Antiwar forces responded with counter-demonstrations—a situation that led to ugly confrontations, as well as a general hostility toward protest of any kind.

In the wake of such unrest, Wood took on a case that joined women's issues to free speech. That June, Margaret Sanger came to Portland to speak on birth control, and the city's guardians of morality acted swiftly to silence her. Sanger was an extraordinary public figure who, in just five years, had changed from a restless young housewife to a free-thinking radical, a fearless advocate for a woman's right to control her own body.

"My welcome to Portland was delightful," Sanger recalled. "The sixty year old poet, C. E. S. Wood, dapper and gracious, made a practice of greeting personally woman speakers, dedicating poems to them on their arrival, and sending bowers of flowers to their hotel rooms."[4] Dr. Marie Equi, a local firebrand, presented herself to Sanger and helped her revise *Family Limitation*, the notorious pamphlet she had written in 1914. A local automobile mechanic printed copies for her and received her permission to distribute it at her lecture.

On June 19, the night of Sanger's first lecture in Portland, Wood delivered an introductory address in which he informed the audience that when Sanger had spoken on birth control in New York, she had been arrested by federal authorities. Wood went on to enumerate the various city and state laws that had been devised to silence advocates of birth control—all in violation of constitutional guarantees of free speech. Meanwhile, the mechanic and two others handed out copies of *Family Limitation*. When policemen arrested the men, a "near riot" ensued.[5] (Whenever radical assemblies showed signs of fervor, "near-riot" was the *Oregonian*'s epithet of choice.) Wood promptly took up their defense.

Ten days later, when Sanger returned to Portland to attend the trial of her loyal supporters, she learned that the city council had passed a bill forbidding distribution of "obscene" literature—a bill tailored to combat her pamphlet. She and Dr. Equi defied the outrageous law. They held a rally at the Baker Theater at which they openly circulated copies of *Family Limitation*. Policemen in the theater promptly arrested them for "selling and distributing obscene

literature." The audience exploded in a "wild demonstration." Wood
spoke out over the bedlam to condemn the arrests and denounce the
city commissioners whose illegal edicts prohibited the pamphlet.[6] As
for Sanger and Equi, they refused bail and spent the night in the
city jail.

Wood took up their defense pro bonum. The trial hearing attracted
intense interest. "Never before," the *Oregonian* observed, ". . . has
a session of Municipal Court been so largely attended by women.
The first three rows of seats were almost solely occupied by keenly
interested femininity." In a learned speech flavored with literary
references, Wood reviewed the legal history of obscenity and ridiculed
the futility of censorship. Judge Langguth disposed of the case in a
way he hoped would quiet the dispute. He ruled that *Family Limitation* was obscene. He supported his decision with the argument that
material that is acceptable in bookstores and medical clinics may
have a wholly different impact if circulated publicly, when it is likely
to excite lascivious thoughts in the minds of impressionable youth.
With that he fined each of the defendants from the original incident
ten dollars. Margaret Sanger and Dr. Equi were also found guilty,
but as they were first offenders, they were let off with suspended
sentences.[7] Unrepentant, Sanger hired fifteen men to walk through
Portland carrying signs that read "Poverty and large families go hand
in hand"; "Poor women are denied what the rich possess."[8]

In San Francisco, Sara became involved in opposing America's
movement toward war. A huge Preparedness parade was planned for
July 21, and four thousand people who opposed war, many of them
members of radical labor unions, gathered for an anti-Preparedness
protest rally at Dreamland Rink on the eve of the great parade. Sara
was the only woman to address the rally. With what she called
"shameless immodesty," she told Wood that people agreed she had
made the only real speech of the evening. "Is This a War for Democracy?" was her subject. She answered her question with a resounding
"No!" When she denounced conscription as unconstitutional, the
crowd gave her a standing ovation. "Oh, it was good," she recalled,
"to feel one's soul thrilling and agreeing with a crowd again, to know
temporary unity with a group."[9]

Wood had planned on coming to San Francisco in early August,
to spend a week with Sara, but at the last minute a swollen prostate

forced him to cancel his visit. Sara assured Wood of the "sorrow and love" she felt for him, but she also reminded him that his behavior brought about their rift: that revelations of his affair with Janina had set off her discontent, what she called her "spiritual reconstruction."[10]

There was nothing more Sara could do. Tired and emotionally exhausted, she set off for Colorado Springs where the National Woman's Party was preparing for the presidential campaign. The Woman's Party resolved to campaign against Democratic candidates in every state where women voted. Their reasoning was simple: Wilson and the Democrats had refused to support the Susan B. Anthony Amendment; since the Democrats were in power, the Woman's Party would do their utmost to punish them. This did not, however, mean that they endorsed Charles Evans Hughes, the Republican presidential candidate, or other members of his party. "We were never a pro party" is how Sara put it.[11]

The decision to turn against Wilson did not come easily. His domestic policies and determination to keep America out of war had won the esteem of many Woman's Party members and their supporters. In condemning Wilson on the single issue of suffrage, the Woman's Party was asking liberal and progressive voters to choose sides. Sara's radical friends on both coasts—Margaret Johannsen and Jo Tvietmoe in San Francisco; Max, Ida, and Louise Bryant in New York—people who had no inclination to idolize Wilson, were dumbfounded by her commitment to what they saw as an obstinate, punitive, counterproductive political strategy.

Wood came out for Wilson a week after the Democratic Party endorsed him for a second term. In a speech delivered in Seattle, Wood argued that nothing was more important than Wilson's commitment to peace.[12] Sara knew that her active opposition to Wilson would worsen her frayed relations with Wood, but she made no apologies. "I was sorry to be yielding up Wilson's black suffrage record," she wrote Wood, "but it has been one of blind obstinacy against every earnest effort of conviction we could bring." She went on to attack Wood's suggestion that suffragists should mute their demands and support Wilson in the face of impending war:

> Men will *always* believe something in their man-made system
> is menaced and that suffrage should "wait." You say it will

come, is bound to come. . . . If [women] don't put their enfran-
chisement first, no one else will. If the situation were reversed
you'd be fighting for manhood suffrage first, I know, as the great
issue against the menace of a privileged sex. But we don't expect
men to get our psychology.[13]

"She has the zeal and the outlook of the fanatic," Sara's sister
Mary remarked to Wood. "It is what gives her conviction and carries
her audience."[14] Mary's admiration was tinged with characteristic
irony, but her point was true enough: Sara's intensely personal identification with women's rights turned her public speeches into a messianic undertaking. "I like to feel," she wrote, "I can give these people,
especially the women, something that momentarily, if no longer, lifts
them out of the muddy streets of Lovelock or Golconda, out of the
monotonous routine of humdrum domesticity and uninspiring personal
life into that touch with the world, the human race, which is the
thrilling part of a social movement."[15]

It was Sara's rare gift that she generally achieved what she set out
to do. She wanted to inspire people, and she did. On her speaking
tour through Nevada, Sara stirred displays of enthusiasm that rein-
forced her sense of purpose, which, in turn, swelled her intuitive
rapport with her listeners.

Wood expressed support for Sara's work, but his tone was paternalistic: "I know neither you nor I are changing, or even fixing, very
many votes, *relatively*. . . . Your chiefest work, though you fail, will
be to compel future Congresses to carefully consider before they treat
you contemptuously. That part of it will grow and grow. In this you
will really someday reap your harvest."[16]

Wood's prediction proved to be true—but just barely. The Wilson-
Hughes election turned out to be one of the closest in history. Hughes
swamped Wilson so soundly in the East that Wilson's only hope was
to win overwhelmingly in the South and West. Had the Woman's
Party campaign succeeded in turning significant numbers of voters
against Wilson, he would have been defeated. But Wilson won. He
carried California by a narrow margin, and he carried ten out of
twelve states in which women voted, losing only Oregon and Illinois.

But Wilson's victory did not herald the triumph of progressive
reform that Wood and so many others had hoped for. On the contrary,

Wilson's second term began with a declaration of war on Germany, followed by a series of measures—the Selective Service Act (May 18), the Espionage Act (June 15), the Prohibition Amendment (December 18), and the Sedition Act (May 16, 1918)—that undermined the democratic ideals that Wilson had so splendidly articulated.

On November 7, while Wilson's reelection still hung in the balance, Wood's attention was drawn to an outbreak of police violence directed against radical labor in Everett, Washington. A group of American Federation of Labor shingle-weavers had gone on strike in Everett, only to have their meetings and picket lines disrupted by police and gun-toting "vigilantes" recruited by lumber interests that controlled the town. When the IWW offered its support, the Everett council passed a bill banning IWW members from setting foot in town. The IWW defied the legislation by chartering two towboats in Seattle to transport three hundred men to Everett by sea. As they approached the shore, a band of sheriffs and deputized gunmen opened fire from three sides, killing five Wobblies and wounding many more. Two lawmen were also killed and sixteen wounded. The IWW had a history of meeting violence with violence and openly boasted of it, but in this case they insisted that they had come unarmed, that the lawmen must have been killed in their own crossfire. The Wobblies were arrested and beaten. Though no firearms were found on any of the demonstrators, seventy-four men were charged with murder.

Wood offered his assistance. He had no doubt that "all truth and justice [is] on the side of Labor, all riot, lawlessness and attack by 'Big Business.' " Everett officials had collaborated with the lumber companies: they had made a mockery of law and, in their effort to crush legal protest, eighteen men had been shot dead. The IWW asked Wood to defend them. "This is a *fine* case to handle," Wood wrote to Sara. "I almost wish I was in it—that is, that they had money enough."[17]

For two days, Wood remained in Seattle to advise IWW organizers on collecting evidence, on legal procedures, on framing the issues of the trial, and on investigating jury bias. He visited wounded protesters in the hospital; he visited the men in jail; he talked with the editor of the local paper and met with the mayor. He did everything short of taking the case. The IWW offered him twenty-five thousand dollars but he refused. "I want my *time* for poetry," he told Sara. "They couldn't collect it anyhow."[18]

Three weeks later, Wood traveled to Washington DC to resume his lobbying for irrigation projects in eastern Oregon. This did not sit well with Sara. The Nevada campaign had left her in such a weakened condition that she admitted herself to a sanitarium. Rest was absolutely essential, but Wood's behavior infuriated her. He had turned down the Everett case in order to press the Wilson administration to support development projects that would make him rich. As she had done in the past, Sara showed her disapproval by taking action of her own. When Alice Paul wired her to come East to participate in a Christmas memorial service for Inez Milholland, she ignored her fragile health and agreed to come.

33. A Revolution toward Real Freedom

Inez Milholland, one of the National Woman's Party's most effective campaigners, died of a blood disease in the autumn of 1916, collapsing on stage at a Los Angeles rally just after she had demanded, "How long must women wait for liberty?"[1] To honor the movement's first martyr, Alice Paul organized a series of memorial services across America culminating in a suffragist deputation to President Wilson.

Sara joined the Woman's Party leaders in their meeting with the president. Once again, she pressed Wilson to support the Susan B. Anthony amendment. Wilson was in no mood to concede the point, nor was he inclined to revise his policy simply because a young woman happened to drop dead campaigning against him.

It was time, Alice Paul decided, to increase pressure on the recalcitrant president. At 9 A.M. the following day, silent pickets marched outside the White House demanding immediate action on a suffrage amendment. From this point on the Woman's Party pursued a course of civil disobedience calculated to lead to physical confrontation, arrests, and jail. Sara approved of these tactics, but she told Alice Paul she could not join the pickets—that a prolonged stay in jail would undermine her strength and might even bring about her death. "Well," Alice Paul replied, "that would be very good for the cause."[2]

Alice Paul never quite forgave Sara for declining to offer herself to the movement as its second martyr. Sara's role in the militant phase of the suffrage movement diminished considerably. Soon she was on her way to Oregon to be with Wood.

*

From early February till the end of March, Sarah and Wood were together in Portland. Wood was still distracted by family obligations and his web of personal attachments. When compared to Sarah's prior visits, however, this one was relatively untroubled.

On March 29, Wood received a wire that Albert Pinkham Ryder had died. Ryder was one of Wood's last remaining links to his youthful days in New York. Wood recalled his "gentle sweet poetic character," the wonderful visions he painted in his ramshackle studio on Fifteenth Street. "He was in painting what Whitman was in poetry," Wood wrote to Sara, "a unique original, America's one and only absolutely *different* genius."[3]

Ryder's death came only a week before the United States declared war on Germany. Most Americans strongly supported the war, but Wilson's progressive supporters felt betrayed. Though he disapproved of the war, Wood remained loyal to Wilson. He condemned the European conflict as a power struggle between an imperial England, determined to protect its world markets, and a militaristic Germany, eager to claim its share of international trade. Yet he declined to join his pacifist friends, Sara among them, who denounced Wilson's policy. In Wood's eyes, German Junkerdom was the greater of two evils; he was in favor of Germany "being whipped to her knees."[4]

That Wood's reactions were inconsistent is hardly surprising. In a sense, his contradictions resembled those of Wilson himself. Here is how Arthur Link described Wilson:

> He was a romantic moralist who, using the poet's hyperbole to express political truth, raised every issue and conflict to a high stage upon which the human drama was being played out. . . .
>
> Certain dangers existed in such excesses of nobility and moral vision. There was always the temptation to idealize unpleasant situations and necessities. . . . It led him to romanticize objectives and to refuse to confront harsh realities.[5]

Link's passage applies equally to Wood. Wood stood by Wilson not only because he supported the president's beliefs and values, but also because he and Wilson shared essential habits of mind. Months later, after the Bolsheviks assumed power and sued for peace (the Treaty of Brest-Litovsk, of March 3, 1918), Wood fantasized that Wilson himself was a revolutionary at heart. In a letter to Hanley, Wood praised the Bolsheviks' "magnificent program" to abolish plutocracy, monopoly, and privilege. The land and all its resources, as well as utilities, transportation, and factories—all were placed in the hands of the people. "I am convinced," Wood wrote to Hanley, "that Wilson in his own heart agrees with the Bolsheviki program but knows what he is able to announce and what he is not able to announce at this time."[6] Wood concluded that revolutionists "must get behind Wilson . . . for a struggle in this country . . . to mould the war to the revolutionary program toward which it seems slowly drifting. I have no objection to oceans of blood if it is for a revolution toward real freedom."[7]

Eventually, Wood discovered that he was wrong in his reading of Wilson's heart and that he had been wildly optimistic in his vision of the revolutionary blessings of war; but in the spring of 1917 events in Russia made even the most unlikely scenarios appear tantalizingly possible. Wood was hardly alone in his optimism. Lincoln Steffens' memorable comment on revolutionary Russia—"I have seen the future, and it works"—expressed the attitude of a significant segment of America's intellectual and artistic leadership.[8] Although the next decades brought some notable defections—most notably, Emma Goldman, Max Eastman, and Steffens himself—for close to twenty years, Russia's revolutionary transformation remained a beacon of hope to those who felt America had betrayed its democratic principles.

Wood joined Sara in San Francisco for the last three weeks of April. Most likely, it was during this visit that he first met the English writer John Cowper Powys. Powys had been coming to the United States since 1905, touring the country with a repertoire of some 150 lectures. At forty-five, he had not yet produced the prodigious novels that are the basis of his literary reputation: he was primarily known as a charismatic lecturer who could speak extemporaneously on seemingly any aspect of literature, history, and culture.

With craggy features, dark piercing eyes, and most of all, his irresistible eloquence, Powys performed with the self-assurance of a gifted actor. An intellectual showman with a gift for transforming high culture into popular entertainment, Powys called his lecture tours a "circus." For all his theatricality, he had the redeeming habit of seducing himself as well as his listeners. "I worked myself up to such a pitch that I *became* the figure I was analyzing," Powys remarked. "It was with almost an erotic emotion, as if I were indulging myself in some kind of perverted love affair."[9] By all accounts, his audiences loved it. Hortense Russell, a critic for the *San Francisco Bulletin*, described him as "the spiritual link between dead writers and their living audiences. He is the literary clairvoyant. He materializes from the shadow-world the creatures of other poets' dreams and fancies."[10]

Prompted by a letter from Harriet Monroe, Wood and Sara went to the St. Francis Hotel to hear Powys lecture on "Shelley, the Ecstasy of the Spirit." Draped in a Cambridge gown, he stepped onto the platform of the Gold Ballroom and scanned the crowd with a searching, hawklike gaze. He spoke of Shelley's passionate commitment to poetry and human affairs, explaining that this remarkable creative soul emerged from a mundane childhood and commonplace parents. With typical audacity, Powys broke forth: "But I don't believe he was their son. . . . I think he was a changeling, brought there by the fairies and just put into that crib!"[11]

Wood and Sara were charmed. Wood invited Powys to be his houseguest when his lecture tour brought him to Portland, and on May 5, Powys arrived to enliven Wood's gloomy household. Their friendship was sealed.

By the early summer of 1917, the Wilson administration had, in the interest of wartime security, begun to institute a series of repressive measures. In April, Wilson appointed George Creel, a journalist with impeccable credentials as a muckraker and progressive crusader, to head the newly created Committee on Public Information designed to run a nationwide propaganda campaign in support of the war. Creel's committee sponsored seventy-five thousand pro-war speakers. In addition, it enlisted Samuel Gompers to head the American Alliance for Labor and Democracy, whose purpose was to ensure that rank-and-file workers supported the war effort. In June of 1917, Wilson signed the Espionage Act, making it a crime "to willfully cause or attempt to cause insubordination, disloyalty, mutiny, or refusal of duty, in the military or naval forces of the United States," or to "willfully obstruct the recruiting or enlistment service of the United States." Most troubling of all, it presented an injunction against circulating through the mails "any matter advocating or urging treason, insurrection, or forcible resistance to any law of the United States."

This revolted Wood. Americans were being asked to fight and die for their country. Surely this entitled them to engage in a searching, open debate of government policy. But the Espionage Act would have a chilling effect: a broad construction of these new provisions gave government officials a free hand to prosecute whomever they pleased. Sure enough, when Eugene Debs, Emma Goldman, Bill Haywood, and various IWW leaders spoke out against the war, they were arrested and prosecuted. That summer, after Max Eastman wrote an editorial for the *Masses* challenging the government's right to draft people who objected to the war, the Post Office promptly banned the *Masses* from the mails. In 1918, after a year of legal and financial struggle, the magazine folded.

In these troubled times, Wood was constantly called upon to lend support and legal aid to groups that defied the government's tactics. He served on the Civil Liberties Bureau of the American Union Against Militarism, a precursor to the American Civil Liberties Union; and he joined Darrow, Amos Pinchot, and Frank Walsh on the legal staff of Anton Johannsen's National Labor Defense Council.[12] (Sara worked on the council's illustrious editorial board along with Ida Rauh, Lincoln Steffens, John Reed, Carl Sandburg, and Fremont Older.)[13] But these groups were powerless to stem the tide of censorship, intimidation, and legal prosecution that accompanied America's entry into the war.[14]

This new crisis spurred Wood to prepare a lucid critique of the American system. On July 20, he spoke on "Industrial Democracy" at a radical labor conference in Los Angeles.[15] America's cherished political democracy was all but negated, Wood argued, by economic privilege and the industrial slavery it produced. When it suited them, private interests circumvented the will of the people, or else they used their overwhelming power to shape public opinion to their own needs. The recent surge of idolatry for the American flag was as good a sign as any that church, schools, and the press were all caught up in the feudal, antidemocratic mentality—that they were becoming pawns of the barons of banking and industry who urged America into the war. The only people who could truly sing "My Country, 'Tis of Thee," Wood remarked, were J. P. Morgan and his class. "When the Standard Oil painted its service stations red, white and blue it was entirely fitting—it was its own coat of arms."

Wood attacked the popular view of the European conflict: that America had joined with England to fight for common democratic ideals. He pointed to England's subjugation of Ireland, Egypt, India, and China and asked how any empire that forcibly governed weaker peoples could call itself a democracy. And what of the United States' intrusion into the internal affairs of her neighbors? What democratic principle permitted us to invade Caribbean and Central American republics, imposing puppet regimes responsive to our economic interests? Imperialism and war are the inevitable result of the disease of industrial feudalism, Wood insisted—the need of the privileged few to find new and larger fields of exploitation.[16]

When Wood finished, his audience rose to their feet in an emotional ovation, cheering and waving handkerchiefs and hats.[17]

That summer, Sara returned East to work with Mrs. Belmont on her autobiography. She had serious reservations about the project (not the least of which was Mrs. Belmont's imperious nature), but after almost a year of rejecting Mrs. Belmont's invitations and turning her back on the opportunity for literary and financial success, Sara finally relented in hope that her work on the autobiography might pave the way for herself and Wood in future creative projects.

By the end of July, Sara had settled in Newport, where Mrs. Belmont reigned over a palatial summer residence built when she was still Mrs. Vanderbilt. Constructed from brown and gold Siennese marble at a cost of two million dollars, Marble House—her summer "cottage," as she liked to call it—was one of the most opulent homes in what was then America's wealthiest community. Mrs. Belmont expected Sara to take up residence as her court scribe, but Sara was sickened by the "selfish indulgence and unvirtuous sloth" of Mrs. Belmont's social set. She rented a room at a sober little boarding house and set about to fulfill her writing commitment, ignoring, as best she could, a community that filled her with loathing and unhappiness.[18]

The life of Alva Erskine Smith Vanderbilt Belmont was not without interest or high drama. Born in Mobile, Alabama, before the Civil War, Alva Smith was brought to New York in the 1870s by her mother in hopes of making a good marriage. New York's social elite received the Smiths and other new arrivals with all the hospitality a treasure ship might show a fleet of buccaneers. The old families closed ranks against what they perceived to be an infestation of parvenus, but young Miss Smith managed to win the heart of William Vanderbilt, scion of the fabulous Vanderbilt fortune. Their marriage in 1875 was the social event of the year—the opening volley of what became a legendary eight-year campaign by Mrs. Vanderbilt to secure recognition from Mrs. William Astor, doyenne of Manhattan's blue bloods.

By 1895, Alva Vanderbilt grew tired of her marriage and her husband's numerous infidelities. She sued for divorce and, a year later, married into a second fortune by giving her hand to Oliver Hazard Perry Belmont. After Belmont died in 1908, his spectacularly rich widow used her resources to advance the cause of woman suffrage.

On the surface, Mrs. Belmont's bold divorce and her active role in the suffrage movement were worthy of Sara's respect. But the more Sara came to know Mrs. O. H. P. Belmont, the more she disliked her. As Sara saw it, Mrs. Belmont used the movement as an extension of her rage against men. Though she displayed an impulse to help women in general, Mrs. Belmont had little sympathy for the working class. She might spend a whole night in court posting bail for women factory workers in a garment union strike, yet she had no qualms about beating her maid with a hairbrush for failing to attend to her in a timely fashion. Even in her dealings with the leaders of women's groups, Mrs. Belmont was often dismissive, dictatorial, even cruel.[19]

Her imperious ways extended into her interviews with Sara. She gave uncensored accounts of her life experiences only when it suited her—which was rarely. More often, she eased into conveniently self-serving versions of her past. This made collaboration on the autobiography distasteful, close to impossible, for Sara.

As Sara struggled with Mrs. Belmont's autobiography, Wood spoke out against the Espionage Act. On August 17, he addressed a rally of six thousand people assembled in Seattle. Police swarmed around the speaker's table, but Wood was not intimidated. He told the huge gathering that First Amendment rights should not be curtailed in times of war: this was the very time when free speech was most needed. He reminded his listeners that, in his first campaign, President Wilson had told the American people that if they did not awaken to their constitutional prerogatives, they would be robbed of their liberties by the great property interests. Wood urged his listeners to follow their president's advice and to exercise their First Amendment privileges. Surely, free and open public discussion was the best way to clarify the values America defended in battle and the principles it sought to perpetuate in peace.[20]

The police were perplexed. They had come to break up the rally and arrest anyone who preached sedition. But what were they to do with a man who quoted the president approvingly and urged his audience to be good American citizens by actively exercising their constitutional rights? Wood's dexterous performance allowed him to set forth his deep conviction that free speech is the essence of citizenship, that any obstacle meant to curtail it is a blight on the vital energies of democratic life. Given the repressive spirit of those times, his argument was a subversive act, a fine display of moral vision supported by wit, poetry, and courage.

While Wood actively challenged odious policies of the Wilson administration, Sara stood against the entire war effort. When antiwar groups banded together to form the People's Council, Sara hurried to Chicago to take part in a Labor Day gathering of the new coalition. In no time, the city was in turmoil. Citing "unlawful assembly," Illinois's governor ordered police to storm the People's Council meeting and seize its chairman. For four days the People's Council remained in Chicago, holding secret meetings at various locations, keeping one step ahead of the police and defying the governor's order to disband. To Mary, Sara wrote: "We have choked the President's own words down his throat and the world may object to what we have done, but it does not evade the fact that 'a war for democracy' is a joke."[21]

From Chicago, Sara hurried back to Washington where the Woman's Party was up against severe pressure. With America at war, Woman's Party pickets brandished placards in front of the White House asking how America could make the world safe for democracy abroad when twenty million women were denied liberty at home.

Banners pointed out that the Russian revolutionary government had enfranchised women as one of its first acts. Other signs cited the Declaration of Independence: "Governments derive their just powers from the consent of the governed." Most grating of all, the pickets quoted Wilson's eloquent words on human liberty and asked how he could say such things and yet oppose woman suffrage.

Through the spring and early summer, the pickets were harassed by mobs and lambasted in the press. Finally, on June 21, Major Pullman, chief of police for the District of Columbia, warned Alice Paul that pickets would no longer be permitted. The following day a handful of suffragists assembled before the White House with a banner that quoted President Wilson's war message to Congress: "We shall fight for the things which we have always held nearest our hearts—for democracy, for the right of those who submit to authority to have a voice in their own governments."

As Major Pullman had promised, they were arrested. Through July and August, the conflict continued: women picketed, mobs tore down their banners, the police continued to make arrests. On one occasion, the police permitted a crowd to storm the Woman's Party headquarters. Even worse, the court sentenced arrested pickets to imprisonment at Occoquan Workhouse in Lortin, Virginia. In response, Alice Paul planned a parade for early September to show that suffrage protesters refused to be intimidated.

Sara was at the People's Council meeting in Chicago when she received a telegram from Woman's Party leaders imploring her to join the demonstration. She wanted to take part, she knew she *should* take part, but she was on the brink of another physical breakdown. She chastised herself for saying no, but she would not jeopardize her fragile health. The suffrage parade took place on September 4. Thirteen women marchers were arrested for illegal picketing and sent to Occoquan Workhouse for sixty days. In the frenetic days that followed, Sara helped manage operations at party headquarters and delivered a number of speeches to rally public opinion behind the imprisoned women.[22]

Wood disapproved of throwing Woman's Party activists in jail. However, he also objected to the women's strategy of picketing the White House, a course of action that he believed was likely to turn public opinion against their cause. "We don't care about popular opinion," Sara shot back. "We care about making the administration so unpopular by revealing their weakness toward internal democracy that they will be forced from self-preservation to pass the amendment. I think 70 years of opportunism applied to woman suffrage is enough of a trial for us to turn to something else."[23]

Sara was fed up with Wood's "reasonable" rationalization for the government's unreasonable actions. "I don't think I want to discuss Wilson with you on paper," she wrote. "He is to all my hopeful friends here, as to me, a colossal failure."[24]

In October, Sara returned to San Francisco. She was physically exhausted and sickened at the thought of Mrs. Belmont and her world. She wrote Wood that "two hundred years from now the book will, I hope, have some significance as a voice from an exterminated class, . . . as an indictment of a monstrosity—for that is what this over-rich element are. . . . I hate them—their ideas, their psychology."[25]

Sara's indignation spilled over into her response to Wood's failure to leave Nannie. "If your freedom is being delayed because you want to maintain Mrs. Wood in an expensive establishment, I do not think you yet want either freedom or your art-expression enough to get it." She told him that if he anticipated being chained to his work, she would return East for the year.[26]

In his personal life, as well as in his political views, Wood longed for a "revolution toward real freedom"—a wish that ran head-on into intractable facts of his own nature. Would he ever find a way to be with Sara and create his artistic retreat? In spite of his promises, in spite of his efforts to settle his affairs, Wood must have doubted if it was ever meant to be. A fatalistic vein entered his thoughts. He reminded Sara of an exhilarating automobile outing they had shared that past April: "Our mad ride along the edge of Death. Yes, we are happy when together. I think we would have been happy in going over those cliffs together."[27] Wood's description of a "mad ride along the edge of Death" was an accurate metaphor for the seven years he and Sara had loved and suffered together. At sixty-six, Wood was, quite literally, traveling along the edge of death. And Sara, with her unrelieved succession of health crises and her periods of profound despair, had also skirted that perilous edge. There were limits to how much either of them could endure. And there were moments, as Wood's fantasy of a lovers' leap suggests, when his exhausted imagination turned to death itself: a vision of romantic oneness that could not be touched by the disappointments of life.

34. Fears and Alarms

Wood turned sixty-six in 1918, and though his health was good, his thoughts often turned to how he would be remembered after his death. He had already taken measures to ensure that future generations would not be deprived of his life's work. Since early 1911, Sara had been sifting through his personal journals, official papers, manuscripts, scores of magazine articles, and thousands of pages of private correspondence—boxes and boxes of material—putting them in order. Wood himself had made a promising start on his reminiscences. There was, in this effort, a wish to do more than merely recount a succession of events. He wanted to claim an afterlife in history.

Age and pride gave Wood's wish greater urgency and, at times, a degree of self-consciousness that irritated Sara. At one point, he lamented that their correspondence, if culled, would not produce much of worth. "All you say sounds as if we had been writing or should write for others to see," Sara replied. "We write for each other. . . . It is absurd to think that every time we were impelled to [share intimacies] we should draw back and say 'No, wait, what would the eyes of a hundred years hence say to this!' We might just as well so measure our kisses and words when together."[1]

In another letter Sara quipped, "Aren't you sorry you can't be in love with yourself and get your own letters?"[2] Yet Sara, too, believed that their lives had special significance. Throughout her career as a speaker for the suffrage movement, she proudly recounted her triumphs to Wood and sent him clippings attesting to her splendid success, all the while insisting she had no taste for celebrity and public acclaim.

Wood and Sara *were* public figures—there was no denying it. In Portland, an air of scandal hung over their affair from the very start; in San Francisco and New York, amidst the congenial society of radical friends, their romance had become a participatory melodrama in which Mary, Margaret Johannsen, Thelma Wold, Louise Bryant, Ida Rauh, Darrow, Powys, Steffens, and a host of others offered sympathy, assistance, and indignation—an ongoing choral commentary. Their love affair was seen as an ardent expression of anarchistic freedom, a challenge to rigid bourgeois values, a compelling vision of true romance. In spite of Sara's aversion to living her private life in public, she was pleased when Powys told her that his memory of her and Wood in their tower room at the Eyrie "was the one classic picture of romantic living in all America."[3]

Sara's satisfaction with Powys's flattering observation shows a habit of mind that had become a kind of reflex for both her and Wood— the tendency to view their love, their lives, as an ongoing work of art, as a beautiful story. This feeling that they were part of something larger than themselves, something they had created and were still creating, sustained them through separation, through personal and political differences, through illness, mental anguish, and utter exhaustion. They needed to believe in their beautiful, unfinished story. When they shared stolen days together, filled with hope and fun and blissful pleasure, it strengthened them and their sense that life itself had become a work of art. When they suffered, or caused one another to suffer, they survived these upheavals by never wholly losing faith that their ordeal was moving toward a radiant conclusion—a secluded retreat where they might realize their abiding wish to be together.

Wood and Sara's penchant for seeing their lives as art was, in large part, the outcome of their repeated separations: months on end, year after year, when their sole contact had been in letters. Impressions of friends, creative projects, politics, accounts of daily life, the most intimate feelings—all this they exchanged in writing. So freighted, personal correspondence tends to create a second self— not a false or fictional self exactly, but a version of one's being, subtly transformed by the process of describing oneself in letters.

It is hardly surprising that when Wood and Sara came together, almost always they managed to overcome whatever tensions flared up in their letters. It was as if the criticism and worried reactions exchanged during their separation had passed between two other people, lesser selves who lived in a real-life epistolary narrative, the work-in-progress that Wood and Sara were still constructing. But it was not *them*, not their true selves—or, at least, they were able to live as if this were so. Neither Wood nor Sara consciously chose this melange of life and art, or even understood that it had come about. But seven years of long separations had conjured this self-division and created the conditions for its sustained existence. Unwittingly, they placed themselves in an exasperating bind: they seemed doomed to inhabit a drama that they alone had created but which they felt powerless to bring to a satisfactory conclusion. This dual life supported their romance, becoming, in a sense, the foundation of their emotional survival. However, in succumbing to his necessary fictions, Wood risked his clarity of vision and, at times, his integrity. In his written exchanges with Sara, he often acted as if saying something made it so. When he showed the same tendency in his public life, he sometimes seemed deluded or hypocritical.

In the first months of 1918, Wood found himself in several situations where his words proved unequal to events at hand. As a result of her anticonscription activities, Emma Goldman was sent to federal prison on charges of conspiracy. Though he had often railed against Wilson's crackdown on free speech, Wood assured his friend that the worst was over: "The Government has deprived you of your liberty during a temporary crisis, for the protection of the Government as it views it, and in my opinion it neither intends to deprive you of more, nor has it the power to do so."[4]

Emma knew better. On the front page of the January number of *Mother Earth*, she had set down thoughts that came from first-hand experience of Wilson's wartime version of the "new freedom": "We cannot refrain from expressing the pain we have felt at the limited social vision of the well-meaning friends who were so naively hopeful of legal justice, in spite of all-too-numerous lessons to the contrary."[5]

Wood should not have needed Goldman to remind him of these "all-too-numerous lessons." Not since Lincoln suspended habeas corpus at the start of the Civil War had the federal government so aggressively suppressed basic constitutional rights. Wood's reaction to what he described as a "temporary crisis" was little more than wishful thinking. In Emma's words, it was "naively hopeful," a sign of "limited social vision."

In truth, Wood was more absorbed in personal issues than in Emma's crisis. At long last, he was close to realizing his long deferred dream of economic freedom. The final details of the land-grant payments were finally settled: Wood could expect his commission in August. In a few months he could make his break, once and for all. Sara and he could begin the life they had dreamed of for so long.

Thelma Wold, Sara's only close friend in Portland, was concerned. Though she was fond of Wood, her feelings for Sara had blossomed to something very much like love. Having counseled Sara through so many upsetting events, Thelma wrote to her to share her concern about what lay ahead:

> The Poet-Man tells me that he is going to you to remain indefinitely and to look for a house for the two of you. Dearest, were it not for little glimpses of your own fears and alarms some weeks ago and my own questionings about all that it involves of sacrifice on your part, this might make me glad. Oh, I have to say it poorly, how full of misgivings I am about your fitness to reach any decision when you are ill and lonely and weary of the conflict.[6]

Thelma saw what neither Wood nor Sara truly comprehended: that their melodramatic romance, so full of intensity, had deprived them of precious clarity. Thelma was deeply worried: Wood believed freedom and happiness were at hand, but to her it seemed that the two lovers were careening along an emotional precipice—they were hurtling out of control.

35. Four

Wood spent May, June, and the first half of July with Sara in San Francisco, which aroused the Reverend Ehrgott's vehement objections. Sara could do as she pleased with her own life, Ehrgott conceded, but he vowed to seek a court order if she ever placed Albert and Kay in the company of the contemptible Mr. Wood.

Of course, Wood had no intention of listening to Ehrgott. It was not in his nature to let anyone tell him what to do—or, more to the point, what not to do. Over the years, he had come to love Albert and Kay as his own children: in many ways he had become a second father to them, or rather, their preferred father. The children adored him; they called him "Pops" and they treasured the days the four of them spent together as a family. But Ehrgott's threat could not be dismissed. If he chose to go to court, Sara's unorthodox behavior was unlikely to win her a favorable ruling.

Ehrgott's injunction against Wood seeing Albert and Kay came only a week or so before Wood returned to Portland to work out final arrangements for his move to California. Thirty-five years in Portland were drawing to an end. At the end of July, Wood concluded his work at the law firm. In early August, he cleared out room 419. "I am sort of making my last will and testament," he told Sara. There, in his private sanctuary, he had sustained himself through his work as a poet, anarchist gadfly, progressive reformer, and legal counselor to radical causes. Now he was free to end his divided life. He stuffed everything in boxes and wastebaskets: poems, newspapers, pamphlets, briefs, essays, the original deeds of the old wagon road—

"the flotsam and jetsam of an era," he called it. It was, as he wrote to Sara, a "psychological housecleaning."[1]

In late August, Wood left Portland to join Sara in San Francisco. It is unlikely that he told Nannie his departure was permanent. He probably told her that he intended to find a quiet place in the Bay Area where he could devote himself to creative work, and that Sara was essential to his work and he would be seeing much of her. Max and Kitty saw him off at the Portland station. "Kit and I felt kind of gloomy when we saw you sailing down the tracks yesterday," Max wrote to his father, "but there was consolation in the thought that you were doing just what you wanted to do. . . . I wish to h— everybody would let every body else do just what they want to without each trying to force the other into his way of thinking."[2]

In San Francisco, the Reverend Ehrgott still refused to permit Albert and Kay to spend time with Sara in Wood's company. If Sara lived openly with Wood as she wanted, she would be cut off from her children; if Ehrgott had his way, she and Wood would be forced to live apart. For most of September there was no danger of the problem coming to a head: Sara and Wood went to Nevada to canvass for Anne Martin, and the children remained with Ehrgott. But Sara dreaded what lay ahead. For her there could be no real peace of mind until she was able to bring Wood and her children together in an undivided life. "The Future looks very dark," she told Wood, "and I am tortured by the conflict of forces within me and confused by the calling of many voices."[3]

Wood and Sara returned to San Francisco in late September. They agreed that until Sara was able to work something out with Ehrgott it would be best for Wood to live on his own. Wood rented rooms across the bay in Corte Madera and settled down to work. After all he had been through, he was at last at peace, or something like it. He had extricated himself from Portland with his health intact; he had every expectation that he and Sara could enjoy his remaining years working together in quiet seclusion. Only Ehrgott stood in their way, but after the many obstacles they had already overcome, he knew they would find a way to live as they chose in spite of him.

Sara remained on edge. As she had done at other times of great distress, she turned to the spirit world for counsel: this time it was a Ouija board. "F–O–U–R," the ouija spelled. "Neither mother or I knew at first what it meant," Kay reported to Wood. "Then it repeated—'Four, mother, Kay, Albert, Pops.' "[4]

Four. It confirmed Sara's deepest wish. Without Wood, Sara and the children were denied the person who completed them, the one who made their three a perfect four. She resolved to defy Ehrgott and claim her happiness. On Saturday, October 12, she piled the children into her motorcar and drove off to visit Wood's place.

The car was Wood's idea. During his last weeks in Portland, he had urged Sara to buy an automobile and to learn how to drive it. They would need it, he explained, during their search for a quiet place to live. At first Sara refused. The thought of driving made her nervous, and she was sure they could manage without a car. But Wood persisted and Sara gave in. She took enough lessons to attain a beginner's grasp of fundamentals: then, to everyone's satisfaction except her own, she bought a new Chandler.

Wood was writing in the arbor when he was roused by calls and laughter—a surprise visit by Kay, Albert, and Sara, who had come to invite him on an afternoon outing. His landlady put up a picnic lunch, and the four of them set out in Sara's motorcar. As a novice driver, Sara tried to avoid steeply graded roads, but in hilly Marin County this was nearly impossible. After a while she came to an incline that made her uneasy, so she turned off the road and they stopped to enjoy their picnic. After lunch, heading back to Wood's home, Sara sought a more level route; but neither she nor Wood were familiar with the roads.

"To the left!" Albert cried, "To the left!" He pleaded with her to follow his directions: a route that ran near a favorite hiking path he knew quite well. "This is the highway," he assured her, "It's perfectly safe."

Sara did what he asked. Within a few miles the road turned up a steep hill running along a washed-out embankment. Halfway up the hill, Sara stopped. The sheer slope made her dizzy and anxious. The only solution, Wood told her, was to back the car downhill till they came to a turning point. Sara shifted into reverse and let the car inch backwards. She struggled with the steering, but the vehicle seemed to have a will of its own. The rear end swung off the roadbed, close to the lip of the embankment. Wood called out, Sara jammed

on the brakes—the car slid closer to the edge. Sara strained to control
the vehicle. At the brink of the thirty-foot embankment, the rear
wheels whirled in loose gravel. Then the grading gave way: the car
and its four helpless passengers tumbled over the edge of Wright's
Hill.[5]

Precious

Hours

1918–1944

36. Recalled to Life

Wood crawled out of the demolished car into glaring sunlight. From within the upside-down vehicle, Kay called for her mother, who lay pinned beneath the wreck. Albert was crushed and unconscious: some involuntary reflex brought forth low mechanical groans, sounds Wood knew from the battlefield at Whitebird Canyon forty years past.

Wood threw open one of the car doors and pulled Kay partly free. He struggled to lift the mangled motorcar to rescue Sara and Albert until the sight of his own blood—he was covered from head to foot—shocked him into realizing that if he did not find help quickly he would be too weak to act at all. He clambered up the steep embankment and staggered along the road until he found two farmers, who hurried back with him to the site of the accident and dragged Sara and Albert from the wreck. Sara's leg was almost severed where the car had fallen on her calf. Albert remained unconscious. Weakened by loss of blood, Wood collapsed by the roadside. Later, there would be time to assess his injuries: a bloody scalp wound, a crushed nose, a gashed elbow, a badly sprained knee, cuts and bruises all over his body. But that afternoon he felt nothing so much as his failure to protect Sara and the children he dearly loved from bodily harm.

Sara's injury required two operations and six months in which to recuperate. Kay had only a few bruises. As for Albert, he had sustained serious injuries but would recover—that is what the doctors told Sara. Sara could hardly believe it. In those nightmare moments when she and her children lay pinned beneath the car, she had felt certain her boy was dying. In spite of the doctors' attempts to soothe her, she could not set her fears to rest. Had he really survived? She begged the staff to tell her the truth, and that night they did: Albert was dead.

The Reverend Ehrgott staged an elaborate funeral for his son. He told the assembled mourners he was glad Albert was at rest; the boy was safe now from those influences that threatened to rob him of his Christian faith. To Ehrgott, it was abundantly clear that Wood and Sara were responsible for what had happened. She had defied his order to keep Albert and Kay from Wood, and now Albert was dead.[1] Ehrgott vowed that so long as Wood remained in Sara's life, he would refuse to let her see Kay.[2]

Ehrgott's anguished accusations and refusal to let Sara see her daughter drove Sara to a near breakdown. Even after Ehrgott permitted Kay to visit her mother on a regular basis, he persisted in his obsessive mission to censure her and to expose Wood's subversive influence.[3]

Sara's leg was in a cast for three months, and she remained incapacitated for half a year. "I have been in great pain," she wrote to Thelma Wold, "horrible, causing me to cry out in the night and to groan thru the day. For myself, since Albert went, I just wait my release. The great, striving world has lost its grip upon me. An old man and a little girl ask me to stay and suffer here for their sakes and the body obeys, but my eyes are turned toward Release. It cannot come too soon for me now."[4] Wood's devotion brought her through. He visited her in the hospital for hours at a time, sitting by her side in silence, patiently holding her hand, hoping his own life-force might somehow restore her will to live.

Sara's despair prompted concern among her friends. "I wish I could say something consoling about Albert," Darrow wrote to her. "I can't. Except that death is better than life . . . I find that pessimism is the most consoling. Life is nothing but a foolishness and a burden and a tragedy. Death is peace—it is nothing. . . . All the rest is delusion and a dream. If you can find some illusion it is good to take, but I fancy that you are so made that you can't find one."[5] Sara sought comfort in spiritualism, but Darrow was right: illusion failed to bring her lasting solace.

During those agonizing months, Wood withdrew almost entirely from public life. Only a few situations aroused his combative spirit.

Three weeks after the accident, he responded to a letter from Wilson's assistant secretary of labor, Louis Post, a man who had been Wood's political ally for close to twenty years. A former editor of the *Public*, Post was one of many notable reformers who had thrown in their lot with Wilson and come to Washington in hopes of turning progressive goals into public policy.[6]

In his letter to Wood, Post had urged him to "patch up the holes in your armor and become a leader." Wood answered with a diatribe against President Wilson's dismal leadership. He reminded Post that one need not move to Washington to serve progressive principles. He had worked long and hard for voting reform; he had spoken out vigorously against America's entry into the European war:

> Do you call these holes in my armor? Do you think they ought to be patched? Because, in a war labeled with a cheap slogan as a war for democracy—every shred of democracy disappeared? Because, under an administration called democratic with its maxim "To make the world safe for democracy"—every shred of freedom of thought or speech or press disappeared and democracy became unsafe for the world? . . . Truth has been prohibited and the great Russian Revolution—the greatest event since the French Revolution—the first and only attempt at the freedom of the land has been met by a conspiracy of lies deliberately arranged by frightened capitalism, and to this conspiracy our Secretary of State and his subordinates have lent their aid. Papers have been seized without a warrant and where no real crime could be found against an agitator or a speaker or a messenger from Russia, some faked up indictment was brought and he was held literally in suspense by the arbitrary power of a little cheap District Attorney. . . .
>
> This administration has sown the wind and is going to reap the whirlwind. They had better a thousand times have let every agitator, pacifist or cantankerous what-not have had his full [say] than have adopted these methods. No war for *real* democracy needs such despotic methods and I repeat—you can't sow tyranny and expect to reap democracy.[7]

Quarreling with his old friend revitalized Wood's spirits, but only briefly. Through the last dismal months of 1918 and on into the new year, he looked after Sara in strict seclusion. By early March, she had recovered sufficient strength to return to the Eyrie at 1601 Taylor Street. A month later, they attended a lecture by Louise Bryant on "The Truth About Russia," their first public appearance since Albert's death.

The previous autumn, when Bryant and Reed returned from the Soviet Union, U.S. Customs officials confiscated Reed's notes and materials for his book on the Russian Revolution. In spite of heavy-handed attempts to silence favorable reports on the Bolshevik Revolution—or rather, because of it—Bryant was determined to share her first-hand impressions of revolutionary Russia with the American public and urge America not to intervene against the new government. She embarked on a national speaking tour which drew large, enthusiastic audiences—though she often had to fight for her right to speak.

Sara had seen little of Louise since 1916, when their friendship blossomed in Greenwich Village. Now, with Louise bravely bringing her report on Russia to the American people, Sara set aside her grief in order to show her support. With Wood by her side, she hobbled down the aisle of the packed hall to take a front-row seat. Wood and Sara continued to be haunted by Albert's death, but that night they were recalled to life. After months of solemn isolation, Louise's exhilarating account of the new Russia overwhelmed them. Their hearts opened with grief and hope. They listened and wept.[8]

37. Clear and Present Danger

The war in Europe came to an end just weeks after the accident that took Albert's life, but military victory did nothing to stem the Wilson administration's chilling exercise of wartime powers. During the six months of Sara's recuperation, the Left was the target of massive police actions. The IWW was broken by a series of arrests made possible by the Espionage Act, and its leadership was decimated by courtroom convictions. When Bill Haywood was sentenced to twenty years in jail, he fled to the Soviet Union, where he spent the remainder of his life.

To make matters worse, Congress had toughened the Espionage Act by passing the Sedition Act in May 1918. Anyone employing "disloyal, profane, scurrilous, or abusive language" about the American flag, the Constitution, or the American form of government was subject to prosecution on the grounds that it interfered with the war effort. The most notable target of the Sedition Act was Eugene Debs, the eloquent Socialist leader. As Debs saw it, working people of all nations were being ordered to sacrifice their lives so that the ruling classes could compete for new markets abroad. Debs openly encouraged men of draft-age to refuse military service—and was duly arrested. Brought to trial, he denied the validity of the law and refused to take any part in his own defense. When finally he spoke out, he condemned all war and expressed solidarity with struggling people everywhere. He was convicted and sentenced to ten years in the federal penitentiary.[1]

Like Debs, Charles Schenck, general secretary of the Socialist Party, was convicted for urging draftees to refuse armed service. He appealed his case to the Supreme Court on grounds that the Espionage Act interfered with his First Amendment right to free speech. The Court upheld the act in a landmark decision that produced Chief Justice Oliver Wendell Holmes's principle of "clear and present danger." In ordinary times, Schenck's leaflets would not be subject to prosecution, Holmes reasoned. But in time of war the government was entitled to place certain restraints on speech whose purpose was to interfere with the war effort. Holmes offered his memorable analogy: "the most stringent protection of free speech would not protect a man in falsely shouting fire in a theatre and causing panic."[2]

With such overwhelming power aligned against them, many on the Left abandoned the struggle. Writing of the postwar period, Frederic C. Howe, a leading figure in progressive politics of the prewar era, glumly asked: "What has become of this movement that promised so much twenty years ago? What has become of the pre-war radicals? . . . Was the fight too hard? Did youth burn itself out?"[3]

Howe's account of a generation of radicals laying down their arms applied, in part, to Wood. He longed to begin his retirement, but he could not turn his back on issues he had fought for most of his adult life.

Three weeks after Wood attended Louise Bryant's speech, he sent a caustic letter to the new attorney general, A. Mitchell Palmer, taking up the case of Dr. Marie Equi, whose conviction for various violations of the Espionage Act had recently been upheld by the Ninth Circuit Court of Appeals.

Dr. Equi's political activism was intensely personal—so much so that even those who shared her beliefs sometimes viewed her as a liability. Wood knew Dr. Equi well. For years she had played an active role in Portland's government reform movement, and she worked energetically in the suffrage campaign of 1913. After receiving her medical degree in 1903, Dr. Equi made her rounds on horseback, often riding into neglected rural areas to treat Indians and the working poor. A woman of passionate political convictions, she displayed a violent temper—almost always directed at men in positions of authority. In one typical incident she horsewhipped a school superintendent for dismissing a teacher in frail health.

In 1913, during a labor strike at the Oregon Packing Company,

Dr. Equi vented her wrath on the Portland Police Department. When Tom Burns, an IWW leader, was hauled off by the police, Equi followed them, delivering a stream of profane curses. At the jail, she forced her way inside and demanded to see Burns. When the officers tried to restrain her, she slugged a deputy sheriff and socked the night watchman in the eye. They heaved her onto the street, but she snuck back in and found her way up to Burns and the police. She shouted at the officer in charge of booking Burns: "You're a cowardly, atavistic creature! You're a primitive puppy. You beat your wife, and you would beat your baby if it cried in the night so that you couldn't sleep. You're a cave man, that's what you are!"[4]

The following day Equi was back again. When police tried to restrain her, she declared: "I started this fight a Socialist, but now I am an anarchist. I'm going to speak when and where I wish. No man will stop me. The first man who touches me will die a slow lingering death. I'll stick him with a pin that contains a certain virus that I can make, this virus will do the work."[5]

The next day, Equi defied a police order against further demonstrations to lead a procession of IWW strikers. She carried a piece of gas pipe in one hand and a club in the other. When police seized her weapons, she cursed the sheriff at the top of her lungs: she became so apoplectic that her anger rendered her speechless. Later, she attacked a patrolman and pricked him with her presumably deadly hatpin. He quickly cauterized his wound. Fortunately for Equi, several friends prevailed on police to let Equi leave town rather than face a trial in which, in all likelihood, she would have faced insanity charges.[6]

In 1916 Dr. Equi's rage against the war came close to turning Portland's Preparedness Day parade into a melee. According to one account, she coopted a telephone lineman's spurs and climbed a telephone pole (she was forty-four at the time) and unfurled a banner that read: "Down with the imperialist war." When a mob of Preparedness supporters demanded that she kiss the American flag and forced it in her face, she refused. The incident led to accusations that she spit on the flag—a charge she vehemently denied.[7]

A second account of the same event has her displaying a banner: "Prepared to die, workingmen. J.P. Morgan & Co. want preparedness for profit. 'Thou Shalt Not Kill.' " An irate mob seized her banner and tore it to shreds. "That's what we do to your banner," they said, "now tear ours!" They thrust an American flag at her.

Equi replied, "Very well, brave American gentlemen. Your flag is no protection to me." She took it and tore two strips off it. A near-riot ensued.[8]

Sara discovered Dr. Equi's mercurial temper during her struggle to extricate herself from her marriage to Ehrgott. Dr. Equi was such a vehement ally that Sara recoiled. In 1913, while Sara was in Goldfield, she told Wood she "had a letter from that strange mixture of Wild Cat and Madonna—Dr. Equi. She has immense impulses for justice and mercy and fair play. She has a great, big maternal heart. She would suffer anything to help a 'down and out.' . . . On the other hand she has an absolutely ungovernable temper and lack of refinement that never holds her tongue back from the vilest language. . . . I firmly believe that at these infuriated times she is really temporarily insane."[9]

Dr. Equi's volatile mixture of abrasive personal qualities and her uninhibited loathing of all restraints on individual liberty made her a highly visible public figure. On June 27, 1918, at a public meeting of IWW members in Portland, Equi declared that she and her fellow workers were not fighting to defend either the American flag or the British flag: their allegiance was to the industrial flag—the IWW's red banner that stood for the blood of industrial workers everywhere. She went on to say that, although it was against the IWW platform to injure or kill another fellow worker, she and every other man and woman who held a red IWW membership card were willing to lay down their lives for the cause of industrial freedom. She pointed to the example of Irish revolutionists who were taking advantage of the European conflict to throw off their tyrannous master while England was weak and unable to stop them. She urged the Wobblies to do the same. Her speech brought her an indictment on eight counts under the Espionage Act (*Equi v. U.S.*, 261 F. 53). She was tried and convicted and sentenced to imprisonment at San Quentin federal penitentiary.

In his letter to Attorney General Palmer, Wood accused the government of falsely invoking the security of the United States in order to satisfy "the privileged, wealthy classes of Portland and those who consider existing conditions sacred." Supporters of the war were free to disapprove of what Marie Equi had to say, but they were not entitled to use the courts to shut her up.[10] Indeed, Wood believed that the court's proper role in the Equi case—its constitutional duty, in fact—was to affirm that she be allowed to be as irritating and inflammatory as she chose to be.

Any hopes that Palmer could be swayed were soon dispelled. Over the next few months the attorney general proved himself to be a formidable enemy of civil liberties. In the last months of 1919, soon after the Worker's Party (forerunner to the Communist Party) was formed, Palmer directed a massive onslaught against the red menace. By his order, thousands of suspects, said to be harboring dangerous anti-American sentiments, were rounded-up in a nationwide series of police sweeps that showed no regard for constitutional rights— the so-called Palmer Raids. (Of the many persons rounded up under Palmer's authority, 249 people of Russian origin were put on a ship and deported to Soviet Russia on December 22, 1919. Among that group were Emma Goldman and Alexander Berkman.)

From the start, Wood regarded the Wilson administration's assault on civil liberties as intolerable. Yet until the Equi case, he managed to separate the high-minded man he had met in Oregon from the vicious actions the wartime president permitted. The trial of Dr. Equi was the final straw. In June, Wood argued Marie Equi's case before three judges representing the Circuit Court of Appeals for the Ninth District in San Francisco. Wood maintained that whatever incendiary words or gestures Dr. Equi may have uttered, in constitutional terms she was exercising her First Amendment right to criticize government actions that she found repellant and undemocratic in nature. Whether she was right or wrong in her beliefs, or whether an overwhelming number of citizens despised her behavior, was quite beside the point. Equi had not conspired with the enemy in treasonous acts; she had not committed acts of violence upon her fellow citizens or deprived them of liberty in any way. She was a firebrand—but then so was Samuel Adams, a national hero.

In the wake of *Schenck v. U.S.*, Wood must have known his arguments would have little impact on the courts. Nevertheless, he filed a lengthy brief lambasting the Espionage Act. His brief was not so much a legal argument as it was a lament over the previous four years in which the progressive temper of the prewar era had been all but obliterated by President Wilson's messianic mission to make the world safe for democracy.

Wood began by calling attention to what he took to be inviolable principles of the First Amendment. It is relatively easy to support the principle of protecting the many from the tyranny of the few, he reminded the court. But the Constitution gives equal importance to safeguarding minority views from the tyranny of the many. Even though the people of the United States overwhelmingly supported the war against Germany, the "insignificant and scattered minority" who opposed war still had a "constitutional right to say their say about the Government's methods and about the war itself."[11]

> *They were entitled to speak, and if by speech and reason they could turn their minority into a majority and by our political methods could upset the administration at Washington, and, as to ourselves, end the war, they had a perfect right to do so.* The Declaration of Independence says so and every principle of free government says so. They had a right to overturn by free speech the very form of government itself. . . . To deny the right of a minority to turn itself into a majority by discussion is to deny free speech and substitute for the tyranny of an autocrat the tyranny of a majority or what the Government pleases to call a majority.[12]

Those who supported the Espionage Act believed that the war effort required national unity. Criticism of government policy was tantamount to giving aid and comfort to the enemy; therefore, it was subject to proper restraint. Wood attacked this line of thought as a grave incursion on the legal foundations of democratic society. The people "have as much right to question the act of *war* as any *other legislative act*," Wood insisted, "as much right to attack the Government's policy of *war* as any other policy."[13] Wood told the court that the Espionage Act had the effect of substituting martial law for civil law—which is to say, "the Constitution was suspended by force."

Wood quoted the First Amendment: "Congress shall make no law respecting an establishment of religion or prohibiting the free exercise thereof or abridging the freedom of speech or of the press or the right of the people peaceably to assemble and petition the government for a redress of grievances." Then he reiterated his point:

> . . . Are not these words clear enough; do they need interpretation? "Abridging" is the word—not "abolishing"—not "preventing"—not "blocking" or "impeding"—but *abridging.* That is, Congress shall not in the least degree *impair, limit* or *pare down* the full freedom of the minority, nor of any *one* person, to protest in *speech* and in *press,* in *war* or in *peace,* against the *government*—freedom to fully criticize every *policy, law* and *act* of *the government without fear for the consequences.*[14]

Wood renewed the argument he had made several years before in Seattle: that it was precisely in times of war, when issues of life and death were decided by tides of popular emotion, that all opinions had to be heard. "If ever individuals need protection for free speech, free press and free conscience," Wood wrote, "it is in time of war. You need a guard in a mad-house more than you do in a cornfield. People don't need constitutional guarantees at their picnics and prayer meetings."[15]

Wood's disdain for the idea that free speech is conditional, that it can be curtailed in times of national emergency, made him particularly critical of Justice Oliver Wendell Holmes's opinion in the Schenck case. Holmes's example of a man falsely shouting fire in a theater and causing a roomful of people to panic was hardly the same as an individual speaking out against her government. Wood pointed out that shouting "fire" in a crowded theater places individual lives at risk and is open to the civil remedy of injunction against private injuries. But how is this applicable to criticism, even deliberate lies, directed against the acts of a government? As a vast network of institutions, governments are not subject to injury in the same way as individuals. Even if a speaker uses false attacks against the government in a deliberate effort to stir up discontent, she is allowed to do so under the First Amendment. If the government is disturbed by what it takes to be subversive criticism or malicious lies, the way to thwart these attacks is for the government to state its own case, combating falsity with truth.

Wood went on to castigate Holmes for his decision in *Patterson v. Colorado.* Holmes ruled that although prior restraints to free speech are prohibited under the First Amendment, this does not prevent the government from subsequently punishing whatever remarks are found to be harmful to the public welfare. "Why, everybody, everywhere, always had the right to speak and *take the consequences*," Wood quipped. "*Free* speech meant that as to attacks on *government* there were to be *no consequences*."[16]

As for Dr. Equi's conviction, Wood challenged the government ruling on several procedural points. At Equi's trial the court permitted the prosecution to show her "intent" by citing her behavior at the 1916 Preparedness Day rally in Portland a full two years before she was indicted, a time when the nation was not even at war and well before the Espionage Act had become law. In other words, a perfectly lawful act by Dr. Equi was used to prejudice the jury against her.

"But . . . what is the use of citing fundamental principles?" Wood asked. In the last pages of his brief he abandoned legal argument to examine the deeper issues that prevented Dr. Equi and many others from receiving a fair trial:

> Just consider the atmosphere of the trial we are discussing. . . . Fences, walls, windows, hotel lobbies and banks were decorated with posters inspiring the most pusillanimous fear and unreasoning hate. . . . Truth was suppressed and lies manufactured and deliberately and knowingly published, atrocities that never happened—fears of invasion, foolish and groundless. Falsities fostered by Government because bonds must be sold and soldiers conscripted—till finally sauerkraut became "Liberty" cabbage; German pancakes, "Victory" pancakes, and American noodles refused to eat German ones. This was the atmosphere. . . . Instead of depending on the spirit of a free people in a true war for true "Democracy" and true "Liberty," the American people were treated as poltroons and imbeciles, too cowardly to face danger and not fit to be trusted with truth. . . . To hint that we were jumping in between two systems of imperialism, fighting to the death, subjected the speaker to prison sentence. That was the atmosphere.[17]

What is most impressive about Wood's defense of Dr. Equi is his willingness to assail the political environment that made her conviction inevitable. Marie Equi's fiery speeches posed no great threat to

America's security. Did the attorney general's office really imagine she would incite the IWW to open revolution? In bold, lively language Wood censured those whom he considered to be truly dangerous people, men whose actions undermined constitutional safeguards of human liberty: the Wilson administration, the attorney general, and the Supreme Court.

"It is a very able document," his friend Darrow observed, "and I do not know of anyone who could have written it better." But Darrow had no illusions about its impact. "I presume the brief will do no good. I wish it would, but what is the use in arguing with the mob. . . ." Constitutions are only good when you do not need them. When they run up against the deep-seated feelings and emotions of man, they are powerless. They help the strong, but they cannot help the weak. The majority in force and power always has its way regardless of its constitutions or laws. . . . In times of great stress, constitutions are always swept away."[18]

Darrow, who aroused others to fervent belief, believed in very little himself; or rather, he believed that ideals, including his own, were relatively insignificant in the real world—that life was essentially a competition of selfish parties trying to manipulate reality to their own ends. Unlike his friend, Wood refused to shrug off the Espionage Act as an unfortunate but inevitable aspect of "the deep-seated emotions and feelings of man." His brief in behalf of Dr. Equi revealed his finest qualities: deep intellectual conviction, moral sympathy, and contempt for the use of force to regulate self-expression. His vehement attack on judicial stupidity and on the anti-democratic temper of wartime America displayed the very values he defended. It was his last important courtroom appearance.[19]

38. The Heart, the World, and
Mr. Wilson

In July of 1919, Wood returned to Portland to close out his business, to see his family, and to attempt the delicate task of asking Nannie for a divorce. In no time at all, he was caught up in the lives of those he had left behind. Once again, Kitty Beck's life was coming apart due to an ill-advised romance. This time it was George W. Vanderveer, chief counsel for the western IWW.[1] Wood had worked with "Van," as he called him, on several occasions and knew him to be a heavy drinker—a horrendous choice for Kitty. After her miserable marriage to the alcoholic Dr. Irvine, it troubled Wood that Kitty had fallen in love with another alcoholic. Haunted as he was by memories of his father's drunken assaults on his mother, Wood saw Kitty's romance with Van as the prelude to disaster.

As for Wood's main mission in Portland, his conversations with Nannie led nowhere. Nannie had no wish to sever their legal ties. It was not a matter of her Roman Catholic faith—she was not especially religious. She was, however, immensely proud of the life she and Wood had built in Portland. She refused to concede that it might be over. She loved him; she made that clear to everyone. She clung to the hope that Wood might eventually tire of Sara and return to her in a show of conjugal devotion that would sustain them, decorously, to their graves. Nannie must have suspected that a change of heart was unlikely. Still, she remained Mrs. Wood, the one and only Mrs. Wood. For almost forty years, she had been Mrs. Wood to every soul who knew her, and her husband's recent defection did nothing to diminish that essential fact. He had done what he pleased in life— done what men do, that is—and she had ignored it, up to a point.

On those rare occasions when an affair wounded her, when a romance went on too long or became too earnest, she pulled herself together and—for the sake of the family, her marriage, her name—bore her head up high. But what he wanted now—legal freedom, the right to give his name to another woman—she would never allow. She could not stop him from abandoning her and the family. There was nothing she could do if, at sixty-seven years, he imagined he could start life anew. Perhaps, as he tried to tell her, she would never again be all in all to him. Still, she would never relinquish their past: their summer courtship at Rosewood Glen; gay military balls; beautiful letters from her handsome young lieutenant; those wonderful first days together as husband and wife; the train ride across America; that early morning at Vancouver Barracks when she heard little Erskine's first cries; their dear children Nannie, Max, Lisa, Berwick, and poor Katherine; their home and garden; Chief Joseph and those stolid Indian chiefs sitting politely in her Portland parlor. Forty years of living memories. No, Nannie would never surrender her pride of name. Till her dying day she would remain Mrs. Charles Erskine Scott Wood.

During Wood's stay in Portland, he wrote a scathing profile of Woodrow Wilson which he sent to his friend William M. Reedy, editor of *Reedy's Mirror* in St. Louis. Over the previous year, the Wilson presidency had unraveled with terrible swiftness. In January of 1918, a triumphant Wilson brought before Congress "the only possible program" for lasting peace, his fourteen points for a new world order. Once Allied forces brought the European war to its end, Wilson planned to call for an international conference to form open covenants of peace. The allied nations would give a sympathetic hearing to colonial peoples' claims for the right to self-determination. Foreign powers would remove themselves from Russian territory to let the Russian people determine their own government and national policy. The Allies would level no punitive indemnities against Germany— Wilson's promise of "peace without victory" would become political reality.

A year later, in January 1919, Wilson traveled to Paris to make good on his plan for universal justice. Jubilant crowds lined the streets to cheer his arrival. But Wilson's program fell apart at the Versailles negotiating table. France, Great Britain, Italy, and Japan

joined in a series of secret agreements: they annexed German territories, extended their colonial designs, and conspired to destroy the
revolutionary Bolshevik government. The Allies spurned almost every
one of Wilson's fourteen points, yet Wilson refused to repudiate the
Versailles Conference or even to admit that his diplomatic mission
had failed. True, Wilson was allowed his cherished League of
Nations—but it was little more than a conciliatory gesture made to
assuage the American leader's affliction of high-mindedness.

Wilson returned to America and demanded that the Senate ratify
the Versailles Treaty. Instead, he was villified by all sides. Opposition
went far deeper than party politics. There were those who worried
that Wilson's League of Nations would entangle America in the
muddle of European politics. Others objected that Wilson had broken
his compact with the American people, that the Versailles Treaty
upended the lofty principles of his fourteen points. Determined to
break the congressional deadlock, Wilson took his case to the American people. In early September he embarked on a speaking tour of
twenty-nine western cities. In three weeks he covered close to ten
thousand miles. Then, on September 25, his health broke down.
Doctors rushed him back to Washington where, on October 2, he
suffered a stroke. Through his last year in office President Wilson
remained an invalid. His dream had come apart, and with it, his
health.

Well before Wilson's health broke down, Wood wrote his devastating analysis of Wilson's presidency. "Some still admire President
Wilson," he began, "many rage against him, but none pities him;
and of all living men, he is most to be pitied. . . . There are failures
which Time lifts up and glorifies, because, though they failed in
accomplishment, they were true to their ideals; and there are failures
which Time leaves crumbled where they fell." Wood left no doubt
which kind of failure Wilson was: he "clothed the ideals of the world
in such perfect phrases that he became the hope of the world," only
to betray his words in a sustained show of "diseased egoism." Wood
denounced Wilson's willingness to support England and Japan's
blockade of Bolshevik Russia—a clear sign that the victorious powers
had no respect for the principle of self-determination. How was it,
Wood asked, that Wilson refused to admit his own failure? How

could he continue to argue, with undiminished eloquence, that he had fulfilled his promises to the American people?

> ... His great egoism reconciles to himself all his inconsistencies. . . . No matter what he does or how he varies, he alone is right, the rest of the world is wrong. . . . He sought to serve mankind, but a supreme egoist can never serve. . . . Debs is serving humanity, and many an humble I.W.W.; but Mr. Wilson cannot serve, for to himself he is greater than any cause on earth. . . . He declared that to alter the treaty by a word would break the heart of the world, mistaking his own heart for that of the world.

Wood excoriated Wilson for his "slaughter of liberty at home":

> ... Wholesale raids, prosecutions, persecutions, mock trials, deportations . . . and he sits, approvingly silent. I ask again, is it because these attacks are against those who have differed with *him* and criticized *him*? . . . Woodrow Wilson knows, if anyone does, that no I.W.W. or any other person brought to trial during the time of war hysteria or during this present time has had or has the slightest chance of a fair trial, yet he permits these wholesale raids and persecutions to go on without a word. . . . Free speech, free press, free conscience and right of assembly have become words, words, mere words to catch school children with.[2]

William Reedy refused to print Wood's pitiless analysis. He admitted to "unstinted admiration" for Wood's piece; still, he confessed that "I cannot go all the way with you in the slaughterous estimate of W.W."[3] Reedy's rejection came only a few weeks after the president's stroke; it may be that this good-hearted man simply could not bear to see Wilson kicked while he was down.

Three months later, Reedy changed his mind. That spring he published Wood's article along with a brief introduction he wrote himself: "The author of this article is probably the best-known of the more advanced Liberals on the Pacific Coast, and he is a veteran of the cause. . . . He supported Mr. Wilson for President on the stump in the campaigns of 1912 and 1915, and now repents."[4]

*

Wood remained in Portland for several months until Nannie rejected his request for a divorce. He must have known from the start that Nannie would hold fast to her convictions and her name; he felt miserable for forcing the issue. Sara was unsympathetic to Wood's protracted effort to spare Nannie's feelings. Furthermore, his lengthy stay in Portland only exacerbated her sense of physical and emotional vulnerability. From afar, Wood urged her to try to assume a more positive mental attitude. After all Sara had been through—divorce, two abortions, Wood's affairs, and Albert's death—it disturbed her that Wood seemed to believe that simply by assuming a more cheerful disposition she could restore her ravaged health: "Now, Erskine, darling, you ought to try to face the characteristics everyone else sees in you. You have a sort of childlike idea that by *wishing* a thing to be, it can be. It is not a fault. It is a charming, fairy-tale sort of attitude which is only difficult to deal with when it prevents you from recognizing insurmountable obstacles to your *wishes*."[5]

These traits that Sara so accurately observed—Wood's wish for the word to become reality; his obstinate behavior when these wishes ran up against "insurmountable obstacles"—bear an uncanny resemblance to Wood's portrait of Wilson. When Wood first met Governor Wilson, he felt an affinity that went deeper than common values and priorities. Wilson and Wood were kindred spirits—or so Wood chose to believe. Well into the war, when Sara and Wood's friends attacked Wilson, Wood defended him as he might have defended himself. Wood was so eager to believe in *his* Wilson that he tried to persuade skeptical friends that Wilson was a bolshevik at heart. Not surprisingly, when Wood turned upon Wilson for his failure at Versailles and his betrayal of civil liberties at home, his dissection of Wilson's character inadvertently exposed much of himself. Wilson's impatience with criticism; his adamant conviction in the overall rightness of his actions; his penchant for masking personal inconsistencies by pointing to an overriding constancy of purpose—these symptoms of Wilson's nature were fundamentally identical with traits that Sara observed in Wood.

Like Wilson, Wood still hoped to impose his heart's wish upon the world. He wrote to Sara: "Let us meet as two young lovers, young in body and soul." But Sara knew this was no longer possible. Sorrow had made her old; she could not "put the soul's clock back."[6] Nevertheless, Wood was determined to live out his dream. After Nannie refused to consent to a divorce, he made the choice he had avoided for so long: to live freely with Sara and share a home with her—to let the law and outraged society be damned.

39. The Flowering Wall

A youthful old man peers into the camera eye. He sports a full beard, proudly unkempt. A mane of white hair falls over his ears, framing his face in wispy ringlets. Bushy eyebrows, arched in recognition of the camera, retain the dark intensity of youth. His eyes look both outward and inward, as if surveying himself in a mirror—assessing not only his image, but his life. Recent tragedy has shaken him enough to disabuse him of any illusions of perpetual youth. At sixty-eight he needs no reminder of his diminished energies, the looming fact of his own mortality.

Even so, his skin is smooth and unlined, that of a person half his years. Alert, strikingly handsome, he seems a young man forced to inhabit an aging body. Some part of him is untouched by time, or, like his youthful skin, seems powerfully resistant to it. He can still exhort Sara, "Let us meet as two young lovers— young in body and soul," as if the mere saying of it might conjure up his lost youth. And there are ways, truly, that his youthful spirit still flourishes. He retains some vital link to that bright-eyed army lieutenant who, forty-five years before, rode forth into the desert vastness of eastern Oregon and came upon its unexpected treasure of rare and beautiful birds. To the young man he once was, that abundant oasis in the midst of splendid desolation came as a radiant omen. Could there be any doubt that he stood upon the threshold of limitless possibilities? One pictures him at that moment of wonder, reining in his steed and pausing to savor his discovery— while heart and mind charge headlong into his imagined future. Then he spurs ahead, bent on joining his life to the bountiful landscape of his dreams.

There are moments when he still believes that all is possible—that happiness lies in sloughing off conventional expectations and prudent self-restraint; that if one dreams the right dreams and pursues them with conviction, one can wish them into being. How can he surrender that hope entirely? How can he possibly concede that growth and change are all but over for him, that there is no more to be gained in living than the muted satisfaction of rest and retrospection?

He cannot. He refuses to become an old man. He is old; he acknowledges this with grudging frankness—but he is old under protest. It shows in his eyes, his expression of candid self-appraisal: the irony and sadness of an unresolved encounter between his life-force, still strong within him, and the hard facts of aging. He remains a rebel, at odds with his situation; a creature of poignant contradiction—a young old man sporting a white gardenia in his lapel.[1]

In the late spring of 1919, before he left for Portland, Wood bought a comfortable three-story house at 1020 Broadway, perched atop a steep hill overlooking San Francisco Bay. An untended garden grew wild over much of the property; a high stone wall, covered with flowering vines, screened it from the street.[2] In the nine years Wood had known Sara it had become a lovers' game for them to give every home they shared a name: "the Flower Pot," "Honeymoon Cottage," "the Eyrie." Now they made "the Flowering Wall" their home: what they hoped would be a quiet refuge in which to renew body and spirit after the last bleak year.

Sara's leg mended slowly, and, as she often warned Wood, her psychic wounds were not easily healed. Nevertheless, when the Democratic Party held its national convention in San Francisco that summer, Wood and Sara took to the convention floor covering events for various radical magazines. Wilson's crippled presidency cast a pall over the dreary affair. The nation had had enough of him and his party: the Democrats stood no chance against the Republican ticket of Warren G. Harding and Calvin Coolidge and their promised "return to normalcy." Delegates, candidates, and reporters endured forty-four ballots before the Democratic Party finally settled on its doomed ticket: James Cox of Ohio for president; and, for his running mate, the young assistant secretary of the navy, Franklin D. Roosevelt.

Wood observed the debacle first hand. He began his report for the *Liberator*, Max Eastman's successor to the *Masses*, with a crowded montage of the political process at its worst: "A band, banners, buncombe, the Democratic donkey braying, the great gloomy auditorium, a flag-draped platform for the Democratic altar and on it A. Mitchell Palmer, the very high priest of liberty. . . . Sharp, lean, keen, smooth-shaven, predacious faces, conferring with unctuous, smooth-shaven, double-chinned faces, politicians all."[3]

Actually, the scene at this convention was not much different than in 1912, when Wood approved of the results. However, for close to six years, many people on the left had suspended their disgust with regular politics in order to share the popular hope that President Wilson might restore government to the common people. Now, as Wilson's second term drew to a close, Wood gave voice to their cynicism and anger. He called one of his convention pieces "View by an Outcast,"[4] an apt name for his *Liberator* article as well, for the underlying theme of his convention report is the renewed alienation of the Left. The president who promised America a "New Freedom" was leaving office with A. Mitchell Palmer ensconced as "the very high priest of liberty."

The one truly gratifying political development of the year happened in mid-August, when Tennessee became the thirty-sixth state to ratify the Susan B. Anthony amendment. Eight days later, on August 26, the Nineteenth Amendment was added to the United States Constitution: woman suffrage became the law of the land. Alice Paul called for a celebration to be held in Washington DC, and she invited Sara to deliver a dedication address for the Suffrage Memorial: triune busts of Lucretia Mott, Elizabeth Cady Stanton, and Susan B. Anthony.

In early February, Sara and Kay left for Washington, where they stayed with Emma Wold, who was then working as Alice Paul's personal secretary. Sara looked forward to celebrating this great victory for women's rights. She soon discovered, though, that the women's movement had been transformed by the changed political environment. The Suffrage Memorial that she had been asked to dedicate was a travesty. She sent Wood a clipping from the *Chicago Daily Tribune* which described the three suffrage leaders as "emerging startlingly from a single block of Carrara marble. Art critics have been perturbed at the strong impression it creates of three startled old ladies sitting up suddenly in bed. 'More like three ladies sitting in a bathtub,' observed a member of the library committee."[5]

Those three eminent women—brave and unyielding in a lifetime of political struggle; yet grotesquely ill-at-ease in their lapidescent afterlife—were a fitting symbol of the changes Sara found in the women's movement. After eight years of militant activity, Alice Paul no longer saw any need for confrontational tactics. In Sara's view, Alice Paul had diverted the party's attention to nonvital measures calculated to "offend *nobody* and—what is more important—keep *wealth* at its command." Sara was disturbed that Woman's Party delegates were so ready to assume the tepid attitudes of mainstream political groups. She joined Helen Todd and Mrs. Robert M. La Follette in a strenuous floor fight for a disarmament platform, which the delegates rejected. She wrote Wood, "I went out of the Convention that day and wept. The militant organization I have loved has become a respectable woman's club."

Along with Crystal Eastman, Anne Martin, and some of the younger women, Sara urged the organization "to swing into a broad, liberal militant program," but to no avail. "They steam rollered that convention like any old Republican machine. . . . I am heartsick. I have refused to join the new organization at $10 annual dues entitling me to the use of the 'Club House' when in Washington. God, it makes me *ill*—the Woman's Party—a Club House!!"[6] The Club House Sara referred to was the gift of Mrs. O. H. P. Belmont, who contributed $146,000 for the purchase of a historic mansion as the party headquarters. The National Woman's Party dutifully elected her their president.

In early summer, Wood went to Portland to settle various business matters and renew his appeal to Nannie for a divorce. In 1921 Lazard Freres paid him a land-grant commission of several hundred thousand dollars, the disposal of which he had to work out with Erskine. He was now in a position to set up generous trusts for Nannie and the children, as well as for Kitty, Sara, and Kay.

Of course, Nannie would hear nothing of divorce. She challenged Wood's supposed anarchism by asking him why divorce was so important to a person who set himself against conventional morality and restrictive law.[7] The situation sickened Wood, and Portland's stifling moral atmosphere only intensified his disgust. His daughter Nan and her husband Dave seemed typical of the life he had fled: "Nan and Dave are the regular decorous married couple of good society and probably think they are as well off as marriage and life permit. . . . No people can decorously tread a treadmill and find it profitable spiritually, intellectually."[8]

In spite of everything, Wood treasured his time with his children and grandchildren. It was time to "shed all remorse through loving memory and meditation."[9] But above all, it was time to enter fully into his life with Sara at the Flowering Wall. "I shall leave [Portland] as if I died," he told Sara, "never to return, and with your hand in mine, . . . really and truly live to ourselves above the clouds—and with our darling daughter."[10]

40. A Man Is More than His Work

Wood's days at the Flowering Wall were crowded with visitors. In the summer of 1921, Sara's sister came by regularly, as did John Cowper Powys, often with his brother Llewelyn in tow. Noel Sullivan, a recent friend, had been an admirer of Sara's since 1916 when he heard her speak at the anti-Preparedness rally at Dreamland Rink. The heir to two substantial fortunes, Sullivan used his resources to support talented African-American artists. At a time when even his radical friends showed little interest in racial issues, Sullivan welcomed black singers and artists into his home as houseguests. In the 1920s and 1930s, he helped launch the careers of Roland Hayes and Marian Anderson, two of the great singing talents of the era. He hosted Bill "Bojangles" Robinson and Duke Ellington. And in 1933 he gave Langston Hughes free run of his home—the first of many generous offers Hughes accepted from the man who became his patron and trusted friend.

George Sterling, the Bay Area poet and presiding spirit of San Francisco's bohemian community, was another regular visitor to the Flowering Wall. In his early fifties, dark-haired, with a strong, square jaw, Sterling cut a rugged, energetic figure. His sportive temperament burst loose in legendary escapades, such as diving for water lilies in the ponds of Golden Gate Park. Yet he remained a member in good standing at the Bohemian Club, the exclusive sanctuary for San Francisco gentry, where he ingratiated himself to people who had little to do with poetry and free-spirited paganism.

Wood received unknown artists in the same engaging spirit with which he welcomed established figures like Sullivan and Sterling.

Through Albert Bender, an enthusiastic patron of the arts, Wood met young Ansel Adams and his wife Virginia well before Adams's photography became widely appreciated. For the next fifteen years Ansel and Virginia were among Wood's closest friends. In March of 1921, Genevieve Taggard and her husband, Robert Wolf, moved into a small apartment across the street. Genevieve was twenty-six, an active socialist and, as Sara observed, "all the poet," whose work was just beginning to appear in national magazines. Along with her lyric talent, she possessed a searching, intuitive intellect. Soon Genevieve was dropping in at the Flowering Wall several times a week. When her first child was born in 1922, she named her after Sara.[1]

In his affectionate memoir, *The Verdict of Bridlegoose*, Llewelyn Powys describes Wood's home in terms that many visitors must have shared:

> We used to see a great deal of Sarah Bard Field and Colonel Wood, the former spirited and generous, and able to wear, prettily enough, flowers in her grey hair, the latter like some magnificent old chieftain, victor of a hundred battles. . . . Never was their bounty exhausted. Truly it was a noble thing to see the old man busy himself with the simples that he was preparing for a salad, or to follow behind him as he walked up Chinatown, white-haired, debonair, and bowed down with parcels. His ways are not my ways, his beliefs are not my beliefs; but I cannot but do homage to this old, unrelenting, white-maned lion of Oregon.[2]

In the last months of 1921 Wood helped establish a theater school in San Francisco. Impetus for the project came from Maurice Browne, a talented young Englishman, and Ellen Van Volkenburg, his American wife. Browne has sometimes been credited with introducing experimental theater to the United States, but though he was not the first person to bring modern drama to the American stage, his creative experiments with the Chicago Little Theatre, which he founded in 1912, made him a vital force in the rapid spread of avant-garde theater. One year after the Chicago Little Theatre gave its first performances, Browne published his credo, "The Temple of a Living Art." Echoing Emerson's "The Poet," he argued that it was pointless for

American artists to duplicate European productions. Why, he asked, was there no truly indigenous theater in America? He found it "utterly incredible" that American artists ignored exciting raw materials in their own culture: in American history, in regional life, and in Indian lore.[3]

In 1921, Browne came to San Francisco where his friend Sam Hume, director of the Greek Theater at Berkeley, had recently opened an experimental theater. Hume urged Browne and his wife, "Nellie Van," to share his rented building and start an associated school. In Browne's words, "the theatre miserably died; the school monstrously flourished." Soon, Browne was issuing regular ultimatums to the city demanding a suitable building.[4]

Wood and Sara took to Browne's project immediately. Wood shared Browne's love of Greek drama, and he admired Browne's determination to pursue his work in defiance of conventional taste. Given the condition of the building Browne was asked to work in, Wood must have been pleased, too, by Browne's cheerful acceptance of hardship. Wood became the angel Browne needed to keep his school alive, and he vowed to raise enough money to build Browne a proper facility.

On a shoestring, Browne and Nellie Van began experimental acting classes organized to explore the underlying principles of commedia dell'arte. They dressed their students in unisex outfits—tight grey caps and overalls—to accentuate the expressive function of face, hands, and body movement. Over the first sessions, students were required to mime objects, events, and emotions. Later, they were given a "language"—the vowels *a, e, i, o, u* in sequence—varying elongation, intonation, and stress to express the particular requirements of their dramatic scene. Still later, they undertook collective improvisation, using their unusual dialect to create thirty minute scenes.

Wood had high hopes for Browne's project. In addition to drama workshops, there was to be puppet theater, Greek plays, and children's theater, as well as instruction in all aspects of acting, playwriting, lighting, set and costume design—the full life of theater.

The Brownes directed several productions, including Wood's one-act play, *Odysseus* (1923). Wood's Odysseus arrives in Thebes an old man who has outlived all the great warriors of his youth as well as Penelope and his son, Telemachus. His clear eyes are clouded and blurred, his "young face now fallen to this wrinkled mask"; he is "a stranger in a stranger world." Two young men greet their hero on an empty beach, but Odysseus debunks his own achievement. "I could make a lie seem very truth," he confesses. ". . . I was the master liar of them all. And I, the master liar, say train your young tongue to truth. There is a jewel for you from an old man—who has seen some things. Yes. Has seen some things; and done some things. . . . How contemptible it was: childish and contemptible."[5]

Odysseus gives his sword to one of the boys, repudiating war as pointless male vanity. Having renounced the martial instincts of his youth, the lover of Calypso and Circe forsakes passionate love as well. Then Odysseus walks into the sea and disappears in the waves— a large sheet of painted canvas, under which several squatting drama students rose up and down to simulate the heaving ocean.

Wood infused his short play with much of his own life. The old man who outlives his contemporaries; the warrior who lays down his sword; the cunning speaker who finally turns to truth; the ardent lover who discovers the greater power of spiritual affinity—Wood's Odysseus is a heroic amplification of himself. In a sense, his play is a reaction to Alfred Lord Tennyson's "Ulysses." Instead of Tennyson's gallant Victorian hero setting off on a last voyage, "to follow knowledge like a sinking star," Wood's Odysseus expresses the chastened idealism of the postwar era. Weighed down by sobering experience, his most heroic act is to reject heroism.

Maurice Browne's school and theater never gained a secure financial foothold. A downturn in the national economy may have reduced the number of potential supporters, but even in the best of times, San Francisco's patrons of the arts were, by and large, conservative. The School of the Arts of the Theatre had no distinct political agenda, but the mere promise of innovation was enough to unsettle cautious souls. Also, among San Francisco's bluebloods and wary philanthropists, "theater" itself held a certain risqué promise—lurid visions of dance hall girls and forbidden pleasures—hardly a fitting venue for discriminating art patrons.

To those inclined to feel uneasy about the unruly possibilities of theater, Blanding Sloan's puppet-play adaptation of Wood's *Heavenly Discourse* was enough to confirm their every fear. Given the nature of Wood's satiric pieces, the idea of enacting them with puppets was inspired. The sight of pompous spokesmen of piety, militarism, and moral censorship portrayed as smaller-than-life puppets fit in nicely with Wood's impudent social criticism. Unfortunately, in attempting to capture the spirit of Wood's writing, Sloan gave himself carte blanche with its content. By conflating material from several dialogues, as well as adding scenes of his own, Sloan disfigured the work. In a scene based loosely on "Preparedness In Heaven"—where God instructs Gabriel on the techniques of propaganda ("Have at every gate and on the steps of the throne posters such as Satan and his fiends clutching virgin seraphs with diabolic intent")—Sloan twisted God's ironic instructions by actually dramatizing the satanic assault. Another scene—nonexistent in Wood's writing—had a puppet of naked Eve sitting seductively on God's lap.[6]

In what must have been one of the most bizarre vice raids of its time, San Francisco police raided the theater to charge Eve with immoral behavior. Given Wood's loathing of comstockery, he might have had a field day in court defending the morals of Sloan's puppets. But Wood was put off by Sloan's misrepresentation of his ideas and insisted that Sloan rewrite the play. This was enough to appease San Francisco's guardians of good taste. However, the possibility of further scandal probably drove more than a few prospective patrons back to orchestras, orphans, hospitals, and other dependably unoffending recipients of their beneficence.

Now that the Flowering Wall had become a gathering point for the Bay Area's creative community, it appeared that Wood was at last living the life he wanted. Still, it upset him that, with the exception of his daughter Lisa, his own children were reluctant to set foot in his home. In mid-September, Max and his wife, Myrtle, came to San Francisco to visit. Of his three sons, Max was Wood's favorite. He spent several days with Max and Myrtle, but the visit was tainted by nagging illness. Max's back ached, he felt rotten; he confided to Wood that he was trying to keep up his spirits for his wife's sake.

Soon after he returned to Portland, Max started discharging blood in his urine. His doctors suspected a kidney problem but an X-ray revealed nothing. A month later, Max developed a high fever, and this time his doctors discovered the cause: an abscess had broken in Max's kidney, causing severe blood poisoning. There was nothing they could do for him.

Wood hurried to Max's bedside in Portland. He assured his son he would be all right. Max responded with feverish talk. Before long he became delirious. A coma exhausted his last reserve of strength. "That's all I had of my boy," Wood wrote to Lisa.

Wood insisted on preparing his son for burial. Erskine and Berwick helped him wrap the body in unbleached muslin winding sheets. Then they set it in a plain pine box covered with black cloth. Wood tried to speak at Max's grave but he broke down. He recovered long enough to talk briefly of Max's life, of his affection and thoughtfulness. Then he broke down again. "Everybody loved him," he added. That was all he was able to say.[7]

Three months later, Wood turned seventy. Though he still grieved over Max's death, on that one day he allowed himself to celebrate with a few friends. John Cowper Powys delivered a poem gorged with hyperbolic praise. Then he lifted his cup and improvised a toast: "A man is more than his work; else his work is but a small thing. And you, my dear lord, who paint life and the old sweet look upon the face of life, you who sing of death and the old strange look upon the face of death, are more than these things; more than the best of these things."[8]

At the heart of Powys's lavish praise were sentiments many of Wood's friends shared: that his stature derived, not from any single accomplishment, but from the caliber of the man himself. His involvement in worthy causes, his vocal criticism of injustice, his writing, his generosity, his sympathy, his abiding love of life—none of these attributes alone accounted for the affection he inspired, the strength and hope he gave others.

Wood was indeed a source of support to many, yet his loving attention failed to shield Sara from her spiritual anguish. Albert's death continued to torment her. For months she had been exploring psychic literature in hopes of finding some supernatural power that might put her in touch with her lost boy. She was not alone in her pursuit. The deaths of so many young men in World War I led to a surge of interest in communication with the "other side," spawning a subgenre of popular books that offered poignant personal accounts of bereaved parents who had spoken to their departed sons.[9]

Max's death only seemed to heighten Sara's fixation with spiritualism. She began receiving "communications" from Albert, bursts of automatic writing that streamed from her in large schoolboy script, the pen never leaving the page: every word and every line linked in the spontaneous flow of mystical reunion with her son. "You were so filled with anxiety that you might not get my message in time," Albert's letter began. "You became a poor channel. Mother dearst [sic] the immense love over here is the key to everything. Its power and possibilities are absolutely unlimited and are a continual joy and revelation. You are such a necessary part of everything. I am always wanting to get you over here only I know the importance of growing to the full on your old plane." Albert's spirit had fond words for Wood. "Pops you are such a picturesque old duck. . . . I am with you very often. You are big you are very picturesque. Please wear a jaunty tie for me."[10]

Albert's transmissions consoled Sara. He had entered a realm of immense love, of acceptance and reintegration. All this was potentially healing—yet it threw everything askew. Sara had been tempted by death before. Now, with Albert speaking to her from "the other side," she felt even more drawn to oblivion. Had Albert not told her he wanted her to join him in a realm of pure love? What held her back? Her anchor, as Albert's message implied, was Wood. When Albert's spirit asked Wood to "wear a jaunty tie," it revealed his power to distract her from her grief. He was her primary link to life, her reason to struggle to be in the world. This time it was not enough. Sara often warned Wood that she had yet to experience the aftershock of Albert's death: that a spiritual and mental crisis was likely to happen, that it *had to* happen; she could not resist it. Sara succumbed to fits of brooding and insomnia that exhausted her and drove her still deeper into herself. She spent days with her Ouija board, hoping to communicate with Albert. At night she stood in her nightgown staring at the moon. In late June, she suffered a nervous breakdown and attempted to take her life.[11]

Wood placed Sara in a sanitarium.[12] For weeks she barely spoke. When she returned to the Flowering Wall, Wood installed bars on her bedroom window and hired nurses to keep an eye on her around the clock. She was, as Kay recalled, "beyond our reach. We had no way of knowing how long this isolation from her would last."[13]

While Sara lay ill, Wood received tragic news from Portland: Janina Klecan had committed suicide. Janina was a talented physician, an intelligent and forceful personality. The vaccine treatment she had pressed upon Wood, the fruits of her studies at the esteemed Virchow Clinic in Vienna, had given him a precious margin of safety at a time when deadly influenza swept across America in epidemic rates. (In 1918 alone, an outbreak of Spanish Flu took half a million lives.) But for all the good she did Wood, and for all his efforts to help her reconstruct a life for herself, their intense relationship was a source of anguish for each of them. When their affair ended, Janina felt all the more isolated; she tumbled again into her melancholic state. In recent years, Janina had done her best to make a life for herself. She had set up a successful medical practice, but she was still trapped within a sphere of spiritual isolation: as she wrote in a suicide note to Marie Equi, she was "worn out." Her sole comfort was that she held the power to deliver herself from despair by prescribing "a long, long rest."[14]

Three months after Sara's breakdown, Wood cabled Lincoln Steffens that Sara was "steadily better."[15] The contest between her crippling grief and Wood's loving attention is given voice in a poem she wrote on Albert's birthday, a year before her breakdown.

> Reach me your hand across his grave
> And let me clasp it tight
> For only Love has power to save
> One who has lost her sight;
>
> A creature blind with agony,
> Bewildered, stricken with the sense
> That he who caught the best of me
> Has vanished and I know not whence.
>
> Taking with him the world I knew,
> Leaving me on a strange, dark shore
> Where all that once seemed good to do
> Has no persuasion any more

Only the longing left to creep
Into the silence where he went,
For where he is—awake—asleep
Is my familiar firmament.

Here there is scarce a crumb for hope;
Here there is nothing we can prove
Only like desperate children grope
For some sustaining touch of Love.

So reach your hand across his grave
And let me clasp it tight
For only Love has power to save
One who has lost her sight.[16]

41. Standing Aside

When he learned of Sara's breakdown, Lincoln Steffens wrote Wood a long letter expressing concern for her well-being. But Steffens had more on his mind. With characteristic enthusiasm, he let fly:

> I think that you and Sara have to learn to practice my theory: that there is a time in life when we should cease to carry the burdens of this world, withdraw from the fighting and the working, and become spectators. You have done your part and certainly Sara has done hers. You have earned the privilege of standing aside. . . .
>
> Let the new generation take up the play, they will take it seriously and, not having thought much, they will play it instinctively, unwisely, probably nearer right than we would. In a word, I think it best for us and for the world that you, Sara and I become watchers and not doers.[1]

Steffens urged his friends to leave America and come to Europe, where they might share with him the joys of a "second childhood." In part, Steffens's advice stemmed from his own romantic renaissance. In 1919, Steffens, who was then fifty-three, fell in love with Ella Winter, a twenty-one-year-old Englishwoman, whose short-cropped hair inspired the nickname "Peter," after Peter Pan.

Wood was tempted by his friend's enticing vision of retirement in Europe, but he was already involved in making plans for a retreat outside San Francisco: thirty-four acres of sloping, tree-covered terrain on a hillside overlooking Los Gatos and the Santa Clara Valley.

He and Sara divided their time between the Flowering Wall and a small shack on the new property. Happy as Wood was at Los Gatos, Steffens's description of carefree life in Europe still appealed to him. With his knowledge of art, music, and literature, Wood did not need to be briefed on the treasures of European culture. Yet other than his trip to Mexico thirty years before, and occasional business sorties into British Columbia, he had lived his entire life in America. Steffens's most persuasive point was the respite Europe offered from political activism. Wood knew precisely what Steffens meant when he said that America presented "too many claims, too many causes and responsibilities that are ours." Now, with money to spend as he pleased, he decided to take Sara and Kay to Europe. They would travel at a leisurely pace, remaining abroad for a year or two, even longer if he found the setting conducive to creative work.

In early January, Wood, Sara, and Kay set sail for Italy. Two weeks later they disembarked at Naples and crossed the bay to Sorrento, where they settled in at Hotel Cocumella, the pension Steffens had recommended the year before. Hotel Cocumella sat atop a high cliff with a fine view of the Bay of Naples, a lovely garden and fragrant orange groves. They stayed there for most of February, making short excursions to Amalfi, Capri, Ravello, and Vesuvius before heading on to Sicily. With its art and architecture, many historic sites, and timeless existence in myth and legend, Sicily delighted him. Yet he was even more drawn to the daily spectacle of peasant life. Wood's sympathetic impressions of Italian villagers, which fill many pages of his journal, make his reaction to the swarms of German tourists all the more striking:

> This perfect exodus or invasion of overfed hoglike people who seem never to have heard or cared that there are millions of starving children in Germany. . . . [This] double-chinned, double-bellied horde scattering money on their own backs, guts and other pleasures. . . . One young ass was fool enough to say: "Wait for the next *war*. It is not ten years off, and it won't be a war of guns and armies. It will be chemical warfare—extermination—and we shall see who triumphs."

To Wood, that young man typified an alarming phenomenon. He worried that the entire German nation might be diseased in spirit, trapped in its own pathology—proceeding down a doomed path that promised the most terrible consequences for its own people and the world at large. "These Germans . . . have done what I had not believed could be done," he confessed, "—made me feel if *any* people are to be wiped off the earth, it had better be the great German people who have given so much to humanity. . . . Today [they] are a smouldering fire—obstinate in their vanity and their hate."[2]

As summer began, Wood received upsetting news. The Internal Revenue Service claimed taxes of $141,000 on his land-grant sale commission and an additional $50,000 for other income. In 1918, when Wood began receiving his commission from Lazard Freres, he claimed a tax exemption by arguing that the work for which he was now being paid had been done before 1913, when the Sixteenth Amendment authorized a federal income tax. If the court ruling went against him, his plans for his family's security and his own future would be shattered.

Wood cut short his open-ended tour of Europe and booked passage home for the end of August. This left three months to visit Rome, Florence, Vienna, Paris, and London. In Florence, he and Sara spent ten days with Steffens and Ella Winter. Ella, who was three and one-half months pregnant, was apprehensive about meeting Steffens's closest California friends, but her concerns were short-lived. When the carriage bearing her and Steffens pulled up at Wood's pensione on the Arno, Wood greeted her with outstretched arms. Ella was enchanted by this "large expansive man with a wild gray beard and flowing white hair." As for Sara, the two women shared important things in common: they were both much younger than their partners, and neither was married. Within a short time they became the best of friends.[3]

Two months later, Steffens and Ella were married in Paris with Wood, Sara, and Kay as their only witnesses.[4] Years later, Ella wrote to Sara: "In my own little personal case you two practically ushered in my whole adult life, our marriage, our baby—the greatest thing in Stef's life, his greatest joy and certainly now mine. From those days in Florence on you always meant more to us, in a deeper and more personal way, than any other element we came in contact with."[5]

At the wedding breakfast they were joined by the sculptor Jo Davidson and his wife, and by Louise Bryant and her new husband, William Bullitt. Billy Bullitt was wealthy, bright, and self-absorbed. Neither Wood nor Sara could imagine why Louise settled for this rampant opportunist after her years with Reed. But Louise, who was thirty-eight when she married Bullitt, was sufficiently determined to snare her thirty-two-year-old lover that she dropped nine years from her age and told him she was twenty-nine.[6]

During his stay in Paris, Wood called on Ezra Pound. In some ways the two men had much in common: Wood's disdain toward America's blustering public figures, capitalism, imperialism, and the unwarranted intrusion of government in individual lives was partially in line with Pound's own political obsessions. Pound, Sara recalls, was "in a ranting mood about how backward America was, how unreceptive to the new writer, how unaware of what was happening in the revolution . . . of writing."[7]

Wood shared Pound's dismay concerning America's parochial outlook, but he had no great liking for the new writing that Pound advocated. Pound was the quintessential experimental artist while Wood, with his embellished poetic diction and his fidelity to traditional rhetoric, represented everything that Pound's rugged modernism rejected. In terms of his own creative work, Wood arrived in Ezra Pound's Paris as a kind of Rip Van Winkle confronted by the jarring fact that he had suddenly aged.

Since his sojourn at Columbia Law School forty-five years before—when he lived in cheerful poverty with Warner, Weir, Pinky Ryder, St. Gaudens, and the gifted new artists of his generation—Wood had felt a natural affinity for bohemian communities, for creative experiment and the lively play of rebellious instincts. With Eastman and his cohorts at the *Masses*, and with George Sterling, Powys, Genevieve Taggard, and Maurice Browne in San Francisco, Wood's role varied from well-heeled patron to trusted friend and creative participant. Yet he always felt a basic commonality, both creative and political, with artists and writers. He arrived in postwar Paris as a welcome visitor, a colorful old man who continued to speak out for all the right things. But he was wholly apart from the creative ferment of the Lost Generation. Pound and Hemingway and their band of exiles jolted American writing into a new age. Wood, a good forty years older than most members of the expatriate community, shared neither their vision nor their methods.

Above all else, Wood's European visit was a pilgrimage to ancient sites of the pagan world and to vibrant villages where peasant life embodied timeless attributes of the poetry and drama he loved. Pound himself was a self-taught classicist, but he and his fellow expatriates viewed Europe less as a repository of cultural tradition than as a congenial haven in which to pursue their radical creative work. One thinks of Pound's friend, the twenty-six-year-old Ernest Hemingway, in his tiny apartment on rue Notre-Dame-des-Champs, turning out spare, oddly affecting stories set in the northern Michigan woods of his youth. In his own youth, Wood had undergone the essential rites that inform Hemingway's fiction: hunting, solitary immersion in the American wilderness, war, disillusionment, and the painful trial of bearing one's wounds in a heartbreaking world. Yet he never turned to the American idiom or to his own rich experience as usable material for his creative work. Wood came to Europe on Steffens's prompting to become a "watcher," not a "doer," and his days in Paris brought home the wisdom of Steffens's advice. The future belonged to a new generation. At seventy-two, it was time to stand aside.

42. The Cats

In early September Wood returned to California after stopping briefly in Seattle to visit with Kitty and George Vanderveer. Kitty and Van had been married since 1922, and from the start, Van disappointed her. His professional ethics, Kitty discovered, did not hold up to close scrutiny. According to her sister, Kitty "learned that the fight against capitalism included shoplifting, manufacturing evidence, and many things her conscience could not stand for, and she just had got into a net and could not get out in any way."[1] On top of all this, Van's drinking was completely out of hand. In a despairing effort to smother her anguish, Kitty began drinking as well. Wood told her she had to stop, that her survival was at stake, but Kitty had lost control of her life.

On the night of October 31, Kitty scrawled a forlorn epitaph on the wall above her bed: "Kitty Beck—sometimes known as Kitty Vanderveer." She sealed herself in an airtight cocoon fashioned from blankets and safety pins: then she inhaled chloroform until she fell unconscious and suffocated.[2] "I wanted to quit many years before," she wrote her sister: she begged Sissy not to blame Van. She sent her love to Wood—then she took her life.[3]

Immediately following Kitty's death, Marie Equi circulated rumors in Portland that Wood was responsible for her suicide. It was perhaps inevitable that Equi's fiery temperament would seize on this event. Coming just two years after Janina Klecan's death, Kitty's suicide revealed a clear pattern to Equi: Wood's love affairs drove women to an early grave. To Equi, Wood was, quite literally, a lady-killer. Kitty's sister, however, placed full responsibility with Vanderveer.

For some time, he had been manipulating Kitty in an effort to seize control of the trust fund and property holdings that had come to her through Wood's generosity. He badgered her and drove her to drink. He had gone so far as to burn her will in an attempt to create enough confusion for him to finagle a stronger claim to her holdings. As far as Sissy was concerned, Van "morally murdered" her.[4]

Just before Thanksgiving, Wood and Sara moved into their new home in Los Gatos. For years, he had envisioned a simple retreat where he could "cast off the tyranny of *things* . . . a house with bare walls, and bare floors, a monastic house."[5] His new home was hardly that. Built into the hillside so as not to "kick the environment in the face," the one-story structure formed a squared off "U" with vine-covered pergolas flanking each wing and a tiled patio and fountain in the center.[6] There were five rooms in all—three bedrooms, a kitchen, and a large living-dining room lined with French doors opening to a balcony. Instead of the bare walls and floors of Wood's "monastic" fantasy, the ceiling was paneled in fine Philippine mahogany. Bookcases lined the walls, filled with rare editions splendidly bound in the finest leathers; the floors were covered with rich Persian carpets. Wood's art and treasured possessions were everywhere.

Wood commissioned works by several artists to enhance the house and grounds. The sculptor Beniamino Bufano created a bronze relief for the living room: a sylvan scene of Wood and Sara seated beneath the tree of Poetry, surrounded by woodland creatures. Later, Buffano fashioned two figures for the courtyard fountain, fired in an exquisite blue glaze he learned in China: a boy and girl, hugging one another with shivering delight beneath the sprinkling water.[7] Ralph Stackpole—whose work was featured at the Panama-Pacific Exposition, and whose sculpture graces the San Francisco Stock Exchange—made a delicate allegorical medallion of "Peace," a mother holding a child, which Wood installed over the fireplace. Stackpole also created an enormous representation of Maia to preside over the courtyard from a pedestal on the rooftop solarium.

The grounds at Los Gatos were lovely: sloping, tree-covered terrain facing east toward the Santa Clara Valley. A series of gracefully curving concrete retaining walls formed terraced gardens interlaced with paths and concrete steps. Thanks to the tireless attention of

Vincent Marengo, Wood's gardener, the land supported a stunning variety of flowers and shrubbery, a grove of olive trees, fruit trees, an excellent lemon crop, and eventually a vineyard.

Wood named his home "The Cats." (The name Los Gatos, "the cats" in English, originated with the first Spanish settlers, who found the hills swarming with wildcats.) He hired the sculptor Robert Paine to create two giant cats to stand on either side of the entrance path to his estate, facing the old Santa Cruz highway. Paine's figures soon became popular landmarks to travelers on their way to Monterey and Carmel. To friends and visitors who turned up the winding road to Wood's home, the cats were emblematic of what Wood and Sara created there: a domain of grace and beauty; a life lavish in its pleasures, yet simple in its essential design; an enchanted realm inviting callers to share Wood's celebration of the precious gift of life.

Except for several weeks of intense, summer heat, Los Gatos was ideally suited for Wood's retirement. It was close enough to San Francisco for him and Sara to visit town for social gatherings, opera, and other cultural activities. And it was not far from Carmel-by-the-Sea, the tiny village that had become a haven for artists and nonconformists in the prewar years. Given Wood's susceptibility to socializing, he did well not to make his home in Carmel. Even so, he and Sara made regular visits to their Carmel neighbors.

By the time Wood moved into The Cats, Carmel's artistic community was diluted by more conventional newcomers, but it still survived. Robinson Jeffers and his family lived there in solitary splendor; Wood and Sara's beloved friend, Noel Sullivan, kept a beach house, "Emmesfree," filled with interesting guests; and a year after Wood took up residence at The Cats, Steffens and his family transplanted themselves to Carmel.

At the urging of George Sterling and Llewelyn Powys, Wood and Sara called on Robinson and Una Jeffers at Tor House, Robin's barnlike granite dwelling built upon the cliffside at Mission Point. Wood and Jeffers already admired one another's poetry. A few years before, Sterling had given Jeffers a copy of *The Poet in the Desert*, which Jeffers found "noble." Jeffers, in turn, sent Wood a copy of *Tamar and Other Poems* (1924), the volume that launched his rise to fame.

Wood and Jeffers had much in common: a Pennsylvania childhood; gifted, demanding fathers; a strong background in classical literature; and, in their own poetry, a penchant for narratives exploring large, philosophic issues. From the mid-1920s through the 1930s, Jeffers was regarded as one of America's foremost poets. Yet, like Wood, he remained an anomaly. His portentous psychological dramas were as far removed from the work of his contemporaries as *The Poet in the Desert*. Jeffers considered most modern poetry to be "thoroughly defeatist." Modern poets fought a losing battle to "reclaim some of the power and reality that it was hastily surrendering to prose." All too often, the result was a poetry that was "slight and fantastic, abstract, unreal, eccentric."[8] Wood thoroughly agreed.

Wood and Jeffers also shared a wish to renounce active life in order to pursue their creative work in isolation. There was this large difference, however: Wood, who was old enough to be Jeffers's father, had led a full life in which he had pursued overlapping careers in the army, law, business, politics, and community affairs. Jeffers became a poet as soon as he left college. His experience of life was limited; his withdrawal from social contact all the more severe. Jeffers seldom called on other people. In the years that followed, he rarely ventured to The Cats. But Wood and Sara visited with Jeffers and Una whenever they came to Carmel, perhaps three or four times a year. Una, who was naturally gregarious, struck up a close friendship with Sara. Jeffers and Wood tended toward abstract, philosophical discussions punctuated by awkward silences brought on by Jeffers's intense inward nature.

In January, Wood traveled to Washington to testify before a subcommittee of the Senate Judiciary Committee on behalf of an amendment designed to bar the United States from conducting war for any purpose. The peace amendment was introduced by Senator Frazier of North Dakota, but much of its support came from the Women's Peace Union, a group of women activists who shared Sara's disappointment at the Woman's Party's reluctance to support controversial issues. No one really expected Congress to amend the Constitution to endorse pacifist principles: the Women's Peace Union viewed the hearings as an opportunity to draw public attention to how America's military budget undermined domestic programs; how saber-rattling affected the minds of America's youth; and how civic organizations had come to reflect the new spirit of militancy. The Peace Union turned to Wood knowing that, with his record of military service, he could set forth their arguments while seizing the patriotic high-ground.

Wood put on a fine show before the committee and the press. He virtually draped himself in the flag: he was a West Point graduate, class of 1874; an old-time Indian fighter who had made the West safe for economic development. When courteous senators chose to address him as "Colonel Wood," he made no effort to correct them. The gist of his testimony was that the nature of war had changed greatly since the battles of his youth. World War I was fought with little respect for human life: killing had become impersonal, a "science" removed from moral principles. With individual combat replaced by mass butchery, even the victors' worthy cause was tainted by unnecessary slaughter. All that Wood said of modern warfare was true, though to enforce his point he expurgated his recollection of the brutal Indian wars, presenting a sanitized fiction of disciplined soldiers inflicting no more suffering than was absolutely necessary.[9]

For the first three months of 1927, Wood divided his time between New York and Washington, waiting for a ruling on his income tax case. In early April he received the news he had been waiting for: the Treasury Department withdrew all claims on his land-grant commission and recommended a refund of twenty-one thousand dollars.[10] Within days, he and Sara were on their way home. Eighteen months before, Wood and Sara had left San Francisco to begin a reclusive life at The Cats, yet it had been several months since they had even seen their beautiful home. Returning West after their long absence, they were in good health and good spirits. It now appeared they would never again have to concern themselves with financial worries. They were free, at last, to live the life they had dreamed of.

43. A Sugarcoated Pill

In March of 1925, Calvin Coolidge was inaugurated president, ushering in a term of do-nothing mediocrity, a comfort to American voters after the scandal-ridden administration of his predecessor, Warren G. Harding. Wood was appalled. At seventy-four, he was determined to stand aside from social issues, but his indignation at what he saw to be a dawning era of callousness, moral lethargy, and continued erosion of human freedom prompted him to defiant action. He gathered the "Heavenly Discourse" pieces he had written for the *Masses* and submitted them for publication.

The eight satirical dialogues that had appeared in the *Masses* added up to less than fifty pages, hardly enough for a book. But Wood had written several additional sketches that were ready for publication when the magazine was suppressed under the Espionage Act. Even after the *Masses* shut down, Wood refused to abide the clear-cut triumph of government censorship. He continued writing as a self-appointed social critic for a magazine that no longer existed, creating new sketches that satirized censorship, sexual prudery, and the government's blatant abuse of law for politically expedient purposes. In all, he produced forty heavenly discourses—a full-fledged assault on American folly through the war years and their aftermath.

Whatever insight or pleasure Wood's pieces may once have given readers of the *Masses*, the publishers to whom he submitted his manuscript in 1926 doubted if anyone still cared to read such stuff. His heavenly discourses "were not timely," Liveright told him, "their occasion had passed." To his friend, Lute Pease, Wood observed that it would take "a brave publisher" to commit himself to these stinging satires at a time when the public temper seemed immune to idealism and thoughtful self-examination.[1] How many editors turned down Wood's manuscript is unclear, but it is likely he received several more rejections before Vanguard Press agreed to publish it jointly with the *New Masses*, Michael Gold's successor to the *Liberator*.

In June 1927, *Heavenly Discourse* appeared in print: a modest edition of three thousand copies. Wood's friends rallied behind him with extravagant praise. Powys called it "a banquet. . . . Perhaps no note is more rare in modern literature than the one that can truly be called Rabelaisian." Genevieve Taggard celebrated Wood as "the last pioneer aristocrat of letters, a man of the proportions of Whitman and Mark Twain." And Max Eastman, who had never much cared for Wood's poetry, found in *Heavenly Discourse* "the irony of a poet— one of the two or three American poets who ever wrote anything sublime."[2]

Wood shrugged off the promotional hoopla. "I never was moved to write [*Heavenly Discourse*] as literature," he admitted, "and only regarded it as a form—a sugar coated pill—for purging the mind."[3] Surprisingly, his "sugar coated pill" attracted a sizable audience. *Heavenly Discourse* saw three more printings before the year's end and five printings in the first four months of 1928. In less than a year and a half it sold seventy-five thousand copies. At a time when sales of one hundred thousand were enough to make a book one of the twenty or so best-selling titles of the year, *Heavenly Discourse*'s success was exceptional.[4]

Though *Heavenly Discourse* was not the pioneering masterpiece suggested by Wood's friendly reviewers, its remarkable popularity suggests that it was more than a sugary palliative. There is no way to say for sure what it was that attracted readers to *Heavenly Discourse*: its appeal stems from a convergence of several factors. To begin with, it was published at a time when progressives were licking their wounds after the government's successful assault on left-wing organizers, unions, and publications. Perhaps because of this, there remained a sizable audience that hungered for literature and criticism to cut through the soporific mental haze. Sinclair Lewis and H. L. Mencken achieved notable success by aggressively attacking prevailing values—what Mencken saw as "a national philosophy which erects conformity into the noblest of virtues and the free functioning of personality into a capital crime against society."⁵ The Babbit mentality of sober respectability spawned its opposite: a constituency eager for satire. When Wood's *Heavenly Discourse* pieces originally appeared in the *Masses*, they were merely an amusing sidelight to a large-scale journalistic campaign against social inequality, injustice, prejudice, war, and intellectual hypocrisy. When they reappeared in 1927, America was greatly changed. Appearing in the face of the "noble" conformity that Mencken described, Wood's satire seemed bolder, more challenging—a vivid assertion of the "free functioning of personality" that Mencken facetiously described as a "capital crime against society."

In "Freedom," one of Wood's early pieces, Mark Twain corrects God after He mistakenly refers to Twain's native country as "Us land." The proper name is the United States of America, Twain explains. "That's it—U.S.," God answers: "They think they are the whole thing so I confused it with 'Us.' Well, that's the trouble with your country. They are always patching, always trying to dodge the great cosmic principles; to dodge freedom. Every blessing has its price and they are never willing to take a chance with liberty and pay the price."⁶

Whether the subject was censorship, education, prohibition, religious intolerance, marriage, the KKK, or the Scopes trial, Wood's discourses dramatized the conflict between "Us land" and those principles of human liberty that his self-deceived homeland regularly betrayed.

For Wood, perhaps, these pieces were merely a means to unburden himself of pent-up indignation at the nonsense allegedly sensible leaders perpetrated in the name of patriotism, religion, law, and public virtue. But for his readers, *Heavenly Discourse* became a source of rebellious delight, a rallying cry when the Left lacked effective leadership.

As literary invention, *Heavenly Discourse* is thin stuff. Yet Wood's one governing conceit—using God as a witty, indignant spokesman for libertarian values—gives his satire a perspective and persuasive authority it might otherwise have lacked. A self-anointed "pagan," Wood understood that Americans have a marked tendency to introduce religious rhetoric into every aspect of political, cultural, and social discourse; he realized that, in many cases, those who claim

intimate acquaintance with God's will are the same people who
favor authoritarian interference with individual liberties. Censorship,
prohibition, prudery, and bigotry have all been justified by holy writ.
With reactionary forces customarily claiming the high ground in the
war against unruly democratic freedom, Wood perversely chose to
invert the situation by expropriating heaven as an anarchist stronghold.

Wood's strategy was doubly perverse since he had nothing but
contempt for institutionalized religion and its convenient fantasies
of heaven and hell. In the suffocating Sundays of his childhood, in
his stubborn attack on Nannie's Catholicism, and in his anguished
struggle with the Reverend Ehrgott for Sara's freedom, Wood had
come to view organized religion as one of the great enemies of human
liberty. What pleasure he must have taken in meting out revenge!
When earthly spokesmen of God's will appear in Wood's heaven,
they are flabbergasted to find themselves in the midst of all they
have condemned.

Anthony Comstock, who for nearly fifty years prevailed as the
dogged guardian of American morals, comes in for a particularly
hard time. A vigorous opponent of birth control, Comstock fails to
win a following in Wood's heaven. When Gabriel informs God that
Comstock "is the man you put in charge of the morals of the earth,"
God responds: "What are morals? . . . I never put anybody in charge
of anybody's life." St. Peter tells God that Comstock "is so pure that
you are impure." He goes on to cite the classic "religious" argument
against birth control: that "it is wicked to interfere with your sacred
laws of life." But God will have none of it: "As, for example in this
wonderful great European War? Or in factories, or the mines, or the
slums, or the gallows? Eh Peter? Let me tell you here in confidence,
Peter, your church and all churches have a lot to learn about me. . . .
Ha—Hm—Censor. Fool. Censor. Hm. (*Yawns.*) Leave me, Peter.
Disconnect the earth."[7]

In the next discourse, Comstock makes the alarming discovery
that heaven is a nudist colony. When poor Comstock arrives at the
gates to Wood's heaven he refuses to enter until St. Peter finds him
something to cover his naked body. "Poor soul," Jesus observes, "he
mistakes cloth for purity."

Next to birth control and abortion, nothing inflamed Comstock's crusading wrath quite so much as the naked human form. A founder of the New York Society for the Suppression of Vice, he raided Knoedler's Art Gallery in 1887 to suppress indecent paintings; and in 1906 he attacked the Art Student's League for showing representations of naked bodies. When the soul of Anthony Comstock appears before Wood's God, it crouches low in shame, holding its knees together, hands between its thighs. To his horror, Comstock discovers that God, Jesus, all heavenly souls, are eternally naked. "Can it be that I am the only pure soul in heaven?" Comstock cries. God answers, "I hope to myself you are." When Eve appears without so much as a fig leaf to affirm her purity, Comstock's beleaguered soul breaks into conniptions and is led away. God observes that "he is too obscene for words."[8]

Wood clearly relished writing his discourse, " 'T. R.' Enters Heaven." Teddy Roosevelt, who died in 1919, erupts on the heavenly scene with characteristic vigor, ready to turn on his famous charm and work the crowd into patriotic frenzy. Roosevelt, whose hyperkinetic idealism so often approached self-parody, conducts himself in heaven exactly as he did during the anguished months of President Wilson's struggle to keep America out of war. In Roosevelt's eyes, the issue of war was a simple matter: Germany was bad and aggressive; America and England were good and stood for democratic world order; therefore, Germany must be crushed. Wood undermines Roosevelt's patriotic blather by having him recite a boastful litany of democracy's recent "achievements." "What the world needs is the democracy of America," Roosevelt declares, "of New York, of Ludlow, of Paterson, of Lawrence, of Bayonne, of Passaic, of the Solid South, united with the splendid democracy of England, of Ireland, of India, of Africa, of Egypt. I shall annihilate this German militarism with a more thorough militarism of my own."

God is so appalled by Roosevelt's jingoism that He adopts the extraordinary measure of leading His followers in a prayer for peace.[9]

In "Noah's Cruise," the final discourse, William Jennings Bryan ascends to heaven following his death at the close of the Scopes "evolution" trial in 1925. "This is the place of infinite tolerance," God tells Bryan, "that is why it is heaven." But Bryan's impassioned support of Prohibition prompts him to object: "I cannot be tolerant with those who attack our religion and our Bible, your sacred word. . . .

I cannot be tolerant to the wine sellers." He remains adamant even after Jesus reminds him that he drank wine at his last supper and gave it to the world as a sacrament. God adds His view that "the only temperance is from within."

After Bryan makes his exit, Jesus asks his father why He is so pessimistic about man? God replies: "Because he does not understand freedom. He is afraid of it. He hasn't the backbone to stand up and take the consequences."[10]

There is little in *Heavenly Discourse* that Wood had not said numerous times before: in speeches, in his writings for the *Pacific Monthly*, and in *The Poet in the Desert*. Yet in these playful pieces he stated his case succinctly, in piquant fragments of dialogue. In Wood's opinion, he had merely skimmed the surface of anarchist thought and his own reactions to antidemocratic tendencies in contemporary America. While this is true, he ignored what his "sugar coated pill" accomplished. By limiting himself to hastily written sketches, he succeeded in dramatizing his views in a manner that was amusing and quietly eloquent. Wood's confident critical intelligence shines through in every dialogue. The human race may, indeed, be damned; but Wood's spokesmen—Mark Twain, Robert Ingersoll, Tom Paine, Rabelais, Voltaire, and several others—never lose their combative spirit or sense of humor. Readers could hardly miss the unspoken fact that none of God's heavenly allies ever held political office or wielded authority over their fellow beings: they are artists and thinkers. Readers of *Heavenly Discourse* might lack their creative gifts, but they were invited to find inspiration in their example. Life is fullest and most joyful when we express ourselves freely, when we question authority and claim our inalienable rights of life, liberty, and the pursuit of happiness: this is what Wood believed and this is what *Heavenly Discourse* dramatized most appealingly.

It is touching, too, that so many of the earthly visitors to this anarchist heaven were Wood's contemporaries. Bryan, Comstock, and Teddy Roosevelt were all born within a few years of Wood. One might also include Woodrow Wilson, who died in 1924. Although Wilson himself never appears among the dramatis personae, several of Wood's most stinging satires take aim at Preparedness, the Great War, and wartime censorship—all features of the Wilson presidency. If there is a quixotic element in Wood's renewed combat against his old enemies, there is also something valorous and characteristically generous in the spectacle of Wood, at seventy-five, interrupting his retirement in order to introduce the old struggles, the old heroes and villains, to a new generation—one that clearly welcomed this blasphemous voice from the past.

44. Courage of Intelligence

Given the unexpected popularity of *Heavenly Discourse*, Jacob Baker, Wood's editor at the Vanguard Press, prevailed upon him to write a second book expounding his political views. Wood needed little coaxing. He set aside his plan to write a history of his father's heroic mission to Mexico and began writing *Too Much Government*: seven philosophic essays, conversational in tone, exploring the fundamental political issues embedded in his *Heavenly Discourse* sketches.

Too Much Government sets forth ideas Wood had already discussed in a variety of formats. In *The Poet in the Desert*, for example, Wood had assumed the persona of a contemporary prophet in search of a saving vision, which turned out to be anarchism. In essays and public speeches over the past thirty years, Wood had taken on the role of soapbox radical, defiantly proclaiming his support of anarchism, the IWW, and the Bolshevik Revolution. In *Too Much Government*, his persona is less dramatic, less removed from the average reader. Furthermore, he appears to have made a conscious decision to forgo radical rhetoric—perhaps in hopes of reaching the same large audience that read *Heavenly Discourse*. He still carries the anarchist banner, but he does not flaunt it. The speaker in *Too Much Government* is part pamphleteer, part cracker-barrel philosopher, and part indignant citizen offering practical criticism of the dangerous machinations of capital and big government. Wood may have had Tom Paine in mind, as well as Thomas Jefferson, Wendell Phillips, Thoreau, and several others: people who believed that human liberty required unflagging opposition to excessive government control.

Wood strikes his essential theme in a short preface:

Each step by "Government" which invades the full freedom of the peaceable individual in his own affairs is a step toward tyranny which, if not instantly resented and resisted, will end in a nation of docile slaves submissive to every despotism.

Constant rebellion is the only safety, and a true equality, economic and political, is the only goal. Disobedience to invasive laws is the greatest virtue.

"Government" is the corporate name for the dominant few who own the wealth of the planet and of society, and so own and exploit the bodies and souls of the people, in war—and in peace; which is only another kind of war.[1]

The first chapter sets out the current crisis in compelling terms. Wood tells his readers that they have passively submitted to tyrannous designs by property-holders and corporate powers, a privileged elite that advances its interests by commanding the machinery of government and law. "We are a stupid people," he insists. "We believe in wealth and in force. . . . Our education is an adoration of wealth and of force, things, and power—the power of money and the power of police, the power of wealth and of jails, and of churchly bigots. These make our ideals and our morals."[2]

Wood continues in this vein; and while he had made all these points before in *The Poet in the Desert* and in his *Pacific Monthly* articles, he had never said them more effectively:

Of all the stupid solemnities of courts I think the stupidest is, "Liberty cannot be permitted to pass into License." If any power can say what *is* Liberty and what *is* License, then there is no Liberty. Liberty means the right to peaceably say all things and peaceably do all things; being answerable for the consequences. All our constitutions say this, but what is the value of a constitution in a graveyard?. . .

. . . "License," "Chaos," "Revolution," "Treason," and all our familiar verbal bricks were thrown at Patrick Henry—Thomas Paine—Hancock—Adams—Washington—Jefferson—Franklin, and the other rebels and traitors we are so proud of. This country is founded on rebellious free speech that led to revolution. . . . Just now the most active traitors against this Free Republic are the Daughters of the Revolution, the American Legion, the A.F. of L.—and such worshippers of force and suppression—and the fascist-minded courts, who oppose free discussion. These seem to act on the idea that this country has arrived at full perfection, and to find fault or advocate any change is treason.[3]

In the second chapter, Wood renews his argument against America's "feudal" economic system, a distribution of natural riches that permits great wealth to reside in the hands of a privileged few. As a case in point, Wood reviews how elected representatives betrayed the American people by parceling the West into land grants to encourage powerful capital interests to develop the Louisiana Territory's immeasurable resources. Wood goes on to show how this policy vanquished the Native American population and how it forsook the pioneer immigrants whose labor developed the land for practical use.

Wood's impassioned historical account would have been even more telling if he had explained his own role in the process. The land-grant case that Wood won for Lazard Freres was a telling example of how unscrupulous dealings in the early days of western development (the activities of the original Willamette Valley and Cascade Mountain Wagon Road Company) became legally sanctioned through the collaboration of capital (Lazard Freres's purchase of the grant) and law (Lazard Freres retaining the finest legal and political support money could buy). "No one ever ought to get an indefeasible right to stolen property,"[4] Wood states at the end of this chapter. Yet his successful defense of Lazard Freres's land grant placed him squarely on the side of feudal property interests.

Wood's third chapter returned to the issue of free speech, though this time he addressed not only America's shortcomings but those of the Soviet Union as well. Among the American Left, this was not a welcome topic. As in *Heavenly Discourse*, Wood called upon enlightened thinkers of the past to add their voices to his ongoing argument with tyrannous modern-day government. His "Russian" chapter begins with a fine quote from Thomas Jefferson:

There are rights which it is useless to surrender to government and which governments have always been found to invade— these are the rights of *thinking* and *publishing* our *thoughts* by *speaking* or *writing*—the right of *free commerce*—the right of

personal freedom. . . . The mass of mankind has not been born
with saddles on their backs, nor a favored few booted and
spurred, ready to ride them legitimately by the grace of God.[5]

Wood picks up from this to comment on how the Soviet Union
measures up to his standards of absolute liberty:

Believing, as I do, that no cause justifies a denial of fullest
freedom to every peaceable man. . . I cannot and do not approve
the denials of political liberty—denial of free thought, free
speech, free press, with which Soviet Russia seeks to bulwark
itself. Instead of approving, I hold this tyranny of the Soviets
up to the American Legion, the A.F. of L., . . . to chambers of
Commerce and fascist "patriots," and beg them not to persecute
communists, socialists, I.W.W.'s, and others who find fault with
our great Republic—because to do so is so exactly like Soviet
Russia that we may be mistaken for Soviet Russia.[6]

Wood went on to deride America's assault on human rights since
World War I. It might appear that he minimizes the Soviet Union's
shortcomings by emphasizing those of America; but this is not really
so. In his description of two powerful nations locked in warlike
contention—each driving the other to despotic measures against its
own people—Wood flashes more than enough indignation to go
around. Because the United States government viewed the Russian
Revolution as a threat to world order, it felt justified in depriving
American Communists and other "troublemakers" of their civil liberties. Crusaders for the American way found it convenient to undermine
the Constitution in order to have a free hand to silence "reds":
jailing them, beating them, deporting them as the situation demanded.
Similarly, because Russia's leaders saw Europe and America aligned
against their new regime, actively seeking its destruction, they felt
justified in taking extreme measures to protect Soviet Russia and its
revolutionary programs, which is to say, they crushed all dissent.
Wood's essay sharply stresses the absurdity of the situation: two great
nations betraying the very ideals they imagine they are defending.

"The trouble is," Wood insists, that

no cause justifies forcible suppression of the thought of any
man; the suppression by force, being inherently an evil, is always

an evil—as much an evil in a good cause as in a bad one. . . .
And not till every government, or dictatorship, realizes that the
greatest safety to itself, as well as to mankind, is absolute
untrammeled expression of thought, in time of war even more
than in time of peace—not till then will intelligence begin. But
such freedom requires the courage of intelligence. The trouble
is, governments and dictatorships—and every government is a
dictatorship—do not want intellectual discussion; for out of
discussion is born truth, and the truth shall set men free.[7]

Wood's chapter stands as a fine example of what he calls "the
courage of intelligence." He did not need to mention Russia at all
in his book; in fact, it appears that his editor at Vanguard Press was
taken aback by his decision. Although some notable figures had
already expressed disenchantment with the Russian experiment,
many more people on the left shared his belief in Russia's glowing
prospects. Certainly, it would have been expedient for Wood simply
to assail the American system, but he held himself to his own high
standards: he could not very well attack the tyranny of *all* government
while excepting the Soviet Union. He could not exalt the necessity
for free speech while muting his own voice.

The remaining four chapters make strong points against bigotry,
censorship, and prohibition, but they tend to ramble. Wood's editor
at Vanguard Press might have done Wood and his work a real service
by eliminating extraneous passages.

In a brief conclusion, Wood challenges his readers to see how
they participate in their own oppression:

We are interfered with and accustomed to control and dictation from the cradle to the grave in thought, speech and act, in
work and play, in morals and manners, in habits and cos-
tumes. . . . We are thoroughly prepared to be submissive slaves
in a great imperialism, and so long as we ourselves are not
smitten we care not that another's freedom is being slain. We
do not fight that others may have freedom in the opinions we
hate. We reverence the policeman's club because it is "Law". . .
and every instinct should teach us that most law is oligarchic
despotism, and no law is entitled to blind obedience.[8]

Wood had little faith in common people's ability to comprehend their situation. The voting reforms that he had worked for—direct election of senators; initiative and referendum; and woman suffrage—had all passed into law. Yet the "people's power" movement achieved far less than reformers had hoped. Whatever the reason—either indifference or the power of ruling elites to manipulate public opinion—voters never used the potent instruments in their possession to gain political leverage over entrenched power and wealth.

In 1931, the same year *Too Much Government* appeared, Lincoln Steffens's autobiography was published. The project gave Steffens a loose, congenial format in which to have his say. The result is one of the memorable books of its time. Part reminiscence, part history, part social criticism, part philosophic reflection, the narrative is held together by Steffens's off-handed charm and the pleasure he takes in telling a good story. Like *The Education of Henry Adams*, which appeared thirteen years earlier, it showed the potential of autobiography as a flexible literary genre: one that gave personal experience the resonance of history, while enlivening history and critical reflection with the engaging particulars of the narrator's own story. If Wood had chosen to return to the reminiscences he had begun just before the war, if he'd continued his autobiography in a narrative that moved freely between his life experiences and his beliefs, he might have produced a lasting contribution to our literature.

That book was never written. *Too Much Government* is pungent and intellectually lively, but as a follow-up to *Heavenly Discourse* it failed to attract the large, enthusiastic audience of its predecessor. If Wood felt any disappointment over this, he left no record of it. A few months after *Too Much Government* was published, he turned eighty, an event that was every bit as important to him as his book. Life itself was his most absorbing undertaking, and he returned to it enthusiastically.

45. We Are Our Own Works of Art

A home movie made at The Cats in 1930: the grape harvest. Vincent, Wood's jack-of-all-trades, pursues his work while Trotsky, Kay's white-haired fox terrier, barks and scampers underfoot. Sara appears briefly, then darts out of the frame to resume her duties as cameraman. Wood bounces here and there in plus fours and full white beard, master of the revels. He and his merry band traipse among abundant vines filling bushel after bushel with ripe grapes, romping and teasing, hamming it up for the camera.

Now they make ready to go. Wood mounts a wooden sled which his retinue drags over the sloping vineyard. He rears back in his marvelous vehicle, dangling bunches of freshly picked grapes above his ears like satyr's horns, laughing, laughing. With rotund belly and white beard he is a bacchic Santa Claus. Buildings of the Jesuit Novitiate of the Sacred Heart lay sprinkled on the opposite hill, but at The Cats pagan gods hold sway.

Back at the house, Vincent dumps the grapes in wooden vats. Wood cannot contain his excitement. Like a boy stripping for his first summer swim, he throws off his shirt and socks, then hops into one of the tubs and improvises a grape-crushing jig. Vincent hands him a cane to steady his balance. He fixes it firmly on the ground and continues to spin and spin in his harvest dance, this celebration of life.[1]

W hen we drove home from the Cats Monday," Steffens wrote to Wood, "I felt that I had been in a place of beauty, and I wondered why we didn't go oftener to you. The drive there is beautiful, the hill is beautiful, the house, the hosts, the guests, the spirit of it all—the whole and every part are beautiful." Steffens continued:

> Los Gatos is a work of art. A play of art. For one feels that
> the design is unconscious, as if it were a garden where beauty

grew and became aware after the blooming. And to me, to a guest, it has the extraordinary effect of taking one in and making you also beautiful, as music and poetry do. You have a rare triumph in your continuous creation of The Cats, for it expresses you & Sarah more completely than anything you two have ever written.

. . . I may be wrong about this, but I am truly telling you the feeling I have after a visit to you. And just this once, let me add that as between the house and yourselves, you, Erskine, and you, Sarah—you are the more perfect. You are, both of you, each one of you, beautiful works of art. One must not say a thing like this twice or to the face of the bearer, and I will not repeat it; and you won't answer it. Please. It is enough that I have got it out of my system, the thought, that we humans can achieve beauty in ourselves & that we are our own works of art. That is what you have proven, that is what you illustrate.[2]

Steffens's tender words bear with them a canny evaluation of his friend's achievement. Wood's powerful effect on people stemmed not from his writing or his political work; it emanated from his remarkable presence—the sum total of what he had become through his long and varied career, enhanced now by the life he made with Sara. It is characteristic of Steffens's lively intellect that the very words with which he praised his friend conveyed gentle criticism as well. A sharp judge of character, Steffens was quick to appreciate originality in whatever form it manifested itself: in the rough pragmatism of city bosses; in gifted proteges like Walter Lippmann and John Reed; in the Bolshevik Revolution; or in his first reading of James Joyce's *Ulysses*. Wood, too, was an original, but not in any one field. Steffens was too fond of Wood to comment frankly on his written work, but it is hard to believe he was much enamored with *The Poet in the Desert* or with the archaic diction of Wood's shorter poetry. When *Heavenly Discourse* was published and Wood's friends responded with fulsome praise, Steffens remained silent. Still, he loved the man himself, like an admiring younger sibling who lived prosaically while his older brother pursued life as a kind of poem.

In a piece originally written for the *Carmelite*, Steffens continued in this vein:

I heard an old anarchist speak on liberty in Los Angeles. A poet, a painter, a gentleman and an ex-army officer, he looked and he spoke like a poet painting pictures. It was a treat: the world is going the other way, but, wherever it goes, men will not be men till they are all like that lovely old anarchist down in Los Angeles and can all say, with his carriage and grace, such lovely things as he sang out of the past into the future. Charles Erskine Scott Wood, is more beautiful than any youth, boy or girl.[3]

As Steffens observed, the world was "going the other way" from Wood's libertarian ideals. The governments of Italy, Germany, and Soviet Russia were being transformed into highly centralized administrations, instruments to execute the designs of dictatorial leaders. In the United States, the New Deal spawned huge new bureaucracies, a higher concentration of governmental authority, and new legal vehicles for coercive force—everything Wood had been combatting for years.

All this gave Wood further cause to dwell in the separate world he made for himself and Sara. The Cats evolved as both Palace of Art and earthly Olympus. A photograph from this time shows Wood in sturdy sandals, a colorless knee-length tunic, and baggy trousers that are tight at the ankle. He has long curling hair and a full white beard: Zeus as bohemian guru.[4]

The Depression did little to curtail Wood's entertaining at The Cats. In 1932 he turned eighty. Friends poured into The Cats from San Francisco and Carmel: Steffens and Ella Winter, Ansel Adams, Noel Sullivan, and many others. Some visitors to the Cats thought that lavish events like these were inappropriate in a time of widespread economic hardship. One such person was Elizabeth Elkus, wife of Albert Elkus, the prominent San Francisco composer. Raised in a working-class London family, an active suffragist and socialist in her youth, Elkus respected Wood and Sara but was rather put off by their costly lifestyle and the peculiar air of elitism she often encountered at The Cats.[5]

It is easy to see why a young radical would feel removed from the goings-on at The Cats. Yet Wood and his friends had proven their generosity and active commitment to radical causes many times over, and they continued to do so. At eighty, he still spoke out against injustice. One event that captured his attention was the Scottsboro case, in which nine black teenagers were falsely accused of raping two white women in Scottsboro, Alabama. The conviction of the "Scottsboro Boys" set off a heated dispute over who would conduct the appeal. The NAACP retained Clarence Darrow, but the International Labor Defense Organization, a Communist group, gained the backing of the defendants and their parents. The NAACP and the Labor Defense group made halfhearted efforts to work together, but Darrow and his associates quickly realized that the Communist Party intended to use the trial to make far-reaching political arguments connecting racial prejudice to class struggle. As a result, Darrow withdrew from the defense.

Wood, who considered himself a friend of the Labor Defense group, inquired about Darrow's withdrawal. They told him that Darrow had never been a part of the defense. Wood challenged this, and they revised their story, claiming that Darrow was invited to participate but that he declined because he thought the case was hopeless. Finally, Wood wrote directly to J. Louis Engdahl, general secretary of the Labor Defense group, to tell him he had been fed nothing but lies. Darrow withdrew, Wood insisted, because the Labor Defense group was determined to pursue a strategy that would "saddle on to race prejudice (the color prejudice) the additional prejudice against 'Communism,' 'The Class War,' 'The Class Struggle,' 'The tyranny of the Master Class,' etc."[6]

Wood was repelled by the Communist Party's willingness to sacrifice human lives to advance their own goals. Darrow could provide the best defense, there was no one better, but he was loathe to use the rape trial as a pretext for condemning America's economic and social system. Wood continued to support Communism and to publicly espouse the promise of Soviet Russia, but clashes like this—when party strategies claimed precedence over the fundamental importance of individual lives—chipped away at his faith.

During his retreat at The Cats, Wood remained in touch with all his family. Few letters between Wood and Nannie have survived from this period: it is likely they only wrote to one another on birthdays, Christmas, and important family occasions. In 1930 Nannie sent him a birthday note, written in crabbed scrawl: "I feel that I should always begin any note or letter by explaining that the reason for my writing such a scratchy bit of a letter is because my hands tremble all the time. I can do no better than to hold a pen. I always want to thank you for your kind & generous thoughts of me."[7]

The rest was indistinct. For close to fifteen years—from the time of their separation—Nannie's letters to Wood conveyed an air of sorrowful dignity. This is what Wood saw of her. But from all accounts, she lived an active life apart from him. She kept up with her wide circle of friends and social groups; there were always children and grandchildren around to brighten holidays and family occasions. Though Nannie's anguish and injured pride never passed, her Portland life remained richly satisfying until age and illness claimed her.

In July of 1933, Nannie fell and fractured her thigh bone. Wood sent her a long letter, expressing his concern. "My dearest Sippy," he began—the old, affectionate nickname from their courtship sixty years before.

This was the last exchange between them. In September Nannie fell into semiconsciousness. At the end, she sank into a delirium: Wood had gone away to San Francisco on a little business trip, she told her family; soon he would return.[8]

Two months before Nannie's death, Wood himself was taken ill. It was nothing serious but enough to prompt Steffens to send him a note. "There's something I'd like to have explained," he teased: "Why is everybody so concerned and anxious when either of you is down? I was in bed for three or four weeks & nobody was—like everybody is when one of you creeps under the covers."[9] Wood and Steffens remained sufficiently well to joke about one another's health, but they had lost enough friends to know how little they could count on their own continued vigor. For the time being, life was sweet: Wood carried on as Zeus at his California Olympus, a grand performance that continued to delight those around him. William Rose Benét had called him "the man of wisdom and unwithering youth."[10] Wood might savor that wishful oxymoron, but he lived with full awareness that the art of living, no matter how fine and generous and beautiful, must finally yield to the inescapable fact of one's own mortality.

46. The Popular Front

With Nannie gone, dear friends like Fremont Older, Bill Hanley, and Lincoln Steffens all ailing, Sara plagued by colitis and coronal angina—and with a sharpened sense of his own mortality—Wood felt a growing interest in leaving a written record of the stirring events from his past. Since the publication of Lincoln Steffens's autobiography in 1931, Wood had received several inquiries encouraging him to tell his story. Around this time, Michael Gold, a veritable dervish of the literary Left, wrote to Sara and Wood from the *Daily Worker*: "I still ask: when is Erskine going to write the Great American Autobiography? From the Indians right smack into the trusts and skyscrapers—it could be the story of America, better and more representative than that of the bookish Henry Adams—if only Gods ever stooped to autobiography."[1] In spite of such encouragement, Wood was reluctant to follow his friend Steffens's lead and undertake such a demanding project.

On March 3, Wood lost one more link with his past when Fremont Older died. As for Steffens, his heart condition continued to worsen, leaving him an invalid at his home in Carmel. Frail, in the final stages of his illness, he managed to send Wood and Sara a New Year's greeting for 1936. In spite of Steffens's hopeless condition, his letter sparkled with lively irony and rich affection:

> I have half a mind to write one New Years's letter just to break my rule, and, to be sure it does no harm, I'll address it to you and Sara, the last old believers in love and justice left in the

whirling world. You two are incorrigible. In spite of all the history we have unrolled at your feet you will not let the light go to your heads. You resist learning. You believe just what you believed when I first met you. War, peace, Ethiopia, Mussolini, England, France, the depression, the recovery and now President Roosevelt and the splitting Republicans have come and—all in vain. You two conservatives have closed your eyes and just stuck. Sometimes I think you have opened your eyes and stuck. Anyhow you have stuck. . . .

It is you, two, not Wall street and not only Soviet Russia which prove that human nature is human nature, that, no matter what you do, flowers will go right on blooming.

I wish you both a Happy New Year in the wide garden of weeds—from my heart I do. Never mind how wrong you are, I bless you as all right all right.

Affectionately and tolerantly[2]

Like Wood and Sara, Steffens too was incorrigibly hopeful about the possibility of social change. For much of his career, he was attacked for the very tendencies for which he affectionately rebuked his friends: his faith in social reform, his belief in spiritual change, and a stubborn refusal to surrender his intellectual independence to political parties and ideologies. Now, at the time Steffens teased Wood for his steadfast fidelity to old principles, the American Left was undergoing a period of rapid transformation. For several years, the Left had been divided over the merits of accommodating independent political and creative expression to Communist Party dogma—or, as the conflict was sometimes defined, over the respective claims of "artistic freedom" and revolutionary solidarity.

By 1935 these heated disputes were superseded by disturbing events in Europe. With Mussolini's assault on Ethiopia (May 1935), Hitler's Germany embarked on a program of rearmament, and Franco and his supporters casting Spain into bloody civil war, people of diverse political convictions united against fascist aggression. The Soviet Union gave these organizations its formal blessing when the Seventh World Congress of the Communist International called for Communist parties in every nation to form a "Popular Front" committed to collaborating with all governments and organizations opposing fascism. Steffens, who only a few years before was taunted by Communist intellectuals for pursuing an independent path, expressed what many felt when he declared that people had to choose between fascism and Communism, between Russia and Germany. "There is a time for thinking and planning," he wrote, but "there comes a time to close our open minds, shut up our talking, and go to it lest Hitler do things his way."[3]

Wood refused to go as far as Steffens. After years of defending free speech, he refused to accept his friend's argument that circumstances created "a time to close our open minds, shut up our talking." Even so, he was pleased with the Soviet Union's new willingness to welcome "fellow travelers." Still, at eighty-four, Wood had no wish to give his time to yet another cause. He wanted nothing more than to live quietly at The Cats, to write poetry and work on his father's history. Also, he had been asked to write a new book of satires, a volume he planned to call *Earthly Discourse*. Most of all, he wanted time with Sara, uninterrupted by the commotion of political activity.

The Popular Front won the support of many of the finest artists and intellectuals of the age. In Europe, André Gide, André Malraux, Bertolt Brecht, Max Brod, Aldous Huxley, E. M. Forster, and Boris Pasternak all attended an antifascist gathering that called itself the First International Congress of Writers for the Defence of Culture. In America, the call for a Popular Front led to the formation of the League of American Writers. Old quarrels were set aside (though not necessarily forgotten) as committed Communists joined unaffiliated radicals and left-leaning liberals. The league's membership included Van Wyck Brooks, Erskine Caldwell, John Dos Passos, Theodore Dreiser, Clifton Fadiman, Waldo Frank, Langston Hughes, Lewis Mumford, Lincoln Steffens, Edmund Wilson, and Richard Wright.

Several months later, Carey McWilliams and Haakon Chevalier, André Malraux's American translator, began organizing a Western Writers' Congress to be held in San Francisco in November. The congress was to continue the mission of the League of American Writers: to bring together enemies of fascism and to clarify the cultural-political tasks created by social turbulence at home and abroad. Over the next few months the congress gathered an impressive roster of sponsors. First and foremost was Steffens, whose name was prominently displayed on the congress letterhead. Other sponsors included Dorothy Parker, Sidney Howard, Robert Benchley, John Steinbeck, Yvor Winters, Upton Sinclair, Robinson Jeffers, Clifford Odets, Irwin Shaw, William Saroyan, Anna Louise Strong, Michael Gold, Kenneth Rexroth, Nathanael West, and Donald Ogden Stewart. Wood was approached by the organizers but declined to take an active role. For once, it appeared, he would really keep to his retirement.

On August 9, 1936, Lincoln Steffens died of arteriosclerosis. In an open churchyard in Carmel, Steffens's friends gathered around his coffin piled high with wreaths and flowers. "We had no service," Ella Winter recalled, "but amidst the flowers, Erskine Wood got up with his broad flowing black bow tie and his gray beard, his gray hair flying, and spoke about his oldest friend."[4]

Three weeks later, Bill Hanley died.

Half a lifetime before, Wood had attended funerals of Portland's tight circle of civic leaders: men who had welcomed him to their raw, energetic town; who had insured his success and social standing. Later, he had mourned his beloved friends: Olin Warner, Weir, and Pinky Ryder. He had seen the passing of General Howard along with a generation of legendary Civil War generals. And he outlived the two most remarkable men he had known: Mark Twain and Chief Joseph. He had faced the suicides of Kitty and Janina. Nannie was gone. And now, in rapid succession, Fremont Older, Steffens, Bill Hanley. Of his closest friends from his active past, only Darrow remained—and Emma Goldman, an exile in France. Wood's longevity thrust him into unexpected prominence as a living link between the Popular Front and radical voices of the past. In spite of his wish to stand aside, Wood was drawn back into the events of his time.

In late October, he received a notice from the Provisional American Committee for the Defense of Leon Trotsky, inviting him and Sara to join. Trotsky, who had fled the hostile political environment in the Soviet Union, was confined in Norway, where he waited in political limbo, deprived of the rights of political asylum. His plight was the most dramatic instance of Stalin's broad crackdown on political opponents. In 1936, in the first of several show trials, Stalin's political enemies were prosecuted for crimes against the state—trials that produced a string of suspicious confessions. Trotsky, who fled his homeland rather than face Stalin's kangaroo courts, sought political asylum and expressed a desire to defend his innocence before an impartial international tribunal.

In no time, Trotsky's American defenders were under attack by orthodox Communists. The March issue of *Soviet Russia Today*, a monthly journal published by the American Friends of the Soviet Union, censured the committee in "An Open Letter to American Liberals," jointly signed by eighty-eight prominent figures in arts and letters, including Heywood Broun, Malcolm Cowley, Theodore Dreiser, Lillian Hellman, Dorothy Parker, Max Weber, and Nathanael West. The Provisional Committee did not back down. They recruited Wood and others like him because, as James Farrell explained, they needed to bolster their forces with "people who we assumed had some integrity and reputation."[5] Wood accepted the committee's invitation. In a letter to John Dewey and the committee, he emphasized what he felt was a crucial task: to educate the public mind at a time when popular opinion was not at all receptive to fundamental principles of justice.[6]

Wood's concern with securing a fair trial for Trotsky was consistent with his lifelong advocacy of basic human rights: his support of Emma Goldman, Margaret Sanger, the iww, Marie Equi, and numerous other defendants. This time, however, Wood's advocacy of free speech had a distinctly personal dimension. At the very time that Stalin was moving to destroy opponents said to threaten the Soviet Union's internal security, anti-Communists in Congress were moving to crush individuals and organizations that they thought imperiled national security. In the autumn of 1936, Wood discovered that he and Sara had been identified as Communists by the House of Representatives's Special Committee on Un-American Activities. From the committee's point of view, Wood was a potential menace to the land he had lived in for more than eighty years.

The avenging angel of the House Special Committee was its chairman, Martin Dies, a Texan who had been elected to Congress in 1930 at the age of twenty-nine. In Dies's eyes, the Popular Front was a "Trojan horse," and its opposition to fascism merely a facade. Its real mission was to swell the membership and influence of the Communist Party, to subvert and eventually destroy the American way of life. Within a short time, Dies's committee released sensational disclosures regarding seditious activities of fascists, Nazis, and Communists in government, labor, and industry. The House Committee's manichaean mind-set hearkened back to the Red Scare of 1919, when an earlier generation of self-designated patriots used the Bolshevik Revolution as grounds to crush the American Left.

To his credit, President Roosevelt would have nothing to do with Dies. He condemned his work as "sordid" and ridiculed the committee's lists of alleged Communists. But Dies persisted. In his book, *The Trojan Horse in America* (1940), he claimed that in just two years his committee "made a record of about twenty volumes which include the names, addresses, identities, methods, and plans of many of the Fifth Columnists in this country and the majority of their leaders."[7] Faced with a Communist epidemic, Dies felt no qualms about denying America's deceitful enemies due process of law. Specifically, he attacked "the false interpretation of civil liberties which permits and justifies the existence of Trojan Horses [Communists]." "How," Dies asked, "can we deal with the enemies of the country when we permit them to operate legally and get their names on the ballot?"[8]

When Wood discovered that he and Sara were targets of Dies's investigation—that unnamed witnesses had assured the House Committee that he and Sara were Communists—he fired a scathing rebuke. "Surely," he wrote to Dies, "so dignified and powerful a body as yours should be particular to see that the person accused has an opportunity to examine the witness against him, and it should be your solemn obligation to examine the witness yourselves if the accused be absent; the more so if some blot of infamy is attached to the word 'communist.' "

Dies kindled Wood's combative moral energy. Wood fought back in language reminiscent of his tirades against former adversaries: General Miles, the Reverend Ehrgott, Anthony Comstock, Woodrow Wilson, and Justice Oliver Wendell Holmes. He showed no concern that his taunting letter might provoke the committee to try to ruin him. If Dies represented himself as the defender of American values, Wood was determined to beat him at his own game: he came back at Dies with his personal history, an American chronicle that required no apologies. He called attention to his appointment to West Point by President Grant and to his record of military service. He mentioned his years as an attorney, and he reminded Dies that his daughter Nan sat with Dies in the House of Representatives. Wood insisted that his letter be entered with the committee's records, "as a correction of careless statements or deliberate lying." "And yet," he said in closing, "Mr. Dies, you know that the correction never overtakes the Lie."[9]

The situation in which Wood found himself—condemning show trials in Stalinist Russia while simultaneously combating threats to free expression in the United States—confirmed the vision of *Too Much Government*. As Wood saw it, true democracy required an economic system based on the communistic principle of shared resources. Equally important, true Communism required democratic governance and unrestricted civil rights. From this perspective both the Soviet Union and the United States were currently betraying their founding principles. The Bolshevik Revolution held forth the promise of economic equality and, therefore, genuine human equality. Yet Stalin's authoritarian rule—in particular, his persecution of Trotsky and other critics—threatened to pervert the revolution's noble vision. However, Wood was also disturbed that in America the rise of people like Martin Dies revealed a widespread tendency to ignore the fundamental principles of liberty and individual rights on which the Republic was founded. The doctrine of freedom of speech permitted every group, no matter how radical or unpopular, the right to be heard. The well-being of democratic society depended on its willingness to tolerate an open exchange of ideas even when these ideas challenged the interests of the status quo.

Faced with these pressing issues, Wood agreed to deliver a welcoming speech at the opening session of the Western Writers' Congress. Had he lived and been well enough to appear in public, Lincoln Steffens would have been the keynote speaker. Now, only Upton Sinclair and Wood had the stature to invoke the rich history of progressive struggle in the West and bring it to bear upon the Writers' Congress's agenda.

Whatever excitement the Congress generated among the literary and political Left, the event went almost unnoticed in San Francisco. On November 12, the eve of the Writers' Congress, the city was preoccupied with pageantry and self-congratulation for the opening of the San Francisco–Oakland Bay Bridge, the longest bridge in the world—or, as the *San Francisco Chronicle* put it, "a seventy-seven million dollar bracelet." All else paled, even the grim news that Franco's Fascist rebel forces had begun an aerial bombardment of Madrid. The Western Writers' Congress held its opening session on Friday night in the Scottish Rite Hall, taking up the theme of "The Writer and Reaction." Upton Sinclair, the first speaker, urged the audience to organize against the fascism of Germany and Italy. Also, he pointed to glaring evidence that America's splintered economic system had pushed the nation to the brink of disorder: ten million Americans were unemployed.[10]

The gathering listened to messages of support sent by Thomas Mann, Sherwood Anderson, Sydney Howard, and Tom Mooney from his prison cell. Harry Bridges, the longshoreman leader, gave a rousing speech, and Ella Winter shared a moving letter from Steffens. Finally, Wood rose to speak. In Ella Winters's account of that evening, she praised him for "raising the key issues that brought the assembly together. All his life he has [fought] for the freedom he cares so passionately about, has helped young writers, poets, artists, to fight the obstacles the young face everywhere: with humor but keen analysis he warned writers 'who are like hens: they like to sit and set and brood before they hatch; but even a hen will fly when it sees a rattlesnake.' "[11]

Wood challenged writers to break from their "brooding cells" and engage issues directly before the impending world crisis propelled them into desperate defensive responses. In Ella's words, "he stole the show." The following day he gave the keynote address to the first working session on "The Writer in a Changing World." Playing on the title of Sinclair Lewis's political novel, *It Can't Happen Here*, Wood assured the assembly "It Can Happen Here."[12]

At eighty-four—most likely the oldest participant at the Congress—Wood presented a striking physical presence. With full white beard and long curling hair, he seemed a cross between Buffalo Bill and Walt Whitman, the living embodiment of the Old West and its code of raucous freedom. His audience saw him as a living link to the men and women whose political and literary work created the heritage on which they now sought to build. Several speakers at the congress called attention to this heritage. Mike Gold praised the congress as "inheritors of the great democratic tradition of Mark

Twain and Jack London."[13] Upton Sinclair recalled George Sterling, Jack London, Fremont Older, and Lincoln Steffens. But no one's life reached back as far, or with such rich associations, as Wood's. Who in that room had been alive to see Abraham Lincoln on his solemn journey east to assume the presidency? Who but Wood could say he had welcomed Mark Twain as a houseguest and had a hand in bringing Twain's writing into print? Who else in that room had the same affectionate ties with Steffens? Finally, there was Wood's friendship with John Reed, the American Bolshevik, honored as a hero of the Soviet Union, his remains buried in the Kremlin—Reed, who had come to Wood as a teenager, eager for advice and encouragement.

After Wood's Saturday morning speech, participants attended workshops and discussion groups devoted to such issues as "Censorship, Suppression, Fascist Trends," "Economics of Writing Profession," "Creative Problems and Criticism," "Writing and Propaganda," "The Screen Writer as an Industrial Worker," and "Writing in a Changing World." Nathanael West spoke on "Makers of Mass Neuroses"; Kenneth Rexroth addressed "The Creative Problems of the Artist"; Sara discussed "The Poet's Responsibility to the New Age"; and Donald Ogden Stewart—whose luminous comedy of elite life, *The Philadelphia Story*, would win him an Oscar in 1941—led a discussion on the problems of Hollywood.

At its final session, the congress elected Upton Sinclair as president. When Sinclair declined, the executive committee turned to Wood. Haakon Chevalier, the group's general secretary, praised him for animating the proceedings:

> I wish I could say something that would adequately express the excitement, the enthusiasm, the warmth, the affection, the feeling of fellowship kindled by your presence among us at the Congress. I think every single soul present at the sessions, even the hostile ones, would agree that no one thing so greatly contributed to the success of the Congress—and it was a *success!*—as your presence and your words. You were the one thing that brought all the diverse elements into focus.[14]

Wood was unanimously appointed president, and the executive committee prepared a list of ambitious plans to turn the congress's concerns into action.[15]

Two months after the congress, Wood received a quirky letter from Ezra Pound offering himself as a "centre of thought" to the newly formed group. Under a letterhead that read "A tax is not a share // A nation need not and // should not pay rent for // its own credit," Pound wrote:

Dear C.E.S.W.

I see you been talkin at a CUNGruss. An' I see how az bro Jeffers haz highHatted thet Kungruss. An I wanna KNOW why the hell the U.S. Can't provide a communications service.

AND when a bloke is INTERESTED in organization and in the means of communication why such a Kungruss shd/ go off and get highatted by a local half wit instead of communicating with the few centres (incarnate) of thought who wd/ willingly have increased the communicativity of the said KINGRUSS.

Instead of having a little local hole in corner dorcas sassiety shindy they might have made the congress a FOCUS.

At present moment there is NO American publication wherein I can find, or whereby I can communicate with, the 12 most intelligent men who are known to me.

cordially yrs. E.P.[16]

By the time Wood heard from Pound, the high hopes of the Writers' Congress were considerably diminished. Few of the executive committee's ambitious projects got off the ground. Over the next three years the group produced a bulletin in affiliation with the League of American Writers. Beyond that, the Western Writers' organization had little to show for their efforts.

What doomed not only the Association of Western Writers but also the League of American Writers and most other Popular Front organizations from the start was fierce ideological divisions engendered by the Moscow Trials. This brutal spectacle disheartened many of the Soviet Union's newfound allies, giving them a chilling glimpse of Stalin's authoritarian methods. There remained those who defended Stalin's measures and who still believed that the Bolshevik Revolution embodied the hope of all oppressed people. In their view Stalin was forced to adopt stern measures in order to protect the revolution from internal unrest. This was no time for dissension and divisive criticism. In a period of world emergency, this only helped the fascist enemy.

American Communists were particularly incensed by the Committee for the Defense of Trotsky. Just a month after the Western Writers' Congress convened, the Defense of Trotsky Committee challenged the American Communist Party to pledge its support for the principle of political asylum. Earl Browder, the primary American spokesman for Communist orthodoxy, shot back a strongly worded response in his column in the *Daily Worker*. The prominent figures who rallied to Trotsky's defense, Browder said, acted "from political naivete or from consideration of factional advantage." The party supported political asylum, Browder wrote, so long as it protected "those who suffer persecution at the hands of the enemies of democracy and progress, the reactionaries and fascists." But Trotsky no longer deserved protection. He had plotted the murder of dozens of Soviet leaders, and now he sought to use political asylum as a cover for these plots. As proof of this, Browder pointed out that sixteen of Trotsky's collaborators had confessed their crimes in open court. To Trotsky's defenders, Browder asked: "Do you defend the right to use asylum to plot and execute assassinations?"[17]

Wood's presence on the Committee for the Defense of Trotsky, provoked a swift rebuke from the Communist Party. As longstanding supporters of the Soviet Union, he and Sara had been invited to a reception at its San Francisco consulate. But after their support for Trotsky's defense became known, the invitation was withdrawn. Wood responded with an angry letter to the consul general in which he argued that Trotsky's predicament touched upon basic issues of human rights:

> The Constitution of the United States requires that every accused person shall have all needed aid in securing testimony for his defence. That is only justice and fair play. It never occurred to us that the Soviet Government, if it really desired justice, could oppose this. . . .
>
> We will say to you what we have not said before, that the evidence produced against him is not convincing—but we did not go on to the Defence Committee as adherents of or partisans for Trotsky, but as partisans for the eternal maxim—"Every man has a right to a full and open trial before an unbiased court: to be confronted with the witnesses against him: to have

his own attorneys and to be allowed to present his evidence."
That is what we are on the committee for—not for Leon Trotsky
. . . . What would have become of Lenin without political asylum?

. . . We did not know your government must be assumed to
be infallible and its conclusions accepted as final—not only by
its officials, but by guests at a social gathering. We think the
Soviet Government makes a mistake in assuming that whoever
differs with it is against it.

Wood gave voice to a dilemma that many progressive Americans
found themselves facing: in spite of his support for the Bolshevik
Revolution and the noble mission of the Soviet Union, he objected
to Stalin's antidemocratic methods:

Over and over again, for years, we have tried, at some cost to
ourselves . . . to counteract the vicious influence of the yellow
press, continually shouting "red", and we shall continue so to
do, for the welfare of our own country. But also we shall not
hesitate to differ and to criticize. We do not hesitate to criticize
our own government.

. . . We have hailed Russia as the Hope of the World—the
one people and political state in all history founded on economic
principles, which in time will produce the world-wide substantial
economic equality which will elevate the race and end war. . . .
She, of all the nations of the earth, has placed her feet on
immortal ground. She alone is holding up the torch. Just as it
is our privilege to believe this of Russia so it is our privilege
to differ with the Stalin or any other Soviet government on matters
of executive conduct and policy whenever we feel compelled to
do so.[18]

Wood refused to let the issue drop. He sent a long letter to Earl
Browder: "Until these recent confessions and executions," he wrote,
"I was a partisan for the Stalin government. It has done much for
the Russian people and to advance the Russian idea. I was very
favorable to it—but now I am disturbed. I do not regard the Stalin
government as *Russia*, nor as the sole repository of the Russian idea.
The Russian idea will live long after Stalin and Trotsky are gone. I
do not regard the Russian government as infallible and not to be

questioned any more than I regard the Roosevelt Administration, from which I have great hope, as infallible and not to be questioned."[19] Wood reminded Browder of basic principles he had always defended:

> You American Communists had better be a little careful how you brush these safeguards away. You may need them sometime.—I know what I am saying is useless, for I am writing against prejudice and emotion: two things quite incapable of appreciating reason.—But let us go on:
> Trotsky has not been convicted of conspiring to assassinate. Whoever says so makes himself a laughing stock in the civilized world. To convict by the confession of others, in the absence of the accused is in the settled law of civilized countries, simply ridiculous, and from such conviction no man is safe. This may be made law under dictatorships. . . .
> Of course I can see the smiles on the pretty faces of my emotional young revolutionists: "Presumed to be innocent till proven guilty?—he is proved guilty—by the confessions of the conspirators. . . . And Mr. Browder says so. What more do you want?"—Only this. Read the constitution of the country which shelters you and to whose laws you owe allegiance.—"*Shall be confronted with the witnesses* against him."—Is that plain? Can you really comprehend its meaning? It is not schoolboy oratory. It is not only our own "Supreme Law"—It is the crystallization of the thought of centuries—crystallized in revolutionary combat with tyrants and autocratic governments—and not to be lightly erased to suit the convenience of Moscow and the emotions of the young American acolytes.—Please use your brains.

As he had done so often in recent years, Wood pointed proudly to the activities of his youth.

> . . . Before these young enthusiasts were out of diapers, long before the Russian revolution, I was preaching the basic principle of "Communism:" No special privileges or monopolies, natural or social, in private ownership.—So were many other "Enemies of Society." Russia has no copyright on the idea. It is in Karl Marx—Prudhomme—Henry George—Herbert Spencer.

Finally, Wood invoked his friendship with Reed.

... There was a boy: a playmate and classmate of my younger sons, who came much to our home in Portland, Oregon, until he went away to college. But when the Russian Revolution shook the world, he hurried there and went through it. When the Revolution was established and things had quieted down a bit, he returned to this country and to his home in Portland. One day he came to my sick bed and said he was going back to Russia. He said he might never return and he could not go without saying goodbye to me. Then he told me, very simply, that I had been a great influence in his life, though he did not appreciate it at the time, but only as he grew older and began to remember my views and utterances. I was surprised at this and the almost emotional though very quiet feeling with which it was said. When he had written me from college he did not write anything of this kind. Usually he asked questions about writing poetry and sometimes submitted verses for criticism.

So we parted. I never saw him again. He lies in the Kremlin, by the side of Lenin.[20]

Wood's letter to Browder never appeared in the *Daily Worker*, but his words found their way into print some twenty-five years later in the closing pages of Daniel Aaron's influential literary history of the 1930s, *Writers on the Left*. Writing in the aftermath of the McCarthy Era, Aaron noted Wood's warning: "You American Communists had better be a little careful how you brush these safeguards away. You may need them sometime." Wood's words were more than stinging rhetoric: the Moscow Trials and his run-in with the Special Committee on Un-American Activities had given him a vision of things to come.

47. *Earthly Discourse*

Wood's participation in the Writers' Congress and his galling clashes with Martin Dies and Earl Browder left him little time for his own projects. With these events behind him, Wood devoted the first months of 1937 to preparing his manuscript of *Earthly Discourse* for publication. He pushed himself hard, hoping that his book would have some influence on the judicial crisis that threatened to bring President Roosevelt's New Deal to a halt.

The predicament arose when the Supreme Court ruled that the National Recovery Act and the Agricultural Adjustment Act, key programs in Roosevelt's New Deal legislative package, were unconstitutional. As the Court saw it, the commissions created to execute these acts represented an unwarranted usurpation of legislative power. In fact, Congress had sanctioned these powerful commissions in order to deal forcefully and promptly with economic emergencies that threatened the nation.

President Roosevelt accused the Supreme Court of obstructing economic recovery and disregarding the mandate he had received from the American people to take extraordinary measures to set the country back on its feet. What right had the Court to supersede both the executive and legislative branches of government? In February of 1937 he retaliated by proposing legislation to increase the Court's membership from nine to fifteen judges—a plan which spurred his opponents to accuse him of trying to destroy the judiciary in order to increase his already substantial powers.

In his lifetime Wood saw only two presidential candidates he believed were truly worthy: Woodrow Wilson and Franklin Delano

Roosevelt. In both cases his enthusiasm led him to take positions that contradicted his ideals. He lauded Roosevelt's ambitious programs for economic and social reform—a start, he hoped, toward reducing the feudal power of wealthy plutocrats and to restoring government to the people. But the New Deal agenda created enormous administrative and regulatory bureaucracies, a decisive shift toward the "too much government" he had always deplored. Wood would have been more consistent if he had attacked Roosevelt's overhaul of American government as an egregious example of the tendency toward centralized power that had already overtaken Italy, Germany, and the Soviet Union. But Wood admired Roosevelt's breadth of vision, his sincerity, his eloquence, and his determination to improve the human condition. This, along with America's grave economic crisis, prompted Wood to support the president.

To this end, Wood wrote "The Supreme Court and the Constitution," a learned hundred-page essay/dialogue, the one substantial piece in *Earthly Discourse*. Wood begins by examining the Supreme Court's extraordinary power to veto acts of Congress. As he points out, the Constitution makes no provision for the Supreme Court to invalidate legislation passed by the nation's highest elected officials. After all, representatives in the House and Senate must answer to the needs and wishes of the their constituents, the American people. Why should nine appointed justices, entrenched in their positions for life, claim the right to override congressional acts? Why should Americans put up with a system in which a simple majority of five justices to four is enough to overturn legislative decisions arrived at by hundreds of elected men and women whose votes express the collective will of the hundreds of thousands of people who put them in office? Are we to have representative government or suffer the tyranny of nine justices?

The lengthiest portion of Wood's piece explores *Marbury v. Madison* (1803), the landmark Supreme Court decision in which Chief Justice Marshall invalidated an act of Congress. (The next such decision came fifty-four years later in the Dred Scott decision.) Marshall's decision, Wood argues, set a disastrous precedent. American democracy is based on the principle of representative government; yet this fundamental idea is at risk if nine appointed judges, with no compunction to answer to the electorate, have the final word over elected representatives of the people.

Wood's thoughtful piece showed an impressive grasp of legal and historic material, but the crisis he addressed was settled through political maneuvering rather than intellectual debate. Roosevelt's battle with the intransigent Court raged on for close to six months, until the Court gave up the fight and sustained several key pieces of new legislation, such as the Social Security Act and the Wagner Labor Relations Act.

Whatever the merits of Wood's criticism of the Court, it had no impact on these events. As for the other pieces in *Earthly Discourse*, most lack the urgency, the irreverent spirit, that made *Heavenly Discourse* an unexpected success. The best pieces in *Heavenly Discourse* were funny, taunting, and provocative; *Earthly Discourse* is, at best, merely well-meaning.

Wood's last discourse, "Still in the Jungle," ends on a valedictory note. God assembles the titans of industry in order to propose a solution to labor unrest. It is time, God suggests, that privileged classes accept the principle of human equality—time to create a new democratic era by surrendering property holdings to the general use of all. Not surprisingly, God's plan is rejected as impracticable, utopian, perhaps even anti-American. God replies with a succinct version of Wood's critique of capitalism:

> Every nation which ever existed—every government that ever governed—has gone to its death because of economic injustice—special privilege secured to a few—the people disinherited—and no freedom for the masses. You must learn to combine economic justice with individual freedom or you will go the same way—it is as inevitable as the wheeling of the stars. There can be no freedom where privilege must be supported and discontent suppressed by force.[1]

Since mankind will have nothing to do with the Eden of true human equality, God consigns his unenlightened creatures back to the jungle. Having washed his hands of the matter, He and Satan adjourn to the seashore "to watch the sea-anemones . . . to hear the cool and timeless rhythms."[2] With that, Wood concluded his work as a satirist and returned to private life.

48. "I Will Write My Memoirs"

Two mammoth concrete cats, twelve feet high, flank the handsome iron grill entrance gate. The cat on the left stares ahead; the one on the right squints, either in sleep or vigilant rest. They recall the sculpted sentinels perched on the entrance steps of Wood's former home in Portland: duplicate castings of Olin Warner's bronze bust of Wood as a young man, his handsome head turned toward itself in self-regard. Just as those twin profiles inadvertently suggested essential qualities of Wood as he then lived—his vanity and self-absorption; the double-nature of his life; his constant self-examination—these twin cats evoke the spirit of his later years. Dignified, ruggedly beautiful, they are, quite literally, larger than life. Though similar in almost every detail, their wholly different counte-nances—one with open gaze, the other with nearly closed eyes—suggest elemental divisions. The cats might be allegorical figures of day and night; or they might signify the dual nature of consciousness: outward-facing to the tangible world, inward to thought and creative imagination. They intimate, too, the transforma-tion Wood so often pondered during his Los Gatos years—from life to death. It is as if these two figures were fashioned with this solemn commission: that the living spirit over which they stand guard is the very one they must finally surrender. The cats do not hold back the world but rather they accept it: greeting not only friends and guests, but also the humbling forces of life; receiving them calmly, reverently, come what may.

On September 12 Wood and Sara traveled to San Rafael to attend the wedding of Lisa's youngest daughter, Katherine. Four days after the wedding, Wood suffered a massive heart attack. For close to two weeks his life hung in the balance, but his strong constitution pulled him through. He remained at Lisa's for months, too weak to return home. On Christmas Eve he summoned his strength to write a Christmas letter to Sara. The strain in his script was obvious, as though each word required a separate act of will. "Once more I have been spared to you my lover," he wrote. "Once more I have felt the hand of Death but your love has pushed it away and drawn me back to you. . . . You drew me back to life with filaments of love stronger and more beautiful than the spider's web, strung with dew, and as I came into myself, to live a little longer, to know the beauty and the joy of life, I followed you as with its eyes an infant follows its mother and I knew without you, life was nothing."[1]

Wood understood that his time was limited. One matter he wanted to settle as quickly as possible was the troubling possibility that his unconventional relationship with Sara might lead to legal problems that could keep her from receiving the substantial legacy he had provided for her. After fifty years of arguing that government had no province over love and sexual union, Wood remarried.

On January 20, 1938, Wood and Sara held a private ceremony that celebrated free love and gave short shrift to the protocols of civil marriage. With Kay and Lisa and their husbands as witnesses, Rabbi Jacob Weinstein joined the two free-lovers in matrimony. The director of a school for Jewish studies in San Francisco, it was Weinstein who, as a young boy, had delivered Wood's daily newspaper in Portland; years later, as a young seminary student, he had written Wood to tell him that *Heavenly Discourse* gave him "the first inkling . . . that the godless are often the most truly religious."[2] Responding to Wood's call, Weinstein hastened to San Rafael to conduct a service that would do justice to the anarchist beliefs of the man he admired. He read love poems by Sara and Wood; then he laid down his notes and spoke directly to his two friends:

In the presence of such a union, made by Power beyond all mortal authority I would feel myself sacrilegiously presumptuous to feel that I, as an individual, had any divine authority to pronounce you husband and wife. Your lives have done that in a manner that has been an example of true marriage far more powerfully than the lives of many whose marriage was, from the first, legalized. This was because, as you say, Sara, "the source of both day and night was the heart of it". So it is only by the civil authority vested in me that, with all humility, I say you are now husband and wife in the eyes of the law of the State of California as you long have been in the eyes of the divine law of the kingdom of heaven.

Wood and Sara were too overcome to speak. Wood went away to a secret drawer in which he kept some treasures and returned with Sara's wedding ring, a great ruby set in heavy Chinese gold, and gave it to her. Later, Sara recalled that "the hour we had both rather dreaded proved one of the most beautiful of our lives together. . . . Nothing was different. Nothing was changed. We told one or two very close friends about it and members of the family. Then we forgot it. But it brought peace to Erskine's mind and heart."[3]

Five weeks later, Sara's sister Mary sent word that Darrow had suffered a terrible blow: "I have tragic word from Chicago; namely that Mr. Darrow has lost his mind, just walks up and down, up and down, mumbling and muttering. Paul, his son, writes that they have no hope of his recapturing his memory. Intimate friends are strangers. I personally think he has retreated from a world that was too inhuman and cruel for him to bear."[4]

Wood's mind remained keen, but he was incapable of sustained work. His eyesight deteriorated rapidly. To Lute Pease, a colleague from his days with the *Pacific Monthly*, he wrote: "Forbidden to use eyes—and now some weeks in bed convalescent but weak—that is the log of the wreck on the beach. . . . My eyesight is gone. I do not clearly see what I write. You must do some guessing. . . . I must quit. Cannot see what I write."[5] Many of the letters Wood managed to write at this time reveal the same vein of candid self-assessment. He was a "wreck"—frail, virtually blind, yet he showed no sign of self-pity. On the contrary, he hoped to gather strength to undertake several ambitious projects. In June of 1939, he signed an agreement with North American Film Corporation, a company that contracted well-known intellectuals such as Bertrand Russell, Hendrik Willem Van Loon, Charles and Mary Beard, and Aldous Huxley to deliver lectures that would be filmed and distributed to educational groups. Wood agreed to speak on four topics: his experiences with the Thlinkits in 1876; the surrender of Chief Joseph; "Is the United States a

Democracy?"; and "How the Supreme Court Usurped the Power to Veto Acts of Congress."[6] Also, he planned to finish his manuscript on his father's role in the acquisition of California. And at long last Wood planned to write his own story.

Each day he walked the flowered path to his writing studio, where he and Sara pursued their work in adjoining rooms. In a large marbled notebook, scrawling in nearly illegible script, he struggled to tell his story. "Surely this mid-twentieth Century will be known as the autobiographic age," he began. "Autobiographies are blossoming as thistles by an irrigation ditch and the thistle flower is blown wherever the publisher listeth. I am not an important item on this planet nor in the horde we call—the people—yet in these later years I have been asked by several publishers to write my biography for publication. Each of these fishers of men has dwelt on my unstable character and chequered career as affording of color. I declined because I felt I had nothing to offer."

He began awkwardly, working his way through doubts about the project, struggling to find an effective narrative voice. "Now that my foot is well over the threshold of my eighty seventh year," he wrote, "a change has come upon me; as in the spring a blush of green steals over the hills. I think of her who has shaped my later life and brought to birth what soul I have. I long for the scrap of immortality which may be found in the memory of great-grandchildren. Shall I be to them no more than one of those parachutes of thistle down dropped into oblivion? Shall my great grandchildren be deprived of a great grandfather because of my mock modesty? By all the good old human pagan gods—No—I want to be remembered!"[7]

Wood seems to have sensed that abstract rumination would only lead him away from the story he had to tell. After another false start, he set down a vivid memory from his youth:

Late summer—and autumn—*1867*. What a miracle, a mystery—an angel or monster is Sex—Holding us helpless its—grip—Belle Painter—a beautiful girl of about fifteen, a neighbor to our home Rosewood Glen at Owings Mills—She came over one day—lovely and brown as a dryad and said lets go chestnutting. . . . We crossed our creek Glenns Falls near Big Rock—

I helping her to come dry shod to almost the last step. Then she slipped and splashed into the shallow [film] over a bed of pebbles—not much of an accident—but she insisted on having off her shoes and stockings. She sat down on the dry grass bed of the creek bank and unlaced her shoes—and held up one shapely leg and foot for me to pull off her shoe or boot— reclining on her back and elbows and holding her foot rather higher than was necessary—but to make it easier for me—then followed the other foot and boot and she began to slip down her stocking—but soon handed the task over to me saying help me off with this stocking Ersk—it is too wet—to help me she pulled her skirt and petticoat up higher. . . . I was as confused and awkward and blushing as any girl ever was—I had been brought up in the utmost Puritan modesty and ignorance as to sex and I had a religious reverence for a girls virtue—This made me very awkward in handling her legs and getting off the wet stockings—

Belle threw them rather testily into the basket and put her shoes in the sun to dry—She walked over to me and stood close in front of me—flushed and her breast heaving—Ersk she said—How far is it from my chin to where Love lies—I don't know said I stupidly—Three spans—she answered and measured off three spans down from her chin to the *mons veneris*, exactly. I'll show you she said and quickly seized my wrist pulled up her petticoat and jerked my hand up between her thighs. When I felt the hair I was frightened to death—I thought it was some animal—a chipmunk perhaps—and jerked my self loose and fled across the creek where I paused and looked back, glad I was safe. . . .

Summer of 1868

I had a number of those experiences. . . . I remember beautiful Blanch Hardesty—standing up in the long swing that dropped from the limb of a great oak behind our barn—As she swung the breeze floated her light summer dress far out and lifted it. "How far can you see up Ern" she called and laughed—She continued this tantalizing until as she swung toward me she leaped down, caught me in her arms—and the impact stretched us on the ground. She on top—I did not then know those amorous lines—

Now are they in the very lists of love
all ready for the encounter
yet will he not manage her although he mount her

Not exactly that. she mounted me—she kissed me violently—
I struggled to be free—And so it was. Scottish Presbyterianism
triumphed—[8]

These frank accounts of sexual discovery—so different from the
autobiographical narratives of Steffens and Henry Adams—were a
promising start. One feels Wood settling into his undertaking, fanning
germinal incidents to life, as he begins to inhabit a comfortable
narrative voice.

The gaiety of those early memories belied his present circumstances. He could only work for brief intervals. His handwriting, so
fluent and graceful in his youth, was painfully clumsy. "Light is
fading," he wrote in early 1941, "and my dim eyes cannot see."[9] By
September he was all but blind. Dr. Lucas, his physician and friend,
loaned him an Ediphone, an expensive recording device, so he could
carry on his work through dictation. In his weakened state, it required
heroic effort for Wood to master the new contraption. Sara looked
on with pity and hope. To Ansel Adams she wrote, "he has for seventy
years thought 'through the point of a pen' as he phrases it. He finds
this new mechanism complicated (simple though it really is) and
strange; but I know, with daily use and his great adaptability, he will
master the technique of dictated composition and in time find it less
tiring than the penned work. His eyes fail entirely, slowly, so this is
his only hope of continuing the work."[10]

In pinched, uneven scrawl Wood began a journal of "Notes to Aid
Memory":

Here begin some memoirs of my life. . . . Why do I now take
up the pen. . . ? The beautiful mother in whose raiment and
embroidery I used to rejoice is putting up the blinds—and
Memory so needed by one who would write memoirs no longer
leaps to my summons.

Now before me yawns a dark cave filled with moving figures
that are lost in the gloom. Now one of these beckons me to
come—It is Death—But I know I shall have no answer.

Wood started again:

> . . . I had ridden over the Great American Desert and like a
> curious child had examined the shells which an ancient sea had
> left. I had lain on my back in the desert sand and examined
> the brilliant mystery when the doors of Infinity were opened.

And later still:

> . . . Oh my beloved mother. How beautiful you were. How
> good you were. O what a hard life the Fates flung down to crush
> you. I am in my ninetieth year but still I see your sorrow chiseled
> lovely face. . . .
>
> I wish I could stand at your grave under the oak in the old
> Garrison Fort Church-yard and whisper to you; asking your dear
> ghost to come to me and say—Forget it all, my dear little curly
> headed boy—as I have forgot. I am at peace. As you will be.
> Then I would like to feel your . . . goodnight kiss.
>
> I am in my ninetieth year and still I long to feel your good
> night kiss. My mother. My dear sweet mother. But O I would
> not bring you back; you have found the everlasting peace.[11]

Wood was adrift in rambling reflections; it seemed impossible that
he would ever again manage to gather his thoughts to renew the story
of his life. "I look into a dark cave," he wrote, "where shadowy figures
move. One beckons me to come. I know I must. That figure is Death.
I must go: but I know I shall receive no answer." Yet even as Wood
imagined his own death—at the very brink of surrendering to it—
he pulled back. "I feel a soft bird fluttering in my hand. I look down.
It is the hand of a little child. I said 'This shall lead me.' I will write
my memoirs though my sight and my memory are dim. So much need
for memoirs, eyes dim. I will write my memoirs."

And he did. Wood mastered the confounding Ediphone; he overcame blindness and frailty; he drew upon a memory that he himself
described as "badly shattered."[12] On cylinder after cylinder he
recounted events from almost a century past. While American planes
and tanks and battleships fanned across the planet, he spoke of
William Maxwell Wood sailing forth with the navy's Pacific fleet to
visit the King of Siam. On the eve of the nuclear age, he recalled
childhood adventures on bustling canals, his glimpse of president-

elect Lincoln, the Civil War, and raucous traffic on the old wagon
road from Baltimore to Rosewood Glen. He tapped fond memories
of the family farm: flying squirrels leaping through locust trees;
possum hunting with former slaves; his mother's garden; and his
romance with Nannie Moale Smith. He remembered West Point:
General Sherman, Ralph Waldo Emerson's address to the cadets,
President Grant's inauguration—the cadet corps marching across a
frozen Hudson River to board the train for Washington. As he
approached his ninetieth year, the days of his youth sprang forth in
luminous narrative. But he had begun his great work too late. Charles
Erskine Scott Wood died on January 22, 1944. His unfinished story
closes on the threshold of adult life: the eve of his wide-eyed journey
West.

49. Final Words

Sara to Erskine:

I will not linger now over the last days your Father spent in his tired, worn body. Those are over and I am glad, indeed, you were spared the pain of them for while Dr. Jones did not let him suffer a moment and he died with no realization death was near, still for those of us who loved the out-worn cloak that had wrapped his great spirit, it was difficult to see the prolonged wracking of his body. Finally at 2.10 P.M. on Saturday, Jan. 22nd, with a deep, strong last breath the body gave up its immortal tenant and he was free. His great soul had long been poised for flight. He had not been concerned with things of this earth. To the last conscious hours nothing but Love and Humor came from his lips. As each face dear to him came close during those conscious moments he would speak the name with such thrilling joy and from such a depth of love and he would hold the loved hand with so strong a clasp. . . .

"Lisa wrote Becky of the last rites, so I'll not repeat. We tried to do all as he would have wished it. Did she tell you of my almost direct message from him through a sonnet I had entirely forgotten? While I still pondered on whether, after all, he would want a grave where people could come to think about him or that 'purification by fire' which he exalts in *The Poet In The Desert*, I opened those Personal Sonnets which he had collected for your Mother and you children. I was looking for a certain sonnet that still eludes me and which I thought was in that collection. (It wasn't)

"At the very end of Personal Sonnets—the last one—was this:

If any would for me build a true bier
Bring my dumb ashes to a pleasant spot
And scatter them without despairing tear
About a young oak. So by time forgot
I shall be joyous in the strong oak's veins
And laugh from out his leaves to the blue sky,
Rejoice in summer sun and winter rains
And know perhaps a gentler ecstasy
Than this world gives. Birds frolic in the boughs
And breezes play. And so the seasons pass.
Lovers I know will come to kiss their vows
And lie awhile upon the whispering grass.
And some who knew me may come here to give
A petal of the heart while yet they live.

"So, then, there was the final word. I ran with it to Lisa and Kay and we were all assured of what was to be done. On his birthday with the family who are near enough to come and a few most close and intimate ones who made his life easier and happier by their devotion and whom he loves, we shall quietly, without formality and without tears, scatter the ashes around the great oak in the grove which is now like a *mille fleur* tapestry with abundant spring bulbs in bloom—snowflakes, jonquils, blue bells and the odor of daphne drifting down from a short distance away. Here, too, when I am gone, I ask that my ashes be strewn as a symbol of the unity which, in my belief, goes on unbroken."[1]

Harry Corbett to Erskine:

"I am glad we talked of your father the other day and if we have sense we will do it again on other days and have the memories of him blow the cobwebs out of our brains. He didn't have any cobwebs in his—all was mostly fresh breezes blowing. I think I owe a good deal of my physical well-being to him and those summer trips. I know I owe to him most of whatever appreciation I have of fineness and niceties, but then hell the whole of Portland as it once was owes much of its culture to him and I doubt that even with the changes that have come on us you can erase real culture ingrained into the foundations of a city. So he has a fine monument. There are few who can shape the trend of thought of a whole city. Certainly he did that for this town and just as certainly that same extraordinary influence of his moved into the most unexpected places. . . .

"I have heard three speeches which I have remembered and thought great. A speech of his was one of the three. I have read biographies of a good many great men, but instead of having to read a biography of his life, I am glad I was close enough to him to have seen and heard him living part of it. I can't be sorry at his death, for his life was so full that death didn't mean anything, but I am sorry he couldn't live long enough to learn what was going to happen to the world. He would have enjoyed finding out."[2]

Rabbi Jacob Weinstein to Sara:

"Of recent months, in the work of the War Labor Board, I have seen evidences of the evil by-products of rugged American individualism and just when I despair of our ever finding the harmonization of liberty and order, of freedom and social responsibility, I think of Erskine and I keep my faith. It was not merely that he balanced these various tendencies in his full, wholesome nature but that he did so in a completely American way. I think that is why he could say and do the most radical things and still hold the respect and admiration of the conservatives. When the liberals of America were being lured and driven from one imported social panacea to another, I often recalled Erskine's counsel. It was so firmly rooted in the American soil and it helped me to keep my balance.

"But it was in the more enduring issues of life that Erskine was of greatest help. He had thought through the political and economic alternatives of modern society fifty years ago. He had seen through them into the pockets of the human soul where the real changes must be made. He could predict with uncanny skill the absorptive capacity, the bending point, and the freezing point of the human will. Because he was so thoroughly honest about his own emotions, he could tell us when we were playing with words and when we were on the beam."[3]

John D. Barry's "Ways of the World" column in the "San Francisco News," *August 7, 1929:*

"Today I saw them walking serenely along the street. I said to myself, 'It would be impossible to think of them in a hurry. They always suggest that they are living in eternity.'

"They were a striking looking pair. He gave the impression of amplitude, not because of any heaviness, but through being built on broad lines. His mild, kindly face, with color that suggested youth, was framed in thick white hair, somewhat longer than convention decreed, pleasantly refractory, and in a white beard discretely trimmed. He had the air of being very much at home in the world, of being intimately related to the elemental forces. She was smaller and younger, with a face of extraordinary sweetness and with a light in her eyes that seemed to reflect an inner glow. 'She's even lovelier than she was when I first knew her,' I thought, and I marveled at the qualities that enabled her to triumph over time. What lessons she was unconsciously offering the followers of the beauty-doctors, with their concern for mere externals. She could show them that the secret of beauty was a profound thing and came from the very essence of being.

"They didn't happen to notice me on the other side of the street and I rather enjoyed letting them pass without holding them up. For the moment I surely couldn't add to their felicity. But, somehow just from observing them I felt better and I walked with a step that was a little more elastic. It was as if they made me recognize that, in spite of certain obvious shortcomings, we were living in a pretty fine world."[4]

Acknowledgments

For many years before I knew of Charles Erskine Scott Wood, I was, in a sense, experiencing the force of his character through my friendship with his great-grandchildren, Bruce and Lisa Livingston. Wood's love of living, his creativity, his generosity, his gift for friendship, his great appreciation of the natural world, his rebelliousness, his social conscience, his resilience, his playfulness—all these qualities shine forth in Bruce and Lisa. In all likelihood, I would never have heard of C. E. S. Wood—certainly, I would never have undertaken writing a book about him—had it not been for their presence in my life. Their mother, Katherine "Tashie" Livingston, was also indispensable. When I think of thanking Bruce, Lisa, and Tashie, along with several other Wood descendants, the whole idea of "acknowledgments" seems small and inconsequential. More than anyone, it was Tashie, the child of Wood's beloved daughter, Lisa, who stood by to help and advise during the writing of this book. How strange and occasionally vexing it must be for her to see her adored grandfather transformed into the subject of a biography!

Three more of Wood's grandchildren generously gave their time, valuable feedback, and moral support to my work: Nan S. Johns, Marian Kolisch, and Alan Kirkham Smith. It is a measure of their faith in Wood that not once did any of these people suggest that I should "go easy" on his peccadillos and prevarications. They understood, I think, that Wood's story would have little significance without a thorough scrutiny of his contradictions and struggles.

Wood's descendants are keenly aware—far more than other readers of this book—how much of Wood's life and spirit are not included in my narrative. They take great pride in Wood's achievements, but they cherish Wood most as "Gaga," their grandfather, the enchanting source of laughter, wisdom, and love. A biography, with its emphasis on public events and social issues, must seem "unfinished," at best a kind of half-truth, to those who knew Wood so intimately. What I want to say to them—along with offering my heartfelt thanks for their trust, their encouragement, and their help—is that I share with them the conviction that Wood's life reaches beyond the version I offer here.

One last word, an anecdote really, that may suggest my debt to Wood's descendants. At the end of my first full day of research on C. E. S. Wood's life, I pulled out a box of photos from the Huntington Library's vast collection of Wood materials. I studied images 125 years old of Cadet Wood decked out in absurd military plumage, his mouth turned in a knowing grin. In four photographs, I saw Nannie Moale Smith—a striking young woman with long hair spilling down her back—transform into a sixty-year-old matron, plump and smiling, in her elegant Portland home. I followed the arc of Wood's life from young attorney, to fin-de-siècle dandy, to the white-haired "living legend" he became in his later years. I gazed at pictures of Sara Ehrgott, so bright and alert, at the outset of her tumultuous romance with Wood. And there were prints of Wood's parents taken in what must have been the earliest years of commercial studio photography. These were timeless moments for me. I was awed at the vast reach of Wood's life, impressed by Wood's presence, and daunted by the task that lay ahead.

In twenty minutes I saw Wood age before my eyes. When I came to the last batch of photos—snapshots from the 1940s—I faltered. At this late date, Wood's achievements were behind him; his children and grandchildren were grown and busy with their lives; his health was waning; his affairs were in order. What remained was his dying. Like the reader of some absorbing novel, I did not want the story to end. When I opened the last folder—identified by the Huntington cataloguer as "2 color snapshots of Charles Erskine Scott Wood (and others)"—my heart stopped. There was Wood at ninety—plump, full-bearded, aglow with the moment—sitting on his terrace in Los Gatos, surrounded by a glorious garden. A satyr head, a reminder of Wood's self-proclaimed paganism, grinned from its place on the wall over Wood's right shoulder. But it was not Wood's sparkling energy or the verdant setting that startled me—it was my unexpected recognition of the "others" in the photo. There before me was Tashie, a shining young woman, and her husband, Ken. And in Wood's lap was a beaming infant, my friend Bruce, brought down to Los Gatos to meet his great-grandfather. Tashie must have been twenty-five at the time, lovely with the flush of new motherhood. Ken, who died so cruelly only a few years ago, was rangy and handsome back then. In the photo, Wood looks right at Tashie—and though he is nearly blind, the bright California light forces him to squint. Light streams through his hair and beard as if he beamed forth his own radiance.

It is difficult to put into words what I felt as I looked at Charles Erskine Scott Wood, a man who began life 146 years ago, tenderly folding his hands around my friend. What I saw at that moment is that America is still a young country. A few generations back, and we are at its origins. I never truly felt this fact until I saw that photograph: there was my friend Bruce, sitting on the lap of a man who had cheered president-elect Lincoln on his way to Washington, a man whose father was a young boy when Thomas Jefferson and John Adams were still alive. More than anything, it was that photograph—and the rush of feeling that accompanied it—that set me on my path.

Working on the life of C. E. S. Wood has been a pleasure from start to finish. I did my research and writing alone, but the help I received from funding institutions, from research libraries, and from caring friends was absolutely essential. My research was launched by a Research Fellowship from the National Endowment for the Humanities and by a grant for Creative Nonfiction from the New York Foundation of the Arts. A Travel Grant from the College Development Fund of Jersey City State College also came in handy. In a time of diminishing resources, I'm keenly aware of the honor and the responsibility these awards entail, and I have worked hard to keep up my end of the contract. One more grant deserves special mention. On three occasions over the past twenty years, I have been invited to pursue my work at the MacDowell Colony in Peterborough, New Hampshire. Once again, MacDowell provided the solitude, the support, and the "magic" that enabled me to complete a substantial chunk of the first draft of my Wood manuscript.

Having worked long and hard on Wood's life, I was delighted when my manuscript found its way into the hands of an editor who knew about Wood and who welcomed my biography enthusiastically. Douglas Clayton, the editor-in-chief at the University of Nebraska Press, was encouraging, demanding, patient, and generous with his time throughout the process of review and revision. I can't imagine a more productive working relationship.

In all probability, I would not be extending thanks to anyone were it not for several scholars and writers who agreed to let me submit their names as referees for my project proposal. Robert Coles and Stanley Kutler have supported my research and writing from the start. Every writer needs an ideal audience, however small: for years it has been a source of pride and personal resilience to know that my books have found their way to two such astute, caring readers. This time around, John Cawelti, Leslie Fiedler, and Daniel Aaron all agreed to write reviews of my NEH proposal. They had no idea, of course, what I would write or how well I would write it—but either their respect for my previous work or their interest in C. E. S. Wood prompted them to respond favorably to my proposal.

I suppose I have C. E. S. Wood to thank for having the good taste and the foresight to place the overwhelming share of his manuscripts, letters, and memorabilia in the sumptuous Huntington Library. At a time when scholarship and reflection on American history have become increasingly marginalized, the Huntington provides an environment that affirms the importance—one might say the "glory"—of serious research. The efficient support of Peter Blodgett, Mary Wright, and Sharon Nemechek provided me with easy access to the Huntington's enormous Wood Collection. I would also like to thank the staffs of the following libraries and research institutions: the Bancroft Library, the University of California at Berkeley; the Portland Public Library; the Peterborough Public Library, Peterborough, New Hampshire; the New York Public Library; the Oregon Historical Society (with special thanks to Terence O'Donnell); the United States Military Academy Archives and Special Collections; and Candace Falk, Editor and Director of the Emma Goldman papers, the University of California at Berkeley.

Had I begun research on Wood's life ten or fifteen years sooner, I could have interviewed scores of his surviving friends and acquaintances. Because so many people from Wood's life are now gone, I treasure the handful of interviews I was able to arrange. Ernst Bacon and Elizabeth Elkus both sat down with me to share memories and reflections of people and events from sixty-five years past. In retrospect, it was not so much their thoughts about Wood that enriched me as it was their own vitality and force of character. These were people who formed an integral part of the cultural and political life in the San Francisco Bay Area during Wood's years at Los Gatos. Their work stimulated Wood, and he, in turn, offered them the powerful presence of his personality. What a lively community it must have been!

Also, I want to thank Katherine Caldwell, Sara's daughter, for inviting me into her lovely home for an afternoon I will always remember. "Kay" was an integral part of Wood and Sara's early years together: it was disarming and immensely moving to spend time with a lively octogenarian whose youth was so deeply merged in the historical narrative I was writing.

When I think back to my months of research at the Huntington Library, I think of Dick and Esther Barthol with a surge of affection and gratitude. Not only did the Barthols welcome me into their home, but Dick was the manuscript's first editor. He gave my work a careful and challenging reading that alerted me to the fact that the enthusiasms of a first draft must yield finally to the rigorous demands of revision. Each evening I would return from the Huntington Library to share my new discoveries with Dick and Esther. Their lively interest in Wood's life assured me that my commitment to my subject was not misplaced. But above and beyond Dick and Esther's absorption in Wood's life, I want to thank them for their warm friendship. When I began my work at the Huntington, I fully expected to live in some nondescript motel room. Instead, the Barthols gave me a home in every sense of the word.

This book is dedicated to my parents, but their support goes far beyond any single project I have undertaken. How lucky I was to grow up in a home where the pleasure of learning, reading, and doing creative work was instilled in me with enthusiasm and love! Since I can remember, my mother and father have tolerated my foibles and shown pride in my occasional achievements. At times, they have wondered what I was up to, but they have never questioned my right to do it. In times of difficulty I have always been able to draw upon their optimism, their belief in the importance of doing one's best, their faith in me, and the joy they take in living. Stating such things seems to diminish them, but there is nothing small about what they have given me or how deep my appreciation is for all we have shared as a family. The more I see of life, the more I realize my great good fortune.

Finally, I want to thank my wife, Ilene Raye Sunshine, and our glowing boy, David. I began my research and writing for this project a few years before Ilene and David entered my life—or, as David would say, when he was "not yet on this earth." Nonetheless, they were with me all through the crucial process of editing and rewriting this book. With Ilene and David close at hand, the daily reasons to rejoice have been far more compelling than the occasional distractions and anxieties of bringing a book into being. Now, with *Two Rooms* completed, we have one more reason to celebrate. But those who know me, know full well that my life has been a continuing celebration since I met Ilene—even more so since David made his surprising appearance to join us here on this earth.

Notes

Abbreviations

By far the most extensive collection of Wood materials is in the Huntington Library, San Marino, California. The Wood collection holds some thirty thousand items, including personal correspondence, journals, manuscript materials, photographs, magazine clippings, drawings, and memorabilia. For the most part, the collection is kept in numbered boxes (over three hundred), each of which holds several folders. Often, as in the case of Wood's voluminous correspondence, each folder is likely to hold a month or two of letters. Because so many of my citations are to the Huntington collection, I have dispensed with any identifying initials. A typical endnote citation might appear as 251 #4, 10/10/1916—which would mean box 251, folder 4, letter dated October 10, 1916.

BL   The Bancroft Library: University of California at Berkeley. Wood's outgoing correspondence from his Portland law office.

EW   Erskine Wood. *Life of Charles Erskine Scott Wood*. Portland OR: By the author, 1978.

NMW   Nanny Moale Wood, "Personal Recollections: Dictated to Dean Fischer, Her Nurse and Companion," c. 1932 (private papers of Lisa Wood Livingston).

OR   *The Oregonian*; earlier *The Morning Oregonian* (until 1937).

OHS   Oregon Historical Society Regional Research Library: Portland OR.

SBF   Sara Bard Field, *Sara Bard Field: Poet and Suffragist*. Interview conducted by Amelia R. Fry, 1959–1963. Regional Oral History Project, University of California at Berkeley.

USMA   The United States Military Academy Archives.

1. An Enchanted Land

1. "Sylvie," written in early 1890s; 66 #54, 11–12.
2. 6 #9, folder 22.

3. 6 #9, folder 25.
4. 6 #9, folder 25.
5. 6 #9, folder 26.
6. 6 #9, folder 28.
7. 251 #4, 10/7/1916.
8. 6 #9, folder 30.
9. 6 #9, folder 31.
10. 6 #9, folder 32.
11. 6 #9, folder 37.
12. 6 #9, folder 38.
13. 6 #9, folder 44.

2. Noah's Ark

1. 6 #10.
2. 6 #1a III, 3.
3. 6 #1a I, 1.
4. Letter from James Wood to Wood: 259 #20, 10/23/1942.
5. 6 #1a I, 2.
6. 6 #1a II, 1; 6 #1a I, 4.
7. Bauer, *The Mexican War: 1846–1848*, 167–68. Also, Wood, *Wandering Sketches of people and things in South America, Polynesia, California, and other places visited*, 366–86. Also, 6 #1a I, 2–3.
8. Wood, *Fankwei; or, The San Jacinto in the Seas of India, China and Japan*, 141.
9. 6 #1a IV, 1–2.
10. 6 #1a IV, 3.
11. 6 #1a V, 2.
12. 6 #1a I, 2.
13. 6 #1a II, 2.
14. 6 #1a VI, 13.
15. Wide-Awake parades, named after the wide-brimmed, low-crowned felt hat—part of the uniform donned by young men who marched in these demonstrations—left a vivid impression on many of those who witnessed them. In his autobiography Henry Adams recalled: "Although no one believed in civil war, the air reeked of it, and the Republicans organized their clubs and parades as Wide-Awakes in a form military in all things except weapons. Henry reached home in time to see the last of these processions, stretching in ranks of torches along the hillside, file down through the November night to the Old House, where Mr. Adams, their Member of Congress, received them, and, let them pretend what they liked, their air was not that of innocence." Henry Adams, *The Education of Henry Adams*, 99.
16. 6 #7.
17. 6 #7.
18. 6 #7.

19. 6 #1a III, 2.
20. 6 #7.
21. 6 #1a III, 1, 5–6.
22. 6 #1b VIII, 3; 6 #1a III, 9–11.
23. 6 #1b VIII, 15–16.
24. 284 #19, 11/13/1863.
25. 6 #1b IX, 11–12.
26. 6 #9, folder 1.
27. 6 #1b X, 2.
28. 6 #9 folder 17.
29. 6 #9, folder 19.
30. Conditional Appointment signed by John Rawlins, June 25, 1869: 187 #77a. See also USMA, descriptive list, 1869.
31. USMA, descriptive list.
32. 284 #23.
33. USMA, annual report of the Inspector, 1870; 6–7.
34. 6 #9, folder 3.
35. 6 #1a I, 2; 6 #1a III, 7.

3. The Best Making of a Man

1. Morrisson, *"The Best School in the World": West Point, the Pre–Civil War Years, 1833–1866*, 5.
2. 6 #9, folder 4.
3. 284 #28, 7/15/1870.
4. "Charge and Specification against Cadet Charles E. S. Wood": 205 #77.
5. 284 #37, 12/20/1870.
6. 6 #9, folder 4.
7. NMW, 10–11. Also, 6 #9, folder 6.
8. NMW, 11–12.
9. James Parker, "My Experiences as a Cadet at West Point." USMA, Special Collections #2623.
10. 243 #11, 12/29/1875.
11. 243 #6.
12. 243 #6.
13. 284 #38, 5/8/1873.
14. Nov. 24, 1873; quoted in EW, 6–8.
15. 284 #40.
16. 6 #1a, III.
17. 6 #1a, III.
18. 243 #7, 10/25/1874.
19. Wood to his daughter Lisa: 237 #26, 12/15/1933.
20. 6 #9, folder 20.

4. A Glade in the Fir Forest

1. Sperlin, "Fur Trade Forts in Washington," 108.
2. 6 #9, folder 46.
3. Wood, "Tales after Mess," 67 #1, 1.
4. 260 #4.
5. 243 #9, 12/21/1875.
6. EW, 131.
7. 284 #41.
8. Special Orders No. 35; Headquarters Department of the Columbia, April 7, 1877. 258 #56a.

5. A Young Chief

1. Wood, "Among the Thlinkits in Alaska," 323. Mount Elias (18,000 ft.) is not "the highest peak in the world." Mount McKinley and Mount Logan are higher North American summits; thirty mountains in South America and Central Asia are also higher.
2. Wood, "Among the Thlinkits," 323–24.
3. Anders, "Settlement of Sitka," 54.
4. Wood, "Among the Thlinkits," 324.
5. 26 #1.
6. Schwatka, "A reconnaissance of the Yukon Valley, 1883," 291.
7. Wood to Lute Pease: 235 #57, 2/22/1928.
8. 238 #7.
9. Wood, "Among the Thlinkits," 339.

6. A Crack at an Indian

1. 26 #1.
2. Howard, *My Life and Experiences among Our Hostile Indians*, 235 (page references are to reprint edition). Anyone seeking a full account of the Nez Perce War would do well to read Bruce Hampton's *Children of Grace: The Nez Perce War of 1877*.
3. In *Annual Report, Department of Interior, 1873*. Quoted in Josephy, *The Nez Perce Indians and the Opening of the Northwest*, 526–27.
4. Howard, *Autobiography*, vol. 2, 454.
5. 26 #1.
6. 26 #1.
7. Josephy, *The Nez Perce Indians*, 542.
8. 26 #1.
9. 6 #7.
10. *Annual Report, Department of Interior, 1877*, 10.
11. Merrill D. Beal, *I Will Fight No More Forever*, 105–6.
12. Howard, *Nez Perce Joseph*, 225.

13. Sutherland, *Howard's Campaign against the Nez Perce Indians, 1878*, 29.
14. U.S. Department of the Interior, *Annual Report, 1877*, 13.
15. *Report of Secretary of War, 1877*, I, 13.
16. Josephy, *The Nez Perce Indians*, 598–99.
17. Beal, *I Will Fight No More Forever*, 200–201.
18. Wood, "The Pursuit and Capture of Chief Joseph," 325–27.
19. Wood, "The Pursuit and Capture of Chief Joseph," 327.
20. Letter from Wood to Elmo Scott Watson, quoted in Western Newspaper Union syndicated release following Wood's death, 1944: 215 #14a.
21. Wood, "The Pursuit and Capture of Chief Joseph," 329–30.
22. In this and many other instances, Bruce Hampton's *Children of Grace: The Nez Perce War of 1877* does a fine job of sifting through diverse and sometimes contradictory accounts of the war.
23. Hampton, *Children of Grace*, 333.
24. Miles to Terry, October 5, 1877, Document No. 6260-77; A.G.O. 3464-77 National Archives; quoted in Beal, *I Will Fight No More Forever*, 232.
25. Wood, "The Pursuit and Capture of Chief Joseph," 333.
26. Wood, "The Pursuit and Battle: Semi-Official Report of a Staff Officer," 5.
27. Chief Joseph, "An Indian's Views of Indian Affairs," 412–33.

7. Lights and Shadows

1. NMW, 17–18.
2. 243 #13.
3. 243 #14, 218.
4. 243 #17, 3/12/1878.

8. The Old Broken Wheel

1. OR, April 3, 1878.
2. 243 #19, 6/14/1878.
3. Canfield, *Sara Winnemucca of the Northern Paiutes*, 38–40.
4. Wood, "Private Journal, 1878," 20–21.

9. A New Life

1. NMW, 21–22.
2. NMW, 22.
3. NMW, 21–22.
4. The anecdote appears in a letter from Wood to his son Erskine, in EW, 30.
5. EW, 33.
6. C. E. S. Wood, "An Unknown Turning-Point in the Destiny of the Republic," *The Californian: A Western Monthly Magazine* 2 (December 1880): 539–43.
7. Bancroft, *History of the Pacific States*, vol. 17, 202n.

8. Bancroft, *California 1846–1848*, vol. 17, 214.

9. *Californian, a Western Monthly* was founded by Anton Roman in January 1880 to fill the gap left by the suspension of the *Overland Monthly* in 1875. In its eight years of existence, the *Overland Monthly* published Bret Harte and Mark Twain at the start of their literary careers. For all practical purposes, the *Californian* was a continuation of its distinguished predecessor. In 1882 its name was changed to the *Californian and Overland Monthly*; in January 1883, the name was restored to the *Overland Monthly*.

10. Ambrose, *Duty, Honor, Country: A History of West Point*, 234.

11. Howard, *Autobiography*, vol. 2, 485–86.

12. Wood's recollection appears as an introduction to a letter by Twain reproduced in facsimile for *The Letters of Western Authors*, no. 9 (San Francisco: The Book Club of California, 1935); 123 #35a.

13. 123 #32.

14. Wood, *The Letters of Western Authors*.

15. Received June 1882; registrar's document dated 1937; 298 #12.

16. Snyder, *Skidmore's Portland: His Fountain and Its Sculptor*, 107–11.

17. Registrar's certification sent in 1937, 298 #12.

18. 235 #7.

19. 235 #7.

20. 251 #4, 10/10/1916.

10. City of Destiny

1. OR 9/9/1883.

2. *West Shore*, September 1883.

3. OR, 9/9/1883.

4. Donald Macleay, President of the Portland Board of Trade, quoted in MacColl, *Merchants, Money and Power: The Portland Establishment 1843–1913*, 225.

5. Wallis Nash, *Two Years in Oregon*, 256–57.

6. Quoted in Zinn, *People's History of the United States*, 149.

7. MacColl, *Merchants, Money and Power*, 30–31.

8. Paul G. Merriam, "Urban Elite in the Far West: Portland, Oregon 1870–1890, *Arizona and the West* 18 (Spring 1976): 47; quoted in MacColl, *Merchants, Money and Power*, 186.

9. OHS #1505; *General Views—1880–89*.

10. OHS # 1504; *General Views 1870–79*.

11. OHS #1817-A, *Portland—Corbett House*.

12. OHS #1820-A.

11. The Sculptor and the King

1. MacColl, *Merchants, Money and Power*, 33.

2. MacColl, *Merchants, Money and Power*, 185–86.

3. EW, 45–46.
4. EW, 45–46.
5. "Chief Joseph, the Nez-Perce," *Century Monthly* 28 (May 1884): 134–42.
6. Original document, 298 #11C.
7. 28 #4, 220.
8. Wood, "The Skidmore Fountain," 97.
9. Wood, "The Skidmore Fountain," 97.
10. Wood, "The Skidmore Fountain," 98.
11. Wood, "The Skidmore Fountain," 100.
12. Ladd, the very epitome of Portland's transplanted New England puritanism, was the subject of one of Wood's favorite anecdotes. Ladd was paralyzed from the waist down, and had been so for many years—though, seated behind his desk, there was no way a stranger could possibly ascertain his condition. One morning, an attractive woman came into the Ladd & Tilton bank and requested a private interview with Ladd in his office. She launched into lively, irrelevant conversation that had very little to do with any services Ladd's bank might render. After twenty minutes, Ladd broke in: "Madam, I've enjoyed your visit and your conversation very much, but what is it you came to see me about?"

    She demanded twenty-five thousand dollars.

    Ladd asked her what security she intended to furnish.

    She said, "I'm desperate for the money. I know you have it right there in the safe. You could give it to me easily. We've been closeted here alone now for about twenty minutes, and if you don't give it to me I'm going to tear open my dress, expose my bosoms and body, tear my hair down, scream, and when your clerks rush in, I'm going to say that you attempted to ravish me."

    Ladd broke into laughter. "Madam," he said, "I want to thank you for the first merry moment I have had in this rather dull day. If you can get anybody in this whole town to believe that I have had a hard-on any time in the last twenty years, I'll give you *fifty* thousand dollars!" EW, 51.
13. Wood, "The Skidmore Fountain," 99.
14. BL:OC, 128.
15. BL:OC, 285.
16. BL:OC, 307.
17. BL:OC, 83–84.
18. BL:OC, 126.
19. NMW, 27.
20. Morgan, *George de Forest Brush (1855–1941): Master of the American Renaissance*, 21.
21. BL:OC, 154–65.

12. The Magic Pearl

1. BL:OC, 284.
2. *House Report #332, 46th Congress, 3rd session*; quoted in Amundson, "History of the Willamette Valley and Cascade Mountain Wagon Road," 30.

3. Amundson, "History of the Willamette Valley and Cascade Mountain Wagon Road," 37.

4. BL:OC, 245.

5. OHS Mss. 307.

6. Hannah Wood to Wood, 258 #48, 9/19/1889.

7. EW, 105.

13. A Labor of Love

1. OHS #1506—"Portland: General Views 1890–94."

2. 26 #7, 28–29.

3. 26 #7, 34–36.

4. 26 #7, 45–46.

5. 27 #7, 48–49.

6. 27 #7, 55–56.

7. 27 #7, 82–83.

8. 27 #7, 86–90.

9. OHS.

10. Writing of Theodore Roosevelt, William James observed that he "gushes over war as the ideal condition of human society, for the manly strenuousness which it involves, and treats peace as a condition of blubberlike and swollen ignobility, fit only for huckstering weaklings, dwelling in gray twilight and heedless of the higher life." (Howard Zinn, *A People's History of the United States* [New York: Harper & Row, 1980], 283).

11. Wood, "Famous Indians: Portraits of Some Indian Chiefs," 436.

12. Wood, "Famous Indians," 445.

13. 26 #8, 11–13.

14. 260 #10.

15. 243 #24.

16. 243 #24.

14. Closet Drama

1. 26 #8, 41.

2. EW, 65.

3. Dictated notes to Frank Ingerson, 1943: 6 #11.

4. 26 #11, 26.

5. 26 #11, 26.

15. Two Rooms

1. The history of "free silver," or bimetalism, is long and complex. Its immediate origins go back to 1873 when, after most European nations adopted a gold standard, the U.S. Treasury demonetized silver (that is, the silver dollar was taken

out of coinage). This happened at a time when silver production was increasing in several western states. The move caused a drop in the value of silver and led to various charges that a "gold conspiracy" comprised of eastern bankers and politicians was out to seize a strangle hold on the national economy. Both the Bland-Allison Act (1878) and the Sherman Silver Purchase Act (1890) were passed to stem the tide of protest from silver and agrarian states. These stop-gap measures came undone in 1893 when foreign investors, worried about America's wavering gold standard, began selling their U.S. securities. As capital fled the country, a banking panic depleted the federal treasury's gold reserves. The U.S. government met the emergency by repealing the Sherman Silver Purchase Act. Western Democrats felt betrayed and powerless, until, with the emergence of William Jennings Bryan, they found a charismatic spokesman.

2. 26, #11, 76–85.
3. Wood's account of the National Democratic Party convention appears in 26 #11, 76–85.
4. 6 #11, 97–99.
5. 26 #11, 108–9.
6. 26 #11, 104–5.
7. 27 #1, 1/12/1897.

16. I Must Unite with Myself

1. Photograph: 296 #39.
2. Albert J. Beveridge, "The March of the Flag"; delivered in Tomlinson's Hall, Indianapolis IN; September 16, 1898; in *An American Primer*, ed. Daniel J. Boorstin, 621–29.
3. Letter written March 20, 1898, to Dr. Edward Holden, who was compiling a Biographical Register for the United States Military Academy; Wood File, USMA Special Collections.
4. Wood, "Imperialism vs. Democracy," 4.
5. Wood, "Imperialism vs. Democracy," 7.
6. Wood, "Imperialism vs. Democracy," 9–10.
7. Wood, "Imperialism vs. Democracy," 15.
8. 240 #23.
9. Quoted in EW, 102–3.
10. *Public* (March 1, 1902), 1.
11. *Public* (March 1, 1902), 1.
12. *Public* (March 1, 1902), 1.

17. The Most Beautiful Theory

1. Published in Chicago and edited by Louis F. Post, the *Public* described itself as "A National Journal of Fundamental Democracy, and Weekly Narrative of History in the Making." From 1898 to 1913, when Post resigned to become

assistant secretary of labor, the *Public* was, as Frederic C. Howe would later observe, "the best mirror of pre-war liberalism that we had":

> Fearlessly honest in opinion, keenly understanding in its reporting, it gave form and direction to the liberal movement and charted the lines of its progress. It was the best mirror of pre-war liberalism that we had; a reading of its pages discloses the fineness, the intellectuality, the hopefulness of that movement which was the last protest of the democracy of the pioneer period still under the influence of the free land of the West. [*The Confessions of a Reformer*, 195]

Over the years, Wood contributed several articles to the *Public* including one, "What Is a Democrat?" (May 18, 1906, 151–54), that Post printed as an editorial because it so closely expressed the guiding principles of his journal.

2. *Public* (March 18, 1902), 826–27.
3. Quoted in DeLeon, *The American as Anarchist: Reflections on Indigenous Radicalism*, 18–19.
4. Thoreau, *Walden and Civil Disobedience*, 225, 232, 236.
5. DeLeon, *The American as Anarchist*, 73, 75, 79.
6. MacColl, *Merchants, Money and Power*, 346.
7. Henry George Jr., *Progress and Poverty*, ix.
8. Ibid., 293–96; 405–6.
9. Ibid., 406.
10. Ibid., 454, 456.
11. Wood to David Schwartz: #236, 10/11/1938, 6.

18. The Course of Empire

1. By 1905 expositions were something of a national growth industry. Beginning with the Centennial Exposition at Philadelphia in 1876, Americans had been invited to visit the Columbian Exposition at Chicago in 1893, Atlanta's Cotton Exposition in 1881 and its Piedmont Exposition in 1887, New Orleans's Cotton Centennial Exposition in 1885, Nashville's Centennial Exposition in 1897, Omaha's Trans-Mississippi Exposition in 1898, the Pan-American Exposition at Buffalo in 1901, and the Louisiana Purchase Exposition in St. Louis in 1904. Still to come were Norfolk's Jamestown Tercentennial (1907), Seattle's Alaska-Yukon-Pacific Exposition (1909), and the Panama-Pacific Exposition celebrated in San Francisco (1915).
2. Abbott, *The Great Extravaganza: Portland and the Lewis and Clark Exposition*, 16.
3. *Oregon Booster*, 2.
4. *Oregon Journal* article, (c. 1934); in OHS clipping file.
5. Duniway, *Path Breaking: An Autobiographical History of the Equal Suffrage Movement in Pacific Coast States*, 216.
6. 66 #14.

7. OR 8/8/1905, 3.
8. OR 3/29/1905, 5.
9. OR 10/3/1905, 1, 11.
10. Wood, "Autobiographic Notes: 1939": 6 #6.

19. A Rebel and a Fanatic

1. 27 #11.
2. Hartwell, *The Wood Household.*
3. 66 #7.
4. OR 11/27/1906, 8.
5. Steffens, "The Taming of the West," 592–93.
6. Wood, "On the Looting of the Public Domain," *Pacific Monthly* (September 1907): 389.
7. NMW, 41.
8. NMW, 41.
9. DeLeon, *The American as Anarchist,* 95.
10. DeLeon, *The American as Anarchist,* 94–97.
11. OR 5/21/1908, 11.
12. OR 5/24/1908, sec. 4, 10.
13. Emma Goldman, *Living My Life,* 430–31.
14. Goldman, "In Portland," 197–203.
15. 27 #8, 54–55.
16. 240 #5.

20. A Versatile Citizen

1. Monroe, *Feelin' Fine!: Bill Hanley's Book,* 63.
2. Monroe, *Feelin' Fine!,* 158.
3. Martin, *James J. Hill and the Opening of the Northwest,* 566–67.
4. OR 11/29/1909, 14.
5. OR 11/29/1909, 14.
6. OR 11/30/1909, 8.
7. OR, 5/15/1910, 1.
8. OR, 5/15/1910, 1.
9. 260 #22, 7/31/1910.
10. When Wood's friendship with Darrow began is unclear. They may have met in November 1907 when Darrow came to Portland to be treated for an ear infection following his defense of Big Bill Haywood in Boise, Idaho. However, Wood might have befriended Darrow in Chicago ten to fifteen years before this on one of his many business trips East.
11. SBF, 200-201.

21. A Deeper Gladness of Soul

1. 80 #11, envelope 3, part II.
2. SBF, 213–16.
3. SBF, 204.
4. SBF, 191.
5. SBF, 220–21.
6. Sara to Wood, 4/11/1912: 267 #2.
7. OR 5/19/1911, 4.
8. *Pacific Monthly* (July 1911), 110–13.
9. Wilson, *The New Freedom*, 10.
10. Wilson, *The New Freedom*, 15.
11. Wilson, *The New Freedom*, 35.
12. Wilson, *The New Freedom*, 283–84.
13. Wilson, *The New Freedom*, 86–87.
14. Wilson, *The New Freedom*, 89.
15. Goldman, *Rendezvous with Destiny*, 213.
16. 266 #3.
17. 266 #3.
18. 244 #5, 9/8/1911.
19. 244 #5, 9/8/1911.
20. 181 #4.

22. The Great Cause

1. SBF, 260. Geoffrey Cowan's *The People v. Clarence Darrow* (New York: Times Books, 1993) presents a thorough, readable account of the McNamara trial.
2. SBF, 261.
3. Cowan, *The People v. Clarence Darrow*, 123.
4. Wood to Sara: 244 #17, 10/17/1911.
5. OR 10/9/1911, 4.
6. 67 #24.
7. 266 #5, 10/13/1911.
8. 266 #5, 10/13/1911.
9. 244 #15, 10/16/1911.
10. 244 #39, 11/25/1911.
11. 244 #40.
12. 244 #5.
13. 244 #40.
14. 244 #50.
15. Sara to Ehrgott: 263 #21, 11/29/1911.
16. Robinson, *Bombs and Bribery: The Story of the McNamara and Darrow Trials Following the Dynamiting in 1910 of the Los Angeles Times Building*, 41.
17. 266 #7.
18. 244 #59.

19. 266 #7, 12/10/1911.

23. All Our Nights Are Bridal Nights

1. Wood to Sara: 244 #73, 4/12/1912.
2. Duniway, *Path Breaking: An Autobiographical History of the Equal Suffrage Movement in Pacific Coast States*, 256.
3. Fremont Older to Wood: 177 #44, 6/21/1911.
4. 235 #31.
5. 130 #20, 6/9/1913.
6. 267 #5.
7. Wood to George Field, Sara's father: 230 #35, 1/15/1913.
8. Sara's account of her divorce appears in a brief filed for the Nevada court, 7/27/1914: 176 #11.
9. 130 #30, 7/29/1913.
10. 257 #7.
11. 267 #7.
12. 245 #15.
13. OR 8/12/1913, 18.
14. 267 #8, 10/3/1913.

24. An Awful Awakening

1. 268 #1, 11/29/1913.
2. William L. O'Neill's *Divorce in the Progressive Era* gives a fascinating account of the social environment of Sara's crisis.
3. 245 #68, 12/17/1913.
4. 130 #18, 12/18/1913.
5. 267 #2.
6. 269 #1, 1/1/1913.
7. 246 #1.
8. 28 #1.
9. Wood to Sara, 246 #1, 1/26/1913.
10. 246 #2.

25. A Dirge unto Civilization

1. 246 #3, 3/16/1913.
2. 28 #1, 3/18/1913.
3. Wood to Max Hayek, 230 #65.
4. 246 #3.
5. 270 #1, 4/23/1913.
6. 270 #2.
7. 28 #1, 5/25/1913.

8. Wood, *Civilization*, 1–5.
9. Wood, *Civilization*, 9–10.
10. 246 #6.
11. 27 #7, 55–56.
12. Herbert Croly, "The Other-Worldliness of Wilson," 194–95.

26. A Day in Paradise

1. 246 #6, 6/8/1914.
2. 28 #1.
3. 246 #8, 8/12/1914.
4. Wood, *Civilization*, 27.
5. 246 #8, 8/12/1914.
6. Wood's wish to separate the "good" rich from craven plutocrats resembles a distinction made the year before by Walter Weyl in his book *The New Democracy*. Weyl found "a cleavage of sentiment . . . between the men who are getting rich and the men who *are* rich" [242]. He felt that "the old wealth . . . inclines, if not to democratic, at least to mildly reformatory, programs" (243).
7. 247 #1.
8. 272 #3, 10/12/1914.
9. 247 #2, 10/8/1914.
10. 247 #3, 10/12/1914.
11. 246 #7, 7/27/1914.
12. 247 #3, 11/8/1914.

27. The Old Man of the Sea

1. 271 #4, 11/30/1914.
2. 247 #4, 12/4/1914.
3. 247 #10, 5/5/1914.
4. 248 #1, 6/6/1914.
5. 273 #1, 6/27/1914.
6. In *The Spirit of Labor*, published in 1907, Hutchins Hapgood devoted an entire chapter to "The Intellectual Proletariat" in which he described the intellectual life of working-class radicals in Chicago. The chapter begins, however, with a sketch of Clarence Darrow:

> More gifted, more clever, and more able than any other Chicago "radical," he is not as consistent or logical as many of them. He is a friend of the proletariat, a philosopher, a literary man and a dreamer, but he is also a lawyer, a politician, and a money-maker. He has a marvelous inconsistency of mind, but a rich temperament and many "parts." Connected as he is, of course, with the "successful" people, and the bourgeoisie, he is not as clear a case as the rank and file of the radicals. He is a friend of the laboring man, not a laboring man either in fact or by instinct. (323–24)

Most likely, Goldman was acquainted with Hapgood's book. Perhaps, Hapgood's description of Darrow's contradictory commitments inspired her to turn the "Intellectual Proletariat" into an ironic portrait of radical labor's well-intentioned, well-to-do supporters.

7. 248 #2, 7/22/1914.
8. 247 #8, 3/23/1914.
9. Letter dated 11/24/1873, quoted in EW, 11–12.

28. The Portland Experiment

1. *Masses* (Oct. 1914), 21.
2. BL:OC, 128.
3. 28 #4, 204–5.
4. 248 #3.
5. Wood to David Schwartz; 10/11/1939, 6.
6. 274 #1, 9/8/1914.
7. In his fascinating book, *American Nervousness: 1903*, Tom Lutz discusses the diagnosis and treatment of neurasthenia—the catch-all designation for illness like Sara's—as a "highly gendered discourse" determined by social convention (31). When men—Teddy Roosevelt is the best-known example—were thought to show signs of nervousness and weakened constitutions they were given the "exercise cure": a rugged environment, fresh air, and plenty of vigorous activity. Women, especially "New Women" engaged in "brain work," who showed neurasthenic symptoms were assigned the "rest cure": sanitariums, passivity, an invalid existence. Sara's good instincts shattered the convention. Arduous campaigning was a source of strength for her. She became "well" only after she defied "sensible" medical therapy and returned to her taxing work as a suffrage campaigner.
8. The Fifteenth Amendment, ratified in 1870, gave the vote to former black slaves, but it said nothing about the rights of women. The amendment reads: "The right of citizens of the United States to vote shall not be denied or abridged by the United States or by any State on account of race, color, or previous condition of servitude." In 1878, Senator A. A. Sargent of California, a close friend of Susan Anthony, introduced a suffrage measure to correct this exclusionary wording: "The right of citizens of the United States to vote shall not be denied or abridged by the United States or by any state on account of sex." Some forty-two years later, the "Susan B. Anthony Amendment" became the law of the land.
9. 274 #2, 10/30/1914.
10. 240 #1, 1/7/1915.
11. 249 #1, 1/25/1915.
12. 275 #2, 4/21/1915.
13. 249 #2, 4/6/1915.

29. The Golden Bars of Your Cage

1. 249 #2. 4/23/1915.
2. 249 #3, 5/4/1915.
3. Wood's criticism of Reitman calls to mind Max Eastman's memorable discussion of Steffens, Older, and Darrow: the three friends Wood had hoped would share his anarchist commune. In his autobiography Eastman disparaged them as "Sentimental Rebels." Pointing to the Protestant origins of their thinking, Eastman remarks that they are "as purely American a phenomenon as the red Indians." In Eastman's eyes, these radicals of estimable American stock were naive and shallow in their political thinking—especially in comparison to Reitman and Goldman—immigrant Jews from Eastern Europe and Russia. (*Enjoyment of Living* [New York: Harper & Brothers, 1948], 424–25.) Without question, Wood's criticism of Reitman and Emma's "un-aesthetic, unbeautiful" qualities suggests a repugnance toward the culture that spawned them. In his most exasperated moments, Wood comes off as outright anti-semitic. "Emma Goldman is now staying with Kitty," he writes to Sara, "brings in her Russian Jew boors at the last moment and says 'Kitten dear, he is such a good worker may I ask him to stay to dinner? . . .' They live so like cattle themselves they do not appreciate what it means to Kitty who is cook, housemaid, and all." (249 #6, 8/9/1915). Yet, more telling than these private remarks is Wood's unwillingness to admit that, in "un-aesthetic" style and "unbeautiful" personal appearance, Reitman and Goldman were far closer to labor audiences than Wood could ever hope to be.
4. Sara Bard Field, introduction to *Collected Poems of Charles Erskine Scott Wood*, viii–ix.
5. 248 #5, 4/25/1915.
6. John Reed, "The Day in Bohemia: or Life among the Artists," 1913. Quoted in Luhan, *Movers and Shakers*, 172.
7. 249 #3, 5/3/1915.
8. 249 #2, 4/23/1915.
9. 249 #5, 7/3/1915.
10. 276 #2, 7/6/1915.
11. 249 #5, 7/16/1915.
12. 276 #2, 7/23/1915.
13. 276 #2, 7/25/1915.

30. I Also Am a Wage Slave

1. Luhan, *Movers and Shakers*, 141.
2. 276 #2, 7/31/1915.
3. 249 #5, 7/10/1915.
4. 236 #10, 7/17/1915.
5. 227 #20, 8/9/1915.
6. 249 #6, 8/10/1915.

7. OR 8/7/1915, 12.
8. OR 8/14/1915, 9.
9. SBF, 304.
10. *Suffragist* (10/2/1915), 5.
11. 276 #4, 9/5/1915.
12. 276 #5, 10/18/1915.
13. SBF, 321.
14. 276 #5, 10/25/1915.
15. 277 #1, 11/3/1915.
16. 277 #1, 11/6/1915.
17. SBF, 565.
18. 277 #1, 11/7/1915.
19. 277 #1, 11/7/1915.

31. Love and Anarchy

1. Photograph: 297 #17.
2. 277 #1, 11/29/1915.
3. 277 #1, 11/25/1915.
4. 277 #2, 12/10/1915.
5. 28 #2, 1/1/1916.
6. 277 #4, 1/2/1916.
7. 277 #4, 1/2/1916.
8. 238 #16, 1/5/1916.
9. 28 #2, 3/11/1916.
10. 277 #6, 4/24/1916.
11. 278 #2, 6/1/1916.

32. Sexual Politics

1. Irwin, *The Story of the Woman's Party*, 160.
2. SBF, 349.
3. Irwin, *The Story of the Woman's Party*, 178.
4. Sanger, *An Autobiography*, 204.
5. OR 6/20/1916, 13.
6. OR 6/20/1916, 13.
7. OR 7/1/1916, 16.
8. Sanger, *An Autobiography*, 204–6; Gray, *Margaret Sanger*, 122–23.
9. Sara to Thelma Wold: 278 #3, 7/23/1916 (erroneously dated "July 1917").
10. 251 #2, 8/7/1916.
11. SBF, 347.
12. 66 #10.
13. 278 #4.
14. 180 #34, 8/10/1916.

15. 278 #6, 10/3/1916.
16. 251 #4, 10/14/1916.
17. 251 #5, 11/10/1916.
18. 251 #5, 11/14/1916.

33. A Revolution toward Real Freedom

1. Irwin, *The Story of the Woman's Party*, 189.
2. SBF, 361.
3. 251 #10, 3/29/1917.
4. 252 #4, 9/7/1917.
5. Link, *Wilson: The New Freedom*, 149–50.
6. 230 #56, 3/18/1918.
7. 230 #56, 3/18/1918.
8. Kaplan, *Lincoln Steffens*, 240.
9. Powys, *Autobiography*, 417.
10. 186 #36.
11. SBF, 458.
12. 99 #21, 9/25/1917.
13. 158 #21, 6/1917.
14. In the September number of the *Masses*, John Reed described the government crackdown in his fine article, "One Solid Month of Liberty."
15. Three years earlier, Herbert Croly, perhaps the most influential political observer of the Wilson years, introduced the concept of "Industrial Democracy" in his book *Progressive Democracy*. Croly used the term to describe his plan to redeem the promise of democratic principles by giving wage-earners a greater stake in management and decision making (378–405).
16. 252 #2, 7/22/1917. Wood revised his speech and had it privately printed as *Ave! Caesar. Imperator. Morituri te salutant.*
17. 182 #14, 7/25/1917.
18. 280 #2, 7/27/1917.
19. SBF, 371–72.
20. 252 #3, 8/17/1917.
21. 265 #25, 9/4/1917.
22. 280 #4, 9/10/1917. The imprisonment of Woman's Party pickets was a turning point in the suffrage struggle. On October 20, Alice Paul was arrested and committed to Occoquan. She began a hunger strike that lasted until she was transferred to a hospital three weeks later, where she was forcibly fed. (After this, she was removed to a psychopathic ward where, in flagrant violation of habeas corpus, she was kept incommunicado for a week.) Just days after her transfer, on November 14, a number of the newly imprisoned pickets insisted that they be treated as political prisoners. They began a new hunger strike that alarmed authorities enough to hasten the course of justice. On November 23, the U.S. District Court ruled that Woman's Party pickets should never have been sent to Occoquan Workhouse: they were offered the choice of posting bail,

pending an appeal, or accepting transfer to jail. For all practical purposes, the Woman's Party had won a great victory.

Six weeks later, on January 9, 1918, President Wilson finally gave his support to a federal suffrage amendment, and the following day the House of Representatives passed the Susan B. Anthony amendment. Though the U.S. Senate did not ratify the amendment until September 1919, the Woman's Party was assured of victory.

23. 280 #4, 9/19/1917.
24. 280 #4, 9/28/1917.
25. 252 #4, 10/13/1917.
26. 281 #2, 11/21/1917.
27. 252 #1, 5/10/1917.

34. Fears and Alarms

1. 279 #5, 3/31/1917.
2. 281 #1, 10/13/1917.
3. 280 #4, 9/28/1917.
4. 242 #18, 2/25/1918.
5. *Mother Earth Bulletin* (January 1918): 1.
6. 221 #44, n.d.

35. Four

1. 252 #10, 8/11/1918.
2. 285 #11, 8/23/1918.
3. 252 #10, 9/21/1918.
4. 115 #22, October 1918.
5. Katherine Caldwell's "Afterword," SBF, 646–47. See also Wood's letter to Max, 254 #31, 10/28/1918.

36. Recalled to Life

1. 130 #48, 12/6/1918.
2. 254 #31, 10/28/1918.
3. Ehrgott's implacable assault on Sara's conscience became his life's purpose and remained so until 1923, when Kay moved in with her mother. With Sara and Kay reunited, Ehrgott lacked the means to torment his former wife. To console himself, he entered into a platonic marriage to a pious, churchly woman with whom he shared his abiding grievances. Then, in 1925, he let it be known that he planned to undertake a worldwide investigation of marriage. "Young people are too superficial in their judgments," he explained. "They hear the same song bird singing their love song, but, unfortunately, many make the mistake of listening to a mocking bird echoing the songs of some one else." With that, the Reverend Ehrgott passed from Sara's life.

4. 265 #70, 1/21/1919.
5. 126 #53, 11/16/1918.
6. In a scathing reassessment of the Wilson years, Harold Stearns observed that "President Wilson not only silenced his critics by putting the outspoken ones in jail but by putting many others in government." [*Liberalism in America* (1919), 109–10]. Louis Post was precisely the kind of person Stearns had in mind. Other notable progressives who served under Wilson were George Creel, Frank Walsh, Newton Baker (secretary of war and a former lieutenant for Tom Johnson, Cleveland's reform mayor and an advocate of Henry George's single tax), Frederic Howe (U.S. commissioner of immigration: another Tom Johnson supporter, writer, and director of the People's Institute at Cooper Union) and Dudley Field Malone (collector of the Port of New York and an active supporter of the Woman's Party).
7. 235 #70.
8. Sara to Bryant, 1/26/1922, John Reed Collection 6. See also, Gardner, *"Friend and Lover": The Life of Louise Bryant*, 162–63.

37. Clear and Present Danger

1. The Supreme Court upheld the decision (*Debs v. U.S.* 249 U.S. 211 [1919]). Debs served two and one-half years in prison before President Harding released him in 1921.
2. *Schenck v. U.S.* (249 U.S. 47).
3. Frederic C. Howe, *The Confessions of a Reformer*, 195–96.
4. OR, 7/16/1913, 3.
5. OR, 7/17/1913, 1.
6. *Oregon Journal*, 7/18/1913, 1, 6.
7. *Oregon Journal*, 11/25/1971, sec. 2, p. 4.
8. *Oregon Journal*, 6/4/1916, 6.
9. 271 #1, 8/15/1913.
10. 235 #39, 4/28/1919.
11. Wood, "Free Speech and the Constitution in the War: Being substantially a reprint of the argument against the constitutionality of the espionage act, from the brief filed in the Marie Equi Case, No. 3328, U.S. Circuit Court of Appeals, Ninth Circuit" (privately printed by author, 1920), 5.
12. Wood, "Free Speech and the Constitution," 6.
13. Wood, "Free Speech and the Constitution," 6.
14. Wood, "Free Speech and the Constitution," 10.
15. Wood, "Free Speech and the Constitution," 12.
16. Wood, "Free Speech and the Constitution," 22. Wood's criticism of Holmes was unduly harsh. That same year, the Supreme Court affirmed the conviction of Jacob Abrams and several codefendants who threw leaflets from a garment district loft onto the streets below. The leaflets attacked the president's support of intervention against the revolutionary Russian government, and they urged workers in munitions factories to form a general strike that would halt production

of materiel that might be used against the freedom-loving Russian people. Though *Abrams v. U.S.* bore significant similarities to the Schenck case, in Holmes's eyes Abrams and his codefendants did not represent a serious threat to America's war effort. To this day, his dissent is cited for its eloquent defense of free speech:

> When men have realized that time has upset many fighting faiths, they may come to believe even more than they believe the very foundations of their own conduct that the ultimate good desired is better reached by free trade in ideas—that the best test of truth is the power of the thought to get itself accepted in the competition of the market, and that truth is the only ground upon which their wishes safely can be carried out. That, at any rate, is the theory of our Constitution. It is an experiment, as all life is an experiment. Every year if not every day we have to wager our salvation upon some prophecy based upon imperfect knowledge. (*Abrams v. U.S.* 250 U.S. 616, 624 [1919])

Holmes never repudiated the Schenck decision, yet his argument in the Abrams dissent shows that he was more committed to protecting speech than to restraining it.

17. Wood, "Free Speech and the Constitution," 26.
18. 126 #46, 8/26/1920.
19. On October 27, the circuit court handed down its ruling against the Equi appeal; the following year, the case was denied by the Supreme Court (252 U.S. 560). After all appeals failed, Dr. Equi served ten months in San Quentin Prison. There too, she showed her solidarity with those in need: she distributed sewing materials to her fellow inmates and when Christmas arrived, she provided them with turkeys. [*Oregon Journal*, 11/25/1971, sec. 2, p. 4.]

38. The Heart, the World, and Mr. Wilson

1. Vanderveer and Wood had worked together on the Equi case and on the Everett Massacre, and Wood respected his professional skill. Yet Van had lost the most important case of all: his defense, in 1918, of the IWW leadership for actions deemed treasonous under the Espionage Act. While Vanderveer doggedly conducted his futile defense, Kitty—who served as head of the Portland Defense Committee—stopped in Chicago to observe the trial. Soon she and Van became lovers. In August of 1918, the IWW defendants were found guilty, and though the verdict had been a foregone conclusion, Van blamed himself. He began drinking heavily and behaving erratically. Soon after, he astonished his wife by surreptitiously selling their home to pay his debts. With his marriage in shambles, Van moved into the Butler Hotel in Seattle where he continued carousing and taxing the patience of his remaining friends. In February of 1919, radical labor crippled Seattle with a general strike. Van's spirits rose, but when the strike disintegrated he fell into despair and called for Kitty to come join him. She hurried up from Portland and settled in with him.

2. Wood, "Woodrow Wilson," 247–49.
3. 188 #22, 10/22/1919.
4. Wood, "Woodrow Wilson," 247.
5. 283 #1, 10/16/1919.
6. 283 #1, 10/9/1919.

39. The Flowering Wall

1. 1920 Photo by William E. Dassonville, a San Francisco neighbor of Ansel Adams. OHS #021696.
2. Photo, 297 #19.
3. *Liberator* (August 1920): 25.
4. Mentioned in a letter from Nannie to Wood, 260 #43, 8/9/1920.
5. Enclosed with letter, 283 #2, 2/9/1920.
6. 283 #2, 2/23/1920.
7. 253 #2, 5/29/1920.
8. 353 #4, 8/11/1920.
9. 253 #3, 5/26/1920.
10. 253 #3, 6/13/1920.

40. A Man Is More than His Work

1. SBF, 466–67.
2. Powys, 49.
3. Browne, "The Temple of a Living Art: Being a Plea For an American Art Theatre," 160–78.
4. Browne, *Too Late to Lament*, 269.
5. Wood, *Odysseus, A Play in One Act*, in *Collected Poems*, 149.
6. Wood to Mrs. H. W. Elliott, 229 #59, 11/8/1935.
7. 237, 11/8/1921.
8. 185 #37.
9. SBF, 394–96.
10. 263 #32.
11. Katherine Field Caldwell, "Family and Berkeley Memories, and the Study and Profession of Asian Art," an oral history conducted in 1992 and 1993 by Suzanne B. Riess, Regional Oral History Office, The Bancroft Library, University of California, Berkeley, 45–47.
12. SBF, 466.
13. Katherine Caldwell, "Afterword." SBF, 650–51.
14. OR 10/10/1922, 1.
15. 200 #4, 10/22/1922.
16. 89 #12.

41. Standing Aside

1. 200 #3, 8/30/1922.
2. 29 #1, 4/3/1923.
3. Winter, *And Not to Yield: An Autobiography*, 102–3.
4. SBF, 507.
5. 200 #16, 2/14/1944.
6. Though he lacked Jack Reed's ingenuous nature, Bullitt was a fascinating character in his own right. Four years earlier, as a twenty-eight-year-old information attaché at the American Commission to the League of Nations, he accompanied Steffens on a secret mission to meet with Russia's revolutionary government. They returned with glowing praise of Lenin and the Russian future—an enthusiasm Wilson did not share. The president worried that any endorsement of the Bolshevik leaders might jeopardize support for the floundering League of Nations. As a result, Wilson refused to give his emissaries an opportunity to report to him on their findings. (Kaplan, *Lincoln Steffens*, 234–45.) Bullitt exacted a measure of revenge by collaborating with Sigmund Freud on a lacerating psychological study of Wilson. *Thomas Woodrow Wilson: A Psychological Study* was not published until 1967.
7. SBF, 503–4.

42. The Cats

1. Sissy Seaman to Wood, 195 #8.
2. Hawley and Potts, *Counsel for the Damned: A Biography of George Francis Vanderveer*, 298.
3. 206 #12.
4. 195 #7.
5. 252 #2, 7/29/1917.
6. 28 #4, 32
7. SBF, 434.
8. Jeffers, *The Selected Poetry of Robinson Jeffers*, xiv.
9. *The New York Times*, 1/23/1917.
10. 28 #4, 191.

43. A Sugarcoated Pill

1. 235 #55, 1/11/1926.
2. Ad in the *Nation* 8/3/1927.
3. 28 #4, 8/3/1928.
4. Vanguard Press kept the book in print for twenty years, through twenty-five printings, before selling the reprint rights to Penguin Books. In 1947, in its first six months as a Penguin paperback, *Heavenly Discourse* sold nearly fourteen thousand copies. (Royalty Statement, 183 #69.)
5. H. L. Mencken, "The National Letters," in *Prejudices: Second Series* (New York: Knopf, 1920).

6. Wood, *Heavenly Discourse*, 14.
7. Ibid., "Birth Control," 26–28.
8. Ibid., "Anthony Comstock in Heaven," 29–33.
9. Ibid., " 'T.R.' Enters Heaven," 118–24.
10. Ibid., "Noah's Curse," 315–25.

44. Courage of Intelligence

1. Wood, *Too Much Government*, 1.
2. Wood, *Too Much Government*, 9.
3. Wood, *Too Much Government*, 16–17.
4. Wood, *Too Much Government*, 46.
5. Wood, *Too Much Government*, 48.
6. Wood, *Too Much Government*, 51.
7. Wood, *Too Much Government*, 53.
8. Wood, *Too Much Government*, 266.

45. Our Own Works of Art

1. Original footage in possession of Kirk Smith, son of Wood's daughter Lisa Wood Smith. The home movie was transferred to videotape by the Oregon Historical Society and is part of their Wood collection.
2. 200 #134, 2/13/1929.
3. Steffens, *Lincoln Steffens Speaking*, 124–25.
4. 296 # 44, c. 1931.
5. Elizabeth Elkus, interview by author, Berkeley CA, June 28, 1989.
6. 230 #31.
7. 261 #13.
8. EW, 138.
9. 220 #20, 10/21/1933.
10. William Rose Benét, *The Dust Which Is God* (New York: Dodd, Mead & Company, 1941), 406–9.

46. The Popular Front

1. 142 #47.
2. 200 #21, 1/10/1936.
3. Winter and Shapiro, *The World of Lincoln Steffens*, 259.
4. Winter, *And Not to Yield: An Autobiography*, 215.
5. Wald, *The New York Intellectuals: The Rise and Decline of the Anti-Stalinist Left from the 1930's to the 1980's*, 132.
6. "To John Dewey, Norman Thomas, and the Others of the Committee for the Defense of Leon Trotsky," 229 #30, 10/28/1936.
7. Martin Dies, *The Trojan Horse in America*, 350–51.

8. Dies, *The Trojan Horse in America*, 365.

9. 229 #31, 11/3/1936. The House Special Committee appears to have let the matter rest. Nevertheless, over the next two years Wood continued to write Dies, constantly haranguing him for his anti-Communism (cf. Wood's letters to Thelma Wold: 242 #26, 27).

10. *San Francisco Chronicle*, 11/13/1936, 9.

11. Winter, "Western Writers' Congress," 345.

12. Cohen, "A Gathering of Literary Lions," 24.

13. Aaron, *Writers on the Left*, 322.

14. 123 #8, 11/17/1936.

15. Carey McWilliams, manuscript collection of papers, BL #12.

16. 185 #18, 2/9/1937.

17. Browder, "Who in U.S. Are Real Friends of Political Asylum?" (Closing remarks at Plenary Session of the Central Committee of the C.P.U.S.A. on 12/8/1936), 3–4.

18. 225 #39, 12/23/1936.

19. 229 #19, n.d., 5–6.

20. 229 #19.

47. *Earthly Discourse*

1. Wood, *Earthly Discourse* 267.

2. Wood, *Earthly Discourse*, 268.

48. I Will Write My Memoirs

1. 253 #8.

2. 215 #37, 1/18/1928.

3. Sara to William Rose Benét, 262 #34, 11/30/1940.

4. 180 #48, 2/27/1938.

5. 235, 6/1/1939.

6. 176 #59, 6/26/1939.

7. 6 #6, 50.

8. 6 #6, 52–55.

9. To Caro Weir (J. Alden Weir's daughter), 230 #28, 1/7/1941.

10. Sara to Ansel Adams, 225 #36, 10/20/1941.

11. 6 #8.

12. 6 #4, 11.

49. Final Words

1. 284 #2, 2/9/1944.

2. 125 #12, n.d.

3. 215 #41, 1/23/1944.

4. John D. Barry, "Ways of the World," *San Francisco News*, 8/7/1929.

Selected Bibliography

Aaron, Daniel. *Writers on the Left*. New York: Harcourt, Brace & World, 1961.

Abbott, Carl. *The Great Extravaganza: Portland and the Lewis and Clark Exposition*. Portland: Oregon Historical Society, 1981.

Adams, Henry. *The Education of Henry Adams*. Boston: Massachusetts Historical Society, 1918. Reprint, Boston: Houghton Mifflin, 1961.

Ambrose, Stephen E. *Duty, Honor, Country: A History of West Point*. Baltimore: Johns Hopkins University Press, 1966.

Amundson, Caroll John. "History of the Willamette Valley and Cascade Mountain Wagon Road." M.A. thesis, University of Oregon, 1928.

Anders, Clarence L. "Settlement of Sitka." In *Alaska and Its History*, ed. Morgan B. Sherwood. Seattle: University of Washington Press, 1967, 47–55.

Bailie, William. *Josiah Warren: The First American Anarchist*. Boston: Small, Maynard & Company, 1906.

Bancroft, Hubert Howe. *History of the Pacific States*, vol. 17, *California 1846–1848*. San Francisco: The History Company, 1886, 201–15.

Bauer, K. Jack. *The Mexican War: 1846–1848*. New York: Macmillan, 1874.

Beal, Merrill D. *I Will Fight No More Forever*. 1963. Reprint, New York: Ballantine Books, 1971.

Bennett, Melba Berry. *The Stone Mason of Tor House: The Life and Work of Robinson Jeffers*. Los Angeles: Ward Ritchie Press, 1966.

Bingham, Edwin R. "Oregon's Romantic Rebels: John Reed and Charles Erskine Scott Wood." *Pacific Northwest Quarterly* (July 1959): 77–90.

————. "The Heavenly Discourse of C. E. S. Wood," *Oregon Humanities* (summer 1990): 7–10.

The Blast. January 15, 1916–June 1, 1917. Reprinted in one volume, ed. Richard Drinnon. New York: Greenwood Reprint Corporation, 1968.

Boorstin, Daniel J., ed. *An American Primer*. Chicago: University of Chicago Press, 1966.

Boynton, Edward C. *Guide to West Point and the U.S. Military Academy*. New York: D. Van Nostrand, 1867.

Broun, Heywood, and Margaret Leech. *Anthony Comstock: Roundsman of the Lord.* New York: Albert & Charles Boni, 1927.

Browder, Earl. "Who in U.S. Are Real Friends of Political Asylum?" (Closing remarks at Plenary Session of the Central Committee of the C.P.U.S.A. on 12/8/1936). *Daily Worker: People's Champion of Liberty, Progress, Peace and Prosperity* (December 17, 1936): 3–4.

Browne, Maurice. "The New Rhythmic Drama," *The Drama* 4 (November 1914 and February 1915): 616–30; 146–60.

———. "The Temple of a Living Art: Being a Plea for an American Art Theatre . . ." *The Drama* 3 (November 1913): 160–78.

———. *Too Late to Lament: An Autobiography.* London: Victor Gollancz, 1955.

Brownell, W. C. "The Sculpture of Olin Warner." *Scribner's Magazine* 20 (October 1896), 429–41.

Bullitt, William, and Sigmund Freud. *Thomas Woodrow Wilson, Twenty-eighth President of the United States: A Psychological Study.* Boston: Houghton Mifflin, 1967.

Caldwell, Katherine Field. "Family and Berkeley Memories, and the Study and Profession of Asian Art," an oral history conducted in 1992 and 1993 by Suzanne B. Riess, Regional Oral History Office. Bancroft Library, University of California, Berkeley, 1993.

Canfield, Gae Whitney. *Sarah Winnemucca of the Northern Paiutes.* Norman: University of Oklahoma Press, 1983.

Carpenter, John A. "General Howard and the Nez Perce War of 1887." *Pacific Northwest Quarterly* (October 1958), 129–45.

———. *Sword and Olive Branch.* Pittsburgh: University of Pittsburgh Press, 1964.

Chalmers, Harvey. *The Last Stand of the Nez Perce: Destruction of a People.* New York: Twayne Publishers, 1962.

Clark, Cleon L. *History of the Willamette Valley and Cascade Mountain Wagon Road.* Bend OR: Deschutes County Historical Society, 1987.

Clemens, Samuel Langhorne (Mark Twain). "Extract from Captain Stormfield's Visit to Heaven." *Harper's Magazine* (December 1907 and January 1908): 41–49; 266–76.

Cohen, Irving. "A Gathering of Literary Lions." *San Francisco Sunday Examiner and Chronicle*, May 24, 1981, 24–25.

Collins, Dean. "Lecture Before I Was Born," *The Portland Journal*, February 12, 1943, sec. 2, p. 2.

Croly, Herbert. "The Other-Worldliness of Wilson." *New Republic* (March 27, 1917): 194–95.

———. *Progressive Democracy.* New York: MacMillan, 1914.

Darrow, Clarence. *The Story of My Life.* New York: Charles Scribner's Sons, 1932.

Deady, Matthew P. Diaries: 1871–1892. Reprint, *Pharissee among Philistines*, ed. Malcolm Clark Jr. 2 vols. Portland: Oregon Historical Society, 1975.

DeLeon, David. *The American as Anarchist: Reflections on Indigenous Radicalism.* Baltimore: Johns Hopkins University Press, 1978.

Dell, Floyd. *Homecoming: An Autobiography.* New York: Farrar & Rinehart, 1933.

DeVoto, Bernard. *The Year Of Decision: 1846.* Boston: Little, Brown, 1943.

De Wolf, Fred. "Early-Day Woman Doctor Made Mark with 'Radical' Reform." *Oregon Journal* (11/25/1971), sec. 2, p. 4.

Dies, Martin. *The Trojan Horse in America.* Dodd, Mead & Company: New York, 1940.

Drinnon, Richard. *Rebel in Paradise: A Biography of Emma Goldman.* Chicago: University of Chicago Press, 1961.

Duniway, Abigail Scott. *Path Breaking: An Autobiographical History of the Equal Suffrage Movement in Pacific Coast States.* Portland OR: James, Kerns & Abbot, 1914.

Eastman, Max. *Enjoyment of Living.* New York: Harper & Brothers, 1948.

Eckford, Henry. "J. Alden Weir." *The Century* (April 1889): 956–57.

————. "Olin Warner, Sculptor." *The Century* (January 1889): 392–401.

Ellis, David Maldwyn. "The Oregon and California Railroad Land Grant, 1866–1945." *Pacific Northwest Quarterly* 39 (October 1948): 253–83.

Erie County Unit of the Federal Writers' Project of the Works Progress Administration. *Erie: A Guide to the City and County.* Philadelphia: William Penn Association, 1938.

"Feccheimer, M. L." *The West Shore* 12 (April 1886): 115.

Fee, Charles Anders. *Chief Joseph: The Biography of a Great Indian.* Introduction and appendix by C. E. S. Wood. New York: Wilson-Erickson, 1936.

Field, Sara Bard. "Colonel Wood: 'Grand Old Rebel.'" *The Saturday Review of Literature* 28 (March 24, 1945): 7–9.

————. Obituary of Charles Erskine Scott Wood. *Assembly* [West Point Alumni Magazine] (October 1944).

————. *Sara Bard Field: Poet and Suffragist.* Interview conducted by Amelia R. Fry, 1959–1963. Regional Oral History Project. University of California at Berkeley.

Flipper, Henry Ossian. *The Colored Cadet at West Point: The Autobiography of Lieutenant Henry Ossian Flipper.* New York: Homer Lee, 1878. Reprint, New York: Johnson Reprint, 1966.

Gardner, Virginia. *"Friend and Lover": The Life of Louise Bryant.* New York: Horizon Press, 1982.

Gelb, Barbara. *So Short a Time: A Biography of John Reed and Louise Bryant.* New York: W. W. Norton, 1973.

George, Henry. *Progress and Poverty.* New York: Robert Schalkenbach Foundation, 1958.

Gidley, M. *Kopet: A Documentary Narrative of Chief Joseph's Last Years.* Seattle & London: University of Washington Press, 1981.

Gold, Michael. "Why a Writer's Congress." *Pacific Weekly: A Western Journal of Fact and Opinion* (November 30, 1936): 308.

Goldman, Emma. *Anarchism and Other Essays.* New York: Mother Earth Publishing Association, 1917. Reprint, New York: Dover, 1969.

———. "In Portland." *Mother Earth: Monthly Magazine Devoted to Social Science and Literature* (June 1908): 197–203.

———. *Living My Life*. New York: Knopf, 1931.

Goldman, Eric F. *Rendezvous with Destiny*. New York: Knopf, 1953.

Gray, Madeline. *Margaret Sanger*. New York: Richard Marek, 1979.

Grisworld, Wesley S. *A Work of Giants: Building the First Transcontinental Railroad.* New York: McGraw-Hill, 1962.

Hampton, Bruce. *Children of Grace: The Nez Perce War of 1877*. New York: Henry Holt, 1994.

Hapgood, Hutchins. *The Spirit of Labor*. New York: Duffield, 1907.

Hapgood, Norman. *The Changing Years*. New York: Farrar & Rinehart, 1930.

Hartwell, Barbara Bartlett. *The Wood Household*. Portland OR: By the author, n.d.

Hawley, Lowell S., and Ralph Bushnell Potts. *Counsel for the Damned: A Biography of George Francis Vanderveer*. Philadelphia & New York: J. B. Lippincott, 1953.

Hendrick, Burton J. "The Initiative and Referendum and How Oregon Got Them." *McClure's Magazine* (July 1911), 235–48.

———. "Law-Making by the Voters: How the People of Oregon, Working under the Initiative and Referendum, Have Become Their Own Political Bosses." *McClure's Magazine* (August 1911), 435–50.

———. " 'Statement No. 1': How the Oregon Democracy, Working Under the Direct Primary, Has Destroyed the Political Machine." *McClure's Magazine* (September 1911): 505–19.

Hofstadter, Richard. *The Age of Reform*. New York: Knopf, 1955.

Holbrook, Stewart H. *James J. Hill: A Great Life in Brief*. New York: Knopf, 1955.

Homer, William Innes. *Alfred Stieglitz and the American Avant-Garde*. Boston: New York Graphic Society, 1977.

Hopkins, Sarah Winnemucca. *Life among the Piutes: Their Wrongs and Claims*, ed. Mrs. Horace Mann. Boston and New York: privately printed, 1883. Reprint, Bishop CA: Chalfant, 1969.

Howard, General Oliver O. *Autobiography*. New York: Baker & Taylor, 1908.

———. *My Life and Experiences among Our Hostile Indians*. Hartford: A. T. Worthington, 1907. Reprint, New York: Da Capo, 1972.

———. *Nez Perce Joseph*. Boston: Lee and Shepard, 1881.

Howe, Frederic C. *The Confessions of a Reformer*. New York: Charles Scribner's Sons, 1925.

Howe, Irving. "To *The Masses*—With Love and Envy." Introduction to *Echoes of Revolt: The Masses 1911–1917*, ed. William L. O'Neill. Chicago: Quadrangle Books, 1966, 5–8.

Irwin, Inez Haynes. *The Story of the Woman's Party*. New York: Harcourt, Brace, 1921.

Jeffers, Robinson. *The Selected Letters of Robinson Jeffers: 1897–1962*, ed. Ann N. Ridgeway. Baltimore: Johns Hopkins University Press, 1968.

Johnson, Tom L. *My Story*, ed. Elizabeth J. Hauser. New York: B. W. Huebsch, 1911.

Chief Joseph (In-mut-too-yah-lat-lat). "An Indian's Views of Indian Affairs." *North American Review* (April 1879), 412–33.

Josephy, Alvin M., Jr. *The Nez Perce Indians and the Opening of the Northwest.* New Haven: Yale University Press, 1965.

Kaplan, Justin. *Lincoln Steffens.* New York: Simon and Schuster, 1974.

Kay, Helena. "C. E. S. Wood, His Life and Works." M.A. thesis, University of Texas, 1937.

Kazin, Michael. *Barons of Labor: The San Francisco Building Trades and Union Power in the Progressive Era.* Urbana IL: University of Illinois Press, 1987.

Leech, Margaret, and Heywood Broun. *Anthony Comstock: Roundsman of the Lord.* New York: Albert & Charles Boni, 1927.

Leonard, Thomas C. *Above the Battle: War-Making in America from Appomattox to Versailles.* New York: Oxford University Press, 1978.

Le Prade, Ruth, ed. *Debs and the Poets.* Pasadena CA: by Upton Sinclair, 1920.

Link, Arthur S. *Wilson: The New Freedom.* Princeton: Princeton University Press, 1956.

———. *Woodrow Wilson and the Progressive Era: 1910–1917.* New York: Harper and Brothers, 1954.

Luhan, Mabel Dodge. *Movers and Shakers.* Vol. 3 of *Intimate Memories.* New York: Harcourt, Brace, 1936.

Lutz, Tom. *American Nervousness: 1903.* Ithaca NY: Cornell University Press, 1991.

MacColl, E. Kimbark, with Harry H. Stein. *Merchants, Money and Power: The Portland Establishment 1843–1913.* Portland OR: Georgian Press, 1988.

Martin, Albro. *James J. Hill and the Opening of the Northwest.* New York: Oxford University Press, 1976.

Marzalek, John F., Jr. *Court Martial: The Army Vs. Johnson Whittaker.* New York: Charles Scribner's Sons, 1972.

Masses (January 1916–November 1917).

McDermott, John D. *Forlorn Hope: The Battle of White Bird Canyon and the Beginning of the Nez Perce War.* Boise: Idaho State Historical Society, 1978.

McWhorter, L. V. *Hear Me, My Chiefs! Nez Perce History and Legend,* ed. Ruth Bordin. Caldwell ID: Caxton Printers, 1952.

———. *Yellow Wolf: His Own Story.* Caldwell ID: The Caxton Printers, 1940.

Meyer, Agnes. *Out of These Roots: The Autobiography of an American Woman.* Boston: Little, Brown, 1953.

Monroe, Anne Shannon. *Feelin' Fine!: Bill Hanley's Book.* Garden City NY: Doubleday, Dorn, 1930.

Morrisson, James L., Jr. *"The Best School in the World:" West Point, The Pre–Civil War Years, 1833–1866.* Kent OH: Kent State University Press, 1980.

Morgan, Joan B. *George de Forest Brush (1855–1941): Master of the American Renaissance.* New York: Berry-Hill Galleries, 1985.

Nash, Wallis. *Oregon: There and Back in 1877.* London: MacMillan, 1878.

———. *Two Years in Oregon.* New York: D. Appleton, 1882.

Nicholas, John, ed. *Art Young: His Life and Times.* New York: Sheridan House, 1939.

O'Callaghan, Jerry A. *The Disposition of the Public Domain in Oregon.* Washington DC: U.S. Government Printing Office, 1960. Reprint, New York: Arno Press, 1979, 52–54.

O'Connor, Richard. *Iron Wheels and Broken Men.* New York: G. P. Putnam's Sons, 1973.

O'Neill, William L. *Divorce in the Progressive Era.* New Haven: Yale University Press, 1967.

———, ed. *Echoes of Revolt: The Masses, 1911–1917.* Chicago: Quadrangle Books, 1966.

———. *The Last Romantic: A Life of Max Eastman.* New York: Oxford University Press, 1978.

Oregon Booster (August 3, 1905).

Overmeyer, Phillip Henry. "Attorney General Williams and the Chief Justiceship." *Pacific Northwest Quarterly* 28 (July 1937): 251–62.

Parsons, Col. William. "The Bannock and Piute War of 1878." In *An Illustrated History of Umatilla and Morrow Counties.* ed. Col. William Pearsons and W. S. Stiach. Portland OR: W. H. Lever, 1902.

The Portland Blue Book: Being the Fashionable Private Address Directory and Ladies Visiting and Shopping Guide. San Francisco: Bancroft Company, 1883–1915.

Portland City Directory. Portland OR: R. L. Polk & Co., 1883–1915.

Post, Louis F. Untitled editorial column. *The Public* (1 March 1902): 737–39.

Powers, Alfred. "Charles Erskine Scott Wood." *History of Oregon Literature.* Portland OR: Metropolitan Press, 1935, 441–52.

Powys, John Cowper. *Autobiography.* New York: Simon and Schuster, 1934.

Powys, Llewelyn. *The Verdict of Bridlegoose.* New York: Harcourt, Brace, 1926.

Pusey, Merlo J. *Eugene Meyer.* New York: Knopf, 1974.

Ridgeway, Ann N., ed. *The Selected Letters of Robinson Jeffers: 1897–1962.* Baltimore: Johns Hopkins University Press, 1968.

Robinson, Corinne Roosevelt. *My Brother Theodore Roosevelt.* New York: Charles Scribner's Sons, 1921.

Robinson, W. W. *Bombs and Bribery: The Story of the McNamara and Darrow Trials Following the Dynamiting in 1910 of the Los Angeles Times Building.* Los Angeles: Dawson's Book Shop, 1969.

Roeder, Ralph. "American Producers: I. Maurice Browne." *Theatre Arts Magazine: An Illustrated Quarterly* (1921), 113–24.

Ross, Steven J. "Struggles for the Screen: Workers, Radicals, and the Political Uses of Silent Film." *The American Historical Review* (April 1991): 333–67.

Sanger, Margaret. *An Autobiography.* New York: W. W. Norton, 1938.

The San Francisco Chronicle (November 12–16, 1936).

The San Francisco Examiner (November 13, 1936).

Schwatka, Frederick. "A Reconnaissance of the Yukon Valley, 1883." In *Narratives of Explorations in Alaska.* Washington DC: Government Printing Office, 1900, 285–365.

Scott, H. W. "The Momentous Struggle for Mastery of the Pacific." *The Pacific Monthly* (July 1905), 3–12.

Sherwood, Morgan B., ed. *Alaska and Its History*. Seattle: University of Washington Press, 1967.

Sinclair, Upton. *The Autobiography of Upton Sinclair*. New York: Harcourt, Brace & World, 1962.

Snyder, Eugene E. *Early Portland: Stump-Town Triumphant*. Portland OR: Binfords & Mort, 1970.

———. *Skidmore's Portland: His Fountain & Its Sculptor*. Portland OR: Binfords & Mort, 1973.

Sperlin, O. B. "Fur Trade Forts in Washington." *The Washington Historical Quarterly* 8 (April 1917): 102–13.

Spurlock, John C. *Free Love: Marriage and Middle-Class Radicalism in America, 1825–1860*. New York: New York University Press, 1988.

Stearns, Harold. *Liberalism in America: Its Origin, Its Temporary Collapse, Its Failure*. New York: Boni and Liveright, 1919.

Steffens, Lincoln. *Lincoln Steffens Speaking*. New York: Harcourt, Brace, 1936.

——— "The Taming of the West: Discovery of the Land Fraud System; A Detective Story." *The American Magazine* (September 1907): 489–505; (October 1907): 585–602.

———. "U'Ren, the Law-Giver: The Legislative Blacksmith of Oregon and the Tools He Has Fashioned for Democracy." *The American Magazine* (March 1908): 527–40.

The Suffragist: Weekly Organ of the Congressional Union for Woman Suffrage. Washington DC.

Sutherland, Thomas A. *Howard's Campaign against the Nez Perce Indians, 1878*. Portland OR: A. G. Walling, Steam Book & Job Printer, & Bookbinder, 1878.

Teiser, Sidney. "Almost Chief Justice: George H. Williams." *Oregon Historical Quarterly* (September and December, 1946): 255–80; 417–40.

Thomas, Dawn F. *The Green Spring Valley: Its History and Heritage*. Baltimore: Maryland Historical Society, 1978.

Thoreau, Henry David. *Walden and Civil Disobedience*, ed. Owen Thomas. New York: W. W. Norton, 1966.

Tucker, Benjamen, ed. *Liberty: The Pioneer Organ of Anarchism* (April and June 1906).

United States Department of War, *Report of the Secretary of War for 1877*, 114–33; 585–660.

United States Military Academy Archives:

Annual Report of the Inspector and Board of Visitors, 1870.

Annual Report of the Inspector and Board of Visitors, 1871–1874.

Annual Report of the Superintendent [in *Annual Report of the Secretary of War*]
— *Report of Maj. Gen. J. M. Schofield, 1880*.
— *Report of Maj. Gen. O. O. Howard, 1881*.
— *Report of Maj. Gen. O. O. Howard, 1882*.

Cadets Admitted Book: 1846–1912.

Circumstances of the Parents of Cadets, 1842 to 1879, v. 1.

Descriptive List of Cadidates for Admission into the United States Military Academy for the Year 1870.

Post Orders, July 27, 1866–December 31, 1871, v. 7.

Register of Delinquencies, Classes of 1873 and 1874, v. 16.

Superintendent's Letter Book, v. 5.

United States Military Academy Staff Records, 1866–1872, v. 8.

Charles Erskine Scott Wood File. Special Collections #2532.

Wald, Alan M. *The New York Intellectuals: The Rise and Decline of the Anti-Stalinist Left from the 1930's to the 1980's.* Chapel Hill: University of North Carolina Press, 1987.

Walker, Franklin. *The Seacoast of Bohemia.* Santa Barbara and Salt Lake City: Peregrine Smith, 1973.

Wecter, Dixon, ed., *Mark Twain in Three Moods.* San Marino: Friends of the Huntington Library, 1948, 27–32.

Weyl, Walter E. *The New Democracy.* New York: MacMillan, 1912.

White, William Allen. *The Old Order Changeth: A View of American Democracy.* New York: MacMillan, 1910.

———. *Woodrow Wilson: The Man, His Times and His Task.* Boston: Houghton Mifflin, 1924.

Whitman, Benjamin, Capt. N. W. Russell, and others. *History of Erie County, Pennsylvania.* Chicago: Warner, Beers, 1884.

Wilson, Kathryn. "The Thing That Impressed Me Most at the Exposition." *The Pacific Monthly* (n.d. 1905, ohs clipping file): 19–20.

Wilson, Woodrow. *The New Freedom.* New York: Doubleday, Page, 1913.

Winter, Ella. *And Not to Yield: An Autobiography.* New York: Harcourt, Brace, 1963.

———. "Western Writers' Congress." *Pacific Weekly* 21 (November 30, 1936): 345–46.

——— and Herbert Shapiro, eds. *The World of Lincoln Steffens.* New York: Hill and Wang, 1962.

Wood, Erskine. *Life of Charles Erskine Scott Wood.* Portland OR: By the author, 1978.

Wood, Nanny Moale. "Personal Recollections: dictated to Dean Fischer, her nurse and companion," c. 1932 (private papers of Lisa Wood Livingston).

Wood, William Maxwell. *Fankwei; or, The San Jacinto in the Seas of India, China and Japan.* New York: Harper & Brothers, 1859.

———. *A Shoulder to the Wheel of Progress.* Buffalo: Derby, Orton and Mulligan, 1853.

———. *Wandering Sketches of people and things in South America, Polynesia, California, and other places visited during a cruise on board of the U.S. ships Levant, Portsmouth, and Savannah.* Philadelphia: Carey and Hart, 1849.

Woodward, Robert C. "William Simon U'Ren: In an Age of Protest." M.A. thesis, University of Oregon, 1956.

Zenker, E. V. *Anarchism.* New York: G. P. Putnam's Sons, 1897.

Zinn, Howard. *A People's History of the United States*. New York: Harper & Row, 1980.

Selected Books, Poetry, Articles, and Printed Speeches by C. E. S. Wood

A Book of Tales; being some myths of the North American Indians: Englished by Charles Erskine Scott Wood. Portland OR: McArthur & Wood, 1901.

"Address of Mr. C. E. S. Wood, at Vancouver, Washington, Memorial services, May 30, 1903." OHS.

"A Heavenly Dialogue." *Masses* (October 1914): 21.
  Six of Wood's dialogues were published in the *Masses*, each bearing the identical title: "Heavenly Discourse." When the dialogues were gathered together in 1927 and published in book form, Wood gave each piece an appropriate name. Dates of the six original "Heavenly Discourses" are listed, followed by the names Wood gave them in his 1927 book.
  April 1915, 13. ("Birth Control").
  June 1915, 19. ("Is God a Jew?").
  September 1915, 18. ("Marriage").
  August 1916, 22. ("St. Peter Loses a Soul").
  January 1917, 12–15. ("Billy Sunday Meets God").
  June 1917, 10–14. ("The Stupid Cannot Enter Heaven").
  Wood's eighth and final heavenly discourse for the *Masses* appeared as "Billy Sunday in Heaven," (July 1917), 33–34.

"A Letter to St. Anthony." *Mother Earth* (January 1907): 31.

A Masque of Love. Chicago: W. M. Hill, 1904.

"Among the Thlinkits in Alaska." *Century Monthly* 24 (July 1882): 323–39.

"An Indian Horse Race." *Century Monthly* 33 (January 1887): 447–50.

Ave! Caesar. Imperator. Morituri te salutant. Privately printed version of his speech on "Industrial Democracy," delivered in Los Angeles, July 20, 1917.

"An Unknown Turning-Point in the Destiny of the Republic." *The Californian. A Western Monthly Magazine* 2 (December 1880): 539–43.

"Chief Joseph, the Nez-Perce." *Century Monthly* 28 (May 1884): 134–42.

"Christ Laughs." *Pacific Weekly: A Western Journal of Fact and Opinion* (November 9, 1936): 299.

Civilization. Portland OR: By the author, 1914.

Collected Poems of Charles Erskine Scott Wood. New York: Vanguard Press, 1949.

"Democratic Democracy." *The Public* (March 8, 1902): 765–66.

Earthly Discourse. New York: Vanguard Press, 1937.

"Famous Indians: Portraits of Some Indian Chiefs." *Century Monthly* 46 (July 1893): 435–45.

"Free Speech and the Constitution in the War: being substantially a reprint of the argument against the constitutionality of the espionage act, from the brief filed in the Marie Equi Case, No. 3328, U.S. Circuit Court of Appeals, Ninth Circuit." Privately printed by author, 1920.

Heavenly Discourse. New York: Vanguard Press, 1928.

"Imperialism vs. Democracy." *Pacific Monthly* II (June 1899): 3–15.

"In the Eyes of the Future." *Blast* (April 1, 1916): 4.

"King of the Magical Pump." *Masses* (December 1914): 3.

Liberty: The Pioneer Organ of Anarchism

> Wood published numerous tales, poems, and essays in *Liberty*, often under the pseudonym, "Francis Du Bosque":

"A Lesson in Crawling." 15 (June 1906): 57–60.

[Francis Du Bosque]. "Carlotta Cortina." 15 (June 1908): 30–52.

"Comstock, St. Paul, et al." 16 (April 1907): 35–42.

[Francis Du Bosque]. "Johann Schmidt." 16 (November 1907): 11–52.

[Francis Du Bosque]. "Mustapha the Wise." 16 (May 1907): 10–34.

[Francis Du Bosque]. "The Angel." 16 (April 1907): 25–31.

"The House of Representatives." 15 (August 1906): 35–43.

[Francis Du Bosque]. "The Truants." 15 (December 1906): 28–34.

Maia. Portland OR: 186 copies printed by F. W. Baltes, 1918.

Mother Earth: Monthly Magazine Devoted to Social Science and Literature.

> Wood contributed these few brief pieces to *Mother Earth*. Emma Goldman needled him over his meager support:

"A Letter to St. Anthony." (January 1907): 31.

"In Memory of Francisco Ferrer." (November 1909): 285–86.

"Truth." (April 1913): 33–35.

"Our Indian Question." *Journal of the Military Service Institution of the United States* 2, no. 6., 123–81.

The Poet in the Desert. Portland: Privately printed, 1915.

The Poet in the Desert, "a new version." Portland: F. W. Baltes, 1918.

The Poet in the Desert, "greatly augmented and revised." New York: Vanguard Press, 1929.

"Preparedness." *Blast* (June 1, 1916): 2–3.

"Private Journal, 1878." Transcribed by Mrs. Peter Voorhies. *Oregon Historical Quarterly* (March 1969): 5–38.

"Private Journal, 1879." Transcribed by Mrs. Peter Voorhies. *Oregon Historical Quarterly* (June 1969): 139–70.

"Socialism or Individualism—The Trend of the Centuries." *The Public* (April 5, 1902): 826–27.

Sonnets to Sappho. San Francisco: Privately printed by Grabhorn Press, 1939.

"The Man Who Is Eastern Oregon" ["Bill" Hanley]. *Sunset, the Pacific Monthly* 28 (May 1912): 594–95.

"The Pursuit and Battle: Semi-Official Report of a Staff Officer." *Chicago Tribune* (October 25, 1877): 5.

"The Pursuit and Capture of Chief Joseph." Introduction and appendix to Charles Anders Fee, *Chief Joseph: The Biography of a Great Indian*. New York: Wilson-Erickson, 1936.

"The Skidmore Fountain." *Oregon Historical Quarterly* 34 (June 1933): 97–102.

"The Surrender Of Joseph." *Harper's Weekly: A Journal of Civilization* (November 17, 1877): 905–6. The article includes seven drawings, almost certainly executed by Wood. They depict the Indian stronghold, their defense excavations in the ravines, the attack of the Seventh Cavalry skirmish line, etc. The entire article may or may not have been written by Wood; however, the glowing centerpiece, a transcription of Joseph's surrender speech, is Wood's.

"The Rabbits and the Goats." *Blast*, February 19, 1916; March 15, 1916.

Too Much Government. New York: Vanguard Press, 1931.

"War and Democracy." In *Is This a War for Democracy?: Two Great Lectures by Two Famous Speakers; Sara Bard Field and Col. C. E. S. Wood.* Oakland: International Press, n.d., 13–22.

"What Is a Democrat?" *The Public,* (May 18, 1906): 151–54.

"What Is the Matter with Labor." *Blast* (January 22, 1916): 3–4.

"Woodrow Wilson." *Reedy's Mirror* (March 25, 1920): 247–49.

Interviews

Ernst Bacon, Berkeley CA, June 26, 1989.

Katherine Caldwell, Berkeley CA, June 25, 1989.

Elizabeth Elkus, Berkeley CA, June 28, 1989.

Index

* 9 7 8 0 8 0 3 2 7 3 1 5 3 *